PENGUIN BOOKS

INVENTING THE INDIVIDUAL

'[*Inventing the Individual*] is a magnificent work of intellectual, psychological and spiritual history. It is hard to decide which is more remarkable: the breadth of learning displayed on almost every page, the infectious enthusiasm that suffuses the whole book, the riveting originality of the central argument or the emotional power and force with which it is deployed. Siedentop takes us on a 2,000-year journey that starts with the almost inconceivably remote city states of the ancient world and ends with the Renaissance. In the course of this journey, he explodes many (perhaps even most) of the preconceptions that run through the public culture of our day – and that I took for granted before reading this book. *Inventing the Individual* is not an exercise in dry-as-dust antiquarianism, still less in pop-historical fun and games. Siedentop's aim has a breathtaking grandeur about it: to persuade us to ask ourselves who we are and where we are going by showing us where we have come from' David Marquand, *New Statesman*

'Extraordinarily wide-ranging, scholarly and beautifully written . . . filled with insight . . . Siedentop has achieved something quite extraordinary. In this learned, subtle, enjoyable and digestible work he has offered back to us a proper version of ourselves. He has explained us to ourselves . . . magisterial, timeless yet timely' Douglas Murray, *Spectator*

'Thoroughly interesting and fundamentally convincing . . . given the range of the material and the audacity of his argument, the account is admirably nuanced . . . formidable . . . *Inventing the Individual* is written with effortless lucidity' Jeffrey Collins, *The Times Literary Supplement*

'*Inventing the Individual* . . . seeks answers to the question, "Is it mere coincidence that liberal secularism developed in the Christian West?" Siedentop argues convincingly that it is not and offers an engaging and timely synthesis reaching back to the Classical world to explain why . . . If there is just one book you read this summer, make it this brave, brilliant and beautifully written defence of the western tradition' Paul Lay, *History Today*

'Erudite and elegantly-written . . . There is much that is intriguing in this audacious argument' Jeremy Jennings, *Standpoint*

'Intellectual history at its best' Nick Spencer, Theos Think Tank

'As Larry Siedentop's erudite and provocative cultural history shows, inhabitants of the pre-Christian world did not think of themselves as "individuals" in the way we understand the world today . . . *Inventing the Individual* spans 2,000 years of history, but it has a 21st century message . . . Siedentop has made an original contribution to this intriguing historical debate – and proved that he at least is not afraid to stand out from the crowd' Andrew Lynch, *Sunday Business Post*

ABOUT THE AUTHOR

Larry Siedentop was appointed to the first post in intellectual history ever established in Britain, at Sussex University in the 1970s. From there he moved to Oxford, becoming Faculty Lecturer in Political Thought and a Fellow of Keble College. His writings include a study of Tocqueville, an edition of Guizot's *History of Civilization in Europe* and *Democracy in Europe*, which has been translated into a dozen languages. Siedentop was made CBE in 2004.

LARRY SIEDENTOP

Inventing the Individual

The Origins of Western Liberalism

PENGUIN BOOKS

PENGUIN BOOKS

UK | USA | Canada | Ireland | Australia
India | New Zealand | South Africa

Penguin Books is part of the Penguin Random House group of companies
whose addresses can be found at global.penguinrandomhouse.com.

First published by Allen Lane 2014
Published in Penguin Books 2015

005

Copyright © Larry Siedentop, 2014

The moral right of the author has been asserted

Set in 9.24/12.40pt Sabon LT Std
Typeset by Jouve (UK), Milton Keynes
Printed in Great Britain by Clays Ltd, St Ives plc

A CIP catalogue record for this book is available from the British Library

ISBN: 978-0-141-00954-4

In memory of my parents

History does not study material facts and institutions alone; its true object of study is the human mind: it should aspire to know what this mind has believed, thought, and felt in different ages of the life of the human race.

Fustel de Coulanges

Contents

A New Model of Government

The Birth Pangs of Modern Liberty

Prologue: What is the West About?

Does it still make sense to talk about 'the West'? People who live in the nations once described as part of Christendom – what many would now call the post-Christian world – seem to have lost their moral bearings. We no longer have a persuasive story to tell ourselves about our origins and development. There is little narrative sweep in our view of things. For better or worse, things have just happened to us.

Some may welcome this condition, seeing it as liberation from historical myths such as the biblical story of human sin and redemption or a belief in progress 'guaranteed' by the development of science. Others will argue that a more inclusive narrative about globalization has made anything like a Western narrative not only obsolete but also morally dubious.

I cannot agree. If we look at the West against a global background, the striking thing about our situation is that we are in a competition of beliefs, whether we like it or not.

The development of Islamic fundamentalism – and the terrorist movements it sometimes inspires – is the most obvious example. A view of the world in which religious law excludes a secular sphere and in which the subordination of women compromises belief in human equality is incompatible with moral intuitions widespread in the West. And that is only one example. The transmuting of Marxist socialism into quasi-capitalism in the world's largest country, China, provides another. In China the governing ideology has become a crass form of utilitarianism, enshrining majority interests even at the expense of justice or human liberty. That, too, offends some of our deepest intuitions.

But do these intuitions mean that the West can still be defined in terms of shared beliefs? It can offer beliefs usually described as 'liberal'. But here we immediately encounter a problem. For in the eyes of Islamic fundamentalists, and indeed in the eyes of not a few in the West, liberalism has come to stand for 'non-belief' – for indifference and permissiveness, if not for decadence. Why is that? And is the charge justified?

This book is an attempt to find out. Its argument rests on two assumptions. The first is that if we are to understand the relationship between beliefs and social institutions – that is, to understand ourselves – then we have to take a very long view. Deep moral changes, changes in belief, can take centuries to begin to modify social institutions. It is folly to expect popular habits and attitudes to change overnight.

The second assumption is that beliefs are nonetheless of primary importance, an assumption once far more widely held than it is today. In the nineteenth century there was a prolonged contest between 'idealist' and 'materialist' views of historical change, with the latter holding that social order rests not so much on shared beliefs but on technology, economic interdependence and an advanced social division of labour. Even the declining appeal of Marxism in the later twentieth century did not discredit that view. Rather, in a strange afterlife, Marxism infiltrated liberal thinking, creating a further temptation to downgrade the role of beliefs. That temptation became all the greater because of the unprecedented prosperity enjoyed by the West after the Second World War. We have come to worship at the shrine of economic growth.

This book, by contrast, will take moral beliefs as seriously as possible, by looking at a series of 'moments' when changed beliefs began to impact on social relations over a period of nearly two millennia. That is not to say that beliefs have been the only cause at work. The story of Western development is not simple or unilinear. No cause has been uniquely powerful at all times. Nonetheless, it seems to me that moral beliefs *have* given a clear overall 'direction' to Western history.

So I tell a story about how the 'individual' became the organizing social role in the West – that is, how the 'civil society' which we take for granted emerged, with its characteristic distinction between public and private spheres and its emphasis on the role of conscience and choice. It is a story about the slow, uneven and difficult steps which have led to individual moral agency being publicly acknowledged and protected, with equality before the law and enforceable 'basic' rights.

A fundamental change in moral belief shaped the world we live in. But this is not to say that those who introduced or promoted that change foresaw or desired its eventual social consequences. My story is, in part, about the unintended consequences of that change of belief. Tracing those consequences is an important part of the story of Western liberalism.

Today many people in the West describe themselves as Christians, without regularly going to church or having even a rudimentary knowledge of Christian doctrine. Is this just hypocrisy or ignorance? Perhaps not. It may suggest that people have a sense that the liberal secular world they live in – and for the most part endorse – is a world shaped by Christian beliefs. If so, by describing themselves in that way, they are paying tribute to the origins of their moral intuitions.

Is it mere coincidence that liberal secularism developed in the Christian West? This book is an attempt to answer that question. Telling a story about the development of a concept over two millennia is, to say the least, not fashionable. Understandably, historians have become nervous of anything like teleological argument, surveying the damage done by historicist theories of 'progress' put forward in the eighteenth and nineteenth centuries. I have tried to avoid that danger.

Nor is that the only danger. The division of intellectual labour and the sheer accumulation of knowledge today pose a great risk for anyone trying to pick a way through such a long period. Specialists are bound to have reservations, noticing omissions and distortions, if not outright mistakes. But must we abandon the attempt to identify and follow longer threads in historical development? In my view, that would be too high a price to pay.

Inevitably, this book is a work of interpretation rather than of primary scholarship. It draws on sources which I have found to be the most penetrating and original, selected from the myriad of sources available. The process of selection has, I am sure, left many valuable sources aside. Nonetheless, there are a number of historians, living and dead, whose writings strike me as both towering achievements and crucial aids in pursuing answers to the questions I explore. I am greatly indebted to their example. They are the real heroes of this book: Fustel de Coulanges, François Guizot, Brian Tierney, Harold Berman and Peter Brown. If this book does nothing more than draw their writings to the attention of a wider readership, it will have achieved something. Yet my hope is that this book may also contribute to a better understanding of that liberal tradition which is at the core of Western identity.

A lifetime of reading, conversation and argument has shaped the pages that follow. Some of the most important friendships which have influenced me are now, alas, matters of memory: friendships with Paul Fried, Myron Gilmore, John Plamenatz, Isaiah Berlin and John Burrow. Burrow read the larger part of the manuscript before his death, providing, as always, comments that were penetrating, helpful and witty. Others who have read and commented on virtually the whole manuscript include Guglielmo Verdirame, Henry Mayr-Harting, Diarmaid MacCulloch and Edward Skidelsky. Their comments and criticisms have been invaluable. To Guglielmo and to Henry Newman I owe a special debt – for innumerable evenings when conversation ranged over all the issues of our time. Their generosity and loyalty helped to make this book possible.

Finally, I want to salute Ruth Dry, at Keble College, Oxford, whose patience in the face of the successive revisions of the manuscript has been remarkably good-humoured.

LAS
Keble College, Oxford,
August 2013

The World of Antiquity

I

The Ancient Family

If we in the West are to understand the world we have created, we must first of all understand another world very remote from our own – remote, not in space, but in time.

The distant past often lives on in surprising ways. Let us take the practice of a man who carries his bride over the threshold of their new home. Who would suppose that this amiable custom is the survival of beliefs that underpinned a society utterly different from our own? It was in many ways a repugnant society. It was a society in which the worship of ancestors, the family as a cult and primogeniture created radically unequal social identities, not just between men and women but also between the first-born son and other male offspring.

So to understand a custom that in its origins was not amiable but stern and obligatory, we must put our preconceptions to one side. We must imagine ourselves into a world where action was governed by norms reflecting exclusively the claims of the family, its memories, rituals and roles, rather than the claims of the individual conscience. We must imagine ourselves into a world of humans or persons who were not 'individuals' as we would understand them now.

Since the sixteenth century and the advent of the nation-state, people in the West have come to understand 'society' to mean an association of individuals. Until recently that understanding was accompanied by a sense of difference, a sense that other cultures had a different basis of organization, whether that was caste, clan or tribe. But in recent decades the Western impact on the rest of the world through capitalism, the spread of democracy and the language of human rights has weakened such a sense of difference. Globalization has made it easier to project an individualized model of society – one that privileges individual preferences and rational choice – onto the whole world.

We have become victims of our own success. For we are in danger of taking this primacy of the individual as something 'obvious' or 'inevitable', something guaranteed by things outside ourselves rather than by historical convictions and struggles. Of course, every human has his or her own body and mind. But does this establish that human equality is decreed by nature rather than culture?

Nature, in the form of genetic endowment, is a necessary, but not a sufficient condition. A legal foundation for equality, in the form of fundamental rights for every person, is also required. In order to see this, it is important to understand how far the Western world has moved away from its origins, as well as how and why. We need to follow the steps between then and now. It will not always be easy. Widespread complacency about the victory of an individualized model of society reflects a worrying decline in historical understanding. For example, to regard Aristotle's definition of slaves as 'living tools', or the presumption in antiquity that women could not be fully rational agents, merely as 'mistakes' – symptoms of an underdeveloped sense of justice – scarcely advances comprehension of the past. After all, radical social inequality was far easier to sustain and more plausible in societies where literacy was so restricted.

It is commonplace to locate Western cultural origins in Greece, Rome and Judaeo-Christianity. Which of these sources should be considered the most important? The question has received different answers at different periods. In the middle ages, Christianity was seen as the crucial source, a view that the sixteenth-century Reformation preserved. The eighteenth-century Enlightenment saw things differently, however. In their attack on 'superstition' and clerical privileges, Enlightenment thinkers sought to minimize the moral and intellectual distance between modern Europe and Graeco-Roman antiquity. They did this by maximizing the gap between the 'dark' middle ages and the 'light' of their own age. For them, natural science and rational enquiry had replaced Christian belief as the agency of human progress. The liberation of the individual from feudal social hierarchies – as well as the liberation of the human mind from self-serving clerical dogmas – represented the birth of modernity.

So the millennium between the fall of the Western Roman empire and the Renaissance became an unfortunate interlude, a regression in humanity. Gibbon's famous history of Roman decline and fall invited modern Europeans to share in elegant mourning for antiquity, mixing sadness with the fun of anti-clerical mockery. As for the moral import of Christian beliefs, it often received short shrift. Gibbon's comment about a late Roman matron who gave her daughter to Christ because she was determined to be 'the mother-in-law' of God says it all. For Gibbon and many of his contemporaries, the modern era of individual emancipation was a return to the freer, secular spirit of antiquity – a view that remains widespread, even if it is now largely purged of virulent anti-clericalism.

But just how free and secular were ancient Greece and Rome? In order to answer that question, we have to probe the religious and moral beliefs that originally gave rise to the institutions of the ancient city-state, the *polis*. For those beliefs shaped a distinctive conception of society, a conception of society that was not seriously challenged until the first century AD.

Once we look closely at the beliefs and practices which shaped Greece and Rome in their infancy, and which survived in large part at their apogee, we find ourselves drawn back to an utterly remote moral world – to an Indo-European world that antedated even the polytheism we normally associate with Greece and Rome. We find ourselves entering a mind-set that generated a conception of society in which the family was everything. It was not only (in our terms) a civil but also a religious institution, with the paterfamilias acting not only as the family's magistrate but also as its high priest.

To recapture that world – to see and feel what acting in it was like – requires an extraordinary imaginative leap. The writer who has best succeeded in making that leap into the minds of the peoples settling Greece and the Italian peninsula several millennia ago was a French historian, Fustel de Coulanges. His book *The Ancient City* (1864), one of the most remarkable books of the nineteenth century, reveals how prehistoric religious beliefs shaped first the domestic and then the public institutions of Greece and Rome. It exposes the nature of the ancient family. 'The study of the ancient rules of private law enables us to obtain a glimpse, beyond the times that are called historic, of a succession of centuries during which the family was the sole form of society.'[1]

Working backwards from the earliest Greek and Roman law codes, Fustel de Coulanges explores a world in which ancestor worship created a domestic religion. His book remains by far 'the most influential of modern works on the ancient city'.[2] Yet Fustel himself distrusted much modern writing about antiquity, apparently considering that terms like 'rationality' and 'private property' can introduce anachronism and prevent us from entering minds and institutions so different from our own. 'If we desire to understand antiquity, our first rule should be to support ourselves upon the evidence that comes from the ancients.'[3] It is that determination that gives Fustel's work its great value.

Fustel draws not only on the first law codes, but also on the earliest historians, philosophers and playwrights in order to recapture the meaning of the beliefs that shaped the ancient family and city. He may at times exaggerate the symmetry and reach of those beliefs, when tracing the emergence of the Greek and Roman polis from a prehistoric society of families. Other causes were at work. The reality was at times more messy than Fustel suggests. For the way humans understand themselves never captures the whole truth. It selects, simplifies and at times distorts. Nonetheless, Fustel's ability to trace the roots of institutions from language itself and early law is remarkable. Thus, his account remains close to the understanding which ancient thinkers – not least Aristotle – had of their own social development.[4] Their beliefs about themselves were Fustel's central concern. They will also be ours.

For Fustel, at its origin the ancient family was both the focus and the medium of religious belief. It was an instrument of immortality, at once a metaphysic and a cult. The practices of the ancient family met the needs of self-conscious creatures seeking to overcome the fact of death. Around the family hearth – with the father tending its sacred fire, offering sacrifices, libations and incantations learned from his father – members of the family achieved union with their ancestors and prepared their future. The fire on the family hearth could not be allowed to die out, for it was deemed to be alive. Its flickering, immaterial flame did not just represent the family's ancestors. It *was* their ancestors, who were thought to live underground and who had to be provided with food and drink, if they were not to become malevolent spirits. Tending the fire therefore became an overarching obligation. The eldest son would succeed his father as custodian of the rites of the family hearth, that is, as its high priest. And his eldest son would follow him.

The circle established by religious belief was exclusively domestic. Gods could not be shared. Only deceased males related by blood could be worshipped as family gods. And it was believed that dead ancestors would only accept offerings from members of the family. Strangers were therefore excluded from the worship of the dead, for fear of gross impropriety or sacrilege. 'The ancient Greek language has a very significant word to designate a family. It is . . . a word which signifies, literally, that which is near a hearth. A family was a group of persons whom religion permitted to invoke the same sacred fire, and to offer the funeral repast to the same ancestors.'[5] If the hearth was not properly protected and tended, the ancestors ('gods of the interior') who 'rested' beneath it would become dissatisfied and wandering, as demons making trouble for the living rather than as gods.

These beliefs in the sacred fire and divine ancestors, revealed by study of the roots of the Greek and Latin languages (which Fustel supplemented with other Indo-European sources such as the Vedas), should not be dismissed as mere anthropological curiosities. For practices established by these beliefs survived, even if modified, into historical times as the domestic practices of Greece and Rome. Indeed, they established the framework of everyday life until the advent of Christianity.

In the house of every Greek and Roman was an altar; on this altar there had always to be a small quantity of ashes, and a few lighted coals. It was a sacred obligation for the master of every house to keep the fire up night and day. Woe to the house where it was extinguished. Every evening they covered the coal with ashes to prevent them from being entirely consumed. In the morning the first care was to revive this fire with a few twigs. The fire ceased to glow upon the altar only when the entire family had perished; an extinguished hearth, an extinguished family, were synonymous expressions among the ancients.[6]

The absolute authority of the eldest male, keeper of the sacred fire and preserver of the family cult, later found expression as paterfamilias. His authority was a direct consequence of religious belief. And for any son to remain single was deemed to be a dereliction of duty, because it was a threat to the immortality of the family.

Other domestic practices in Greece and Rome – the subordinate role of women, the nature of marriage, property rights and inheritance rules – were also direct consequences of religious belief. Let us take the role of women first. Women could participate in the worship of the dead only through their father or husband. For descent was traced exclusively through the male line. But even then religion governed the definition of relationships so entirely that an adopted son, once he was admitted to the family worship, shared its ancestors, while a son who abandoned the family worship ceased altogether to be a relation, becoming unknown.

If we return to the example of a bride being carried across the threshold of her new home, we can now begin to understand the origins of the practice. In a world where the family was the only social institution, and the family worship the source of personal identity, the move from one family to another was a truly momentous step for a young woman, a step that changed her identity completely. So what had to happen for a marriage to take place? First, the daughter had to be separated for ever from her own family, in a formal ceremony before its sacred fire. But in renouncing her family worship, she lost all identity. She became, temporarily, a non-person. That is why her future husband had to carry her across the threshold of his family house. Only when she had been received into the worship of her new family, in another solemn ceremony before their sacred fire, did she acquire a new identity – an identity that enabled her to enter and leave the house of her own accord. Now, once again, she had ancestors and a future.

Clearly, the family – past, present and future – was the basic unit of social reality. It was necessarily the building block of any larger social units. Nothing could legitimately violate its domain. Fustel argues that this reflected a prehistoric period when the family, more or less extended, was the only social institution, long before the growth of cities and governments. Beating the bounds of the family domain was understood as establishing not just a physical but also a moral frontier. Outside that frontier were strangers and enemies. Nor were these two sharply distinguished. Initially at least, those outside the family circle were not deemed to share any attributes with those within. No common humanity was acknowledged, an attitude confirmed by the practice of enslavement.

There was an intimate connection between these beliefs about the nature of the family and the origin of the idea of property rights. The family hearth or altar, and with it the divine ancestors or gods of the family, provided the focus of a sedentary life, of a fixed relationship with the soil.

> There are three things which, from the most ancient times, we find founded and solidly established in these Greek and Roman societies: the domestic religion; the family; and the right of property – three things which had in the beginning a manifest relation, and which appear to have been inseparable. The idea of private property existed in the religion itself. Every family had its hearth and its ancestors. These gods could be adored only by this family, and protected it alone. They were its property.[7]

The boundaries of the family property were also the boundaries of a sacred domain. Just as two sacred fires and the gods they embodied could not be merged, even through intermarriage, so family enclosures had to remain distinct.

This primitive belief survived in practices centuries later, when the Greeks and Romans first built cities. For while urban houses had to be much closer together, they could not be contiguous or joined – some space, however slight, had to separate them. 'At Rome the law fixed two feet and a half as the width of the free space, which was always to separate two houses, and this space was consecrated to "the god of the enclosure".'[8] No doubt the building of tenements later compromised this prohibition. But it shaped Roman property law at the outset.

Today when we see other humans, we see them first of all as individuals with rights, rather than family members, each with an assigned status. That is, we now see humans as rational agents whose ability to reason and choose makes it right to attribute to them an underlying equality of status, a moral equality. We are even inclined to see this moral equality as a fact of perception rather than a social valuation, so ingrained is our assumption that rational agency demands equal concern and respect.

Yet as we can already see it was not always so. In recapturing the prehistoric religious beliefs and practices that gave rise to the Greek and Roman city, the roots of their domestic institutions, we find ourselves entering a world of, so to speak, small family churches. No one was allowed to worship at more than one hearth or sacrifice to more than one series of divine ancestors – for each series constituted a perpetual divinity, joining past, present and future family members and protecting them exclusively. To be involved in sacrifices at more than one sacred hearth would have been seen as monstrous, an impiety likely to bring disaster to both families.

As each family had its own gods, from whom it sought protection and to whom it offered sacrifices, separation from the family worship involved losing all personal identity. That is why Fustel de Coulanges was right to insist that the ancient family was founded, not on birth, affection or physical force, but rather on religion. Powerful religious beliefs that antedated belief in the gods surrounding Zeus or Jupiter shaped the domestic institutions of the Greeks and Romans. These beliefs reflected a period when there were only families, more or less extended – that is, a period before the creation of cities.

Larger associations did, however, gradually develop. And the emergence of polytheism was a symptom of the development of such associations. If, originally, the only unit of lasting human association was the family, and the basis of that association was religious belief, then certain conditions had to be satisfied before wider associations became possible. Before cities could emerge, new associations of families had to develop – first the *gens* or extended family, then clans (called phratries in Greek and *curiae* in Latin), and finally tribes. Fustel did not claim that there was always a tie of family within these larger associations. But when they were formed, their beliefs obliged them to find a common divinity. Each extension of human association required the establishment of a new worship, recognition of a divinity superior to the domestic divinities.

Vestiges of these intermediate associations long survived amid the institutions of the Greek and Roman city. In so far as each step forward in human association required an extension of religious belief – the acknowledgement of shared divinities – the original model of the domestic religion continued to impose itself. Its tenacity still strikes ancient historians.[9]

Evidently we are a long way from the Enlightenment's vision of a free, secular spirit dominating antiquity, a world untrammelled by religious authority or priesthood. Driven by anti-clerical convictions, these eighteenth-century thinkers failed to notice something important about the Graeco-Roman world. They failed to notice that the ancient family began as a veritable church. It was a church which constrained its members to an extent that can scarcely be exaggerated. The father, representing all his ancestors, was himself a god in preparation. His wife counted only as part of her husband, having ancestors and descendants only through him. The authority of the father as priest and magistrate initially extended even to the right to repudiate or kill his wife as well as his children. Celibacy and adultery were accounted serious crimes, for they threatened, in different ways, the family worship.

Yet the father exercised his authority on the basis of beliefs shared by the family. His was not an arbitrary power. The overwhelming imperative was to preserve the family worship, and so to prevent his ancestors, untended, being cast into oblivion. This restriction of affection to the family circle gave it an extraordinary intensity. Charity, concern for humans as such, was not deemed a virtue, and would probably have been unintelligible. But fulfilling obligations attached to a role in the family was everything. 'The sense of duty, natural affection, the religious idea – all these were confounded, were considered as one, and were expressed by the same word.'[10] That word was piety (*pietas*).

Nor should we suppose that the claims of family piety were much weakened in later, historical times, when families were joined in larger associations. Observing those claims continued, for example, to shape the daily routine of the Roman citizen. 'Morning and evening he invokes his fire . . . and his ancestors; in leaving and entering his house, he addresses a prayer to them,' Fustel notices. 'Every meal is a religious act, which he shares with his domestic divinities; birth, initiation, the taking of the toga, marriage, and the anniversaries of all these events, are the solemn acts of his worship.'[11]

Virgil's great epic, the *Aeneid*, written when the Roman republic was giving way to the empire, is a testament to the claims of piety in circumstances of distress. Bernini's statue of Aeneas, Anchises and Ascanius – kept today at the Villa Borghese in Rome – embodies those claims. It shows Aeneas, after the fall of Troy, carrying away his father Anchises and the household gods, while his son Ascanius carries the household fire. Father and son are carrying away what mattered most to them. It is a powerful visual representation of the idea of piety.

On close inspection, then, the domestic institutions of the Greeks and Romans – institutions that provided the foundation for their public law and political institutions – were shaped by beliefs about the claims of sacred ancestors. Nowhere is this clearer than in the idea of property rights that resulted. In the earliest Greek and Roman law, the sale of property was virtually forbidden. And even in later, historical ages such a sale was surrounded by prohibitions and penalties. The reason is clear. Family property was integral to the family worship. 'Religion required that the hearth should be fixed to the soil, so that the tomb should neither be destroyed nor displaced. Suppress the right of property and the sacred fire would be without a fixed place, the families would become confounded and the dead would be abandoned and without worship.'[12] It followed that property belonged not to an individual man, but to the family. The eldest male possessed the land as a trust. The rule of succession made this clear. For property followed the same rule as family worship. It devolved upon the eldest son, or, in the absence of male children, it went to the nearest male relative. Daughters could not inherit. In Athens if the deceased had only a daughter, she was required to marry the heir – even if the heir or she was already married!

The disposal of property was not a matter of contract or individual choice. In the earliest period the Greeks and Romans understood property primarily as a means of perpetuating the family worship. In Athens, the will or right of testament was unknown until Solon's time (sixth century BC), and his innovations only permitted it for the childless. It later made headway only against very strong religious scruples. Fustel de Coulanges has no difficulty finding examples of the survival of such scruples even in Athens' greatest period. Plato, in his *Laws*, treats contemptuously the wish of a man on his deathbed to dispose of his property as he pleases: 'Thou who art only a pilgrim here below, does it belong to thee to decide such affairs? Thou art the master neither of thy property nor of thyself; thou and thy estate, all these things, belong to thy family; that is to say, to thy ancestors and to thy posterity.'[13]

It is tempting for a moment to adopt the idiom of the eighteenth-century Enlightenment and call these beliefs 'prejudices'. These prejudices founded a hierarchical conception of society in antiquity, and they long survived the earliest, undiluted forms of ancestor worship. It is true that many legal arrangements founded on these prejudices were modified in historical times: the disposal of property was made easier and paternal authority came to be somewhat restricted. Changes occurred which prepared the ground for a moral revolution.

Yet the Greeks and Romans continued to understand 'society' as an association of families, each with its own cult – and not as an association of individuals. Hence justice within the family remained basically a matter for the paterfamilias, not for the city. Paternal authority deriving from the domestic religion entailed the subordination of women.

> The Greek laws and those of Rome are to the same effect. As a girl, she is under her father's control; if her father dies, she is governed by her brothers; married, she is under the guardianship of her husband; if the husband dies, she does not return to her own family, for she has renounced that forever by the sacred marriage; the widow remains subject to the guardianship of her husband's agnates – that is to say, of her own sons, if she has any, or, in default of sons, of the nearest kindred.[14]

Thus, the inviolability of the domestic sphere and the exclusive character of family worship were intimately joined together. They established a moral boundary that the ancient city, as it developed, was obliged to respect. The domain of legislation stopped at the property of the family. Interfering with property was interfering with a domestic religion, that is, with the most sacred obligations. The treatment of debtors confirms this. For while a debtor lost control of his own labour, his property could not be touched.

We are now in a better position to understand the chief consequence of Greek and Roman religious beliefs for the ordering of their society and government. It is a consequence which even Fustel does not identify clearly enough. In order to understand it, we must abandon the modern distinction between public and private spheres, the distinction that underpins our notions of civil society and individual liberty.

For the Greeks and Romans, the crucial distinction was not between the public and private spheres. It was between the public and domestic spheres. And the domestic sphere was understood as the sphere of the family, rather than as that of individuals endowed with rights. The domestic sphere was a sphere of inequality. Inequality of roles was fundamental to the worship of the ancient family. Little wonder, then, that when the ancient city was created citizenship was available only to the paterfamilias and, later, his sons. Women, slaves and the foreign-born (who had no hearth or worship of their own, no recognized ancestors) were categorically excluded. Family piety ruled them out. Piety raised a barrier that could not be scaled.

There was an intensity of feeling within the ancient family unknown to us. But this intensity came at the price of moral transparency – of what we could call the claims of humanity.

2

The Ancient City

We have explored a pre-historic world in which the family was everything, a world in which obligation, gods and priesthood were exclusively domestic. How do we get from such a world to the world of cities and historical memory in Greece and Italy? How did the range of human association increase, gradually giving birth to political institutions, to the polis or city-state – indeed, to the very idea of politics?

It is important to find out, because the city-state later gave rise to a tradition of political discourse – usually called classical republicanism – which is still influential. It is a tradition that has at times been invoked to condemn such basic institutions of the modern world as the nation-state, the market and representative government. This was particularly the case during the second half of the eighteenth century. Perhaps inspired by the writings of Jean-Jacques Rousseau, leading French revolutionaries began to invoke the 'virtue' of ancient citizens – their single-minded concern with *res publica* or the public weal – in an attempt to remould European society and government. The rhetoric of Robespierre, for example, suggested that ancient citizenship provided the test of 'true' liberty. For him, ancient liberty became the most authentic liberty.

This claim ought to give us pause. We have already discovered an ancient world which was by no means secular. We have discovered that the family and its worship of sacred ancestors – veritable small churches – were the building blocks of ancient society. If that society did not sustain anything like the role of the individual, with equality before the law and individual rights, how can its political institutions be identified with liberty? What kind of liberty is being spoken of, when such a claim is made? Did the development of the ancient city lead, after all, to the destruction of the family as a cult and the emergence of individual rights? Did ancient citizenship mark the advent of secularism? And if not, what was the meaning of ancient liberty?

To answer these questions, we must look more closely at the transition from a world of families to a world of cities – moving from the third and second millennia to the first millennium BC.

Although the family which shaped pre-Greek and Roman institutions was our point of departure, it would be a mistake to conceive of that family in modern terms, as anything like a modern nuclear family. The very religious beliefs which helped to constitute that family led to its rapid expansion in size. Younger sons and their offspring remained attached to the family hearth and its sacred fire. Moreover, as the number of subordinate families grew in successive generations, the patriarchal family (or *gens*) acquired dependants. Some became permanently attached to the family by being admitted to an inferior role – resembling that of women – in the family worship. There might also be slaves, with no religious connection, attached to the family.

How did such patriarchal families or *gentes* eventually form larger associations? They did so in the only way known to them. That is, they came to acknowledge a shared ancestor and founded a common worship. An altar was raised to a divinity or 'hero' held in common. A ceremonial meal – comparable to the 'sacred' repast of the household – was then established. These wider associations required their own priesthood, assembly and rites. For a new religious identity sustained the phratry or *curia*, what we might call a clan. When these new associations, in turn, increased in size and proximity, they came to establish a still wider association, called a tribe. The tribe too required its sacred altar and a god. That god was also generally 'a man deified, a hero'.

The ancient city came into being when several tribes became associated, by founding a common worship, a worship that supplemented rather than replaced the pre-existing worships of *gens*, phratry or curia and tribe. Here Fustel de Coulanges's account has come in for criticism. He may well have exaggerated the coherence attending the founding of cities. Were they always founded by clans having familial origins? Probably not.[1] Yet, as we have seen, Fustel did not claim that there was always a tie of family within these larger associations. Nor does his argument exclude the likelihood that incorporation in a polis changed the role of associations. And one fact remains. In terms of their formal organization, both Greece and Rome built civic institutions around the claims of such subsidiary groups. They catered for the claims of phratries or *curias* as well as tribes, giving each a formal role. The city that emerged was thus a confederation of cults, an association superimposed on other associations, all modelled on the family and its worship. The ancient city was not an association of individuals.

Religious ideas expanded with the increased scale of association. Fustel does not argue that religious progress brought about social progress in any simple way, but he does emphasize the intimate connection between the two. Thus, as the scale of association increased, the gods of nature or polytheism became more important – for these were gods who could more easily be shared, gods less exclusively domestic than ancestors, gods associated with the forces of nature rather than with divine ancestors. These were gods who represented the sea, the wind, fertility, light, love, hunting, with familiar names such as Apollo, Neptune, Venus, Diana and Jupiter. The building of civic temples to these gods offered physical evidence of the enlargement of religious ideas. Still, the gods of each city remained exclusive, so that while two cities might both adore 'Jupiter', he had different attributes in each city.

Particularism was the rule. Even after a city was founded, it was inconceivable for the city not to respect the divine ancestors, the sacred rites and magistracies of the different groups that had attended its foundation. For the souls of the dead were deemed to live on under the ground of the cities they had helped to create. The statesman Solon, who in the sixth century BC endowed Athens with laws, was given the following advice by the oracle of Delphi: 'Honour with worship the chiefs of the country, the dead who live under the earth.'[2] The city had to respect their authority in matters concerning their descendants. For the city's authority was all of a piece with theirs. Gods and groups marched hand in hand.

This corporate, sacramental character of the ancient city dominated its formal organization. Whether it was a question of procedures for voting, military organization or religious sacrifices, care was taken to represent tribes, *curiae* and families – and to conduct civic life through them. It was deemed important that men should be associated most closely with others who sacrificed at the same altars. Altars were the bonds of human association. That emerged in the Greek and Roman conception of warfare. In one of Euripides' plays, a soldier asserts that 'the gods who fight with us are more powerful than those who fight on the side of the enemy'.[3]

The progress of a young Athenian or Roman towards full citizenship recapitulated the progress of association that underpinned the city. Born into a family and joined to its worship a few days after birth, the youth was years later initiated successively into the cults of curia and tribe (each involved a ceremonial meal, a 'sacred' repast), before in his late teens being formally accepted as a citizen in a public ceremony.

> At the age of sixteen or eighteen, he [a young Athenian] is presented for admission to the city. On that day, in the presence of an altar, and before the smoking flesh of a victim, he pronounces an oath, by which he binds himself always to respect . . . the religion of the city. From that day he is initiated into the public worship, and becomes a citizen. If we observe this young Athenian, step by step, from worship to worship, we have a symbol of the degrees through which human association has passed. The course which this young man is constrained to follow is that which society first followed.[4]

The successive worships into which the ancient citizen was initiated left no space for individual conscience or choice. These worships claimed authority over not just his actions but also his thoughts. Their rules governed his relations with himself as well as others. There was no sphere of life into which these rules could not enter – whether it was a matter of dress, deportment, marriage, sport, education, conversation or even ambition. If a citizen was deemed likely to acquire too much influence over others, and thus become a potential threat to the government of the city, he could be ostracized, that is, driven from the city. No subversive action or proof of intent was required. The safety and welfare of the city was everything.

The religious character of the ancient city was stamped on its form of government. 'If we wanted to give an exact definition of a citizen, we should say that it was a man who had the religion of the city.'[5] Originally, the magistrates of the city were also its priests; the two functions were not distinguished. The ceremonies attached to every association, the sacred meals dedicated to their presiding deities, were in the city the responsibility of the magistrates. Honouring the gods of the city was their primary duty. And just as the gods had originally been exclusively domestic, the gods of the city were not shared with strangers. Even gods of nature adopted by a city became, as we have seen, patriotic. Thus, the priesthood of one city had no connection with the priesthood of another city. There were no doctrines held in common. For the gods of the city were exclusively interested in its welfare, its protection. They were 'jealous' of it.

Kingship was the highest priesthood, presiding over the cult established with the city itself. The king was hereditary high priest of that association of associations that was the ancient city. The king's other functions, as magistrate and military leader, were simply the adjuncts of his religious authority. Who better to lead the city in war than the priest whose knowledge of the sacred formulas and prayers 'saved' the city every day? And, later, when kingship gave way to republican regimes, the chief magistrate of the city – the archon in Athens, the consul in Rome – remained a priest whose first duty was to offer sacrifices to the city's gods. In fact, the circlet of leaves worn on the head of archons when conducting such sacrifices became a universal symbol of authority: the crown.

Just as the highest magistrate was a priest, so the laws he defended were originally the laws of a religion, a perpetual endowment transmitted to the city by its heroic founder. Laws were the necessary consequences of religious belief. There was nothing like the modern notion of sovereignty, of a merely human agency with the authority to create new law. The priests jealously guarded the laws of the city, for the laws were understood to be the work of the gods. Indeed, they probably took the form of prayers before they came to be written down, and at first they may have been sung.

These ancient verses were invariable texts. To change a letter of them, to displace a word, to alter the rhythm, was to destroy the law itself, by destroying the sacred form under which it was revealed to man. The law was like a prayer, which was agreeable to the divinity only on condition that it was recited correctly, and which became impious if a single word in it was changed. In primitive law, the exterior, the letter, was everything; there is no need of seeking the sense or spirit of it. The value of the law is not in the moral principle that it contains, but in the words that make up the formula. Its force is in the sacred words that compose it.[6]

Even when laws were written down and became more numerous, they continued to be deposited with the priests. They could not be inspected by just anyone. For the laws were civil in a stringent sense: that is, they applied only to citizens. Living in a city was by no means to be placed under the protection of its laws. For example, neither slaves nor strangers resident in the city had such protection. Laws could establish a relationship only between men who shared in the worship of the city, sacrificing at the same altars. They alone were citizens.

Religious belief shaped the character of ancient 'patriotism'. Serving the 'fathers-land' emerges in the word itself. The defenders of an ancient city under siege were not moved by interest as we understand the term. They were not defending a public institution that had created and guaranteed individual rights. Neither were they inspired by the kind of historical narratives that have been created to celebrate and reinforce the identities of modern nation-states. There was nothing self-serving, abstract or sentimental about ancient patriotism.

The ancient citizen saw himself as defending the land of his ancestors, who were also his gods. His ancestors were inseparable from the ground of the city. To lose that ground was to lose the gods of the family. Indeed, the loss of the city meant that the gods had already abandoned it. That is why, whenever a new city was about to be founded, the first public rite involved its members digging a trench to receive soil carried from their previous city, representing the soil in which their ancestors had been buried. Citizens could then still say this was the land of their ancestors, *terra patria*. In Plutarch's account, Romulus, the founder of Rome, did exactly that, in order to establish a new residence for his ancestral gods. The foundation of a city was not the construction of a few houses, but the assertion of a hereditary religious identity, 'patriotism'.

When defending his city, the ancient citizen was therefore defending the very core of his identity. Religion, family and territory were inseparable, a combination which turned ancient patriotism into an overwhelming passion. The enslavement that often followed the unsuccessful defence of a city merely confirmed a truly dreadful anterior fact: the loss of identity that necessarily accompanied the loss of domestic gods.

We can now understand why patriotism was not only the most intense feeling but also the highest possible virtue for the ancient citizen. Everything that was important to him – his ancestors, his worship, his moral life, his pride and property – depended upon the survival and well-being of the city. That is why devotion to the 'sacred fatherland' was deemed the supreme virtue. In devoting himself to the city before everything else, the citizen was serving his gods. No abstract principle of justice could give him pause. Piety and patriotism were one and the same thing. For the Greeks, to be without patriotism, to be anything less than an active citizen, was to be an 'idiot'. That, indeed, is what the word originally meant, referring to anyone who retreated from the life of the city.

So it is no accident that exile was the most severe punishment the citizen of a polis could suffer. It was worse than death, or rather it was a living death. To be exiled meant to be separated from the religious rites and relationships that were the source of personal identity. The city-state or polis was not simply a physical setting or place for the citizen. It was his whole life.

> Let him leave its sacred walls, let him pass the sacred limits of its territory, and he no longer finds for himself either a religion or a social tie of any kind. Everywhere else, except in his own country, he is outside the regular life and the law; everywhere else he is without a god, and shut out from all moral life. There alone he enjoys his dignity as a man, and his duties. Only there can he be a man.[7]

This, of course, is why Aristotle later famously argued that the life of the citizen was the only life worth living.

Fustel de Coulanges illustrates the nature of the ancient city by noticing that the ancients made a distinction we do not make. They distinguished the *urbs* from the *civitas* when referring to the city.

What is the difference? The *urbs* is the physical location, the place of assembly and worship. But the *civitas* is the moral nexus, the religious and political association of the citizens. And in unusual circumstances that association might survive the destruction of the *urbs*. That, for Fustel, is the significance of the story of Aeneas, as told by Virgil. By preserving the sacred fire of Troy, after the sack of the city, Aeneas has preserved the moral basis of its association – which is to say, its gods. His quest thereafter is really their quest. It is they who identify their new home as Rome, and their will that prevents him settling anywhere else, even in Dido's Carthage. The epic, then, is not about one man's struggle, but about the successful struggle of the gods of Troy to become the gods of Rome.

Gods gave the lead to their cities. Only by taking this assumption seriously can we understand the practices of Greek and Roman cities in historical times, when republican regimes had replaced the original kingships. Votes were not enough by themselves to confer legitimacy on magistrates. In Athens, drawing lots was deemed to be the best means of ascertaining the choice of the gods. In Rome, election to consulships could only take place from a list offered by the presiding priest, who had spent the previous night observing the skies while intoning the names of candidates. If the auspices were deemed unfavourable, a name was excluded. That is why the Romans sometimes found themselves electing candidates whom they despised, rather than popular figures. The will of the gods was what mattered.

It was this belief that led the Greeks and Romans into their (to us) strange practices of divination. 'If Romulus had been a Greek, he would have consulted the oracle of Delphi; if a Samnite, he would have followed the sacred animal – the wolf or the green woodpecker. Being a Latin, and a neighbour of the Etruscans, initiated into the augurial science, he asks the gods to reveal their will to him by the flight of birds.'[8] These practices did not disappear in the later development of cities. They survived long into Greek and Roman history.

By the sixth century BC, nonetheless, things had begun to change. In both Greece and Italy, a radically hieratic society – in which paterfamilias was combined with priesthood – came under attack from the lower classes, classes that previously had no part in the government of the city. We must remember how few in numbers the citizens originally were. Citizens were originally simply the *patres*, something surviving in Roman usage when senators were called the 'fathers' of the city. In many cities younger sons could not become citizens while their father, the family's priest, was alive. Nor could the heads of junior branches of the family, formed over generations, claim that status. Even less could clients, who had no blood relationship to the family and its cult, have the privileges of citizenship.

Of course, to describe what was originally an unquestioned superiority of status as 'privilege' already suggests changing beliefs. It was symptomatic of a period when class conflicts began to erode the social structure on which the ancient city had been raised – conflicts between the 'equals' and 'inferiors' in Sparta, between the Eupatrids and thetes in Athens, and between the patricians and plebeians in Rome. But we ought not to exaggerate the extent or rapidity of change. Ancient beliefs, and the social structure they had created, were tenacious.

Even when social conflicts began to widen membership of the citizen class, the original basis of citizenship – sharing in the worship of the gods of the city – long remained. Evidence of the resistance of beliefs to change was the extreme difficulty of founding a single state in Greece out of its many city-states, a difficulty resting finally not so much on geography or technical backwardness, but on obstinate attachment to civic gods, who did not welcome strangers. Even marriage between people from different cities was viewed as strange, if not immoral. And when circumstances forced temporary alliances between cities, these would be represented on medals as two gods holding hands. The gods were not to be confounded!

Fear of the gods governed Greek and Roman conduct in war and in peace. Even if all the preparations had been made, an expedition or a battle could be postponed if the priests suddenly reported unfavourable auspices – a comet or partial eclipse perhaps, a flight of birds or something missing in the entrails of a sacrifice. Spartan campaigns were always regulated by the phases of the moon, while Athenian armies never undertook a campaign before the seventh day of the month. During the Peloponnesian War, the destruction of the Athenian fleet outside Syracuse – which led to the decline of Athens – owed not a little to reliance on omens. 'The Athenian, like the Roman, had unlucky days; on these days no marriage took place, no assembly was held, and justice was not administered.'⁹ To do otherwise, was to tempt the gods.

The intermingling of religion and government remained complete. From the sixth to the third century BC changes in the form of polis government – from monarchy to aristocracy, from aristocracy to democracy – did not reduce the authority of the city-state over its members. There was no notion of the rights of individuals against the claims of the city and its gods. There was no formal liberty of thought or action. Participation in the assembly and service as a magistrate, if chosen, were obligatory and enforced. Citizens belonged to the city, body and soul.

The liberty of the ancient citizen – celebrated by the classical republican tradition – was thus far removed from our own idea of liberty. Ancient liberty consisted of having a share in the government of the city, in public power. It consisted of the privilege and duty to attend the assembly, speak in debates, judge the arguments, take sides and vote, with the further possibility of serving as a magistrate or on a jury, if required. Ancient liberty did not tolerate indifference to the political process. The public thing, *res publica*, was everything.

The domestic sphere, with its personal attachments or relationships, might count as nothing. Fustel de Coulanges tells a story about Sparta, drawn from Plutarch, that Rousseau later held up to the eighteenth century as exemplary. The Spartan army had suffered a serious defeat at Leuctra, with terrible loss of life. When the news reached the city, relatives of the dead were required to appear 'with gay countenances', while the mothers of those who survived were required to weep and lament their survival. There is probably an element of myth here. Yet nothing better illustrates the unlimited demands of the ancient city – the absence of a private sphere with legitimate claims – than this story.

Citizenship, with its superior status and its share in public power, was demanding. Citizens were constantly on display – like actors performing before their public, a public consisting, however, of their inferiors, of younger sons, clients, women and slaves. If divested of the religious beliefs that had created the role, citizenship retained great aesthetic appeal, the appeal of superiority and power, gravitas and pride. Or so it must have seemed to a class of men who gradually increased in numbers, a class settled in the polis but not forming part of its 'people'. Why not? The defining feature of this class, called in Rome the plebeians or *plebs*, was that it had no religious connection with the city or its foundation. Probably formed of later arrivals, the *plebs* had no domestic altars, and therefore no ancestors, no gods. The plebs did not have even that indirect connection with a family worship shared by clients. It was this class that, along with the clients, began to contest the limits of citizenship.

So the history of Greek city-states from the sixth century BC until the advent of the Roman empire is dominated by class conflict – by argument about who should be included in the citizen class. But argument was still limited by assumptions inherited from the cult of the ancient family. That is, there was no question of women, slaves or the foreign-born being included in public life. They remained confined to the domestic sphere, the sphere of inferiority. Only one city, Rome, offered an important exception to this rule.

The long period of aristocratic ascendancy in Greek and Italian cities, founded on the family and its worship, had already reduced kingship to a religious role, stripping kings of political authority. The reason for this is clear enough. Kings had frequently made common cause with the lower classes. They had formed alliances with clients and the *plebs*, directed against the power of the aristocracy. Challenged both from without (by a class which had no family worship or gods) and from within (by clients questioning the traditional ordering of the family), the aristocracy of the cities carried through a political revolution to avoid a social revolution.

Nonetheless, a social revolution slowly took place. Fustel de Coulanges, living in the mid-nineteenth century, drew on modern European history in order to understand that revolution. For it was a question of understanding a very gradual, incremental process, a transformation of social structure not unlike the process which had eroded feudal institutions in France from the thirteenth to the eighteenth century. Two of Fustel's immediate predecessors, François Guizot and Alexis de Tocqueville, had explored the role of class conflict in forwarding that process. Fustel finds something remarkably similar when trying to understand the social forces that undermined the aristocratic institutions resting on the ancient family and its worship.

Analysing a social revolution involved going beyond what could be found in the narratives of ancient historians. Their focus had been primarily political. They were concerned to describe and analyse observable political events in the world of city-states. Alliances, foreign wars and civil wars – these were their bread and butter. Even the subtlest of the ancient historians, Thucydides, takes the social structure of the polis largely for granted. Fustel, on the other hand, seeks to understand a fundamental change in that structure, drawing on incidental information in ancient sources, especially information about the nature and distribution of property.

The first major change took place within the patriarchal family. Primogeniture came under attack and gradually gave way, with the consequence not only that younger sons inherited and became full citizens, but also that junior branches of the ancient families or *gentes* became independent. These developments greatly increased the number of citizens, and reduced the power of the ancient family heads as priests.

A second major change followed. The clients of the family were gradually liberated, becoming free men. At the outset clients could not own property. They did not even have any security of tenure on land they worked for the paterfamilias. They were little better than slaves. 'Possibly the same series of social changes took place in antiquity which Europe saw in the middle ages, when the slaves in the country became serfs of the glebe, when the latter from serfs, taxable at will, were changed to serfs with a fixed rent, and when finally they were transformed . . . into peasant proprietors.'[10]

Fundamental to these changes was a rise in expectations. That rise was, in turn, due to the comparisons that became possible once the patriarchal family was merely part of a larger association, the polis or city-state. No longer was the paterfamilias, the magistrate and priest, the only representative of authority in sight, the only spokesman of the gods. The paterfamilias gradually lost his semi-sacred status through being immersed in civic life. His inferiors now 'could see each other, could confer together, could make an exchange of their desires and griefs, compare their masters, and obtain a glimpse of a better fate'.[11]

Obtaining the right of property was their first and strongest desire, preceding any claim for the full privileges of citizenship. But the latter was bound to follow, for obtaining greater equality on one front only increased a sense of exclusion on the other. Citizenship, in turn, unleashed a process of abstraction which could and did threaten inherited inequalities.

No one understood this better than a series of rulers called tyrants. Tyranny was acceptable to the previously underprivileged classes because it was a means of undermining the old aristocracy. Tyrants were so called because 'kingship' evoked a religious role, a role that recalled the subordinations based on the ancient family and its worship. The lower classes supported tyrants in order to combat their former superiors. Tyranny was an instrument that could be discarded when it had served its purpose, unlike the sacred authority claimed by the original kings. It was an instrument serving a sense of relative deprivation.

The dynamics resulting from a sense of relative deprivation slowly destroyed the hold of the original aristocracy on the city. But it would be utterly wrong to conclude that it destroyed aristocracy as such. On the contrary, what moved the younger sons, clients and *plebs* was a desire to share in the privileges of the citizen class – to cut a figure comparable to that of a class which had hitherto combined the gravitas of priests, the pride of rulers, and the glory of warriors. It was a class that enjoyed being seen in a heroic pose, stripped for action. The ancient taste for nudity was no mere accident. Nudity expressed a sense of social superiority – the superiority of citizens who rose above mere domestic concerns, seeking glory for themselves through the city, and for the city through themselves. To be seen naked was to be seen as superior to the meretricious and even sordid wants of women, merchants and slaves.

The domestic sphere, a sphere of radical inferiority, remained. The social revolution, which reshaped ancient city-states in the centuries before their eclipse under the Roman empire, did not tamper with that sphere. The social revolution was a struggle of the underprivileged for greater privilege. It was not a struggle for justice, as we understand the term.

The claims of the city remained pre-eminent. An enemy of the city had no rights. A Spartan king, when asked about the justice of seizing a Theban citadel in peacetime, replied: 'Inquire only if it was useful, for whenever an action is useful to our country, it is right.'[12] The treatment of conquered cities reflected this belief. Men, women, children and slaves were slaughtered or enslaved without compunction. Houses, fields, domestic animals, anything serving the gods of the foe might be laid waste. If the Romans spared the life of a prisoner, they required him to swear the following oath: 'I give my person, my city, my land, the water that flows over it, my boundary gods, my temples, my movable property, everything which pertains to the gods – these I give to the Roman people.'[13]

When the fortune of their own city was at stake, the Greeks and Romans were implacable.

3

The Ancient Cosmos

The heroic role played out by the Greek and Roman citizen constantly confirmed his superiority. But it was not just a matter of ritual or public theatre. Whether as magistrate, priest or warrior, the citizen's actions were deemed to incorporate a powerful rationality. His actions were proper responses to the claims of the city and its gods. Decisions by the assembly of citizens allowed for no independent review. The idea of individual rights was absent. Social subordinates were, after all, not deemed to be fully rational. No doubt women, merchants and slaves had important social functions, but their minds did not rise to the public sphere and its concerns. Instead, gossip, mercenary calculation and uncomplaining obedience were their respective lots.

We are encountering a conception of 'reason' very different from that of the modern world, for it 'carried' within it hierarchical assumptions about both the social and the physical world. We can see these assumptions about the superiority of the citizen and his cult of honour emerging in Xenophon's dialogue, the *Hiero*:

> All creatures seem in a similar fashion to take pleasure in food, drink, sleep and sex. But that love of honour does not grow up in animals lacking speech. Nor, for that matter, can it be found in all human beings. The lust for honour and praise grows up only in those who are most fully distinguished from the beasts of the fields: which is to say that it grows up only in those judged to be real men and no longer mere human beings.[1]

The citizen was a kind of superman. Public life, founded on religious observances, gave citizens the opportunity to express both their piety and patriotism. For citizens, it was assumed, joined a sense of the proper ordering of things to their taste for glory. What we would call their 'status' was understood rather as natural endowment. This assumption probably had roots in a period when citizens, relatively few in number, were not only priests and magistrates, but also had a virtual monopoly of literacy – with the status it conferred. However that may be, the assumption of superiority was later reinforced by the role of oratory in enlarged assemblies, the sophistication of public argument and the military prowess expected of citizens.

Yet gradual expansion of the citizen class did change the nature of its prestige. The sacerdotal family had to share the stage with new ways of organizing the citizenry. Family piety had to combine with new ways of thinking. In Athens, the move from aristocratic to democratic government altered the nature of the tribes. They became, in a sense, offshoots of the public assembly, reflecting the claims of citizenship and voting rather than of the sacerdotal family. A similar symptom of social change in Rome appeared when the army was no longer organized simply according to family and *gens*. Instead, centuries – that is, numbers – became the basis of its organization. Former clients and plebeians had often become rich (the introduction of money facilitating the circulation of property) and they played an increasingly important military role. The original aristocratic means of making war, the cavalry, had declined as compared to expensive, heavily armoured infantry: Greek hoplites and Roman legionaries. Thus numbers and money – introducing a touch of abstraction – came to count for more within the privileged citizen class, supplementing its religious foundation.

Wider participation in the government of the city, and the importance of public debate which resulted, had formidable intellectual consequences. New skills were fostered, skills required for careful argument and effective persuasion in the assembly. Logic and rhetoric thus came into existence as public disciplines. The ability to make a coherent case, defend it and present it persuasively to an audience of equals became a sine qua non for leadership in the city. The development of these critical and imaginative capacities contributed, by the fifth century BC, to the emergence of abstract, philosophical thinking out of religion and poetry. Athens became both its centre and a symbol.

Yet these developments had an important unintended consequence. Reason or rationality – *logos*, the power of words – became closely identified with the public sphere, with speaking in the assembly and with the political role of a superior class. Reason became the attribute of a class that commanded. At times reason was almost categorically fused with social superiority. So the assumption grew that reason could command – even when, paradoxically, it involved defining an immutable order or 'fate'. Thus the Roman writer Seneca felt able to prescribe the role of the stars: 'On even the slightest motion of these hang the fortunes of nations, and the greatest and smallest events are shaped to accord with the progress of a kindly or unkindly star.'[2]

The assumption that reason 'governed' shaped the understanding of both the social world and the physical world. In the physical world, the assumption emerged as a belief that purposes or ends (what Aristotle called 'final causes') governed all processes and entities. In that way, relationships within the non-human world were assimilated to reasons for acting in human life. It followed that reason could identify that towards which each thing 'naturally' tends, finding its proper place in a 'great chain of being'. In the social world, the assumption emerged as belief that there was a natural hierarchy, a superior class entitled by 'nature' to rule, constrain and, if need be, coerce. Thus, in a society where some were born to command and others to obey, the motivational power of reason seemed self-evident. Out of its own resources, reason could guarantee action.

This assumption deserves our attention. For it runs contrary to a central tradition in modern philosophy, especially to an empiricist tradition that gives reason a merely instrumental role. In this modern view, reason as a faculty cannot motivate: it does not move us to action. Reason merely provides us with the means of calculating the consequences of different courses of action. Characteristically, modern thought interposes a separate event in the individual – 'willing' – between deliberation and action. Yet even today it remains a matter of controversy whether Greek philosophers had a distinct concept of the will. If they did, it seems to have developed relatively late. What is more immediately striking is that Homeric Greek, the Greek of the *Iliad* and *Odyssey*, did not even have a word for 'intention'.[3]

By identifying rationality with social superiority – by taking for granted the deference of inferiors, of a domestic sphere – the ancient world had less need for a doctrine of the will. It had less need to posit a separate event or faculty preceding action in every person. The notion of human agency was shaped by the structure of society. Some were simply born to command and others to obey. Hence there was no ontological gap between thought and action. The status of the person who reasoned guaranteed the availability of action if required.

We can see the persistence of this assumption in antiquity, even after philosophy had emerged from the critical habits fostered by public debate in the assemblies. In the *Republic*, Plato asks what a just society would be like. He replies by arguing that we can most easily understand what it would be like by analogy with a just person. So what is characteristic of a just person? A just person is governed by reason, the highest faculty. Reason governs actions, and draws on the appetites for fuel. What are the social implications, according to Plato? As reason is the attribute of only a few – in fact, only of philosophers – it is philosophers who therefore ought to govern. They ought to direct the actions of a warrior class, which is in turn sustained by a large inferior class of what we might now be inclined to call workers.

Plato's use of this analogy is revealing. While he ostensibly argues from a picture of the just self to that of a just society, it is hard to resist the conclusion that the argument really proceeds in the other direction – and that he conceives of a just self on the model of a radically stratified society, a society in which there are groups ready-made to act on the conclusions of deductive argument. Of course, Plato's argument does not necessarily identify philosopher-kings with the traditional citizen class. To that extent, we can see the impact of more abstract, philosophical reflection. But his conception of society remains one in which radical status differences ensure the harmony of thought and action. For Plato, everyone is born with an attribute that fits him or her for a particular social role, his or her 'proper' place.

Several features of the ancient world make sense against the background of these assumptions – its contempt for labour and distrust of commerce, its admiration for military valour and, not least, its conception of the universe or cosmos.

We have already seen that civic virtue or patriotism, unlimited devotion to the welfare of the city, was accounted the highest virtue. Now the chief threat to civic virtue was deemed to be a taste for 'luxury', a taste that the development of money had no doubt fortified. The admirers of Sparta often attributed this taste to Athens and Corinth. In their view, luxury led inexorably to the corruption of a city. Luxury distracted citizens from their proper concern, which was the public weal. By indulging a taste for luxury, citizens were led instead into a preoccupation with wealth and its perquisites: consumption, display and pleasure. By contrast, Sparta was cited as the model for citizens living an austere common life, always ready to answer the call of duty, with weapons at hand. Spartans were stripped for action.

Doubtless there was more than a little propaganda in this view. But that did not make it any less influential, either at the time or later, when it became a stock-in-trade of the classical republican tradition. For this rhetoric captured an important aspect of thinking about the city-state. The growth of luxury represented a withdrawal into the domestic sphere, and a weakening of the citizens' public ardour, fostering instead a kind of self-indulgence and even effeminacy. And the latter quality was a symptom of the inferior nature of the domestic sphere.

Honour, rather than pleasure, ought to be the concern of the citizen. For honour or 'glory' was the public reward for virtue. Socrates dramatized the choice facing citizens when repeating the story of a debate between 'Vice' and 'Virtue' staged before the young Heracles. After Vice has offered the boy rapid access to happiness through pleasure, Virtue exclaims:

> What can you know of real pleasure . . . ? You fill yourself full of everything even before you feel the need. Before feeling hunger, you eat; before feeling thirst, you drink. In order that you may take pleasure in dining, you contrive the presence of chefs; in order that you may take pleasure in drinking, you equip yourself with expensive wines and rush about in search of snow in summer; and in order that you may take pleasure in sleeping, you provide yourself not only with soft bedding, but with a frame for your couch as well . . . You force sex before it is needed, contriving everything and using men in place of women. You train your friends, behaving arrogantly at night and sleeping through

the most useful hours of the day. You never hear praise, the most pleasant of all things to hear; and you never see the most pleasant of all
things to see: for nothing is more pleasant to see than one's own noble
work.[4]

The admiration of other citizens – not to mention inferiors – was
what mattered. And that admiration had to be won through single-
minded devotion to the public weal. It was a goal that required clear
thinking and self-control. The heroes in Thucydides' account of the
war between Athens and Sparta (the Peloponnesian War, 431–404 BC)
are the prototypes, making a contrast with the self-indulgent, aber-
rant behaviour of an anti-hero like the traitorous Alcibiades.

At the heart of this rhetoric was a simple contrast between mascu-
line hardness and feminine softness. If the former was associated
especially with the warrior citizens of Sparta and early Republican
Rome, the latter was associated not only with the more pleasure-loving
societies of Athens and Corinth but also, later, with Imperial Rome.
Thus commerce became associated with 'giving in' to appetites – with
refinements, sensual pleasures and a narcissism that subverted civic
spirit. Commerce became the enemy of simplicity. It became almost a
synonym for decadence. Commerce, along with the taste for luxury it
promoted, turned men into quasi-women. Cicero, the orator and
Roman moralist, liked to cite a saying by Archytas of Tarentum on the
evils posed to the polis by luxury and sensuality: 'the greatest of these
evils is that it predisposes men to unpatriotic acts'.[5]

The cult of the heroic male nude, who steadfastly resisted the lure
of 'mere' appetites, served to complete the contrast between the qualities required for public life and the qualities fostered by the domestic
sphere. For the citizen had to be prepared to be a warrior. He had not
only to defend the territory and gods of his city, but also be ready to
take part in any expeditions the assembly might decide upon. The
Spartan warrior was always on call.

As we have seen, military expeditions against other cities were not
judged on abstract grounds of justice. What alone mattered was the
prospect of success. The king of Sparta, Archidamus, urged war
against Athens in the following way: 'Remember, then, that you are
marching against a very great city. Think, too, of the glory or, if events

turn out differently, the shame which you will bring to your ancestors and to yourselves, and, with all this in mind, follow your leaders, paying the strictest attention to discipline . . .'[6]

Apart from glory, the advantage to be gained by success was as much economic as political. For in antiquity there was no clear distinction between military and economic activity. How could there be? Part of the point of warfare and conquest was enslavement of the enemy. War was also the recruitment of labour. Little wonder, therefore, that labour was seen as dishonourable. It was associated with defeat and permanent social inferiority.

Inevitably, such radical status differences spilled over into judgements about the proper uses of the mind, that is, about rationality. The contrast between the 'noble' qualities of the citizen and the inferior skills of the merchant were a case in point. The grave reflection and persuasion that fostered knowledge of the public weal stood in sharp contrast to the bargaining and calculation of the marketplace. It was deemed demeaning for the citizen to use his mind in such a way. He had better things to do. (Is this why Romans regarded the enormous wealth accumulated by generals and governors in their service as 'inadvertent'?)

Of course, the faculty of speech and reason – logos – carried with it another possibility: disagreement. If men could disagree about how words were to be used in the most mundane, domestic matters, how much greater were the discords that might result from arguments in the assembly. At worst, appeals to the public good might simply cloak citizens' defence of partial interests, while the pursuit of honour might become the plaything of vanity, in what might be called the Alcibiades syndrome. When such things happened, the polis had become corrupt. The domestic sphere had come to overwhelm the public sphere, alone the sphere of nobility.

The danger of civil war always lurked in the background of public argument. For it could undermine the city entirely, leading to the destruction not just of the *urbs* but also of the *civitas*, the moral community or nexus of association. This extreme danger could take the form of one faction or class within the city appealing to another city for its intervention – a tactic that helped the neighbouring Macedonian kingdom gradually to subdue Greek cities. Such action amounted to the renunciation or abandonment of logos, of rational argument in the assembly. It was the collective equivalent of the penalty of exile for particular citizens, because it plunged the city into a similarly strange world without norms, a world without family or civic gods whose aid could be counted on.

The threat that held the prospect of *stasis* or civil war at bay was the threat of conquest. The citizen class were necessarily also warriors, concerned to protect the independence of the city. That concern helped to unify factions. It turned the idea of the public weal or common good into a kind of glue. For, as we have seen, conquest could lead to enslavement, to sudden, total loss of that superior status which defined ancient citizenship.

For citizens, conquest involved not merely the loss of goods but of gods, of personal identity. It may be that what finally sweetened a bitter pill, the loss of complete autonomy for the city, was an overlordship which preserved the outward forms of civic independence and worship – and with them, the superior status of the citizen. Thus domination by Philip of Macedon and Alexander the Great, who had overcome the cities of the Greek heartland by the late fourth century BC, was preferable to slavery.

Just as previously inferior groups had acquiesced in tyranny within the city, in order to enter the citizen class and share in its privileges, that enlarged citizen class eventually sacrificed self-government – very reluctantly – to the preservation of its privileges. But, in consequence, its superior social status, which was deemed to incorporate a superior rationality, was forced to come to terms with a wider world and a more remote form of government. It has been argued that by the third and second century BC many Greeks welcomed the 'imperial' progress, first of Macedon and then of Rome, as a relief from the incessant social conflicts within their own cities.

This created a serious crisis of identity. For if the need to defend the independence of the polis had hitherto justified the primacy of the public sphere – underpinning the self-abandonment of citizens to the excitements of government and warfare – what could now prevent citizens retreating into the inferior pleasures of the domestic sphere? What could prevent them forfeiting the claims of rational superiority that had been central to their role and their self-respect?

With the decline of the polis, a whole conception of society and of the rational self was at risk.

For most citizens of Greek cities, 'law' and 'justice' had been identical. Participation in making the law helped to give citizens a sense that obeying the law was an imperious duty. It was at the core of a citizen's rightful pride. And it was cited to explain the Greeks' superiority over mere 'barbarians'. Herodotus tells the story of a deposed Spartan king, Demaratus, who took refuge at the Persian court of Xerxes. When the Persian king, planning his invasion of Greece, asked whether the Greeks would resist, given their very inferior numbers and the fact that they had no master to compel them to fight, Demaratus replied:

> They are free, yes, but not entirely free. For they have a master, and that master is Law, whom they fear even more than your subjects do you. Whatever this master commands, they do, and his command is always the same. He does not permit them to flee in battle, against whatever odds, but compels them to stand firm, conquer or die.[7]

The decline of the polis threatened to undermine such pride – and with it, the whole aristocratic model of society.

Little wonder that some philosophical movements, notably that of the Sophists, had already begun to speculate whether law or justice was anything more than the rule of the strongest. Both struggles within the citizen class and constant warfare between cities, culminating in the prolonged struggle between Athens and Sparta, had lent plausibility to their arguments. But such scepticism came up against impressive intellectual resistance. In the ancient world it was not only the conception of the self – of rationality and action – that carried the imprint of a highly stratified society. That imprint can also be detected in the conception of the universe or cosmos which prevailed in Greece and Rome.

After all, we should never forget that it was the Greeks who invented 'nature'. That is, they invented the concept that has had such a long and varied career, being turned to the uses of very different societies and cultures during two and a half millennia. In its original form, which the Romans accepted from the Greeks, the concept of nature was about as far removed from the nineteenth-century Darwinian

picture of nature 'red in tooth and claw' as it could be. It was originally a concept that conveyed a rational order or hierarchy of being.
Everything had a fixed place in 'a great chain of being'.

The Greek conception of nature did not at first make any sharp distinction between nature (*physis*) and culture (*nomos*), between the
cosmos and the social order. Instead, it presented the two as a single
continuum. Binding them together was the assumption of natural
inequality, the assumption that every being has a purpose or goal
(*telos*), which fits it to occupy a particular place in the great chain of
being. Only when tending towards that goal is it fulfilling its nature
and contributing to the preordained harmony of things. To be fully
rational was to be able to grasp this 'natural' order.

When the Greeks turned to speculating about the order of the heavens, these habits of thought came into play. Greeks projected their
hierarchical vision onto the universe. That vision shaped their understanding of the heavens, an understanding elaborated by Aristotle
and, later, turned into a sophisticated model by Ptolemy. Accepted by
the Romans, the Ptolemaic model of the cosmos would not be seriously challenged until the late middle ages.

We can see the impact of this hierarchical vision in the way a difference of opinion among Greek thinkers about the cosmos was resolved.
One of the first cosmologists, Aristarchus, had placed the sun at the
centre of things, with the earth orbiting around it. Yet the very idea of
the earth moving around the sun proved uncongenial to the Greek
mind. How could their stable, 'rational' hierarchy be founded on
movement? So a rival model was increasingly preferred, which placed
the earth at the centre of things, surrounded by eternal and incorrupt-
ible heavens.[8]

In that way the assumption of natural inequality shaped the Greeks'
understanding of the planets as well as the stars. For them, these
were 'heavenly' bodies in more than one sense. That is, they encir-
cled the earth in a series of ever-larger crystalline spheres, with the
outer and 'higher spheres' of the stars beyond the inner and lower
planetary spheres. The more distant the sphere, the purer and more
spiritual it was assumed to be. Aristotle assigned a separate intelligence to each of the spheres. The moon, so close to the earth, was the

least refined of the heavenly bodies – the lowest in intelligence. The most remote stars of the final sphere represented the most refined intelligence and controlled the others. 'Ancient thinkers were alternately inspired and oppressed by a vertiginous upward view. As they stepped out under the night sky, they thought of themselves as looking upward at layer after layer of vibrant beings, each more glorious than the last, each very different from their heavy selves.'[9] Distrust of matter informed this view of things celestial. The visible cosmos was represented as a spiritual ascent, by analogy with the assumption that the mind should govern the body, which was, after all, mere 'base matter'.

Despite the constraints imposed by these hierarchical assumptions, Greek cosmologists and Ptolemy did display extraordinary ingenuity in charting the movements of 'heavenly' bodies without the aid of telescopes. Drawing on Babylonian sources and developing sophisticated mathematical techniques, the Ptolemaic model of the cosmos accounted for much of what could be seen with the naked eye, making it possible for the ancients to predict eclipses and solstices. Yet what we would call physical events continued to be seen by them as signs or 'auspices' – signals revealing the will of the gods. Thunder and lightning, the movements of birds, the behaviour of an animal when released from its cage – all of these 'portents' could influence decision-making in the ancient polis. Despite the emergence of more abstract thought, nature remained full of purpose for the Greeks and Romans. Divination was the art of identifying those purposes. While the Greeks appealed to oracles as well as omens, the Romans had 'a doggedly enduring faith in the predictive power of astrology'.

So even the powers of abstraction, whether in the form of mathematics or philosophy, appeared to confirm the claims of rational superiority through the imagery of ascent. It is no surprise that Plato's so-called 'Neoplatonic' followers relied so much on that imagery. By definition, the superior mind was able to disentangle itself from 'base' matter, enabling it to hear 'the music of the heavenly spheres', a trait which, for Plato, created the philosopher-king's right to rule.

The Sophists, however, began to challenge this view of things. They were a fascinating group. They were the first professional teachers or intellectuals, that is, they were paid for their services – which immediately brought them up against a deep prejudice in a residually aristocratic society. Even more importantly, perhaps, the Sophists, who often came from small cities and modest backgrounds, wandered from city to city. They were not citizens anywhere, which placed them outside the sphere of morality in the eyes of traditional Greeks. Sophists were literally 'amoral', because they did not belong to the moral world of any polis. Even the way they taught seemed to undermine their claims to teach the skills required by citizenship. For they prided themselves on being able to show, with equal ease, how to defend or refute successfully any particular proposition.[10]

When Socrates argues with Protagoras, the leading Sophist, it is clear that he greatly respects Protagoras' dialectical skills. The Sophists had begun to distinguish 'nature' from 'convention'. Often they made the two antithetical. Yet they did not pursue a single strategy. Some might champion what existed 'by nature' – brute rule of the strongest, for example – while others defended what existed by 'convention' or custom, unwritten moral rules on which, it was claimed, positive law depended. But whatever strategy they pursued, the Sophists fostered habits of thought which disturbed the assumption that nature and culture belonged to a single moral continuum, a hierarchical order in which the gods lay behind the laws on which society was founded. In this way they encouraged a kind of scepticism.

Was reason really the anointed instrument of moral and social order? Or did the claim that reason can and should rule merely mask the role of appetites, vanity and mere force in human affairs? Did reason provide not a privileged access to the nature of things but rather a means of manipulation? Whether the Sophists intended it or not, such questions began to be asked. For the Sophists' approach raised doubts about a teleological understanding of the world.

To be sure, the Sophists met powerful philosophical opposition. Responding to 'sophistry', Plato and Aristotle sought to place social and political argument once again within the framework of a world order defined by purpose or *telos*. Anxious about the future of citizenship in the polis – for Aristotle 'the only life worth living' – their efforts restored teleology to a dominant position. Whether it was Plato's mathematically inspired forms, or Aristotle's typology of causes, rational understanding was the crux. Such knowledge was presented not only as a necessary but also a sufficient condition for achieving harmony – for identifying and conforming to the rational order or logos behind the material world of sensations and shifting appearances. Knowledge of goals was the key to both natural and social order.

This defence of teleology enabled philosophers to see themselves as the vanguard of a superior class, the class of citizens. For a long time their concerns remained tied to the concerns of the polis, to fostering the skills of the citizen. As we have seen, the idea of logos or rational order was fused with the idea of public speaking and with the vocation of the citizen. Even when the persistent asking of questions and pursuit of rational conclusions stirred unease in the city – and might lead, as in the case of Socrates, to charges of subversion – a case could still be made that fostering self-awareness gave a city such as Athens an important competitive advantage, an advantage in knowledge and therefore power. For just as thought and action were fused in the Greek mind, so were knowledge and skill. In the fifth century BC, the astonishing defeat of the Persians by the Greeks and the growth of the Athenian empire had seemed a vindication of such associations of ideas. Yet in the following centuries these near certainties were shaken.

The idea of logos had shaped Greek understanding of law as well as the cosmos. The original sanction of the gods of the city gradually took refuge in the idea of logos. But if debates in city assemblies promoted abstract argument at the expense of domestic worships and civic gods, the weakening of the Greek city-states after the Peloponnesian War and the rise of Macedonian power – reducing formerly proud city-states almost to colonies – gave the idea of logos an even more powerful impetus. The logos which had been embodied in the city and its laws began to make way for a logos embodied in a universal rational order, in what would be called 'natural law'.

Observing the shift of power from cities to large military empires had an important effect on minds. The new scale of social organization could not be ignored. The centralizing of power at the expense of local autonomy led philosophers to question assumptions that had previously sustained the life of the polis. Was the life of the citizen really the only life worth living? Was the virtually complete hold of civic life over body and soul justified when the city had ceased to be autonomous and self-governing? Was it really 'idiotic' not to be totally immersed in the life of the polis?

In the Hellenistic period – following the apogee of the city-state – philosophers began to speculate about a universal or 'human' nature that underlay different social conventions. Yet their speculations were directed especially at demonstrating their rational superiority, an ability to rise above the local and parochial. To that extent, it was a reassertion of the assumption of natural inequality which had for so long sustained a hierarchical conception of society. These philosophers' speculations did not have any radical moral import. They were not subversive. They were not designed to challenge or undermine the 'aristocratic' beliefs and practices of the ancient world, though the weakening of the city-state and the advent of large empires, first the Macedonian and then the Roman, no doubt influenced them.

Aristocratic assumptions about the proper ordering of society began to take refuge in a larger world. That is the strategy – irresistible in its way – that can be detected within newer philosophical movements such as Stoicism. In its austere message of self-control, Stoicism brought to a new height the assumption that reason can and should govern, with the passions entirely subjugated to reason. The model of motivation Stoics relied upon still bore the impress of a superior class commanding subordinate social forces. Becoming a 'citizen of the world' offered a new form of privilege, even if it was the privilege of renunciation, withdrawal and contemplation rather than of civic participation. It rested on the same postulate of rationality that had set citizens of the cities apart from their inferiors, a postulate that preserved a sense of superiority and provided a citadel for pride when the walls of the city had been breached.

Such a refuge exacted a high price, however. It divorced social superiority from observable local power. It weakened the hold of the citizen class, previously religious, military and theatrical, over their inferiors. For during the Hellenistic period the splendid monuments, buildings and games sponsored by civic notables – as in Alexandria, the city founded as a memorial to Alexander the Great – could not entirely conceal the loss of self-government. Are we to suppose that their inferiors did not notice?

A Moral Revolution

4

The World Turned Upside Down: Paul

At the core of ancient thinking we have found the assumption of natural inequality. Whether in the domestic sphere, in public life or when contemplating the cosmos, Greeks and Romans did not see anything like a level playing field. Rather, they instinctively saw a hierarchy or pyramid.

Different levels of social status reflected inherent differences of being. The paterfamilias, priest or citizen did not have to win or justify his status. His superior status reflected his 'nature'. It was self-justifying. And so entrenched was this vision of hierarchy that the processes of the physical world were also understood in terms of graduated essences and purposes – 'the music of the spheres'. Reason or logos provided the key to both social and natural order. Thought and being, it was assumed, were correlative. Each, in the end, provided the guarantee for the other. These assumptions about reason ensured that the categories of the mind could, in a sense, 'command' reality, even when that involved defining an immutable order or 'fate'.

Natural inequality meant, however, that rationality was not equally distributed among mankind. The distractions of the senses, vagaries of desire, the snares of imagination – all of these drastically restricted the distribution of rational understanding. Nor could the social role especially identified with rationality – that of the citizen – always be counted on to deliver it. A life governed by reason required that the pride given by status be joined to discipline and self-denial. For Plato, only a select few, the guardians, were able to leave behind the unreliable world of sensations and gradually ascend to knowledge of the forms. Even followers of Aristotle, who viewed the physical world with less suspicion, did not doubt that their *telos* or 'function' in a hierarchy of being established that some humans were slaves 'by nature'.

Thus, reason or logos and a hierarchical ordering of things – everything 'in its place' – were virtually inseparable. From a modern vantage point, both rested on an assumption that looks irredeemably aristocratic. In the first century BC, however, this aristocratic model came under threat.

We have already encountered one threat. The relentless spread of Roman power, until the Mediterranean became a Roman basin, was accomplished even before the Roman Republic became an empire under Augustus. In terms of political life, Rome had become the centre and the rest of the Mediterranean world the periphery. Rome was like a giant theatre or stage, with the citizens of subjugated and dependent cities reduced to mere spectators sitting on its benches. They were ceasing to be actors on their own stages. Their inherited roles were jeopardized.

The undermining of local autonomy – of that civic life which provided the justification of citizenship and its privileges – had profound social and intellectual consequences. The ancient family had given birth to an aristocratic model of society, while polytheism had expressed the self-esteem of so many autonomous centres of political life. Just as the ancient citizen class was stricken by a mortal illness, because of centralization, so the familiar civic gods were fading into mere ghosts. In their place was a fierce, remote and often unfathomable power: Rome.

Where were people, not least the citizen classes, to turn in such an unfamiliar landscape? It is hardly surprising that a period of religious ferment coincided with these institutional changes. Mithras, Osiris and other exotic deities attracted followers. The growth of mystery cults, the search for personal 'salvation' and a new openness to foreign beliefs reflected the displacement of ancient citizenship. And this weakening of local identities afflicted inferiors as well as superiors, for it was not only the civic gods who began to lose their hold. So too did the whole structure of ancient rationalism, which – as we have seen – had been complicit in hierarchy, identifying reason as the attribute of a superior class.

Developments in Platonic philosophy provide an uncannily accurate picture of these wider developments. Instead of being content with the model of a rational ascent up the great chain of being by a few – that ascent which tied thought and being so closely together – philosophers began to worry about the source of all being. They began to worry about what was called the Absolute, a first cause that was beyond comprehension. This search for the power that lay behind everything turned philosophy in a more mystical direction. It began to reshape ethical thinking as well. For it led to moral rules being considered, not so much as rational conclusions derived from the nature of things, but as commands issuing from an agency that was 'beyond' reason.[1]

It was as if the trials of dealing with Roman power were being projected onto a universal screen. Was 'will' rather than 'reason' the key to things? If so, could a philosophical tradition that presented reason as the key both to nature and to right living provide an adequate conception of the will? Already, the attraction of mystery cults suggested that intensely personal acts of faith or dedication were gaining ground against the claims of a 'rational' order.

Such new questions gave, inadvertently, an enormous advantage to a religious tradition which, by the first century BC, had ceased to be a merely local tradition. An important Jewish diaspora was bringing radical monotheism to the attention of many Greek- and Latin-speaking urban dwellers around the Mediterranean. Synagogues became centres of interest in many cities. They attracted numerous followers, even while ritual requirements such as circumcision and diet preserved the tribal identity of Judaism. Eventually these followers acquired a name. They were 'God-fearers'.

Just what was it that, rather suddenly, made Jewish beliefs so interesting? It was partly a matter of imagery. The image of a single, remote and inscrutable God dispensing his laws to a whole people corresponded to the experience of peoples who were being subjugated to the Roman *imperium*. But it was not just imagery. It was also a question of meaning, the meaning of law. For the Jews 'law' meant not logos or reason, but command. The law, properly so called, was Yahweh's will.

The feeling of privileged control that had accompanied ancient citizenship – the product of taking part in public discussion and decision-making in the polis – had infiltrated the ancient sense of rationality itself. It had led to the conclusion that reason could govern. Now both the feeling and the conclusion were compromised by the decline of the polis.

Conforming to an external will was becoming the dominant social experience. And the voice of Judaism spoke to that experience, as no other did. The message of the Jewish scriptures was radical. Virtue consisted in obedience to God's will. His will was not something that could be fathomed by reason. It could not be deduced from first principles. Nor could it be read in the book of nature. Scripture alone mattered, because it was the record of God's commands and promises. Historical events – the medium of God's will – were privileged over deductive reasoning. The Jewish God refused to be pinned down: 'I will be who I will be.'

A new sense of time thus went hand in hand with the new awareness of will. For both Greeks and Romans the dominant model for understanding change had been cyclical – the cycle of birth, growth and decay had seemed to fit only too well their experience of political constitutions being corrupted, of 'virtue' being undermined by 'luxury'. Only the efforts of heroic legislators could restore virtue, and that but temporarily, before the cycle reasserted itself. Permanence was provided by the cycle itself. And that predictability fitted well into the framework of ancient rationalist thinking.

The Jewish sense of time was different. It was unilinear rather than cyclical. Even the repeated lapses of Israel into idolatry did not dispel belief in God's overall control and direction of events. Had he not led his people to the 'promised land', and saved them repeatedly? The Jewish God expressed himself in time. Nothing would ever be the same as before. That was the nature of time. Is it fanciful to trace this sense back to the experiences of a nomadic people in the desert, aware that wind blowing across the sand transformed their landscape from one day to the next?

But there was something else. Although the law had always been understood as the inheritance of Yahweh's 'chosen' people, the law embodied his will for all of his people. And all were deemed to be capable of sinning against that law, even the most famous Jewish kings such as David. Law therefore did not have the aristocratic connotations it had acquired through its identification, by Greeks and Romans, with the logos of a citizen class. Nor did Yahweh's will have the static quality conveyed by logos or reason. It was as if the imagery surviving from their nomadic past provided a different simile for the Jews' monotheism. God's will was like the wind shifting the desert sands. Nothing could resist it.

The concept of the will began to provide a new foundation for philosophical reflection by the first century AD. A gap opened up between the rationalism of earlier thought and this new voluntarism. Typical of the older view was Seneca's comment on the gods: 'They who believe the gods do not want to do harm are mistaken; the gods cannot.'[2] That is, the gods themselves are constrained by the rational structure of reality. They too must submit to a comprehensible natural order.

Later Platonists had, it is true, begun to compromise that rationalism in their account of the Absolute. They held that, because the first cause of being was beyond rational understanding, it could only be revealed in momentary illuminations to those whose rational discipline had led them away from sense experience to knowledge of the forms. But what such moments of illumination revealed was ineffable, beyond the resources of language to express. All that could be said about the Absolute was negative: that it was not limited, not necessitated, not the subject of knowledge. But if that was so, then the Absolute was not constrained by the supposed unity of thought and being, indeed by anything at all. The Absolute could act as it chose, whenever and however.[3]

The experience of submitting to a remote Roman ruler may well have contributed to such philosophical preoccupations among learned members of the citizen class. But for the urban populations of the Mediterranean at large that experience was more likely to result in a religious disposition than philosophical conviction. The set of roles provided by the city-state was disturbed. Withdrawing from accustomed roles into the self – a kind of inner exile – was often the result. The drama of the polis was losing its hypnotic hold. Instead of acting out parts written by their prescribed 'natures', people had little choice but to identify themselves in another way. An act of submission now seemed to be the precondition of knowledge. So it began to appear that obedience led to understanding, rather than the reverse. It was a remarkable turnabout. For making obedience precede understanding, rather than follow from it, amounted to an intellectual revolution. It was a revolution that overturned the basis of the claim to superiority of the citizen class.

By the second century AD the new direction taken by argument made philosophers more self-aware. They no longer claimed that Moses and Plato had taught the same truth. Galen, writing about AD 170, contrasted Jewish belief in a creator whose unconstrained will brought everything into being, with Plato's and Aristotle's conception of a creator whose work is constrained by the dictates of reason – 'even a god is not able to change his nature.'[4]

If the God of the Old Testament was known through the dictates of his will, his reasons were beyond human comprehension. 'For my thoughts are not your thoughts, neither are your ways my ways . . . For as the heavens are higher than the earth, so are my ways higher than your ways, and my thoughts than your thoughts.' A new sympathy with these words of the prophet Isaiah was a sign that the ancient Mediterranean world was on the brink of a profound change. Postulating an act of will was becoming necessary to understand that world.

It might, indeed, look as if Jewish habits of thought were about to triumph completely over Graeco-Roman habits of thought, as if, in a battle between the idea of agency on the one hand, and that of rationality on the other, agency was about to drive rationality from the field. Did not the Jewish idea of 'law' correspond more closely to everyday experience – and help to cope with it – than 'reasons' founded on nature? Yet no such complete victory of Jewish thinking took place. And it did not take place at least in part because of the vision of a young Jew, Saul of Tarsus.

We have been looking at the impact of a religious tradition issuing from Palestine, a tradition that privileged time and will as against reason and nature. But Palestine itself had not been immune to outside influences. Ever since the Greek-dominated kingdoms established following Alexander's conquests, the Near East had been exposed to Greek influence in both obvious and less obvious ways. The Greek language had become virtually a lingua franca. Few among the Semitic peoples had not encountered it and learned a smattering of Greek, while some, like Saul of Tarsus, had become wholly proficient in its use. Hellenized Jews were not uncommon. Greek culture had a very significant presence in all major cities, even in Jerusalem. Altogether, after three centuries of exposure the Near Eastern world was deeply Hellenized.

The spread of Roman power added to this intermingling of cultures. But it also created a new threat to Jewish nationhood and identity – an identity that had been defended stubbornly for centuries, in the face of repeated invasions and periods of exile. Little wonder that Judaism became increasingly volatile at this period, with the growth of Messianic movements, some of which looked forward to the advent of a national saviour, others of which renounced the world in anticipation of 'the last days'.

One of these movements was the Jesus movement. Jesus of Nazareth seems to have begun as a disciple of one who later became known as John the Baptist. But Jesus came into his own and acquired followers, who accompanied him as he preached in the Galilean countryside. Just what did he preach? As far as we can tell, he preached repentance and the imminent end of the world. He spoke of God as his 'father' who loved all his children, not least the socially marginal. Those who truly repented of their sins could hope to enter the Kingdom of God. They should become like children, showing charity and trusting in God's mercy.

Apparently there was no unanimity among his followers about the exact nature of Jesus' mission. Some were probably still tempted to see him as the Messiah, in the sense of a leader who would lead Israel to victory over its enemies. Others understood the 'kingdom' in more mystical terms. Uncertainty about the nature of his claims, on the part of the Jewish and Roman authorities, may have contributed to his arrest, trial and crucifixion in Jerusalem. Shortly afterwards, the conviction that Jesus had survived death and that his work must go on gave this movement ('the way') new life in Jerusalem, where it was led by his brother James and disciple Simon Peter, the so-called 'Jerusalem church'.

Beyond these sparse facts, little can be asserted with confidence about the historical Jesus of Nazareth. What we do know, however, is that Jesus' followers very soon perceived his crucifixion as a moral earthquake. And the aftershocks of that earthquake continue into our own time. Followers of Jesus began to claim that his sacrificial life and death amounted to a dramatic intervention in history, a new revelation of God's will. Understanding that revelation would, in due course, provide crucial underpinning for what we understand as the nature and claims of the individual. It provided the individual with a foothold in reality.

First, Jesus crucified; then, Jesus resurrected. Previously in antiquity, it was the patriarchal family that had been the agency of immortality. Now, through the story of Jesus, individual moral agency was raised up as providing a unique window into the nature of things, into the experience of grace rather than necessity, a glimpse of something transcending death. The individual replaced the family as the focus of immortality.

The earliest surviving writings about Jesus are the work of Saul of Tarsus, who, of course, became St Paul. It is Paul who, translating the word 'Messiah' or 'anointed one' into Greek, began to speak eloquently and with determination to a non-Jewish world about Jesus as 'the Christ' – the Son of God who died for human sins and whose resurrection offers mankind the hope of eternal life. 'The Christ' thus was not a proper name but a title and an idea. It originally referred to an anointed one who would deliver Israel from its enemies, but Paul gave the term a new meaning and spoke of the Christ offering salvation to all humanity. 'The Christ' stood for the presence of God in the world.

It is hardly too much to say that Paul invented Christianity as a religion. Paul felt that through Jesus he had discovered something crucial – the supreme moral fact about humans – which provided the basis for reconstructing human identity, opening the way to what he called 'a new creation'. 'Even though we once knew Christ from a human point of view, we know him no longer in that way. So if anyone is in Christ, there is a new creation: everything old has passed away; see, everything has become new!'[5] For Paul, it was through the Christ that God was reconciling the world – individual souls – to himself, 'not counting their trespasses against them, and entrusting the message of reconciliation to us'. Spreading that message of love became Paul's great missionary enterprise.

So we must now do our best to enter into Paul's mind.

Paul, who as Saul of Tarsus had persecuted members of the Jesus movement, had a famous conversion experience when travelling from Jerusalem to Damascus. He was thrown from his horse, according to a New Testament account, by the power of a vision of Jesus. But whether his conversion was quite so instantaneous and complete is open to doubt. It is more likely that he spent some years pondering the significance of Jesus of Nazareth, finding the terms in which to express his new convictions. Paul's vision gradually became a conception, his remarkable conception of the Christ.

In Paul's eyes, the Christ reveals God acting through human agency and redeeming it. The Christ reveals a God who is potentially present in every believer.

> Who shall separate us from the love of Christ? Will tribulation, or distress, or persecution, or famine, or nakedness, or peril, or sword? No, in all these things we are more than conquerors through him who loved us. For I am sure that neither death, nor life, nor anything in all creation . . . will be able to separate us from the love of God in Christ Jesus our Lord.[6]

Through an act of faith in the Christ, human agency can become the medium for God's love – what Paul sometimes calls 'faith acting through love'. The faith accepting that love amounted to an inner crucifixion, from which could emerge a transformed will, embodied in the person of Jesus. For Paul, it was a personal transaction, the creation of another, better self. 'I have been crucified with Christ. It is no longer I who live, but Christ who lives in me. And the life I now live in the flesh I live by faith in the Son of God, who loved me and gave himself for me.'[7]

In effect, Paul's vision of a mystical union with Christ introduces a revised notion of rationality – what he sometimes describes as the 'foolishness' of God. It is a foundation for a rationality reshaped through faith. It constitutes a depth of motivation unknown to ancient philosophy. 'No one can lay any foundation other than the one that has been laid; that foundation is Jesus the Christ.'[8] For the sacrificial nature of love is open to everyone. And it counts everyone as a child of God. 'Let it be known to you, therefore, my brothers, that through this man forgiveness of sin is proclaimed to you; by this Jesus everyone who believes is set free . . .' Paul's message is directed not merely to Jews but to all humanity. It is an invitation to seek a deeper self, an inner union with God. It offers to give reason itself a new depth. Rationality loses its aristocratic connotations. It is associated not with status and pride but with a humility which liberates.

Paul's conception of the Christ overturns the assumption on which ancient thinking had hitherto rested, the assumption of natural inequality. Instead, Paul wagers on human equality. It is a wager that turns on transparency, that we can and should see ourselves in others, and others in ourselves. A leap of faith in human equality reveals – beneath the historical accumulation of unequal social statuses and roles – the universal availability of a God-given foundation for human action, the free action of love. That action is what Paul's vision of the Christ revealed. As deployed by Paul, the concept of the Christ becomes a challenge to the ancient belief that humans are subject to an immutable order or 'fate'.

Paul's vision on the road to Damascus amounted to the discovery of human freedom – of a moral agency potentially available to each and everyone, that is, to individuals. This 'universal' freedom, with its moral implications, was utterly different from the freedom enjoyed by the privileged class of citizens in the polis.

In his conception of the Christ, Paul brings together basic features of Jewish and Greek thought to create something new. We can see this in a famous passage from his letters, the letter to the Galatians, dating from about twenty years after Jesus' crucifixion. Paul uses Jesus' emphasis on the fatherhood of God to insist on the brotherhood of man and, indirectly, to proclaim his own role as apostle to the Gentiles. 'There is neither Jew nor Greek, there is neither slave nor free, there is neither male nor female; for you are all one in Christ Jesus.'[9] Paul's 'one' signals a new transparency in human relations. Through his conception of the Christ, Paul insists on the moral equality of humans, on a status shared equally by all. And his great mission becomes the salvation of individual souls, through sharing his vision of the Christ – a vision which makes it possible to create a new self.

The argument that all humans can become 'one in Christ' – and that through him all may share in the righteousness of God – reveals

Paul grafting a new abstractness onto Jewish thought. It is an abstractness that would foster Christian understanding of community as the free association of the wills of morally equal agents, what Paul describes through metaphor as the 'body of Christ'. The metaphor conjures up a mystical union which moralizes individual wills by relating them to the source of their being. This mixture of elements which became Christianity was profoundly indebted to developments in Greek thought. For the discourse of citizenship in the polis had initiated a distancing of persons from mere family and tribal identities, while later Hellenistic philosophy had introduced an even more wide-ranging, speculative 'universalist' idiom. That intellectual breadth had, in turn, been reinforced by the subjection of so much of the Mediterranean world to a single power, Rome.

What Paul did, in effect, was to combine the abstracting potential of later Hellenistic philosophy – its speculations about a universal or 'human' nature – with Judaism's preoccupation with conformity to a higher or divine will. In order to do so, Paul ceases to think of that will as an external, coercive agency. For him, the death of Christ provides the symbol and the means of an inner crucifixion, of leaving behind the life of 'the flesh' for the life of 'the spirit', that is, leaving behind inclinations and desires that will die with the flesh. 'Dying in Christ' means acquiring a will properly so called. It is a liberation or, as Paul often calls it, the beginning of a 'new creation'. And the act of faith required is an individual act, an internal event.

Paul overturns the assumption of natural inequality by creating an inner link between the divine will and human agency. He conceives the idea that the two can, at least potentially, be fused within each person, thereby justifying the assumption of the moral equality of humans. That fusion is what the Christ offers to mankind. It is what Paul means when he speaks of humans becoming 'one in Christ'. That fusion marks the birth of a 'truly' individual will, through the creation of conscience.

When human action had been understood as governed entirely by social categories, by established statuses and roles, there was no need for another foundation for shaping intentions. But introducing the assumption of moral equality changes that. It obliges Paul to look deeper into the human agent. Suddenly there is a need to find a standard to govern individual action and a force within each person to act. In his conception of the Christ, Paul claims to have found that standard and that force. Now, the identity of individuals is no longer exhausted by the social roles they happen to occupy. A gap opens up between individuals and the roles they occupy. That gap marks the advent of the new freedom, freedom of conscience. But it also introduces moral obligations that follow from recognizing that all humans are children of God.

For Paul, belief in the Christ makes possible the emergence of a primary role shared equally by all ('the equality of souls'), while conventional social roles – whether of father, daughter, official, priest or slave – become secondary in relation to that primary role. To this primary role an indefinite number of social roles may or may not be added as the attributes of a subject, but they no longer define the subject. That is the freedom which Paul's conception of the Christ introduces into human identity.

Yet the individual freedom implied by the assertion of this primary role did not mean that Paul dissolved traditional social bonds without replacing them. His was not an 'atomized' model of society. Far from it. Rather, Paul creates a new basis for human association, a voluntary basis – joining humans through loving wills guided by an equal belief. In his eyes, the motivating power of love is the touch of divinity within each of us.

> If I speak in the tongues of mortals and angels, but do not have love, I am a noisy gong or a clanging cymbal. And if I have prophetic powers, and understand all mysteries and all knowledge, and if I have all faith, so as to remove mountains, but do not have love, I am nothing. If I give away all my possessions, and if I hand over my body so that I may boast, but do not have love, I gain nothing . . . Love is patient; love is kind; love is not envious or boastful or arrogant or rude . . . It bears all things, believes all things, hopes all things, endures all things . . . Love never ends.[10]

Love creates what Paul calls a mystical union in the 'body of Christ'. The metaphor conveys what, in his eyes, is distinctive about Christian association. An unseen bond of wills joined by conscience identifies this mystical body, distinguishing it from associations founded on birth, gender or social status. Human agency acquires a new independence and dignity.

Paul thus attaches to the historical figure of Jesus a crucial moment in the development of human self-consciousness. Before Paul, speculation about a 'human' nature had not carried a strong moral message. By contrast, Paul's Christ carries a revolutionary moral message. For Paul, the Christ is a God-given challenge to humans to transform their conception of themselves and reach for moral universality. Through faith, they can achieve a moral rebirth. They can move beyond the Jewish law or mere rule-following. Baptism became the symbol of receiving that 'Holy Spirit', which meant that believers were henceforth 'in Christ' and free. Paul relies on the imagery of casting off the shackles of slavery, a potent image in a world where slavery remained such a basic institution. His message is one of universal hope.

In his preaching, as he moved from city to city along the Anatolian coast and into Greece, Paul insisted that his God was a God who is 'with us'. The age of the 'spirit' has succeeded the age of the 'flesh'. The resurrection of Jesus (with a spiritual body rather than a body of 'flesh and blood') heralds the beginning of that new age – which is not to say that 'the saints' would not falter or often relapse into old ways. In fact, Paul spent much of his time corresponding with churches he had founded, fighting against habits of thought which, in his view, recreated forms of bondage, neglecting charity in favour of rules and attributing to 'principalities and powers' a reality they did not possess.

Despite constant setbacks and eventual martyrdom, Paul may be said to have prevailed. For his understanding of the meaning of Jesus' death and resurrection introduced to the world a new picture of reality. It provided an ontological foundation for 'the individual', through the promise that humans have access to the deepest reality as individuals rather than merely as members of a group. Here we see the power of abstraction, which had previously led Hellenic philosophers to speculate about a human nature prior to social conventions, being turned to a new moral use. The self can and must be reconstructed. That conviction enabled Paul to conclude that Christian liberty supersedes the Jewish law. It provided the justification for his mission to convert the Gentile world to the God of Israel revealed in the Christ.

The wish of some Jewish Christians to make conversion to Judaism a prerequisite for becoming Christian – requiring circumcision for males, for example – aroused Paul's fury and contempt, not least because it jeopardized his conception of his own mission. For Paul, Christian liberty is open to all humans. Free action, a gift of grace through faith in the Christ, is utterly different from ritual behaviour, the unthinking application of rules. For Paul, to think otherwise is to regress rather than progress in the spirit. That is how Paul turns the abstracting potential of Greek philosophy to new uses. He endows it with an almost ferocious moral universalism. The Greek mind and the Jewish will are joined.

Individual rationality, rationality in all equally, is purchased at the price of submitting to God's will as revealed in the Christ. For Paul, when rationality and the will are presented as alternatives, they are false alternatives. In the Christ, both the power of God and the wisdom of God are revealed. Jesus is the Christ because his death and resurrection give humans, as individuals, access to the mind and the will of God. God ceases to be tribal. 'The law was our guardian until Christ came, so that we might be made righteous by faith. But now that faith has come, we are no longer under a guardian, for in Jesus Christ you are all sons of God, through faith.'[11]

Often, it is true, 'I do not do what I want, but I do the very thing I hate'.[12] Yet through the gift of faith, human actions can cease to be bound by mere habit. For Paul, only in the Christ are wisdom and power joined. Only through faith are the human capacity to act and the faculty of reason reconciled. 'For Jews demand signs and Greeks desire wisdom, but we proclaim Christ crucified, a stumbling block to Jews and foolishness to Gentiles, but to those who are called, both Jews and Greeks, Christ the power of God and the wisdom of God.'[13]

So what has Paul achieved by arguing in this way? What does abandonment to the love of God as 'revealed' in the Christ entail? We cannot know everything this meant to Paul. But we can identify at least part of what it meant to him, disengaging moral principles from his apocalyptic vision of a universe transformed. In order to do that, we must look closely at one premise of Paul's argument. The premise of moral equality requires a human will that is in a sense pre-social. It is that will which Paul's great discovery, his mystical vision of the Christ, provides. The Christ provides a foundation in the nature of things for a pre-social or individual will. Individual agency acquires roots in divine agency. The Christ stands for the presence of God in the world, the ultimate support for individual identity.

Delving below all social divisions of labour, Paul finds, beneath the conventional terms that confer status and describe roles, a shared reality. That reality is the human capacity to think and choose, to will. That reality is our potential for understanding ourselves as autonomous agents, as truly the children of God.

But if thought depends upon language, and language is a social institution, how can rational agency have a pre-social foundation? That is the dilemma Paul's argument comes up against. For Paul, the gift of love in the Christ offers a pre-linguistic solution, through a leap of faith – that is, a wager on the moral equality of humans. Faith in the Christ requires seeing oneself in others and others in oneself, the point of view which truly moralizes humans as agents. So Paul's solution – a paradoxical one, to say the least – is that human autonomy can only be fully realized through submission, through submitting to the mind and will of God as revealed in the Christ. That act of submission is the beginning of 'a new creation'.

Was Paul wrong? His expectation of the imminent return of the Christ was disappointed. And the postponement of the 'last days' led to considerable embarrassment for 'the saints' in the churches he established during his journeys. By the end of the first century what became the Christian church was abandoning its emphasis on the imminent end of the world. Yet Paul's vision of a world transformed may have been more misleading in form than in content. For, in fact, his conception of the Christ laid the foundation for a new type of society: 'The present form of the world is passing away.'[14] While that insistence by Paul in a letter to the Corinthian church is open to more than one interpretation, Paul himself seemed to believe that the new creation was already under way.

What did submission to the Christ involve? In religious terms, it called for human relationships in which charity overcomes all other motives. But, even when separated from an apocalyptic vision of human community (the 'body of Christ'), the promotion of 'Christian liberty' involves submitting to the premises of moral equality and reciprocity. 'You were called to freedom . . . Only do not use your freedom as an opportunity for the flesh, but through love serve one another. For the whole law is fulfilled in one word . . . Love your neighbour as yourself.'[15] Those premises promised to create a transparency and freedom previously lacking in human relations.

So in Paul's writings we see the emergence of a new sense of justice, founded on the assumption of moral equality rather than on natural inequality. Justice now speaks to an upright will, rather than describing a situation where everything is in its 'proper' or fated place. Paul's conception of the Christ exalts the freedom and power of human agency, when rightly directed. In his vision of Jesus, Paul discovered a moral reality which enabled him to lay the foundation for a new, universal social role.

5

The Truth Within: Moral Equality

The imagery that dominated Paul's teaching was an imagery of depth – of going 'beneath' and finding 'the depths of God'. Despite Paul's conflicts with leaders of the Jerusalem church over the Jewish law, the extent of its obligations for Gentile followers, his emphasis on innerness and freedom spread through churches developing around the Mediterranean. These churches, which at first were really Christian synagogues, increasingly conveyed a Pauline message, proclaiming that, through the gift of grace in the Christ, 'the Kingdom of God is within you'.

Fierce Jewish opposition to the Jesus movement helped to give it a more distinct identity. Moreover, the destruction of Jerusalem by the Romans in AD 70 reinforced the role of Gentile converts and Paul's influence. In the following decades what was beginning to be called the 'Christian church' ceased to be primarily a Jewish sect, as it had been when dominated by Jesus' brother James.

The development of that 'church' at the end of the first century and early in the second century remains largely a matter of surmise. There was as yet no fixed canon of Christian gospels, nor any agreement about the relationship between Christian writings and Jewish scriptures. Indeed, disagreements about some matters soon became so important that they became the means of beginning to define Christian 'orthodoxy' later in the second and in the third century. It is by looking at those disagreements that we can get a sense of the nature of a movement now so widespread that it was coming to the attention of the Roman authorities.

As apocalyptic expectations weakened, the need for Christians to explain themselves grew. From the middle of the second century Justin

67

Martyr and Irenaeus of Lyons wrote the first significant apologetics. Echoing Paul, Irenaeus argued that 'it is not sacrifices that sanctify a man; for God has no need of sacrifices', rather, 'it is the purity of the offerer's disposition that sanctifies the sacrifice.'[1] The quality of the individual will or disposition was becoming the Christian leitmotiv. Paul's imagery of depth had fostered the sense of a realm of conscience that demanded respect. Individual agency and divine agency were now understood as parts of a continuum.

Slowly that sense or intuition was formalized. The church which presided over major developments in thinking systematically about the core of Christian beliefs was the church of Alexandria. The church of that sophisticated city came to count among its membership intellectuals formed by the schools of Greek philosophy, particularly later Platonism. Their attempts to adapt the categories of Greek philosophy to their new belief in a God who had revealed himself in Jesus – in Paul's 'the Christ' – led to arguments over imagery, over the role of human agency or freedom and over the claims of reason. These arguments became the first important steps in developing the notion of humans as morally equal agents, as individuals properly so called. The arguments also reveal how Christian beliefs caused trouble for minds shaped by the rationalism of the ancient world. For that rationalism was impregnated with assumptions about natural inequality, hierarchy and fate.

The argument over imagery was more implicit than explicit. It was a struggle between the imagery of descent and the imagery of ascent. Paul's conception of God 'with us' had privileged the imagery of descent. The incarnation was a matter of knowledge, but it was knowledge of an inner event and reality – as Clement of Alexandria, writing late in the second century, emphasized by quoting from Paul on 'that knowledge of God in Christ in whom all the treasures of knowledge and wisdom are hidden'. Clement was aware that the new emphasis on descent made a contrast with the traditional Platonic imagery of a rational ascent, of climbing a mountain that led away from unreliable sense experience to certain knowledge, for at least a few. So Clement quotes from the Gospel of John in order to present the Christian God as the ground or foundation of individual being:

John the apostle writes: 'No one has seen God at any time; the only-begotten God, who is in the bosom of the Father, he has declared him.' (John 1.18) He (John) uses the name 'bosom' of God to refer to his invisibility and ineffability; for this reason some people have used the name 'depth' to indicate that he is inaccessible and incomprehensible, but embraces and enfolds all things.[2]

Knowledge of the depths revealed by the Christ – the discovery of a will that redeems – raised, in turn, the question of human freedom. For if faith in the Christ can free humans from the bondage of sin, then each must have a potential for freedom, a free will.

Yet old habits of thinking were not overcome easily. The reality of time, will and sin – imports from the Jewish tradition – had now to be joined to a Greek framework which prized knowledge, orderliness and control. We can observe such joining in the arguments of Origen, a pupil of Clement who wrote early in the third century. Origen reflects on the nature of religious language, in order to show that God's dealings with man can only be described in human terms, with all their limitations. Thus, to say that God is 'angry' or that he 'repents' should not be taken literally. These terms are rather like the language adopted by a loving father when dealing with his children.

So it is with human freedom and God's 'foreknowledge' of the outcome. The two are not inconsistent, Origen insists:

> In the passage, 'Speak to the children of Israel; perhaps they will hear and will repent' (Jer 26 2.3), God does not say 'perhaps they will hear', as if he were in doubt about it. God is never in doubt and that cannot be the reason ... The reason is to make your freedom of choice stand out as clearly as possible and to prevent your saying: 'If he foreknows my loss then I am bound to be lost and if he foreknows my salvation then I am quite certain to be saved.' Thus he acts as if he did not know the future in your case, in order to preserve your freedom of choice by not anticipating or foreknowing whether you will repent or not. So he says to the prophet: 'Speak; perhaps they will repent'.[3]

Divine government of the world or providence does not exclude human freedom. On the contrary, when properly understood, individual choice, action and the consequences of action are evidence of providential government, which is not the same as fate.

For Origen, God had created 'rational creatures endowed with the faculty of free choice', who were led 'each one by his own free will, either to imitate God and so to advance or to ignore him and so to fall'. The variety of the human world reflects a freedom that is the crux of human agency. Thus the 'diversity between rational creatures' had its origin 'not in the will or judgement of the creator, but in the choice made by the creature's own freedom'.[4]

In these attempts to join Jewish and Greek categories of thought, there is a quite new emphasis on demonstrable fact as against metaphysical speculation. There is a new prejudice against multiplying entities or essences, a reluctance to populate the world with beings intermediate between God and man. Early Christians saw themselves as involved in a war against 'demons', even suggesting that the demons existed only so long as people believed in them. Here we can perhaps see Paul's inveighing against belief in 'dark' powers or rudiments taking hold, although references to 'angels and demons' long survived in Christian discourse. But, at bottom, the new structure of ideas was hostile to them.

It is no accident that early Christian apologists emphasized the simplicity of their faith – the way it focused on human intentions or the will, rather than on spurious beings that give an inflated impression of what humans might control or influence. 'I am fully convinced that the solemn ceremonies and secret rites of idolatry build up credence and prestige for themselves by means of their pretentious magnificence – and by the fees that are charged,' Tertullian, a formidable Carthaginian convert, insisted early in the third century. 'For God, being the creator of the whole Universe, is in no need of smells or of blood. That is the fodder of petty demons. We do not merely despise these demons; we subdue them; we put them to daily disgrace; we drive them out of people, as multitudes can testify.'[5] These apologists were implacable opponents of black magic. In a sense they were redefining the sphere of human action, laying the foundation for what eventually became a clearer distinction between 'internal' reasons for acting and the physical causes of external events.

Critics of Christianity like Celsus late in the second century were disturbed by such attitudes. Celsus argued that Christianity separated man too sharply from the rest of nature and demeaned nature by reducing it to a mere instrument for human purposes. 'They say that God made all things for man,' he complained. 'He forsakes the whole universe and the course of the heavenly spheres to dwell with us alone.'[6] Celsus had a serious point. But he failed to see the importance of clarifying the sphere of human freedom for identifying individual moral responsibility. For Christian converts, receiving the 'holy spirit' in baptism stood for liberation from the confusions of paganism as well as the literalism of Judaism. Being 'in Christ' meant receiving that spirit. It directed attention where it ought to be directed: to real moral choices and works of charity. It made sacrifices in the temples of local deities and male circumcision unnecessary.

'What wretched unbelief to deny to God his distinctive attributes – simplicity and power!' Tertullian once exclaimed.[7] In a way, his attitude anticipates a principle laid down by an Oxford philosopher in the late middle ages. 'Ockham's Razor' insists that explanations should always be made in the simplest terms possible, avoiding the multiplication of entities. Human desires and intentions should not be confused with natural processes. It may not be far-fetched to suggest that Ockham's principle had its roots in early Christian reassessment of the role of human agency, roots which nourished a sense of the difference between nature and culture, of the limits of human reason.

For there is no doubt that early Christian apologists associated the polytheism of paganism with misuse of the mind and the will. In deifying natural forces and creating local gods, paganism drew attention away from crucial questions about the individual will and man's God-given responsibility. Even Judaism had fallen into the trap of largely identifying the will with external conformity to the law, which had led Paul, in reaction, to look 'inward', to motivation. This Christian awareness of the 'love of God' as the source of upright action was intensely practical. Something of this can be glimpsed in the fourth century in St Basil's apology for Christianity against those who, defending once again the assumptions of ancient rationalism, condemned Christians for worshipping 'what they do not know'. In reply, Basil turned the distinctions of Greek philosophy against its latest defenders:

They should not be asking us whether we know God's essence; they should be enquiring whether we know God as awe-inspiring, as just, or as merciful. And these are the things that we confess that we do know. If on the other hand they say that God's essence is different from these attributes, they must not produce spurious arguments against us on the basis of the simplicity of that essence. For in that case they have themselves admitted that his essence is something different from every one of his attributes. His activities are various but his essence is simple. Our position is that it is from his activities that we come to know our God, while we do not claim to come anywhere near his actual essence. For his activities reach us, but his essence remains inaccessible.[8]

What emerges from these early texts is a chastened conception of the role of reason – what might be described as a more democratic, less aristocratic conception of reason. Deductive reason can aid in the discovery of truth, but it cannot lay down the truth out of its own resources. Reason cannot and indeed should not try to coerce reality. Christian humility was presented as a precaution against that error. The 'foolishness' of God's revelation in the Christ was a permanent warning.

What adds to the interest of these texts – and what became important for Christian 'orthodoxy' – is that they responded to the arguments, not just of pagans or Jews, but of other Christians who found it hard to give up the framework of ancient rationalism. As late as the fourth century Gregory of Nyssa, one of the Fathers of the Church, speaks with an unreconstructed Platonic voice, when describing Moses receiving the law on Mount Sinai. 'When the herd of irrational animals is driven as far as possible from the mountain, he [Moses] approaches the ascent to higher thoughts,' Gregory comments. 'The fact that no animal is permitted to appear on the mountain indicates, in our judgement, that in the vision of intelligible reality, one is passing beyond knowledge derived from sense experience.'[9]

Gregory does not hesitate to draw conclusions about the proper ordering of the Christian Church:

The multitude could not hear the voice from above but left it to Moses to learn for himself the hidden secrets and to teach the people whatever divine truths he might acquire from the teaching coming from above. The same is true of the ordering of the Church. It is not for everyone to push themselves forward to try to comprehend the mysteries. They should select one of their number who is able to grasp divine truth; then they should give careful attention to him . . .[10]

The aristocratic bias of his Platonism is clear enough. For Gregory, reality continues to be essentially intelligible, but only for a few. His imagery remains that of Platonic ascent. In his view, most people are incapable of reaching further than the foot of what is truly a mountain – 'for such indeed is the knowledge of God'.

Ancient rationalism was not defeated rapidly. In fact, in the second century it had already mounted a powerful rearguard action, an action associated with the movement known as Gnosticism. Gnosticism was in part a reaction against Jewish influences. The Gnostics fell back on the Platonic assumption that knowledge was the condition of enlightenment and that a hierarchy of being stigmatized 'base matter'. They too relied on the imagery of ascent, an ascent possible for the elect. Self-liberation required renunciation of the material world and its 'darkness', in order to return upwards to the world of 'light'. For Christian Gnostics, the Christ provided knowledge of that world of light. Yet those capable of achieving that knowledge strongly resembled Plato's guardians. In effect, the Gnostics moved away from Paul's assumption that liberation through faith was the condition of knowledge and salvation. The 'foolishness' of God was not altogether to their taste.

Christian Gnostics did not hesitate to multiply essences and entities: in one Gnostic text no fewer than thirty 'highest' levels of being or light were enumerated! These highest levels of being were pure thought, flowing from the transcendent God. They were uncontaminated by matter or 'darkness'. However, this descending order of pure being reached a point of impurity, when the lowest of these beings – Sophia or wisdom – succumbed to sexual desire and gave birth to a material world ruled by Yahweh, an inferior god. When Adam, in turn, was created, he retained a vestige of the world of light or pure being, but through his body was joined to the material world and its temptations, the world of Yahweh. Only the advent of Christ, the very figure of light, revealed again the true nature of God and made salvation possible for the elect.[11]

These Gnostic ideas reveal the problems that marrying Christian convictions with Platonic metaphysics introduced. They introduced a disdain for the material world foreign to Judaism, a flirtation with the assumption of natural inequality that Paul had overturned, and a doubt about whether Yahweh and the Christian God were one and the same. Indeed, the radical dualism of the Gnostics threatened the very conception of the incarnation – for it made problematic the intimate union of God and man in the Christ. For the Gnostics, spirit and matter could not be combined.

If the Gnostics represent – in relation to ancient rationalism – a conservative or even reactionary wing of the Christian movement, there was another wing. And that wing reveals the socially subversive potential of Christian beliefs, a potential that would take many centuries to emerge fully. Still, we can get an impression of its potential by looking at a text and at a man. The man is Marcion, the most controversial figure to emerge in Christian thought since Paul. Born towards the end of the first century, Marcion was the son of a presbyter-bishop on the Black Sea coast, and became a wealthy merchant and shipowner. But he was also a frustrated intellectual, with a passion for finding out and defining what was new and distinctive about Christian beliefs. That passion finally led him to Rome and into what the 'orthodox' began to call 'heresy'.

In Marcion's eyes, Paul's letters and the Gospel according to Luke provided all that was necessary. He presented a radical and simplified version of Paul's teaching. Free from Paul's anxiety about dealing with the Jerusalem Church, Marcion issued a kind of declaration of independence. The loving God revealed by the Christ was not the jealous God of the Old Testament, who was a primitive, tribal being. The revelation of Christ needed no support from the Jewish scriptures. It was a new revelation, sufficient unto itself, the means of salvation for those who trusted in God's goodness. Marcion wanted to purge the Christian gospel – indeed, he was perhaps the first to try to assemble 'the' gospels – of irrelevant Jewish elements.[12]

Marcion fastened onto the universal dimension of Paul's conception of the Christ, emphasizing the abstract individualism latent in the conception rather than presenting it – as Paul had done – as a new covenant with the God of Israel. Evidently Marcion was influenced by

Gnostic ideas. But he avoided the dualism which turned the Christ into a purely spiritual being with only the appearance of a human form. What he did not avoid, on the other hand, was the temptation to understand salvation as the return of disciplined souls to God. Marcion neglected those features of Paul's thought that depicted Christian churches as 'loving' associations founded on belief in human equality, a new type of community.

The fate of the individual soul rather than a community of 'the saints' became the focus of Marcionism. Apparently the churches Marcion established were rather hieratic, perhaps a hangover from Gnosticism. Nonetheless, his churches were also criticized for giving women an important role. If Marcion was a heretic, it was probably because he developed the individualism latent in Paul's thought to the point where he would one day be considered a proto-Protestant.

The other source which gives a glimpse of the potential for Christian radicalism is a text discovered about fifty years ago in the Egyptian desert, the Gospel of Thomas. There is doubt about its exact date, though most scholars believe that in its present form it dates from the mid-second century. Certainly it reveals Gnostic influences. But it probably also incorporates an important early Aramaic tradition of Jesus' sayings, a survival of what scholars suppose may have been many 'sayings gospels'. In any case, the Gospel of Thomas contains extraordinary passages devoted to what can only be described as women's 'liberation'.

We have seen that the conventional view in antiquity was that women could not be fully rational beings. Their subordination, like that of slaves, was justified in that way. The Gospel of Thomas urges a new project on believers: nothing less than turning women into men! They are to become as 'one'. By that it is clearly meant that women should be enabled to become rational agents, to recognize that they have the same rational and moral capacities as men. 'When you make the two into one, and when you make the inner like the outer and the outer like the inner ... and when you make male and female into a single one, so that the male will not be male nor the female be female, then you will enter (the kingdom).'[13] That reconstruction of the self, which Paul had urged on his followers, is here tied overtly to a change in the status of women. The implication of the text is that only when women are free can men also be truly free – that the reciprocity which belief in human equality entails is only possible when their shared nature is fully acknowledged.

In the Gospel of Thomas the proper use of the mind leads to moral transparency. It continues the work of liberation from hierarchical agencies that Paul had urged. As reported by Thomas, Jesus' words overturn the subordination of women, one of the pillars on which the ancient family – and with it a whole conception of society – had rested. His words are consistent with passages in the canonical gospels in which Jesus asks that his followers be prepared to throw over even the ties of family, rejecting parents and siblings when the service of God so requires.

Such injunctions privileged individual agency over corporate agency, conscience over inherited social roles. They may also throw light on the roots of Pauline individualism in Jesus' sayings. Certainly they make it easier to understand Paul's conviction that faith, which reveals the foundation of human agency, liberates. In the Gospel of Thomas we can see the moral intuitions generated by Christian beliefs being given a new application. Belief in the moral equality of humans was beginning to threaten fundamental status differences.

Of course, the Gospel of Thomas was a minority report. But it reveals that the moral intuitions generated by Christianity were hard to contain, even when the organized church was anxious to placate Roman authorities and deny that it had any conspiratorial or subversive character. Paul had already firmly asserted that the 'powers that be are authorized by God'. By and large, the early Fathers of the Church agreed. To combat Celsus' argument that Christians' loyalties made them bad citizens, Origen argued that Christian morality offered a better foundation for public power: 'The more pious a man is, the more effective he is in helping the emperors – more so than the soldiers who go out into the line and kill all the enemy troops that they can.'[14]

This was a fateful argument. For what does it suggest? Origen was meeting Celsus' complaint that the Christians' unwillingness to sacrifice to the civic gods, accept public office and take up arms when asked was compromising the safety of the Roman empire and undermining the piety that sustained it. In reply, Origen argued, at least by implication, for a wholly different conception of society. He argued for a society that recognized moral limits to the claims of public power, invoking a sphere of individual responsibility that transcended the traditional duties of citizenship: 'We know of the existence in each city of another sort of country, created by the Word of God.'[15] Origen's implication was that a society founded on Christian morality offered, in the long run, a better prospect of stability and survival. 'We who by our prayers destroy all demons which stir up wars, violate oaths and disturb the peace, are of more help to the emperors than those who seem to be doing the fighting.'[16]

Thus, even before Augustine's 'city of God', Christian apologists were invoking 'the country of God' to assert the claims of the individual conscience. Such claims of conscience seemed to follow irresistibly from the assumption of moral equality. Equality, choice and responsibility hung together in their minds. Irenaeus repeatedly insisted on this as early as the mid-second century: 'God's just judgement falls equally on all men, and never fails.'

If God has created humans as equals, as rational agents with free will, then there ought to be an area within which they are free to choose and responsible for their choices. Identifying such an area was at first a means of self-defence by Christians. But soon it was also more than that. Tertullian saw clearly the implications of Christian moral beliefs. 'Here lies the perfection and distinctiveness of Christian goodness,' he argued. 'Ordinary goodness is different; for all men love their friends, but only Christians love their enemies.'[17] Respecting a range of freedom of choice in all humans might be seen as one aspect of the latter.

The suggestion that belief in 'equal liberty' appeared in early Christian apologetics will surprise many and irritate some. For the anti-clericalism which has been an integral part of liberal historiography does not lend itself to such a conclusion. Besides, the distrust of anything like teleological explanations in history – of what is often called the Whig interpretation of history – reinforces such scepticism. But texts are facts. And the facts remain. In the mid-second century Irenaeus of Lyon asked, 'what new thing did the Word bring by coming down to earth?' For Tertullian, writing only a few decades later, the answer was clear. 'One mighty deed alone was sufficient for our God – to bring freedom to the human person.'[18]

Tertullian was perhaps the most remarkable of the Church Fathers before Augustine. And he was in no doubt about the claims of conscience.

> We worship the one God ... There are others whom you regard as gods; we know them to be demons. Nevertheless, it is a basic human right that everyone should be free to worship according to his own convictions. No one is either harmed or helped by another man's religion. Religion must be practised freely, not by coercion; even animals for sacrifice must be offered with a willing heart. So even if you compel us to sacrifice, you will not be providing your gods with any worthwhile service. They will not want sacrifices from unwilling offerers – unless they are perverse, which God is not.[19]

Here we may find one of the earliest assertions of a basic right, a rightful power claimed for humans as such, that is, as individuals. Did Tertullian's argument also imply that authority, founded on consent, was different from mere physical power, the ability to constrain? Probably. That seems to lurk behind the suggestion by many early apologists that Christians might, after all, be the 'better citizens', despite their unwillingness to sacrifice to civic gods or the emperor. For they gave social order a foundation in consciences. In any case, Tertullian's determination to defend the claims of conscience – a sphere of personal choice – is unmistakeable.

But would such a determination survive after the Christian Church was recognized by the Emperor Constantine in 313 and, in due course, became the official religion of the Roman empire?

6

Heroism Redefined

By the second half of the third century Christianity had become a major phenomenon in the Roman empire – and Christians a group that could not be ignored. Intermittent persecution gave way to more determined campaigns, by Decius and Valerian in the decade after 250, to impose on Christians the worship of civic gods and the emperor. Yet the campaigns were soon abandoned. Christians, especially in the East, were now too numerous, too wealthy and too well placed to be persecuted for long, though they were still far from being a majority.

In any case, the 'martyr's crown' may have increased the moral appeal of Christianity. The sight of individuals from all classes of society – women as well as men, slaves as well as patricians – enduring suffering and death, often without complaint, sometimes even with a kind of triumph, dramatized the character of the new faith. It was, in a dreadful way, powerful theatre.

Later Christian apologists probably exaggerated the number of martyrs, but that scarcely matters. The important thing is that the cult of the martyrs began to redefine heroism as previously understood. The ancient hero had been – Odysseus-like – an aristocrat. Springing from a leading family and often associated with the foundation of cities, the ancient hero was typically male, strong, wily and successful. His conversion into a demigod reflected the nature of ancient polytheism. Fame was the medium of heroism. Family and civic piety preserved the hero's reputation. He was an eminently social being.

By contrast, the Christian martyr – whether facing stoning by a crowd, ferocious animals in a crowded stadium or burning on a pyre – was defying society. The refusal of martyrs to bend under the claims of family and civic piety or to worship the Emperor meant that they were alone. They were unwilling to submit. Little wonder that the Roman authorities described martyrs as 'enemies of the human race' because of their insistence on standing alone.

But were they really alone? The martyrs claimed to be acting in the name of a more important relationship, a relationship that underpinned their wills. Apparently they had found something within themselves more precious than social conventions or conformity. But that was not all. The interior conviction that marked them out was something that disregarded gender, class and status. Martyrdom illustrated the exercise of an individual will, founded on conscience. It made that will visible.

In making martyrs of Christians, the ancient world was consecrating what it sought to destroy and destroying what it sought to preserve. For the Christian martyrs gained a hold over the popular imagination. And it is easy to see why that should have been so. The martyrs offered a model of heroism open to all, a democratic model of heroism. As Tertullian remarked early in the third century, the martyrs' blood provided 'the seed of the church'.

The idea of the individual – of an underlying moral status shared equally by all – may first have entered the minds of many non-Christians reflecting on scenes or tales of martyrdom. That there was something to be admired in the martyrs may have made at least some pagan persecutors, as well as their audiences, at times rather wistful. Thus an unintended consequence of the persecution of Christians was to render the idea of the individual, or moral equality, more intelligible. The glimpse of a depth of motivation, at once individual and potentially universal, was not easily forgotten.

Christianity was still primarily an urban phenomenon, attracting at first especially the 'middle sort' of people. It spread through persuasion and example, in ways that upper-class pagans found demeaning. 'We see them in our own homes, wool dressers, cobblers and fullers, the most uneducated and common persons, not daring to say a word in the presence of their masters who are older and wiser,' Celsus famously complained. 'But when they get hold of the children in private, and silly women with them, they are wonderfully eloquent, to the effect that children must not listen to their father, but believe them, and be taught by them.'[1]

Was it an accident that women and even slaves also played an important part in the growth of Christianity, and that, through them, it spread into the upper classes? The Christian movement gained from being marginal. The offer of dignity through belief in the Christ did not openly challenge patriarchy or servitude. But it offered self-respect. A moral revolution was under way.

The church had already found it necessary to organize itself. A hierarchy of offices emerged. The informal distinctions of the first century gave way to a structure of bishops (for each city), aided by presbyters and deacons. 'The exact history of this transition within two generations from apostles, prophets and teachers to bishop, presbyters and deacons is shrouded in obscurity, though our sources give occasional glimpses of the process.'[2] But adjusting to hierarchy did not stop there. By the later third century Christians also occupied important positions in the Roman administration, at the centre and in the provinces. Christians were to be found even among high officers in the army. The church had, moreover, acquired rich benefactors, and the largest episcopal sees developed elaborate welfare organizations. Indeed, they amounted to mini-welfare states, through their provision for poorer members. Bishops were fast becoming important civic figures.

This penetration of the Roman state by the church had important consequences for each. On the one hand, it led to striking changes in the rhetoric and the behaviour of the urban governing classes. On the other hand, it threatened the sense of an egalitarian 'community of saints' that had sustained the church as a persecuted minority, and led to a movement within the church to reject the world and its 'temptations'. Let us look now at each.

Peter Brown has brilliantly explored the changing rhetoric and behaviour of the urban governing classes in late antiquity. Their emphasis on proper deportment – on noble birth and *paideia* or culture – had an important function in the empire. Dignified carriage, formalized speech and elaborate manners were meant to convey their superior status. Such attributes amounted to the only available restraint on the exercise of unbridled power. It was an unbridled power that was constantly on view, both in domestic and public life. 'From wives and slaves in the household to the abject courtiers of tyrannical rulers, the lives of so many persons in so many situations appeared to depend on the whim of their superiors.'[3]

The anger of superiors was exceedingly dangerous. Unsurprisingly, the upper classes seized every occasion to remind the Imperial government that, thanks to their codes of deportment and public speaking skills, they were indispensable for the control of the cities. Education, manners and ceremony, binding the emperor to the upper classes of his cities, offered the only thing approaching a constitutional restraint on the exercise of power. So it was no accident that this *paideia* of the upper classes increasingly focused on the subtleties of decorum, even if at times it was hardly more than a tone of voice. It was a form of self-defence. And it was frail enough.

A defining characteristic of belonging to the class of civic notables (and condition of its self-confidence) was exemption from corporal punishment. But as the class of notables was expanded to increase the range of tax gathering, the privileges that had previously protected noble birth and *paideia* were put at risk. Incidents of flogging and torture were no longer restricted to the lower classes. It was a dreadful breach of decorum. In consequence, anxiety about their status increasingly afflicted civic notables. Nudity, once the badge of social superiority, was becoming instead nakedness in the face of a remote, capricious public power.

However, by the end of the third century one section of the urban elites embarked on a different course for dealing with the emperor and provincial governors, a course which drew on their Christian beliefs and enabled them to become the spokesmen of the lower classes. A new rhetoric served their bid for urban leadership. It was a rhetoric founded on 'love of the poor'. Drawing on features of the Christian self-image – the church's social inclusiveness, the simplicity of its message, its distrust of traditional culture and its welfare role – 'love of the poor' made possible, Brown argues, a regrouping within the urban elites. It was a rhetoric that reflected and served an alliance between upper-class Christians and the bishops of cities, who were themselves often men of culture or *paideia*.

This new rhetoric was put to use 'in the never ending task of exercising control within the city and representing its needs to the outside world.'[4] It was a kind of Christian populism, which served notice on

the emperor and his servants that the bishops were now an indispensable factor in urban government. The bishops claimed to be better
able to mobilize and shape opinion than members of the urban elite
who continued to worship civic gods, for the bishops' 'love of the
poor' now extended beyond their congregations and embraced the
whole urban population. 'In the name of a religion that claimed to
challenge the values of the elite, upper-class Christians gained control
of the lower classes of the cities.'[5] They drew on a long-standing
Christian rhetoric that attributed the spread of the faith to the humility of its unlettered preachers – to men who, like the apostles Peter
and Paul, conspicuously lacked the *paideia* and manners of the traditional urban elites.

Yet the fact that this new rhetoric of the poor made possible a
regrouping within the urban elites should not distract us from its
wider significance. Its advent marked a fundamental change in the
terms of public discourse. The aristocratic values that had previously
shaped that discourse – conveyed by such terms as piety and *paideia* –
were displaced by values that can properly be called democratic. The
rhetoric of the poor carried within it the seeds of a new form of society. 'Urban notables had presented themselves as standing at the head
of an entire social hierarchy, made up of all active participants in the
life of the city. The Christian bishop, by contrast, erected his claim to
authority over a social void. The poor were defined as those who
belonged to no social grouping.'[6] Thus, 'love of the poor' extended
public concern beyond the citizen class, a privileged class. Bishops'
'love of the poor' reached out to the servile, destitute and foreign-born,
to groups without standing in the hierarchy of citizens. They were
offered a home. It was an irresistible offer.

In this way the inclusive character of the Christian church – its
'universality' – could be proclaimed long before it had anything like a
majority of adherents in the city. This claim also enabled it to begin to
turn a moral status (the 'equality of souls') into a visible social role,
the individual. For it was as individuals that both the rich and the
poor, including those who had previously existed outside the bounds
of the citizen class, approached the sacraments of the church. They
were baptized and received the Eucharist as individuals seeking salvation, rather than as members of a group.

Christian churches thus began to dissolve the corporate character of an aristocratic society. However, at the same time that the church was penetrating urban society with new moral norms, a protest movement developed within the church, a movement expressing anxiety about any such embracing of the world. It took the form of a withdrawal from urban life. And it presented the character of Christianity in a peculiarly vivid way.

The instinct of withdrawal had antecedents in Judaism. Groups such as the Essenes had fled to remote regions to embrace an ascetic life. But the Christian form of withdrawal was, especially at the outset, far more individualist. It began in the later third century in Egypt and Syria, with individuals withdrawing into the 'wilderness', individuals who gradually became known as 'anchorites' or 'monks'. It is important to note that they withdrew as individuals rather than as members of previously organized groups. For it throws light on the nature of their goal. Their goal was salvation. But it was salvation understood in a particular way. They sought to develop a higher will by overcoming their personal appetites. St Antony, the most famous early monk, described their goal as seeking the help of the Holy Spirit to gain 'control over their souls and bodies in order that both may be sanctified . . .'

The era of martyrs had come to an end. But in many Christians the need to demonstrate the depth of motivation released by their new beliefs had not. For some, ascetic practices at home no longer seemed to suffice. These ascetics at first took up residence in caves and other deserted areas outside cities and villages. Gradually some moved further away, building mud-brick cells on mountainsides or occupying abandoned military outposts. These monks cultivated a life marked by celibacy, poverty and self-denial – away from the clamour of the agora and forum, away even from the ceremonies of the church. They sought to overcome the temptations of the world, its demons, by communing with God in solitude, that is, through themselves.

The monks sought to gain control over their bodies – to create wills properly so-called – through study of the scriptures, meditation and prayer. It seemed to them the principal step required by Christian belief. The withdrawal into the self was at the same time a reach for moral universality. 'Therefore brothers, let us be equal, from the least to the greatest, whether rich or poor, perfect in harmony and humility,' urged one leading monk.[7] By renouncing selfish, transient desires, monks sought, through the habit of obedience, to incarnate a superior will. Innerness was everything. The story of a young anchorite trying to learn from a venerated elder tells us as much:

> As far as I can I say my little office [says the younger man], I fast a little, I pray and meditate, I live in peace and as far as I can, I purify my thoughts. What else can I do? The old man stood up and stretched his hands towards heaven. His fingers became like ten lamps of fire and he said to him, 'If you will, you can become all flame.'[8]

Many urban Christians who did not share their solitude, but imposed austere practices on themselves at home ('dedicated virgins' were not uncommon), shared the monks' view that an ascetic life was 'the whole yoke of the lord'. That widely shared view helped, in turn, to give the monks great prestige.

Of course, for many monks solitude remained relative. They were city-dwellers by origin, and what they understood by 'wilderness' could be rather suburban. Often their cells were within easy walking distance of the cities. And as the monks' reputation for austerity spread, they became the object of solicitous visits from their urban Christian brethren, who were perhaps moved as much by curiosity as by piety.

There was undoubtedly a degree of extravagance in the way some monks renounced the world and communed alone with their God. Simeon the Stylite, who lived on top of a column outside Antioch for years, is the most obvious example. One of Simeon's disciples is said to have lived on a column outside Constantinople for thirty-three years. But other forms of self-mortification – such as wearing a heavy iron chain or feeding on grass – also flourished. Such anchorites often described their ways of defying society as 'becoming fools for Christ's sake'.[9] It is hardly surprising that many of the urban clergy deplored what they saw as these monks' theatricality. Nonetheless, the self-image projected by the monks gave them a remarkable moral authority. The charisma attached by city-dwellers to 'isolation' resulted in healing powers being attributed to monks. They were sometimes called 'practical' philosophers – philosophers who did not rely on literacy or bookish learning for wisdom or influence.

A democratic, if not populist, message was lurking. When the Copt who became St Antony was questioned by a visiting philosopher about the absence of books in his mountainside refuge, he replied that all he needed for contemplation was 'God's creation'. Antony, a wealthy farmer's son, had given away his inheritance, and retreated to the countryside, where he relied on the Bible, prayer and manual labour to resist the 'demons' that tempted him. He had no Greek, the language of high culture, but felt no need to apologize for the fact. 'My book . . . is the nature of God's creation; it is present whenever I wish to read His words.'[10] Struggles with sexual temptation – whether in the form of women or boys – were continual. 'He kept vigil to such an extent that he often continued the whole night without sleep,' Antony's first biographer, Athanasius, reports. 'He ate once a day, after sunset, sometimes once in two days, and often even once in four, while his food was bread and salt and water only.' (The Egyptian climate must have helped, for Antony allegedly lived to be 105.)

When we imagine away the more extreme manifestations of a movement that quickly assumed large proportions in Egypt and Syria, we are left with something revealing about the character of Christianity: its egalitarianism, its potential for inwardness. As long as churches had been small and persecuted, a strong sense of community ('of the saints') had to some extent obscured that character. Such besieged communities constrained, so to speak, the moral impulses released by Christian belief. But the monks gave those impulses a dramatic release. Traditional urban spaces were far too constricted for their message.

No one understood this more completely than St Augustine. Knowledge of the monastic movement in Egypt and Syria took some time to reach the West. But when Augustine was first told about the movement associated with St Antony (*circa* 386), he grasped its inward and democratic import at once. 'The uneducated rise up and take heaven by storm, and we, with all our learning, here we are, still wallowing in flesh and blood . . .'[11]

The movement of monks into the wilderness involved a rejection of traditional forms of community, in particular the city or polis – without at first pretending to any organization or common life. Solitude, prayer and the scriptures were enough, it was claimed, to lift monks onto a higher moral plane. Undistracted by crowds and the noise of the city, they sought God in solitude and silence, overcoming temptations, demons and natural hazards. If the martyrs had offered a more democratic model of heroism, the monks could be portrayed as a new type of athlete, an athlete who sought not physical perfection or competitive glory but conquest of the will. The desert rather than the amphitheatre was the setting for victory. The audience was God rather than crowds. An inner voice rather than outbursts of applause was the medium of success.

By the end of the third century some parts of the Egyptian and Syrian countryside were becoming 'crowded' with monks. A century later tourists from Rome visiting Egypt, who were curious about what was initially an Eastern phenomenon, complained about the overcrowding. Some sites in Egypt were occupied so intensively that a form of community sprang up, at first very loose and informal. Monks would gather together once or twice a week for services, served by priests from a neighbouring city. No doubt the urban clergy encouraged this regularizing of the religious life of the monks and the promise of discipline it brought to what must have seemed an anarchic development of Christianity.

7

A New Form of Association: Monasticism

The equality of souls in search of salvation was at the heart of Christian beliefs. It was the dominant moral fact about the movement that created the church. Yet during the first century that fact had been embedded in a mystical vision of 'the last days' approaching – a belief that the return of the Christ would soon usher in a new creation.

It was the weakening of expectations about an imminent second coming of the Christ that led to rethinking in the following centuries. If the Christ was already in the world, as Paul had suggested, how did that change things? If the Holy Ghost made it possible for believers to become 'one in Christ', what should 'the saints' bring to the world around them? What should be their attitude to the society and government of the Roman empire?

Historians have often discussed early Christian attitudes towards the government of the Roman empire. But they have been less attentive to the question of how Christians began to conceive of society in view of the moral intuitions generated by their new beliefs. That is a pity. For Christian beliefs had begun to impinge on the traditional conception of society by the later second century. Indeed, these beliefs began to lay the foundation for a new conception of society.

Why have historians been slow to explore this matter? Two reasons stand out. The first is that they have been impressed by the determination of the early church not to offend the Roman authorities – by its anxiety to establish that the Christian movement was not subversive or conspiratorial. Some have even traced this self-protective instinct back to 'prudent' Gospel accounts of the Roman governor Pilate declaring that he could attribute no crime to Jesus. The second reason has to do with the formidable influence of St Augustine. Augustine wrote the *City of God* after the sack of Rome by Alaric's Goths in AD 410. He denied that, by overthrowing the old civic deities, Christianity was responsible for that disaster. Instead, he sought to minimize the significance of the event, arguing that all human institutions were subject to decay and disaster. He insisted that the city of God could not be identified with any institution, not even with the church itself. Augustine's argument could easily be construed, however unfairly, as rejecting any interest in social reform or reconstruction.

It is a mistake, however, to suppose that Christian beliefs had not already begun to reshape the prevailing conception of society. One symptom of change, fifty years earlier, can be found in the Emperor Julian's attempt to restore paganism as the official religion of the empire and reopen the temples. For Julian's version of paganism was of a paganism 'purged' by Christian moral intuitions. The new priesthood he sought to create was to have as its test 'the love of God and of fellow men', while 'charity' was to be its vocation. Indeed, Julian often complained that what pagans failed to understand about Christians was that 'their benevolence to strangers, their care for the graves of the dead and the pretended holiness of their lives' explained the rapid spread of Christian 'atheism' – by which he meant the Christian rejection of polytheism.[1]

Evidently Julian was sensitive to the egalitarian moral thrust of Christianity. And he hoped to reconcile polytheism with that thrust, removing its traditional involvement with hierarchy, its association with the assumption of natural inequality. Yet removing such features threatened paganism with a complete loss of identity. So Julian's project was probably doomed from the outset.

Christianity was turning outward and visible things inwards. The basilicas built in Rome by the Emperor Constantine, after his conversion in 312, gave architectural expression to the difference of focus between paganism and the new moral beliefs. In place of the ancient temple, with its splendid columns and decorations on the exterior, the Christian basilica was simple, unadorned brick on the outside, with columns and decorations reserved for the interior. The change was symptomatic. Where paganism had concerned itself primarily with external conformity of behaviour, Christianity now concerned itself especially with inner conviction.

During the fourth and fifth centuries heated debates raged throughout Christian churches. For this was the period when Christian 'orthodoxy' was defined against other views that came to be regarded as heresies. It was the period of 'universal' church councils, those of Nicaea (325) and Chalcedon (451), held under the patronage of Christian emperors. Heresies described as Arianism, Docetism, Sabellianism and Donatism were identified, which turned on difficult questions about the Trinity, the relationship between Father, Son and Holy Ghost. Fortunately, we do not have to concern ourselves with most of the issues debated. But one cannot be ignored. That is the issue about the nature of the Christ, what theologians have since called the Christological question. Just what was the relationship between the human and the divine in the Christ? How were the two natures related in Jesus?

The answers given to these questions differed between east and west, north and south, within the now far-flung Christian churches. The positions taken up can easily seem abstruse – whether, for example, the Son was coeternal with the Father, or whether divinity was fully present in Jesus throughout his life or developed gradually. However, lurking behind all the variations in argument lay an issue central to the development of the conception of the individual.

What does it imply about human nature to say that, in Jesus, God became 'flesh of our flesh'? In what sense can it be said that God is active in the world, and that God is 'with us'? These questions raised others, especially after the appearance of Christian emperors. Just how should Christians conceive of society? And what sort of government is appropriate to such a society? Behind apparently abstruse theological debates, intensely practical issues were emerging. The Christological debate carried them, although in other terms and concealed beneath its surface.

Historians have been struck by the extent to which theological issues became matters talked about in the streets of Alexandria and Constantinople, capable of arousing strong, even violent, popular feelings. In a famous sermon, Gregory of Nyssa described his encounters with public opinion in fifth-century Constantinople. 'If in this city you ask anyone for change, he will discuss with you whether the Son is begotten or unbegotten; if you ask about the quality of bread, you will receive the answer that the Father is greater, the Son is less; if you suggest that a bath is desirable, you will be told that there was nothing before the Son was created.'[2] Were these preoccupations simply a matter of fashion?

Such popular feelings ought to have alerted historians to the larger issue at stake. For at stake was nothing less than how society should be conceived, something in which people in the street were deeply involved, even if they were unable to identify the nature of their concern. By itself, their involvement in these abstruse discussions suggests a progress of the idea of equality, the idea of a shared human nature. The *demos* – the 'people' – had ceased to refer merely to the privileged citizen class. Even slaves, after hearing passionate sermons in churches, might develop theological opinions. But this progress of equality could and did point in very different political directions. The fourth and fifth centuries give evidence of two opposed conclusions about the proper form for government, drawn from the Christian assumption of the moral equality of humans.

The first conclusion was drawn at the expense of the traditional urban upper classes and their *paideia*. It was the conclusion that the new moral beliefs entailed equal subjection to a central government, that is, to Rome's imperial majesty. This conclusion was parasitic on monotheism. It likened the imperial role to that of the divine ruler of the universe. The emperor's role provided a foretaste of the role of the Godhead, linking every person directly to the font of authority. Intermediaries became suspect. The cult of the ancient family, the association of citizens in the polis, local notables: these could no longer legitimately interpose themselves into the only relationship which had a divine sanction. Humans, despite their manifold inherited social roles, were becoming individuals, each deemed to have a soul. The ancient vision of hierarchy, social as well as natural, was fading.

Here we begin to see the impact of the Christological controversies. Peter Brown has noticed and described that impact.

> The emperor no longer yielded to the philosopher because he shared with him the same restraints imposed by an elegant and ennobling paideia. He yielded to bishops and to holy men because even Christ himself had yielded, to become a man like those he ruled. Swathed in majesty,

the emperor made plain, not that he shared a culture with his upper-class subjects, but, rather, despite all appearances to the contrary, he shared a common humanity with all Christians.[3]

This assimilation of imperial power to a Christ-like authority began to transform not only the perception of government, but also the conception of society, through its insistence on equal subjection and its distrust of intermediaries.

One of the earliest Christian historians, Eusebius of Caesarea, was a contemporary of the emperor Constantine. At times his writings amount to an apology for the analogy between divine majesty and imperial majesty. Eusebius too was influenced by what Brown calls the mood accompanying the Christological controversies, an awareness of the 'awesome condescension' of God in stooping to identify himself with the human condition, through the incarnate Christ. In a sense the analogy made it easier to understand each party. If God became the emperor of heaven, the emperor was 'very much God on earth'. In principle, the emperor claimed an unmediated connection with each of his subjects, and was equally concerned for each.

Of course, the condescension of God in assuming a human nature also imposed a decisive obligation on individuals. Here too the analogy held. The new Christian Roman empire took the first steps along a very long road, which would transform the older Roman idea of imperium into the modern notion of sovereignty, substituting the individual for the family as the unit of subjection. What have been described as the 'individualist' trends in later Roman law – the weakening of paterfamilias, improved status for women and changes in inheritance rules, for example – probably both contributed to this Christian mind-set and reflected it.

Yet if the incarnation revealed God as present to the world in a new way – if individual agency and divine agency were now understood as parts of the same continuum – then another line of argument, yielding a different political conclusion, was also plausible. For 'Christian humility' might be invoked as effectively as 'Divine Majesty'. This alternative could present the claims of authority as moving 'from within or below' upwards, rather than as descending from 'on high'. In that sense, the assumption of moral equality proved to be double-edged.

The early church illustrated this alternative road, although in a patchy, incoherent way. For once the age of apostles and prophets had passed, presbyters and bishops were chosen by general consent of believers. The 'laying on of hands' on candidates for presbyters, from which group 'bishops' gradually emerged as the senior figures, illustrates earliest practice. The choice of bishop was itself often the result of popular 'acclamation', even when the candidate had been pre-selected by virtue of his learning and *paideia*. Here we can see a kind of compromise between the traditions of the urban notables and a more egalitarian emerging culture.

The choosing of 'superiors' by 'inferiors' was the norm, though it was not formalized or systematic. It was only later, when the church became closely joined to the Roman empire, that this norm had to compromise with another, that is, with the practice of 'superiors' choosing 'inferiors'. Even before the official toleration and then adoption of Christianity by the empire, the role of the bishops as spokesmen for their cities in dealings with the emperor had given an aristocratic turn to the proceedings of urban churches. Nor did wealth hurt. It contributed to the clergy becoming an autonomous, self-perpetuating body – coming to resemble in that way the class that had traditionally provided the curia of the ancient city. For the superior magistrates of the city had exercised their jurisdiction as a personal right, as an undoubted inheritance or birthright. Their authority was not a matter of delegation or representation.

Yet while urban churches compromised with the aristocratic world in which they had developed, the new, chaotic movement of monks preserved the primitive norms of the church. As the monks became more numerous and concentrated in certain places, the first steps in organizing monasticism were taken. As we have seen, the urban clergy encouraged this development, since the monks had often lived apart from the rites and sacraments of the church. Nonetheless, the gradual organization of monasticism reveals more about the moral thrust of Christianity than what had become the 'state' religion of the Roman empire by the late fourth century could do. As hermits or anchorites became cenobites – that is, as asceticism became communal – Christian beliefs began to generate a new conception of 'community', an utterly new form of social organization.

The need for organization was made obvious by the scale of the movement of monks into the countryside or 'desert'. Take, for example, the mountain of Nitria in Egypt. By the fourth century it had become exceedingly populous. 'On the mountain live some five thousand men with different modes of life, each living in accordance with his own powers and wishes, so that it is allowed to live alone or with another or with a number of others,' observed Palladius, in his *Lausiac History*.

> There are seven bakeries in the mountain which serve the needs of both these and also of the anchorites of the great desert, six hundred in all . . . In the mountain of Nitria there is a great church by which stand three palm trees . . . Next to the church is a guest house where they receive the stranger who has arrived until he goes away of his own accord, without limit of time, even if he remains two or three years . . . In this mountain there also live doctors and confectioners. And they use wine and wine is on sale. All these men work with their hands at linen-manufacture so that all are self-supporting. And indeed at the ninth hour it is possible to stand and hear how the strains of psalmody rise from each habitation so that one believes that one is high above the world in Paradise. They occupy the church only on Saturday and Sunday.[4]

Recent studies emphasize the extent of organization all this implied – with monks employing an agent to sell their products and purchase supplies, while in some places the monks also established proto-hospitals.

Little wonder, then, that monasticism was acquiring a group identity, both in the eyes of the monks and for outsiders. The first striking thing about that new identity was that its basis lay in voluntary association, in individual acts of will. This was a radical departure from the beliefs and practices of the ancient world. Family cult, civic status and servitude had been assigned by birth or imposed by force. It is true that the mystery cults had developed through individual adhesion. But it was as if they could not show their face in a world organized so differently, and hence they remained semi-secret, 'mysterious' societies.

The primitive church had also developed through individual 'conversion'. But in the face of official hostility and even persecution, the 'saints', too, remained concealed from the world, in an enforced solidarity. Their beliefs and practices were at least half-hidden – giving rise to the lurid stories about cannibalism and sexual promiscuity which long circulated among pagans. Secret meetings in private houses, burials in catacombs: these were the practices of the earliest Christians. There was little or no self-advertisement. Rather, martyrdom, rumour and discreet proselytizing were its modes of development.

Monasticism was different. Even its exaggerations announced a new confidence when challenging the form of existing society. Separating themselves physically as well as morally from the ancient family and the polis, monks offered the picture of a world founded on different principles. Their struggles to subdue themselves by means of a deeper relationship – despite the many offences against good taste and civility involved – suggested how the individual conscience could and should constrain social relationships, giving them a new foundation.

The transition from solitary hermits to communal monasticism confirmed a new form of sociability, a sociability founded on the role of individual conscience, on accepting the claims of a universal moral law. In no sphere did this emerge more clearly than in the status and treatment of women. We have seen that women had played an important part in the growth of the early church. By the third century 'dedicated virgins' had acquired a new prestige in upper-class families and, indeed, in the Christian community at large. What was the most striking possible evidence of a woman's freedom in the 'new age'? The answer was sexual renunciation, a manifest act of individual will.[5] Monasticism soon gave these moral developments further impetus. The creation of ascetic communities for women – what were to become convents – marked the emergence of women from the ancient family, from the permanent subordinations of the domestic sphere. It is hardly surprising that upper-class women led the way.

But that was not all. The way of life associated with the monks also had another important, if unintended, consequence. It rehabilitated 'work'– separating work from its association with a servile status, from the stain of ancient slavery. Work acquired a new dignity, becoming even a requirement of self-respect. Basil of Caesarea urged that 'we must not use the ideal of piety as an excuse for idleness or a means of escaping toil'. After all, idleness opened the door to 'demons', to images, fancies and appetites, which undermined the construction of a morally upright will. And it was to such a will that the monks sought to subordinate themselves. Personal salvation was understood as a laborious, lifetime quest. It was not a matter of momentary ecstasy or sudden initiation.

The idea of mutual support, through work, became central as the isolated life of anchorites gave way to communal monasticism or cenobitism. At first there was resistance to relinquishing the belief that solitary communing with God was the highest possible calling. But by the early fourth century the Egyptian monk Pachomius, who helped to shape a more communal asceticism, was inclined to the opposite view. One source has Pachomius saying that while 'in the view of people living as anchorites' the life adopted by cenobites 'does not seem perfect', in truth 'they are far superior to those who live as anchorites for they walk in the obligingness of the Apostle'.[6]

Sharing a common life, while seeking personal salvation, seemed to conform more closely to the Gospels. The form of community consistent with equality of souls was essentially a community of shared values. Such a communal life ought, according to an early life of Pachomius, to 'fashion the souls of men so as to present them pure to God'. Working and sharing, on the basis of equality, contributed to forming 'a perfect koinonia like that of the believers which Acts describes: "They were one heart and one soul".'[7]

Gradually work was assimilated to prayer. It became almost a form of prayer. St Basil of Caesarea (c. 330 – c. 378), who gave Eastern monasticism its Rule, did not see any conflict between the two. For 'it is God's will that we should nourish the hungry, give the thirsty to drink, and clothe the naked'.[8] Such a reconciliation of the claims of conscience with an emphasis on social obligations was to shape the future of monasticism, Western as well as Eastern.

For Basil, the scriptural foundation of the monastic life – a life both solitary and social – was summarized by the first two commandments of Jesus: 'Thou shalt love the Lord thy God with all thy heart and with all thy soul and with all thy mind. This is the first and great commandment. And the second is like unto it, Thou shalt love thy neighbour as thyself.'[9] This joining of equality with reciprocity provided the basis for Basil's conception of a monastic community. Together, the two assumptions created an unprecedented version of authority. To be in authority was to be humble. 'Let meekness of character and lowliness of heart characterize the superior,' Basil urged.

> For if the Lord was not afraid of ministering to his own bond-servants, but was willing to be a servant of the earth and clay which he had made and fashioned into man . . . what must we do to our equals that we may be deemed to have attained the imitation of him? This one thing, then, is essential in the superior. Further he must be compassionate, showing long-suffering to those who through inexperience fall short in their duty, not passing sins over in silence but meekly bearing with the restive, applying remedies to them all with kindness . . .[10]

This remarkable new model of authority – and the rhetoric it inspired – had a long future ahead of it. It would receive a crucial elaboration in the sixth-century Rule of St Benedict, which shaped later Western monasticism. Benedict's Rule reinforced the democratizing of the idea of authority, insisting that monastic leaders temper their government with a 'listening' culture and respect the different needs of individual monks. The object was 'to work towards the fellow citizenship of the heavenly kingdom'. To promote such moral equality, Benedict sought to eliminate social distinctions within the monastery.

How were the new monastic communities governed? The answer seems to be that at first it was by a mixture of antecedent practice and the authority of elderly monks who had proved their holiness. In the Egyptian desert, Pachomius and Shenoute took the earliest steps by organizing houses of monks, standardizing their dress and establishing a routine of worship. Shenoute introduced monastic vows and a period of probation. But, once again, the crucial figure was to be Basil, who insisted that monasteries should be relatively small, that they might even be located in cities, that monks share property, and that their time be divided between work and prayer, with six services during the day and two during the night. Basil discouraged exaggerated asceticism. Instead, monks were to involve themselves in the life of the world around them, by founding schools and hospitals.[11]

Basil accepted that final authority over the monasteries belonged to the local bishop. But he also believed that this authority should be exercised only intermittently. For the monks should govern themselves, guided by those who had proved their worth, led by an abbot. So the ideal was clear enough. The ideal was self-regulation, often summarized as the monks being of 'one heart and one mind'. Such self-regulation was meant to minimize the need for sanctions.

By taking individual responsibility so seriously, the ideas of moral equality and limited government became closely associated. Outward conformity of behaviour was all that had been expected in the ancient family and polis. But monasticism consecrated a vision of social order founded on conscience, on hard-won individual intentions rather than publicly enforced status differences. However difficult to achieve, there was in theory 'no distinction' between persons on the grounds of social status, whether of higher or lower class, slave or free-born.

The struggle for self-control, which had marked monks from the outset, led to calls for an obedience that was stringent but self-imposed. That is why we find a paradoxical joining of the Pauline celebration of Christian liberty with the emphasis on monastic obedience. Liberty, it now seemed, consisted in obedience to rules that an individual's conscience imposed on itself, in the self-imposition of rules. The authority of the abbot should be like that of an unerring conscience.

Of course, these principles were often compromised in practice. Social conditions changed, particularly in the West, as the Roman empire succumbed to successive invasions by Germanic tribes in the fifth century. The habit of families 'giving' their children to monasteries and convents developed, in part as a reaction to growing social disorder. And the notion that the children's 'vocation' had to be confirmed by themselves when they reached maturity – in a free act of will – tended to be more theoretical than real. As a result the authority of the abbot had to be reinforced. With many younger novices, and in the face of 'barbarous' social conditions, Western monasteries did not so much establish schools for the laity (as with Basil's Eastern model) but became schools themselves.

Yet something survived the chaos and the compromises. Today, the mixed reputation enjoyed by monasticism since the sixteenth century makes it hard to recapture the prestige it had enjoyed in its earlier centuries. Yet at the end of antiquity the image it offered of a social order founded on equality, limiting the role of force and honouring work, while devoting itself to prayer and acts of charity, gave it a powerful hold over minds. Monasticism preserved the image of a regular society when the *pax romana* was being undermined, first by the overthrow of the Western empire (476) after the Germanic invasions, and then by Muslim conquests in the East.

The image of social order that monasticism preserved was not that of the ancient world. Rather, it suggested a new foundation for social order. For, despite its many failings and compromises, monasticism associated the ideas of law and of obedience not with unthinking custom or external force, but with individual consent and the role of conscience. Monasticism offered the glimpse of 'another world', a world that at least approximated to Christian moral intuitions. Slowly, but surely, that glimpse of another world further eroded beliefs and practices surviving from the ancient world.

8

The Weakness of the
Will: Augustine

The apostle Paul deployed his vision of the Christ to call for a reconstruction of the self. He did so in terms that were passionate, direct
and poetic. At the end of the fourth century Paul had a worthy successor, whom we know as St Augustine (354–430).

Augustine sprang from Thagaste in Roman North Africa. His
devout and determined mother, Monica, brought him up as a Christian. But when studying in Carthage, his search for 'wisdom' led him
into dualist, Manichaean beliefs. Later, while making a career as a
rhetorician in Rome and Milan, he was attracted by Neoplatonic
philosophy. Christianity, however, retained a hold on his conscience.
Immersing himself in Paul's letters while in Milan, he underwent a
profound conversion in 386. In his *Confessions*, Augustine describes
how, reduced to tears by an inspection of his conscience, he picked up
the volume of Paul's letters he had been reading.

> I seized it and opened it, and in silence I read the first passage on which
> my eyes fell: *Not in revelling and drunkenness, not in lust and wanton-
> ness, not in quarrels and rivalries. Rather, arm yourselves with the Lord
> Jesus Christ; spend no more thought on nature and nature's appetites.*
> I had no wish to read more and no need to do so. For in an instant, as
> I came to the end of the sentence, it was as though the light of confidence
> flooded into my heart and all the darkness of doubt was dispelled.[1]

Paul permanently changed the orientation of Augustine's mind. That
new orientation enabled him to give a more systematic and philosophical form to Paul's project.

Reconstructing the self – by opening the self to the work of grace –
led Augustine to focus on the human will and on the conditions of its

exercise. It led him in due course to write a spiritual autobiography of genius, the *Confessions*. That intense account of Augustine's relations with himself and with his God (the *Confessions* takes the form of a long prayer) has led some to attribute the birth of the individual to Augustine. For he portrayed 'the will' as the indispensable middle term between 'reason' and 'appetite'. He embedded the will in our conception of the self. Certainly there is an almost incredible self-consciousness in his writing. The fall of man is not a second-hand story for him. Augustine sees himself in the human species and the human species within himself. The equality of our plight underpins everything he wrote as a Christian.

Augustine drew on the resources of ancient thought and literature to make the case for Christianity. For he not only had a great love of the Latin classics. He had also argued his way through many of the standard positions of ancient philosophy. In particular, his mind had been susceptible to that deep suspicion of the material world – to the contrast between mind and matter – which had been its hallmark. Even after he left behind the extreme dualism of the Manichaean philosophy, Augustine remained attracted to aspects of the Neoplatonism of Plotinus, with its vision of ascending from the everyday world to purer realms of thought and being.

Augustine was no stranger to the appeal of elitism. When he took up residence in Milan, he found himself surrounded by a refined and congenial company, which for a time impressed him with what cultivated and philosophically inclined minds could achieve. The imagery of ascent was seductive. It enabled Augustine and his friends to think of moving towards 'perfection'.

Augustine's conversion, however, exploded his previous certainties. The imagery of ascent began to seem a delusion, the goal of achieving personal perfection through cultivation of the intellect unattainable. Paul's imagery of depth was far more compelling, while his insistence on the role of feeling in motivation – as against pure acts of judgement – corresponded more closely to human experience. In Augustine's view, Paul's conception of the Christ rightly made humility the key to salvation: 'I beseech You, God, to show my full self to myself.' The 'rational' self cannot forsake the source of its own being without falling victim to self-delusion: 'Work out your salvation in fear and trembling: for it is God that works in you, both that you should wish and act with a good will.'[2] Only the pride of the intellect could suppose that the human will can be completely self-determining. The incarnation revealed that something more is needed. 'My mind, questioning itself upon its own powers, feels that it cannot rightly trust its own report.' Augustine's conception of the self became a subtle mixture of autonomy and dependence.

Feelings or the calls of 'delight' are the springs of human action. 'Who can embrace wholeheartedly what gives him no delight?' Augustine asked, under Paul's sway. 'But who can determine for himself that what will delight him should come his way, and, when it comes, that it should, in fact, delight him?'[3] Paul's ecstatic awareness that the centrality of the will was matched, in the absence of grace, by a weakness of the will, overwhelmed Augustine. His writings became and remained to a large extent a commentary on Paul.

Augustine continued the demolition of the foundation of ancient beliefs and practices that Paul had begun. Equal subjection to divine power – in the depths of motivation – now seemed to make a mockery of the assumption of natural inequality. Belief in the innate superiority of some souls had to be discarded. 'I just cannot find what criterion to apply in deciding which men should be chosen to be saved by grace. If I were to reflect on how to weigh up this choice, I myself would instinctively choose those with better intelligence or less sins, or both; I should add, I suppose, a sound and proper education . . .' Almost bitterly, Augustine added: 'And as soon as I decide on that, He will laugh me to scorn.'[4] These new convictions obliged Augustine to reassess the claims of the superior intellect and, along with those claims, indirectly, the whole aristocratic structure of ancient society.

The Christ had revealed that God's love is available to all. It is simply a fact that not all avail themselves of it. For Augustine, this is a mystery beyond human comprehension. The right response to the mystery is humility, a constantly renewed innerness, not a reassertion of the belief that superior minds can leave behind the common lot of mortals. When he became a bishop at Hippo in North Africa, Augustine was confronted daily with the diversity of human motivation. For a Christian, there was only one option. 'One depth calls to another.'

Augustine revises the Neoplatonic account of the soul's journey and adapts it to Pauline imagery. It is no longer a process of ascent or moving beyond the physical world. The answer lies within. As Peter Brown has observed:

> The *Confessions* are a manifesto of the inner world: 'Men go to gape at mountain peaks, at the boundless tides of the sea, the broad sweep of rivers, the encircling ocean and the motions of the stars: and yet they leave themselves unnoticed; they do not marvel at themselves.' A man cannot hope to find God unless he first finds himself: for this God is 'deeper than my inmost being', experience of Him becomes 'better' the more 'inward'. Above all, it is man's tragedy that he should be driven to flee 'outwards', to lose touch with himself, to 'wander far' from his 'own heart': 'You were right before me: but I had moved away from myself. I could not find myself: how much less, then, could I find You.'[5]

The *Confessions* provide us with a story, not primarily about the development of Augustine's mind, but rather about the development of his 'heart' or 'feelings'. The search for God proves to be a search for the only 'delight' that is not precarious or illusory.

For Augustine, the conscious action of the individual has now to be understood as a mysterious merger of intellect and feeling, the result of an obscure process in which the heart is 'stirred'. By understanding the will as a compound of intention and feeling, Augustine in effect repudiates the assumption that had pervaded ancient thinking: the assumption that reason, largely from its own resources, can motivate. For Augustine, conversion is the work of grace. And that opening of the self to grace begins with the realization that 'He hath made us and not we ourselves . . .'[6]

Even conversion is only the beginning of a difficult journey, a journey during which the new self is assailed by doubts and temptations that can be overcome only with the help of grace. Augustine's emphasis on the role of grace enables him to give a more realistic account of the confines of human choice:

> It will not be held against you, that you are ignorant against your will, but that you neglect to seek out what it is that makes you ignorant; not that you cannot bring together your wounded limbs, but that you reject Him that would heal them. No man has been deprived of his ability to

know that it is essential to find out what it is that it is damaging not to be aware of; and to know that he should confess his weakness, so that He can help him who seeks hard and confesses.[7]

With this analysis of the complex nature of the will, Augustine completes the demolition of ancient rationalism. The patriarchal family, the aristocratic society underlying the polis, the cosmos as a hierarchy of ends or purposes: all of these became suspect and vulnerable without its support. Instead of confidence in deduction, we have prayer. For through prayer humans can seek the support of grace for their better intentions. Only with such support can they hope to act as they ought to act. So confessing one's weakness to God is 'the countenance of true piety'.

Deductive reasoning is downgraded in relation to fact. Reason – no longer identified with social superiority – has to confront and make sense of a world it cannot entirely control. And that is true even within the self. Intentions, however upright, are often constrained by fact. And nothing is more factual, in Augustine's eyes, than the shackles we forge for ourselves. Therein lies the human predicament – the corruption of the will. Through the faculty of memory, humans become subjugated to their acquired tastes and sensibilities. They find themselves at the mercy of the consequences, often unforeseen, of their previous choices.

> In our present state, we do have the free power to do or not to do anything, before we are caught up in any habit. When we do have this freedom to do something, the sweetness and pleasure of the act holds our soul, and it is caught in the sort of habit it cannot break – a habit that is created for itself by its own act of sin.[8]

The pleasure springing from past actions is 'inflicted' on the memory, a pleasure that is 'mysteriously' intensified through recollection and repetition.

In that way feelings or dispositions become compulsive and freedom of choice is constrained. Augustine thus presents previous actions rather than the world of matter as the source of corruption of the will. His analysis enables him to understand the Pauline dilemma: 'that which you wish not, that you do.' And, again following Paul, Augustine identifies prayer – opening oneself to the action of grace – as the only way out of such a vicious circle: 'We had destroyed ourselves, but He who made us made us anew.'

So, for Augustine, the inwardness of the individual is by no means a sphere of silence. It is a sphere of dialogue, of conversation with God. No wonder that the *Confessions* take the form of an extended prayer. Inventing the individual – in the sense of acknowledging the equality of humans in the face of their maker – is not an exercise leading to isolation. Instead, it is the creation of a self-consciousness that undercuts merely social identities, statuses conferred by the conventional terms of a language. The deepest struggles of the self are pre-linguistic. They are struggles to find words that do justice to our feelings both of freedom and of dependence.

Augustine's conception of God makes him a crucial agent in our innermost struggles. Yet by recognizing the need for human intentions to seek support in an even deeper agency, Augustine does not deny the reality of free will. Rather, he tries to clarify the conditions that make 'true' freedom possible, the conditions in which good or just intentions can become effective. For so often our habits trap us in previous decisions: 'If you want to know what I mean, start trying not to swear: then you will see how the force of habit goes on its own way.'[9]

The transformation of the will – escape from undesirable habits and dependencies reinforced by 'memory' – requires more than a mere act of judgement. Only when the very ground of our being is involved, Augustine insists, can we hope to escape from 'darkness' into the 'light' of moral transparency. Yet even then we shall have only intervals of relief and serenity. For habits fight back.

> Sometimes You fill me with a feeling quite unlike my normal state, an inward sense of delight, which, if it were to reach fulfilment in me, would be something entirely different from my present life. But my heavy burden of distress drags me back: I am sucked back to my habits, and find myself held fast; I weep greatly, but am firmly held. The load of habit is a force to be reckoned with![10]

Following Paul, Augustine becomes the incomparable champion of human frailty, of the dependence of an upright will on divine support. That, in turn, makes Augustine an obstinate opponent of anything like a perfectionist ethic. On his understanding, the reality of free will does not mean that human intentions – or even a sudden 'conversion' – can be a sufficient condition of acting rightly.

It is that conviction that underpinned the greatest philosophical dispute of Augustine's later years, the dispute with Pelagius over the will. Whereas Augustine was an African by origin, Pelagius hailed from the British Isles. Unusually gifted, both men had made their way to Italy and Rome. Yet Augustine's stay had been relatively short. After his conversion Augustine became a priest and, soon afterwards, bishop of the city of Hippo in North Africa. That meant that his convictions were informed by his heavy pastoral duties. By contrast, Pelagius remained a layman in Rome and open to the intellectual currents circulating around the Mediterranean world – not least to the strenuous achievements of Eastern monasticism.

Pelagius, too, made his reputation through writings inspired by Paul's letters. But his message was very different. For Pelagius, God was the lawgiver who created obligations which humans could satisfy if they chose to. God demanded a complete obedience that was within the power of man to achieve. In an eloquent exposition of the thirteen letters of Paul, Pelagius did not mince his words: 'Since perfection is possible for man, it is obligatory.' But that conception of the power of the will jeopardized Augustine's emphasis on its fallibility.

Pelagius did not have the systematic mind of Augustine. It is probably best to understand him as a reformer, someone who sought to raise the level of moral ambition in souls informed by Christian belief. His acolytes in Rome often belonged to senatorial families. They hoped to carry his arguments about human freedom and responsibility into law and public administration. Little wonder that Pelagius deplored what he saw as a kind of fatalism or quietism about the action of grace implicit in Augustine's *Confessions*. Might not such overly subtle probing of the conditions of exercising the will weaken the role of good intentions? Might not an exaggerated emphasis on the sinfulness of mankind hinder Christians becoming what they ought to be?

The relationship between Augustine and Pelagius can perhaps be understood by analogy with that between the great European philosophers of the seventeenth century and their reformist successors, or philosophes, in the eighteenth century. Unlike Descartes, Hobbes and Spinoza, who became remarkable for their comprehensive philosophical systems, eighteenth-century writers like Voltaire and Diderot were far more polemical, more directly involved in social reform. Like Pelagius, the latter were less concerned with elaborating ideas than with changing the world around them. Yet there is an even more striking comparison available with the most formidable eighteenth-century philosopher. For Immanuel Kant resembles Augustine, holding that, while we must seek to perfect ourselves, what we 'can' achieve will always fall short of what we 'ought' to be. The fact that moral perfection is unattainable, and that we are all stuck in a struggle in which we shall not fully succeed, conjures up Augustine's anguished insistence on the weakness of the will, on the moral equality of humans.

For Augustine (and Kant), none of us can ever claim to be a success in moral terms. We all fail, and it is this failure – tragic, but also humbling – that contains a powerful egalitarian message. But that need not obscure the nature of Pelagius' reformist ambitions. Pelagius and his followers were greatly influenced by the Eastern monastic movement. They interpreted monasticism as a challenge, a challenge to convert a Roman world that was now 'officially' Christian into a 'truly' Christian society, that is, a society trying to live up to the moral demands of Christianity. In pursuing their goals, the Pelagians in Rome spoke to the Christian members of a governing class – a class with influence – whereas Augustine dealt with a humbler, provincial audience.

Where Augustine struggled to bring an awareness of the action of grace into the humdrum life of his parishioners, Pelagius and his followers attacked the hypocrisy of a society which had officially adopted Christianity but which remained saturated with traditional pagan beliefs and practices – a society in which 'giving' often became a vehicle for the pride of the rich, in which the cult of the family and the paterfamilias remained powerful, and in which slavery and torture were still publicly unchallenged.

Just as the monastic communities of the East had begun to offer the image, however blurred, of a new form of society, a society founded on the assumption of the moral equality of humans, so the followers of Pelagius sought to introduce a new moral stringency into the Roman world, to make what was officially the norm into what was really the norm.[11] This perfectionism was perhaps also a response to the needs of a governing class living through a crisis, the loss of control following the Germanic invasions of the Western empire and, not least, the sack of Rome by Alaric's Goths in 410.

Pelagius sought a strict, universal observance of the new Christian law. Thus, Peter Brown quotes from the fervent letter of a Pelagian follower in Sicily: *'Who believes in God, attends to His commandments; this is love of God; that we do what he commands.'* All believers should therefore approach something like the condition of monks. For Christian obligations did not vary according to social status.

> Surely it is not true that the Law of Christian behaviour has not been given to everyone who is called a Christian? . . . Do you think that the fires of Hell will burn any less hotly for men licensed (as governors) to give vent to their sadism, and will be made hotter only for those whose professional duty it is to be pious . . . There can be no double-standard for one and the same people.[12]

Evidently Pelagius, in his exhortations, wanted Christians to be seen to change their behaviour, to become a visible, distinctive and irreproachable society, a manifest reproach to surviving pagan habits and attitudes.

Augustine could not accept this. Was there not a real danger that the grace of God revealed in the Christ was being sacrificed to a more sophisticated version of the law? Augustine's exploration of human motivation, drawing heavily on Paul's letters, led him to see in Pelagian arguments a return to the rationalism of the ancient world, and to the elitism which it sustained. For Augustine, it was a fundamental mistake to suppose that the church could become a conspicuous society of 'perfect' Christians. Grace did not work like that. The mind could not command love. Reason, through intentions, could not motivate in the fashion required by Pelagius' exhortations. No human institution could attain perfection.

Augustine's insistence on the complexity of the human will – and the role of grace in human motivation – would leave a permanent mark on later Christian thinking about the self. The dominant ancient view portraying the will oversimply as 'an act of desire (whether rational or not)' gave way to 'a concept of the will as a power of the soul distinct from the intellect and from appetite'.[13] Understanding the complexity of the will as a motive force and the frailty of human intentions led Augustine to oppose 'naive' views of the transformative potential of the church. It also helped him to deal with pagan arguments exaggerating the church's impact on recent events.

Countering claims that the adoption of Christianity and abandonment of the 'pagan' gods had led to the sack of Rome in 410, Augustine insisted, in his great work, the *City of God*, that human weakness and vices beset all societies (the 'earthly cities'). All were subject to the vicissitudes that follow from the weaknesses of human nature. Nor was the church exempt. The city of God (or 'eternal city') could not therefore be identified with the organized church. At best, the church could help to open the individual soul to the work of grace, encouraging humility, continence and prayer. 'From the raised benches of the clergy, the precept "Render no man evil for evil" is read out as given by divine authority, and wholesome counsel is proclaimed in the midst of our congregations, as if it were in school rooms open, now, to both sexes, to all ages and to all ranks of society.'[14] The appeal of the church was universal. But the outcome lay in the hands of God. Conscience could not be created or directed so simply as Pelagius required.

Nonetheless, it was the task of the church to try to create and tend consciences. For conscience provides access to the city of God, a sense of belonging to another, a better or 'heavenly city'. In conscience the quality of what the self loves must be the test. Although in human affairs good and bad are always – like motives – mixed, and all that can be expected of public policies is that they strike a balance of advantage, what the evangelist John spoke of as the 'glance of the heart' still makes it possible to distinguish the 'faithful' from the 'faithless'.

The faithful are far from perfect. When Augustine describes the Christians familiar to him in Hippo, he does not exaggerate their propensity for good works, nor underestimate their pleasure in sexual relations and eating. He acknowledges their occasional flights of vanity and bouts of anger. They are not above litigation to protect their property. But they also possess something that gives them moral perspective, a conscience. That possession made for a decent Christian, 'looking on himself as a disgrace, and giving the glory to God'.[15]

For Augustine, the faithful are those who see themselves as sojourners on earth. It is not that they refuse to take part in public affairs or fail to try to improve things here and now. But, finally, they identify themselves in another way. They are not the slaves of worldly ambitions or pleasures. They are not restricted to the conventions of their society or the boundaries set by their government. They have a better hope, a hope that they carry into their relations with others. It is a hope that can make them stern judges of themselves. But it is also a hope that can nourish charity towards others.

His Christian beliefs had now led Augustine outside philosophy, outside the Neoplatonic concern with the fate of the individual mind. He no longer saw the faithful soul in isolation, bent on 'escaping' from an inferior material world. Christians neither could nor should turn their backs on the world. But they should bring to that world the attitudes of what Peter Brown – in a happy phrase – calls 'a resident alien'. And here I must let Brown have the final word: 'So the *City of God*, far from being a book about flight from the world, is a book whose recurrent theme is "our business within this common mortal life"; it is a book about being otherworldly in the world.'[16]

Little wonder that Augustine became the greatest single influence on Western theology for the next thousand years. His writings would be copied, studied and venerated in monasteries and cathedrals by Latin-speaking clergy who shaped the culture of the lands which became Europe. Before Augustine, theology had been largely the preserve of the Greeks. He inspired the Latin church with a new confidence in its own intellectual and moral resources, endowing it with an incomparably subtle account of human agency.

Towards the Idea of
Fundamental Law

9

Shaping New Attitudes and Habits

So far we have been looking chiefly at the impact of Christianity on beliefs. We have seen the extraordinary process by which Christian thinkers drew on the resources of Greek philosophy to give their new convictions a systematic and public form. It was a drawing together that involved compromises on both sides. Christian convictions were submitted to the disciplines of logic and metaphysical speculation, to the requirements of disciplined argument. In doing so, those convictions sometimes lost the poetic fervour they had carried in the primitive church. But at the same time Greek philosophy was also transformed. Its traditional assumptions about natural inequality and the motivating power of reason were gradually abandoned.

Yet if reason had lost the almost coercive power attributed to it by much ancient philosophy, the habit of disputation – of disciplined argument – was preserved by the church in later antiquity. From the fourth century onwards nothing was more characteristic than the holding of church councils, local, provincial and universal, to discuss matters of doctrine and discipline. It is tempting to see these councils as insinuating a form of representative government into a Roman world which, after the decline of the polis and the influence of local notables, had become centralized and authoritarian. But in any case, the habit of disputation became engrained in the life of the church. Paradoxically, the need to define 'the truth' contained in what were now regarded as canonical scriptures – to defend that truth against false opinions or 'heresy' – ensured that the de facto multiplicity of opinions on many points was constantly on display.

Historians often emphasize that in the sixth century the Emperor Justinian closed the philosophical schools of Athens. In so doing, they imply that rational argument was giving way to an age of faith. But it is a mistake to conclude that the philosophical tradition the schools represented was entirely lost as a result. It had already penetrated and helped to shape the doctrines of the church, while leaving in contention such basic matters as the nature of the Christ and of the Trinity, free will and the role of good works, the operation of grace and predestination.

It is true that argument came to rest on a new set of assumptions – assumptions about the relationship between individual souls and God being fundamental, about the limits and fallibility of human reason, and about the moral dangers springing from polytheism. But, as we have seen, ancient philosophical argument had also rested on a distinct set of assumptions – assumptions that privileged the identity of the family and the polis over the individual, that cast some humans as by nature slaves or 'living tools', and that often presented the higher faculties of the mind as making possible a liberation from the physical world into a superior realm of pure ideas.

Any set of basic assumptions opens up some avenues for thought, while closing down others. Is it too much to suppose that new assumptions in later antiquity opened up new opportunities for human understanding and action? Is it fanciful to suggest that the individualist implications of Christian moral beliefs had the potential to change not only the prevailing conception of society but that of the physical world as well, 'nature' as well as 'culture'? Finally, is it surprising that a religion which postulated the incarnation – a God who is 'with us' – would change the understanding of time itself, holding out a hope that undermined older beliefs in a relentless cycle of growth and decay?[1]

I think not. But, that being said, it would be folly to suppose that such fundamental changes in mind-set could take place overnight. Centuries would be required for the implications of Christian moral beliefs to be drawn out and clarified – and even more time would pass before long-established social practices or institutions were reshaped by these implications.

That is not to deny that some changes took place rapidly. We have seen that the monastic movement in Egypt and Syria involved a radical departure from the world of the polis, a movement so individualist that at times it bordered on the anarchic. Nonetheless, it laid down markers of a new world, a world in which individual conscience rather than assigned status provided the foundation for social relations, and in which work was rehabilitated, becoming almost a form of prayer.

Paganism was in retreat, though its powers of resistance – not least among the old Roman aristocracy – should never be underestimated. Later emperors prohibited public sacrifices, which had been central to the polis as a religious association. The closing of pagan temples was followed by attacks on rural shrines associated with animistic cults, both carried out in the name of a triumphant monotheism that opposed the multiplication of moral agencies as a distraction from the all-important relationship between individual souls and their God.

Of course, older polytheistic beliefs and practices hung on, especially in rural areas. The cults of local divinities and festivals honouring personified natural forces – not least those associated with generation and regeneration – were sometimes overcome only by being reprocessed as Christian. Assigning a date for the birth of the Christ, just after the winter solstice, is only the most obvious example. In order to appropriate the advantages both of change and of continuity, Christian buildings or altars were also often raised on the ruins of earlier temples and shrines. The church of San Clemente in Rome illustrates just such a transition; below the foundations of the original fourth-century church lie the remains of a temple of Mithras.

For a long time such concessions to popular tastes probably limited the intellectual impact of Christianity on the less educated, as did the cult of 'the saints' which grew out of the stories of martyrdom in the early church. The veneration of saints and their relics – which would assume major importance in the middle ages – gave polytheism a benign afterlife. That veneration re-peopled the religious world with more familiar and approachable, less intimidating figures.

Nonetheless, Christian beliefs did reshape practices in one crucial area from an early date. They destroyed the ancient family. That is, they destroyed the family as a cult or religious association. We have seen that the beliefs and practices of the ancient family had provided the building blocks for an entire society underlying the ancient polis or city-state. The privilege as well as the duty of the eldest male in the family was to act as its priest or pontiff. He was in charge of preserving the sacred flame of the family hearth – which was, after all, the living expression of its ancestors – and all the rites associated with it.

The authority of the paterfamilias over other members of the family sprang directly from this priestly role. This religious character of the ancient family made it, rather than the individual, the fundamental social unit. The unequal statuses of the public institutions of Greece and Rome had their origin in the unequal statuses consecrated by the cult of the ancient family. By transferring religious authority from the father to a separate priesthood, the Christian church removed the religious basis of the paterfamilias. It curtailed the claims to authority of the family head, relaxing the ties of subordination that had previously bound its members.

An early symptom of this was the changed role of women. It became much harder to look upon women as mere chattels, as completely subject to the authority of the paterfamilias. The early church insisted on the equal obligations imposed by the bond of marriage. When a priest became the authority on matters of conscience, women could look outside the family for guidance and support. Clergy provided a new moral space and served as a kind of court of appeal, something that probably benefited younger sons as well as women.

We have seen that women had played an important part in conversions to Christianity – leading to complaints by some pagan writers about their 'unfortunate' and 'credulous' influence on children and spouses. By the third and fourth centuries this new role was confirmed in the role of the 'dedicated virgin', a role which did not make any sense unless it was assumed that the woman had a mind and will of her own. Such women were no longer confined by the statuses of the ancient family.

Nor is it surprising that such declarations of independence by women seem to have been especially frequent in upper-class families. It is as if the confidence engendered by the superior status of a family was appropriated by some women and put to a new use, helped by Christian belief in the equality of souls. With social confidence and also, no doubt, financial means, such Christian women took on new roles. They became patronesses, disciples and travellers. They prized associations with leading Christian intellectuals. They use associations with such men to further their education.

The career of St Jerome, who translated the Bible into Latin (the famous Vulgate version), suggests as much. Both in Rome and, later, in Palestine, Jerome attracted the attention of 'pious matrons'. In Rome, he created a salon in the household of a rich woman called Paula, a salon which became a major centre of Christian learning, argument and devotion. When Jerome left Rome and took up residence in Bethlehem, he became part of the larger attraction of Eastern monasticism for visitors from the West. In what he called his 'cave', he received far more visits from Roman matrons than he had bargained for, leading to moments of extreme irritation . . .

By the late fourth century it had become fashionable for rich heiresses in the West to make a tour of the sites associated with Eastern monks and ascetics, not least St Antony. For example, Egeria, an aristocratic lady from Spain, travelled first through the Egyptian desert to Sinai, then through Palestine to Jerusalem, and finally to Constantinople, 'determined to see everything from monastic cells to the rock which Moses struck'.[2]

It is not easy to trace exactly the route of other changes in the ancient family, under the influence of new Christian beliefs. But it is clear that husbands were enjoined, in the name of the Christ, to treat their wives, at least spiritually, as equals. So the condemnation of adultery was extended to include husbands as well as wives. On the other hand, debates about divorce and remarriage did not at first yield any clear conclusions. But the fact of argument itself reveals how far the ancient family had travelled since the time when husbands had the power of 'life and death' over their wives and children.

The power of fathers over sons was steadily reduced in later Roman law. And other changes, which we might call 'humanitarian', are noticeable. In 316 Constantine decreed that criminals should not be branded on the face, for 'man is made in God's image'. The Romans had long given slaves more protection than had the Greeks. The law was already deemed to forbid treating slaves 'with excessive or causeless harshness'. But in the fourth century the process for freeing slaves – manumission – was made easier. Constantine decided that slaves could be freed before a bishop as well as before a magistrate.

Were these developments results of the infiltration of Christian norms? No doubt in Christian circles attitudes towards slavery were changing. There was no direct challenge to the law. But the freeing of slaves was accounted an important virtue. Paul's letter about a run-away slave, Onesimus – in which Paul had made clear his hope of manumission 'for the sake of the gospel' – could always be cited in support. And within churches, masters and slaves were counted as 'brothers'. Indeed, several slaves succeeded in becoming bishops.[3]

The relationship between Christianity and the eventual abolition of slavery in the West is a complicated and contested subject. There is no doubt that extravagant, over-simplified claims have been made about the role of the church in opposing slavery. In fact, the early church was extremely cautious about pronouncing on the subject. And that was for at least two reasons. The first had to do with the law. Since the time of Paul, the church had tried to avoid confrontation with the Roman authorities, enjoining obedience to the law and established authorities in the name of peace and order. The second reason was habit. It was exceedingly difficult for those brought up in a radically stratified or aristocratic society to see any alternative. Thus as late as Augustine we find some Christian apologists explaining the institution of slavery as an unavoidable consequence of human sin. In their eyes, trying to save the souls of slaves – and in that sense admitting their spiritual equality – did not require an onslaught on the institution itself. Not unlike the Stoics, such Christians urged that slavery of the soul was the real problem, rather too easily sidestepping the question of legal slavery.

Nevertheless, Christian norms were making a difference. There had been critics of slavery in antiquity, such as Seneca, who urged gentler treatment of slaves and were uneasy about the institution for pruden-tial reasons. A revolt of the slaves was a terrifying prospect. There were also critics who acknowledged cases of 'unjust' slavery, where the fortunes of war had resulted in the enslavement of someone who was not 'by nature' a slave. However, the usual bias continued to be that of Aristotle, who insisted that 'some are free men and others slaves by nature'. The contrast between 'barbarians' and citi-zens was extreme. The usual presumption remained one in favour of inequality.

By contrast, Christian insistence on the equality of souls in the eyes of God reversed that presumption. It reversed the burden of justification, obliging believers to find other reasons to tolerate slavery, if they so wished. We can, for example, detect that reversal in Augustine, who wrestled uneasily with the question of slavery, before coming to the conclusion that slavery of the soul was more important than, and independent of, legal slavery. But already there were Christians who had gone much further. A presumption in favour of equality shaped the attitudes of Gregory of Nyssa, who in fourth-century Constantinople delivered a fierce attack on slave-owning, in one of his most eloquent sermons.

Gregory's sermon is a meditation on the statement: 'I bought male and female slaves.' Gregory does not mince his words. In his view, buying a slave denies, by implication, the jurisdiction of God:

> For what price, tell me? What did you find in existence worth as much as this human nature? What price did you put on rationality? . . . God said let us make man in our image, after our likeness. If he is in the likeness of God, and . . . has been granted authority over everything on earth from God, who is his buyer, tell me? Who is his seller? To God alone belongs this power; or rather, not even to God himself. For his gracious gifts . . . are irrevocable. God himself would not reduce the human race to slavery, since he himself, when we had been enslaved to sin, recalled us to freedom.

The owners of slaves are pretending, in effect, to be 'masters of the image of God'.

> What does this power contribute to you as a person? Not longevity, nor beauty, nor good health, nor superiority in virtue. Your origin is from the same ancestors, your life is of the same kind, sufferings of soul and body prevail alike over you who own him and over the one who is subject to your ownership – pains and pleasures, merriment and distress, sorrows and delights, rages and terrors, sickness and death. Is there any difference in these things between the slave and his owner? Do they not draw in the same air as they breathe? Do they not see the sun in the same way? . . . If you are equal in all these ways, therefore, in what respect have you something extra, tell me, that you who are human think yourself the master of a human being and say, 'I brought male and female slaves', like herds of goats or pigs.[4]

Gregory of Nyssa was not expressing the dominant opinion in the church, yet neither was he a lone voice in the wilderness.

Two things were coming together in a way that made a central tactic of ancient philosophical argument – a tactic which many Christian thinkers took on board from the Stoics – less and less plausible. That tactic was to separate body and soul sharply, insisting that everything the soul required could be achieved independently of social status or bodily condition. What now made that tactic less plausible was that Christians of all social conditions, even slaves, met together in the same urban space. They shared Christian sacraments in the basilica.

The Christian basilica was an architectural form taken over from the Romans. Originally it had been simply a rectangular meeting hall. But of course in its original form its use was hedged around by the unequal statuses of the ancient city. In its Christian form, however, in principle no one was excluded. The pride of citizenship and the indignity of being an inferior had less place in the Christian basilica. While a degree of segregation survived, people assembled essentially as 'souls'. Here they were exposed to a horizon that extended beyond the walls of the city and to a rhetoric that portrayed them all as children of God. From the pulpit it was emphasized that the judgement of God would fall on all equally and that God's love was available to each. Popular processions to the tombs of local 'saints' and martyrs, involving a mixing of social strata and sexes, also promoted a more democratic form of sociability.

It was in the Christian basilica that a new social form was born, a form that gave birth to the medieval city. The early medieval city in Western Europe came to differ significantly from the cities of antiquity. The most important figure in urban life during the transition from antiquity to the early middle ages was the local bishop. In the last century of the Western empire it was the bishops who became the de facto rulers of the cities, taking up many of the functions previously provided by the imperial administration and gradually supplanting the hereditary urban elite or *curiales*. The law codes of two emperors, the Theodosian (438) and Justinian (529–33) codes, testify to this changed role. It involved not just humdrum matters of administration, but the defence of the city as well. Justinian ordained: 'We desire that the defenders of the cities, being well instructed in the holy mysteries of the orthodox faith, be chosen and instituted by the venerable bishops, the priests, the notables . . .'[5]

Now the distinctive thing about the bishops' new urban role was that it was based on an appeal that was 'democratic' rather than 'aristocratic'. This appeal – as 'the love of the poor' – had emerged earlier in the cities of the Eastern empire. But there it remained circumscribed by the survival of the Imperial administration and the emperor's authority. In the West, the decline and fall of the empire by the end of the fifth century led to greater fluidity and uncertainty, but also, perforce, to more innovation.

Although the bishops often came from the traditional urban elite of the empire, their local authority now had a different foundation: it was founded on a faith shared with much of the urban population. The rhetoric that such bishops relied upon was, as we have seen, inclusive rather than exclusive. It was a rhetoric that encouraged women, the urban poor and even slaves to feel part of the city in a way that had not previously been possible. This rhetoric had its physical counterpart as well. In contrast to the segregated spaces of the ancient city, the Christian population of the cities began to share the same spaces, hearing the bishops' *ex cathedra* words in the basilica or principal church, and taking part in the same rites, that is, baptism, the mass and funerals. Processions to the tombs of local martyrs were for everyone.

It would be a mistake to suppose that the ceremonies of the church at this period closely resembled those of the middle ages, after an increase of pomp had proved useful in impressing the invaders of Western Europe and when the separation of the clergy from the laity was more complete. Perhaps no one has captured the dignity and simplicity of the sacraments of the early church more successfully than the seventeenth-century French painter, Nicolas Poussin. An extraordinary intensity and innerness leaps from his cycle of paintings on the sacraments, which conjure up an urban space and social relations that were being transformed.

The sacraments of the church fostered social relations that prefigured the end of antiquity. The hierarchical order of the polis began to fade. Its remnants – deference to the notables and the partial segregation of males and females, even in church – mattered less than a new sense of sharing something on an equal basis. Civic notables were introduced to a new moral world by the words they heard and repeated. The equality of souls postulated by Christian beliefs began to be seen and felt. The translation of moral equality into the primary social role was under way. The result, ultimately, was the destruction of the aristocratic character of the ancient city.

Did the bishops, who so frequently sprang from aristocratic families, really intend such an outcome? The answer is almost certainly not. They lived what seems in retrospect a strange life. Their instincts and habits belonged to one world, while their new convictions belonged to another. Yet they moved between the refined pleasures of an aristocratic society and the moral challenges of a more egalitarian or democratic order without noticing the contrast – or, at least, without feeling any great discomfort. In his shrewd assessment of the moral condition of Christian notables in the later fifth and sixth centuries, the nineteenth-century French historian François Guizot emphasizes that, while notables could be found at the extremes both of a pagan style of life and of a life of pious austerity, the larger number combined elements of the two in a rather surprising way.

At one extreme some notables in the south of Gaul led a life of scarcely diminished grandeur, the life of Roman aristocrats. Having occupied leading posts in the Western empire during its last years, they had come to terms with the Germanic invaders, and retired to their country estates. Even then there were uncomfortable moments. There is a hilarious description by one patrician of the ordeal of breakfasting with foul-smelling 'barbarians' whom he had been obliged to lodge. Unsurprisingly, their manners left much to be desired in his eyes. While many of these patricians had become Christian, it is difficult to know whether their faith was more than nominal. In any case, Guizot describes how

> they lived on their lands far from the mass of the population, passing their time by hunting, fishing and in all sorts of amusements. They had fine libraries, and often a theatre where plays by some rhetorician, often a client, were performed. On Ausonius' estate, the rhetorician Paul had his comedy *On Extravagance* performed himself composed the music for the intervals, and presided over proceedings. On such

occasions there were intellectual games, literary conversations. The ancient authors were discussed . . . and verses were written celebrating even the smallest episodes of life.[6]

Altogether, Guizot concludes, the life such notables led was elegant, varied and agreeable. But it was also 'soft, egoistical and sterile, removed from any serious occupation, from any urgent and general interest'.

At the other extreme was the life of bishops such as Hilaire, bishop of Arles in the fifth century. Hilaire passed his life almost entirely in the confines of the city.

> As soon as he wakened, whoever wanted to see him was received. He heard complaints, and sought to accommodate differences, acting as a justice of the peace. Afterwards he made his way to the church, where he celebrated mass, preached and taught, often for several hours. Returning home, he had his meal, and during this time he listened to the reading of some edifying text or else he dictated, while people could freely enter and listen. He also worked with his hands, sometimes spinning cloth for the poor, at other times working in the fields of his church. In that way his day passed, in the midst of his people, given over to serious and useful occupations.[7]

Such bishops could not avoid involvement in the affairs of the city. Concern for the public weal was forced on them almost hourly. But the conception of the public weal they brought to bear was no longer that of the radically stratified ancient polis.

The assumptions of ancient citizenship were being discarded – and discarded, tacitly, even by bishops far more worldly than Hilaire of Arles. Such bishops led a life that combined serious public duties with the pleasures of an aristocratic past. Trained in law and rhetoric, they savoured elegant literary pursuits and a cultivated social intercourse. But they also understood that they could not afford to stand apart from the great moral revolution of their age, 'if they wished to preserve some real importance and exercise an active influence'. It was probably this motive which led many members of the former Roman senatorial aristocracy to become bishops.

One such fifth-century bishop stands out: Sidonius Apollinaris, bishop of Clermont. Sidonius sprang from a rich and distinguished senatorial family. Yet he was able to adapt to the tenor of his age, without abandoning tastes that had long set his family and class apart. To illustrate this, Guizot quotes a light-hearted but revealing letter that Sidonius, a native of Lyons, wrote to his friend Eriphius: 'You tell me to send you some verses I wrote at the request of your father-in-law, that respectable man, who in the midst of a society of equals, is equally ready to command or to obey.' Sidonius goes on to describe a procession to the sepulchre of St Just outside Lyons: 'Before daybreak, we made the annual procession in the midst of an enormous crowd of both sexes, which the basilica ... could not contain, despite its being surrounded by such spacious porticos.'[8]

When matins had been celebrated, with choirs of priests and monks singing the psalms in alternation, the 'diverse classes of society' dispersed in a 'suffocating' heat, to await the celebration of mass. The 'principal citizens' made their way to the tomb of the consul Syagrius, where on a fine lawn surrounded by vine-covered trellises, they engaged in animated conversation – not allowing their gaiety to be compromised by talk about 'tributes' or 'the powers that be' (references, surely, to the Germanic invaders ...).

After a certain time, however, boredom set in. So 'we separated into two groups, according to age, with some calling loudly for a game of tennis, the others calling for tables and dice'. Philimathius, the father-in-law of Eriphius, did not take sufficient account of his age. He was soon prostrate with heat and fatigue from playing tennis. While recovering, he asked Sidonius to compose a verse in honour of the damp cloth he had been given to cool his forehead! Sidonius warned that 'the Muses' might be offended by such a public display. Philimathius countered that Apollo might rather be offended by his disciples working in secret. 'You can judge what applause met such a rapid and well-phrased response.'

The quatrain then produced by Sidonius, and its sequel, tell us more about an age of transition than pages of analysis: 'On another morning, whether when leaving a hot bath, or when hunting has covered your forehead with sweat, may the handsome Philimathius still find this cloth to dry his moistened brow, so that water may flow from his brow into this cloth as into the throat of a heavy drinker.'[9] Hardly had this quatrain been composed, however, when the bishop of Lyons appeared. Sidonius' company jumped to their feet and joined the others moving towards mass.

Such processions were, in fact, an important part of early Christian solidarity, whether they were processions inside churches or to them, into cities or to visit the tomb of a founding 'saint'. How were they organized? We do not really know. They may have reflected the older social hierarchy to an extent, though the passage above suggests a traditional elite feeling the need to 'catch up' with a popular movement.

Fear of boredom pointed to their privileged past. But new convictions, even if mixed with a large dose of opportunism, opened up a different future for such men.

IO

Distinguishing Spiritual from
Temporal Power

Every set of beliefs introduces its own logic and its own constraints. This was certainly true of Christianity. We can see this if we ask about the impact of Christian beliefs on law and government in the two or three centuries after the end of the Western empire in 476.

It was, of course, a period marked by terrible disorder. The decline of cities and shift of power to the 'barbarians' in the countryside, the rise and fall of new kingdoms established by Germanic leaders who sought to imitate Roman ways, the successful struggle of the Christian church to convert the newcomers, the conflict between orthodox and Arian Christians (who denied that the Son was 'of one substance with the Father'), uncertainty about the legal condition of persons and property – all of these things marked the period.

Yet despite the disorder – and, if truth be told, at times because of the disorder – important innovations took place. These innovations were halting and far from consistent. Yet they were pregnant with the possibilities of further change. By the ninth and tenth century they began to give Western Europe a distinct identity, an identity distinct not merely from the surrounding Islamic world, but also from the Eastern or Byzantine empire.

The first of these innovations was an unintended consequence of the new urban role of the bishops and clergy. As the bishops were so often the de facto rulers of the cities, they assumed – and had to assume – a primary role in dealing with the Germanic invaders of the empire. At stake was not only the safety of the cities and their Romanized populations, but also the very future of the church. It was a pope, Leo the Great, who succeeded in 'dissuading' Attila and his Huns from sacking Rome itself in 452, with the help, perhaps, of a quantity of gold. This new role of the clergy in defending the cities and dealing with the 'barbarian' invaders confirmed their ascendancy over the traditional magistrates of the city. The clergy became diplomats and administrators.

In fact, the new role of the clergy was undermining the very foundation of traditional urban government. The ancient city had been founded on the privileges of birth, which included the hereditary possession of leading urban magistracies by particular families. The ancient family was both a civic and a religious institution. And just as the transfer of religious authority to the clergy had weakened the authority of the father in the family, so it also compromised hereditary claims to urban magistracies.

Even in the late empire, when wealth as well as birth had led to membership of the curia (the governing senate), the position of *curialis*, once conferred, was hereditary and could not be abandoned – something demonstrated by laws that forbade *curiales* joining the army, clergy or civil service, at a time when the fiscal burdens imposed on them had become onerous. In a sense, the *curiales* themselves began to revolt against their own status, against the burdens of a birthright.

That civic magistrates should continue to occupy positions as a birthright began to seem anomalous, especially in view of the importance of the clergy as administrators, judges and diplomats. The traditional claim to civic authority based on birth confounded a property right, a civic function and a religious duty. New distinctions were needed, and – indistinctly at first – began to be made.

When the clergy found themselves performing major civic functions, how did they conceive of their task? Their view of the world privileged the salvation of souls. Their range of concern – as Augustine had so eloquently argued – was the whole human race. Nobody was excluded in principle, from the clergy's concern. So it is hardly surprising that, when they were considering the interests of the city, the clergy's view tended to include everyone, not just the traditional, privileged citizen class. A church council in late sixth-century Gaul went so far as to ban bishops from having dogs – for fear that they might frighten away supplicants!

This is not to say that bishops were unaware of inherited status differences or innocent of deference to wealth. The force of habit saw to that, especially if – as was often the case in the fifth and sixth centuries – they came from an aristocratic background themselves. But the beliefs the clergy shared with the urban populace, and which now provided the foundation of their authority, were not based on the claims of family or class. Rather, they were based on the claims of the individual. The church had long since become a refuge for those excluded from the citizen class.

By making the clergy as a class the spokesmen of religion, the church had downgraded not only the role of the family and of birthright, but also, indirectly, the juridical foundation of urban government. The rhetoric that the new, de facto rulers of the cities relied upon – what might be called 'the rhetoric of the Christian people'– rested on belief in the equality of souls. So it is not surprising that the first impact of this rhetoric was on urban government.

If no one was born with a right to rule, then upon what could the right to rule be based? The role of the chief magistrates could be understood as that of representing the curia and deriving their authority from it – while the curia, in turn, could be understood as representing the community, the entire *urbs* rather than just the traditional citizen class. By the early sixth century these new attitudes became formalized in the law code of the Visigothic kingdom.

This development amounted to nothing less than the emergence of a principled basis for representative government. In his *History of Civilization in France*, Guizot drew attention to these changes in urban government after the fall of the Western empire. He emphasized that in the fifth and sixth centuries southern Gaul was the most prosperous and cultured region in the West. Urban life retained considerable vitality not only in Lyons, Nîmes and Bordeaux, but also in a city such as Toulouse, which became the first capital of the Visigothic kingdom. Guizot's conclusions deserve more attention than they have received. They will shape much of this chapter.

In the ancient Roman municipality the superior magistrates ... exercised their jurisdiction as a personal right not at all by way of delegation and as a representative of the curia; it was to themselves, and not to the curia, that the power belonged. The principle of the municipal regime was more aristocratic than democratic. That had been the result of the ancient Roman *mores* and especially of the primitive amalgam of religious and political powers in the superior magistrates. In the Breviarium (Visigothic Code), the aspect of the municipal code changes; it is no longer in his own name, but in the name of and as a delegate of the curia that … (the magistrate) exercises his power. To the curia as a whole now belongs the jurisdiction. The principle of its organization has become democratic; and so is underway the transformation that will turn the Roman municipality into the medieval commune.[1]

Yet there is one thing – perhaps the most important of all – which Guizot does not make clear.

This legal development is important not only for what it reveals directly, about government, but also, indirectly, about society. It reveals that the rhetoric of the Christian people was undermining a whole conception of society. The conception of society as founded on 'natural inequality' was giving way to a conception of society as founded on 'moral equality', as an association of individuals rather than an association of families. Sidonius Apollinaris was hardly alone when he noted, with ill-disguised regret, that (after the fall of the Western empire) society was no longer formally – that is, legally – classified.

A new world is announced by this development – a world whose underlying principle, as Guizot observes, would be democratic rather than aristocratic. And it is suggestive that this development – a new juridical basis for urban government – first appeared in the Visigothic code. For, among all the Germanic kingdoms established on the territory of the former Western empire, the Visigothic kingdom was the one in which the clergy had far the greatest influence.

Yet it was not only church doctrine that pushed the clergy in the direction revealed by the Visigothic code. Antecedent practice also contributed. For although the clergy had become formally separate from the Christian laity by this period, the practice of the early Church survived in the election of bishops and abbots, sometimes even of popes. Underlying this practice was the principle that superiors should be chosen or elected by those who would then be subordinate to them. Not only did the local clergy often elect their bishops; the urban populace as a whole played a part in the choice of a bishop. 'By acclamation' – even if it contained an important element of deference – meant more than simply perfunctory ratification. It meant something like election.

There were no fixed rules about the election of bishops. The election of Ambrose as bishop of Milan in 374 is often cited as an example. The young Ambrose had just been sent to Milan as governor by the emperor, when the death of the local bishop led to a fierce struggle between two parties of the clergy and people – the Catholics and Arians – about who should succeed. Ambrose decided to visit the cathedral and observe the conflict for himself. Hardly had he arrived and made enquiries, however, when someone in the crowd (the voice of a child, by some accounts) cried: let us name Ambrose bishop! And so it happened that the young governor entered on a career that would lead him to become St Ambrose.

A century later the involvement of the people and clergy was scarcely less noticeable. In a letter Sidonius Apollinaris describes the tumultuous election of a new bishop at Châlons. The people of the city were divided:

> The assembly of clergy found a number of factions ... having been inspired by a triumvirate of competitors. One of them, who was without merit, proclaimed his illustrious descent; another ... relied on the vociferous support of parasites who had been won over by (the offerings) of his kitchen; a third had made a secret deal, if he achieved his ambition, to divide the domains of the church among his supporters.[2]

A group of bishops, who had arrived in Châlons to preside over the election, grasped the nature of the situation. Consulting among themselves, they suddenly put forward the name of a modest and honest deacon, John. Although he was not a priest, John – a man of unquestioned virtue – was proclaimed bishop, 'to the great astonishment of the intriguers'.

These are glimpses of a society in which the ancient hierarchy was in shambles. Not only had the Roman army and the imperial administration withdrawn, the class of local notables or *curiales* had lost all vigour and independence. The intensity and turbulence of life was now to be found in the church, rather than in traditional institutions. 'The Roman people' had become, as Guizot suggests, 'the Christian people'. In the church, the principle that superiors should be chosen by inferiors – the principle of consent – had not yet given way to the principle that superiors choose their inferiors, though the latter gained ground after the adoption of Christianity as the official religion of the empire. It is tempting to see the 'progress' of the latter principle as a symptom of attitudes of the ancient world leaving a final mark on the new faith. Nonetheless, the crucial moral fact about this period of transition is that there was a fierce, prolonged competition between the two principles.

Even when, in the later middle ages, the church had come to be dominated by the second principle – that superiors choose their inferiors – the first principle survived in the medieval commune. And the roots of that new juridical basis for urban government can be traced back to the fifth and sixth centuries, when the bishops and clergy held sway over cities. In retrospect, this domination of the cities by the clergy might seem worrying. Did it not pave the way for theocracy, for later papal claims that could be interpreted as a threat to the independence, even perhaps the existence, of secular authorities? Such a conclusion would, however, be mistaken.

We must try to put ourselves into the minds of the clergy who were faced with the collapse of the empire. They had to deal with invaders with whom they did not at first share any beliefs and who had a virtual monopoly of material force. They were overcome by fear. What they sought was not supremacy but survival. And survival involved getting some access to the minds of the invaders. Rather than directly challenging Germanic customs, the clergy sought to identify a sphere of their own, a sphere where force, by its very nature, could not prevail. And they had long since been used to distinguishing the 'sacred' from the 'profane', invoking the Christ's injunction to give to Caesar what is Caesar's and to God what is his. Now they pointed to a 'God-given' law that offered to mortals the hope of life after death, a 'moral' law distinct from custom or human command.

When dealing with the Germanic invaders the clergy could therefore hardly fail to dwell upon the difference between eternal or 'spiritual' and mere temporal concerns. The clergy defended a realm to which they alone offered access. The law of an invisible king – the Christ who offered the hope of 'salvation' to individuals – became a moral sword wielded with dramatic effect by the hard-pressed clergy. An eloquent sixth-century Irish missionary to the continent, Columbanus, conjures up their frame of mind: 'I am coming from the end of the world, where I have seen spiritual leaders truly fighting the Lord's battles.' The strength of their convictions, acting without the benefit of force (though reinforced by the wealth and elaboration of life in episcopal cities), mightily impressed the invaders.

The sharp edge of the moral sword wielded by churchmen cut through to – and exposed – an 'awareness of self'. For it turned on a day of judgement, that moment at death when the soul would be summoned by its maker, before being directed to heaven or hell. The widely copied homilies of the late sixth-century Pope Gregory the Great spread the message. 'Let us consider how severe a Judge is coming, who will judge not only our evil deeds but our every thought.'[3] The clergy were certainly not above manipulating credulity or relying on material analogies. Often they referred to what they offered as 'medicine' for souls. (Even Gregory the Great liked to call the clergy 'doctors of the soul'.) Yet, in its essentials, the realm the clergy claimed for themselves and sought to defend was unseen. It was within. Columbanus made the point to his converts: 'This is no god which dwells far from us that we seek ... For He resides in us like the soul in our body ... Ever must we cling to God, to the deep, vast, hidden, lofty and almighty God.'[4]

Of course, the self-interest of the clergy played a part in their efforts at conversion. The relics and tombs of saints and martyrs – together with the 'miracles' often attributed to them – sustained the importance of the episcopal cities and gave bishops useful bargaining counters in their dealings with the invaders. These dealings were complicated by the fact that the Goths had been converted to an Arian understanding of Christianity relatively early, while the Franks, under their leader Clovis, only converted to the 'orthodox' or Catholic faith in AD 506. As a result, the finer, controversial points of doctrine were often subordinated to the immediate needs of the clergy.

Nonetheless, the nature of their beliefs pushed the clergy beyond mere self-interest. Under the Franks' Merovingian dynasty, sixth- and seventh-century church councils were dominated by questions of public morality and welfare. Without claiming the right to settle secular matters, the clergy succeeded in introducing the norm of 'charity' into the sphere of public policy, where it had not previously had any acknowledged role. The idea of an overarching moral framework for legislation made its appearance.

> If the Christian Church had not existed, the . . . world must have been abandoned to purely material force. The Church alone exercised a moral power. It did more: it sustained, it spread abroad the idea of a rule, of a law superior to all human laws. It proposed, for the salvation of humanity, the fundamental belief that there exists, above all human laws, a law which is denominated, according to periods and to customs, sometimes reason, sometimes the divine law . . . [5]

Whereas later anti-clericals would interpret this proclamation as a form of oppression, Guizot argues that it laid the foundation for a development that would take centuries to accomplish, a formal separation of spiritual from temporal power and liberation of the human mind.

> With the church originated a great fact, the separation of spiritual and temporal power. This separation is the source of liberty of conscience; it is founded on no other principle but that which is the foundation of the most perfect and extended freedom of conscience. The separation of temporal and spiritual power is based upon the idea that physical force has neither right nor influence over souls, over conviction, over truth. It flows from the distinction established between the world of thought and the world of action, between the world of internal and that of external facts. Thus this principle for which Europe has struggled so much, and suffered so much, the principle which prevailed so late, and often, in its progress, against the inclination of the clergy, was enunciated under the name of the separation of temporal and spiritual power, in the very cradle of European civilization.[6]

That is not to say that the clergy understood the implications of the principle they began to defend. For them, it was a principle that offered protection against brute force that might extinguish the church and its mission. It was their own sword, the sword of spiritual power.

Few if any among the fifth-century clergy would have realized – or readily accepted – that freedom of conscience might be invoked not just to defend the church, but also to limit its claims. Nonetheless, in putting forward this principle the church was being true to the logic of its belief in the equality of souls. Distinguishing spiritual from temporal power rests on the premise of the individual conscience. For that premise can be construed as meaning that there must be a sphere within which everyone ought to govern his or her own actions, an area of choice, governed by conscience. Some early Christian thinkers had moved tentatively towards that conclusion: Tertullian, Ambrose, Martin of Tours and Augustine (for much of his life). Yet they would remain a 'liberal' minority for a long time to come.

Another innovation that impinged on developments in law and government was the alliance of the new religion with the cause of learning, a merger of Christianity and the philosophical tradition. Some will be surprised by this claim. For it is true that those teaching in surviving ancient schools – whether as grammarians, rhetoricians or philosophers – were usually sympathetic to paganism and hostile to the new religion. But the reality was that vigorous intellectual debate had already largely deserted these survivors of ancient learning.

The dependence of professors on Imperial favour and the strict regulation of students in the ancient schools had resulted in forms of servility and a sadly devalued syllabus. Often literary production consisted of slight variations on established forms and abridgements of earlier grammatical, historical and philosophical texts. With students coming mostly from privileged classes in the process of dissolution, the ambition to learn faltered. Ancient learning – crafted for a social structure in tatters – did not engage with the problems of the age. It became a matter for display, not least to impress the Germanic invaders. At the Visigothic and Frankish courts 'displays of old-fashioned Latin rhetoric and poetry were still appreciated'.[7] Sons of the invaders' leaders were frequently sent to the new royal courts to learn the 'subtlety of words'. But it was ornament rather than the substance of ancient learning that appealed.

The contrast with the Christian world could not have been greater. Two things especially contributed to its intense intellectual life, a life reflected in the constant circulation of letters and longer writings about both church discipline and philosophical issues such as the nature of the soul, freedom of the will, grace and necessity. First, the bishops, though often recruited from the old privileged and instructed class, were immersed in the affairs of the world. They could not indulge in 'pure' speculation, speculation for its own sake. They had to respond to unexpected events and new arguments. Secondly, they had the advantage of debating issues of Christian doctrine that were not yet settled – which is to say that there was an extraordinary freedom of discussion. The canon of the gospels was now settled, but interpretation of the gospels over the most basic questions was still open. Despite social and political instability, at least thirteen church councils, debating both theological and practical issues, took place in Gaul during the sixth and seventh centuries.[8] The church gave ancient philosophy an 'afterlife'.

Lacking any inherited Christian schools, learning in what had been the Western empire – especially in Gaul – took refuge in the monasteries being created in the fifth century. Western monasticism rapidly came to differ from that in the East. Where monks in Egypt and Syria had originally sought the solitude of the 'desert' to escape worldly temptations, Western monasteries – in the face of invasions and the fall of the empire – became refuges for community and learning. Monasteries became schools. Young men from noble families who gathered at a monastery like Lérins, near Marseilles, did not seek isolation, but rather deeper instruction in the new faith. 'The monasteries of southern Gaul became the philosophical schools of Christianity: it was there that people meditated, discussed and taught; it was from there that new ideas, boldness of thought, even heresies came.'[9]

Why was that so important? Historians frequently emphasize how these monasteries were crucial for the transmission of classical culture, especially through the copying of ancient texts. But the monasteries assured something else that was just as important, yet more immediate. They laid the foundation for the emergence of an educated clerical class, drawing heavily from the former class of notables, but weaning them from the attitudes and habits of social privilege.

Lérins sent out into the world zealous thirty-year-olds from old families, fully capable of deploying the old skills of rhetoric and government, but in a new manner, for a new, high cause. The transformation of the old order began with the body. A harsh ascetic regime changed the

body out of recognition. It lost all of its previous aristocratic ease. Lux-
uriant hair was cut short. The flush of high living was drained from the
face by penitential fasting. The proud eye and haughty step of the 'natural born' leader of Gallic society were curbed by a monastic discipline
of humility.[10]

Not all monasteries would perform this role. In the seventh and
eighth centuries many became virtual refuges for landless younger
sons of the nobility. Yet others remained open to a wider social intake.
We have seen that Eastern monasteries offered at least a blurred image
of a new form of society, a civil society founded on belief in human
equality. Western monasteries, perforce, did more. They began to form
a class of clerics who, as bishops, brought more egalitarian attitudes
to the government of society.

The urgent need for the church to create a tolerably educated clerical class contributed to an important difference between Western
Europe and the Eastern empire. In the latter, the imperial administration remained in place. The Eastern empire preserved – in aspic, as it
were – relations between church and state that had been characteristic
of the whole empire in the century after Constantine's adopted Christianity. Those relations were marked by a considerable deference of the
church to the state. Memories of subordination died hard, especially
when mixed with gratitude for the official adoption of Christianity. In
consequence, the clergy in the East did not feel any need to reshape the
state.

In the West, by contrast, the clergy developed a different attitude
towards the Germanic invaders of the empire, whether Visigothic,
Burgundian or Frankish. Not only had the clergy succeeded in converting the newcomers, they retained a marked intellectual superiority
over them. In the fifth century leading figures from the former imperial administration at times became advisers to the new kings, who
were clad 'in furs' rather than arrayed 'in purple'. But by the sixth and
seventh centuries that role fell increasingly to the higher clergy, who
had become, in effect, the only educated class. The fact that bishops
were often recruited from old patrician families probably increased
their influence over the newcomers. They became advisers, confessors,
tutors and even, at times, critics. They introduced the new rulers not

merely to the 'subtlety of words' and complexities of Roman law and public administration, but also to the elements of Christian doctrine and morality.[11]

The clergy thus acquired a significant role in the creation of the new kingdoms in the West. Indeed, by the sixth century Frankish kings were complaining, according to the chronicler Gregory of Tours, about the power and wealth of the bishops: 'There is no one with any power left except the bishops,' King Chilperic lamented. 'No one respects me as king; all respect has passed to the bishops in their cities.' Gregory of Tours' *History of the Franks* gives an extraordinarily vivid picture of the turmoil that reigned in post-Roman Gaul, turmoil that was not merely physical but also moral. The quandary of the bishops emerges in Gregory's wonderful opening sentence: 'A great many things keep happening, some of them good, some of them bad.'

What did these bishops want? And what did they combat? To be sure, they combated the survivals of paganism – a struggle that, in the countryside (the word *pagani* originally meant simply countryfolk), would continue for centuries. But at the courts of the new kings, the bishops' influence was directed at preserving Roman law (the Theodosian Code) for the benefit of the urban population and at softening the customary 'laws' of the invaders. In due course they developed a larger ambition. That is suggested, at least, by the course of events in the Visigothic kingdom, where, as we have seen, the clergy played an even more important part than they did in the Frankish and Burgundian kingdoms.

The social evolution of the new kingdoms can be inferred from the successive law codes that they promulgated from the fifth to the seventh century. There has long been controversy about the dating of the Salic law of the Franks, which set down in writing what had hitherto been the unwritten customs of the Franks, many of them dating from the period before they settled in the empire. Other provisions of the Salic law suggest a later date, when the Franks had already been settled among the Romans. In any case, the Salic law was a code that applied only to the Franks. The Roman population continued to be governed by its own laws. So law was entirely 'personal', that is, applying to men of the same race. Law was not territorial.

This system of 'personal' rather than 'real' legislation (legislation that applies to everyone in a territory) became the rule in the new kingdoms for two centuries or more. Nonetheless, as Guizot shows, important changes can be detected in the successive codes promulgated during those centuries. These changes reveal a gradual fusion of the two societies, Roman and Germanic – a fusion in which the Germanic tribes, giving up the customs of a wandering life and acquiring fixed property, adopted elements of Roman civil and criminal law. Thus, 'the Ripuarian law is less Germanic than the Salic law; the law of the Burgundians less Germanic than the Ripuarian law; the Visigothic law even less than the Burgundian law'.[12]

Guizot may oversimplify. But there was a trend. For in acquiring fixed property, the invaders acquired more permanent relations both among themselves and with the Roman population. Roman civil and criminal law catered for those relationships in a way that traditional Germanic customs could not. In the cities of Italy and southern Gaul this process had begun early, but it was the clergy who became central in promoting it throughout all the new kingdoms. Indeed, it was the clergy of the Visigothic kingdom who carried the process to an original conclusion. Visigothic law was debated and shaped by a kind of parliament, the Council of Toledo (their second capital), in which the clergy played the leading part. Under their influence, Visigothic kings in the seventh century abandoned the system of personal legislation for the system of real or territorial legislation. Roman and Germanic laws were fused, with the formal abolition of Roman law. The two peoples became one. The code that resulted, the Forum Judicum, was incomparably more sophisticated than earlier Germanic codes, having a subtlety and consistency that owed much to Roman law.

But the Visigothic code was territorial legislation with a difference. It was Roman law tempered by moral intuitions generated by Christian beliefs. It was not a return to the rule of law under an imperium that had traditionally considered the domestic sphere, the sphere of the family and its cult, as 'sacred'. Nor did the Visigothic code preserve the basic distinctions of 'barbarian' law. 'Among the barbarians, men had, according to their relative situations, a determinate value; the barbarian, the Roman, the freeman, the vassal, etc., were not held at the same price, there was a tariff of their lives.'[13] The Visigothic code left 'personal' law behind. Suddenly, a stronger commitment to equality emerges. What the clergy introduced into the Visigothic code – although not without ambiguities and vestiges of the past – was the principle that all men have 'equal value in the eyes of the law'.

That egalitarian emphasis was even more pronounced in the regulations for monastic life laid down by Benedict of Nursia (*circa* 540). His 'Rule' would provide a blueprint for the reform of Western monasticism. It elaborated the new conception of authority springing from the writings of St Paul and St Augustine. For Benedict's Rule 'was one of simplicity and self-discipline, not of penitential austerity or self-inflicted mortification'. Benedict emphasizes an equal 'innerness'. He appeals to the 'ears of the heart' in order to found a community based on consciences. The authority of the abbot over fellow monks becomes a matter of 'mutual listening'. Thus, even the voice of the youngest, latest recruit should be treated with respect. 'Now the reason,' says Benedict, 'why we have said that all should be called to council, is that God often reveals what is better to the youngest.'[14] In particular, Benedict takes pains to shield the monastic community from the social distinctions of the outside world. Patronage and favour for particular monks are forbidden. Monks are to wear the same clothes, eat the same food and do the same tasks.

Such uniformity served a moral purpose. The Life of Benedict (written by Pope Gregory the Great) describes how the son of a local notable, having became a monk, reacted when obliged to share the task of holding a lamp behind Benedict, so that the abbot could have his dinner: 'Who is this', he thought to himself, 'that I should have to stand here holding the lamp for him while he is eating? Who am I to be acting as his slave?'[15] Alert to the recalcitrance of social status and worldly pride, Benedict's Rule was designed to create a far more egalitarian community.

Benedict's Rule gives the abbot great authority, it is true. But it is essentially a moral authority, founded on and constrained by the consent of the community. For the monks are assumed to share a common goal, a sense of justice that should govern the relations of ruler and ruled. 'As to Benedict's idea of authority as stewardship, it passed directly into a work by the greatest of Benedict's admirers, Gregory the Great, a work which would shape the notion of authority for centuries to come, *Regula Pastoralis* (*Pastoral Care*).' The *Pastoral Care* was in large part given over to the responsibilities and subtleties of exercising spiritual power. Thus, 'the care of souls' requires diverse forms of encouragement and moral guidance, irrespective of social standing – 'mixing soft words with threats, the sternness of a school-master with the tenderness of a father'.[16]

Subjection to the abbot's authority was a way of affirming the moral equality of souls and the importance of caring for them. And that mandate would be extended, not only to bishops but also to lay rulers. Gregory's emphasis 'on the heavy responsibilities of the ruler for the souls of his subjects' was diffused throughout Western Europe from the seventh century onwards.

> In what he wrote on the duties of the Christian rector (ruler), he created the language of an entire governing elite. With the *Regula Pastoralis* to guide them, the kings and clergy of Latin Europe no longer needed to look to the surviving 'Christian empire' of east Rome to guide them. Gregory had given them a mission to rule and code of conduct as clear and as all-embracing as any that had once inspired the governing classes of the Roman empire.[17]

Increasingly, acknowledging that subjects had souls was making a difference to the question of what constituted proper governance. It was another step in inventing the individual.

I I

Barbarian Codes, Roman Law and Christian Intuitions

Language itself provides important evidence of social and intellectual change. In the period that was long called the 'dark ages' – the sixth, seventh and early eighth centuries – this evidence is particularly important. Urban life was under threat during this period. But it was far from being almost extinguished, as historians once supposed.

In the south, a life that was still recognizably Roman survived, though churches and markets were now more central to life than temples or amphitheatres. Indeed, the latter often served chiefly as quarries for building material. In the north, where cities had been smaller, new religious building more often took place outside the Roman walls, in sub-*urbs*.

The meaning of basic terms referring to life in the cities was shifting. Two terms, *urbs* and *civitas*, began to be confused. Under the empire, *urbs* had referred to the physical city and its walls, whereas *civitas* referred to the larger association of citizens, some of whom might live outside the *urbs*. Isidore of Seville, in the seventh century, tried to defend the original meaning. 'The *civitas* is a multitude of men united by a bond of association, so-called from the citizens . . . For although the *urbs* itself is made by its walls, the *civitas* gets its name not from stones, but from the inhabitants.' [1]

Unwittingly perhaps, Isidore's distinction reveals the changes taking place in minds. His reference to 'inhabitants' as well as 'citizens' suggests why the term *civitas* began to take on a more territorial meaning. The citizenry in the ancient world had, of course, formed only one class among the inhabitants. But as the forms of ancient civic government decayed, and the clergy assumed an ever more important role, 'inhabitants' came to refer to 'souls' rather than citizens. It became inclusive rather than exclusive. The idea of the *civitas* began to merge with that of the bishop's seat and territory, the ecclesiastical diocese. The result was that in the Merovingian period *urbs* and *civitas* were used almost interchangeably. 'There was no unambiguous word in Merovingian Latin for town as such; both urbs and civitas could mean the town with its rural surroundings.'[2]

Viewing the population as a whole, rather than merely in terms of status, was reshaping linguistic usage. The old social classifications were eroding. Perceptive members of the former privileged classes grasped soon enough that superior status would now have to rest on something other than formal classification. In 478, two years after the fall of the Western empire, Sidonius Apollinaris remarked that 'since old grades of rank are now abolished, which once distinguished the high from the low, in future culture must afford the sole criterion of nobility'.

It was not only statuses previously attached to civic government and public law that were being undermined, however. The beliefs the clergy propagated also threatened attitudes and habits that had sustained the family among the Germanic tribes. These attitudes and habits bore a considerable similarity to those that, more than a millennium earlier, had first given rise to the institutions of the Greek and Roman city-state. Paterfamilias, the subordination of women and inflexible rules of inheritance provided the core, though paternal authority among the Germans was less priestly and allowed more freedom to younger sons, at times even to women.

The influence of both Christian doctrine and late Roman law began to challenge these attitudes and habits among the Goths, Burgundians and Franks. The process can be seen in law codes issued by the new kings, who were inspired by the Roman idea of imperium. Instead of simply confirming antecedent practice, the kings began to legislate – to do what the emperors had done. For example, important changes emerge between the earliest collection of Frankish customary law, the Salic law (*circa* 510), and the second major compilation, the Lex Ribuaria (after 600). Famously, the former prohibits any female inheritance of ancestral land, while the latter relaxes such restrictions. The absorption and development of Roman law in the successor kingdoms – something which should never be underestimated – testifies to the prodigious moral effort made by the clergy to influence Germanic manners.

Of course, it would be a mistake to exaggerate the pace of change in Germanic manners. The church and the survivors of a Roman educated class met with reverses more often than successes in dealing with the newcomers. Any reader of Gregory of Tours' sixth-century *History of the Franks* will soon be convinced of that. Habits of violence, lack of foresight and the ingrained pleasure of leading an unregulated life meant that betrayal and murder were commonplace in the ruling families of the new kingdoms. Among the Franks, in particular, there was widespread suspicion of the Visigoths, who were perceived as having become unduly submissive and over-impressed by 'Roman ways'. Frankish opposition to the rule of King Sigibert's widow, the Visigothic princess Brunhild, stemmed partly from that.

Yet a remarkable example of change even among the Franks can be found in a seventh-century collection of legal formulas edited by Marculf. In it we find King Chilperic, who reigned from 561 to 584, expressly rejecting ancestral customs: 'A long-standing and wicked custom of our people denies sisters a share with their brothers in their father's land; but I consider this wrong, since my children came equally from God ... Therefore, my dearest daughter, I hereby make you an equal and legitimate heir with your brothers, my sons.'[3] How tempting it is to imagine a priest, his face full of encouragement, writing down these lines dictated by Chilperic! For the church became a major beneficiary of changes following the introduction of wills and weakening of family control over property. It was not long before the cathedral churches and monasteries became major landowners.

But we ought not to be distracted by what was, in part, an unintended consequence of new beliefs. Far more important is the fact that Christian insistence on the equality of souls suggested, although at first only in an indistinct way, a new image of reality. Concern with the fate of the individual soul was nibbling away at a corporate, hierarchical image, along with the polytheism that had traditionally expressed it.

Church councils and missionaries from the fifth to the seventh century regularly attacked the multiplication of moral agencies, which they understood as pagan survivals – 'demons'. Thus, one Visigothic priest, Martin of Braga, asked his Galician congregation: 'How can any of you, who have renounced the Devil and his angels and his evil works, now return again to the worship of the Devil?' Just what did Martin have in mind? He had in mind practices such as 'observing the first days of the month, burning candles at trees and springs, marrying on the day of Venus (Friday), invoking the names of demons, and so on'.[4] Successive church councils condemned, in particular, the cult of angels – prayers and amulets invoking Uriel, Michael and Raguel – as demon-worship and idolatry. Such cults threatened the all-important relationship between God and the individual soul.

Later sixth-century Merovingian councils reveal the church fighting not merely an entrenched paganism, but also – something considered even more dangerous – a widespread willingness to combine pagan and Christian practices.

> It is not permitted to dress up as a calf or a stag on the Kalends of January or to present diabolical gifts . . . it is forbidden to discharge vows among woods or at sacred trees or at springs . . . nor let anyone dare to make feet or images out of wood . . . it is forbidden to turn to soothsayers or to augurs, or to those who pretend to know the future . . .

Such church legislation probably had little effect at first. For the Merovingian church remained primarily urban. There was as yet little attempt to establish it in any comprehensive way in the countryside. That attempt – and with it the creation of a more or less instructed rural priesthood, capable of delivering sermons and trying to set a moral example – was made rather by the Carolingian church, from the later eighth century.

An extraordinary example of the persistence of ancient beliefs and practices – and their ability to infiltrate Christian rites – is the way the mass was widely understood in the sixth century. Peter Brown shows how it was assimilated to the immemorial habit of offering 'sacred' meals to ancestors. Despite their new beliefs, Christians continued to feed the dead. 'Families offered food, wine and money at the Christian Eucharist so that their dead should still be "remembered" as part of the Church.' The seventh century saw a dramatic change. 'Only in the seventh century did the Eucharist – the Mass – lose this quality of a "meal" relayed from the family to the dead. The Mass came to be spoken of as a "sacrifice" which only a priest could offer. The laity could contribute nothing to this "sacrifice".[5] The displacement of moral authority from the family to the clergy reveals the subversive side of the new religion. The clergy focused attention on the fate of the individual soul, rather than on the claims and continuity of the family.

Nothing shows more clearly the individuation encouraged by Christian beliefs than what Brown calls the 'Christianization of death'. He detects a profound change under way in the seventh century – a new fascination with the 'day of judgement', the fate of the individual soul after death. This fascination overwhelmed an older sense that Christian beliefs and practices already gave glimpses of paradise in this world, foretastes of eternal bliss. Instead of such confidence, seventh-century Christians – living in a far less stable world – worried increasingly about sin and its consequences for the individual on that final day of reckoning.

There was less hope of communal salvation, more anxiety about 'the dread last journey of the soul'. Brown tells the story of Barontus, a late seventh-century nobleman turned monk at Bourges, who had a fearful dream about what awaited him on his deathbed. Suspended in the air above his native city, would his soul belong to the angels who beckoned him to paradise or to the 'clawed, toothed demons' who sought to pull him down below earth? Could his sins be purged before that decisive moment?

> Previously Christian believers had been, perhaps, more confident of salvation. But the other world to which they hoped to come had been more faceless. Apart from great, well-known saints, the identity of individual believers had tended to be swallowed up in the golden haze of paradise. By contrast, the timorous Barontus had a face. It was a face etched in terms of his 'purged' and 'unpurged' sins. These sins made him distinctive. He saw himself built up, like a coral reef, by his individual sins and his individual virtues ... Barontus' otherworldly experiences may seem bizarre to us. But they addressed with a new precision the problem of how much of the present self survives, as a unique individual ... beyond the grave.[6]

Little wonder that Brown and others identify in this questioning a new depth of self-consciousness – which is to say, a more individualized picture of the way things are.

Despite frequent reverses at the hands of ancient beliefs and practices, the church persisted in its moral enterprise, which was, after all, its *raison d'être*. It is impressive how its frontal attack on 'superstition' survived even the decline of formal education and literacy by the seventh century. The beginnings of a clearer separation of moral from physical phenomena was lurking in the habits of mind fostered by Christian beliefs. For that all-important struggle within the self to create an upright will, portrayed eloquently by Augustine, sharpened a sense of the involuntary. Even in the self, not every event embodied an intention, while the old habit of discovering intentions behind non-human, physical events now risked the charge of impiety.

The church's struggle against polytheism began to tell. A complete knowledge of the reasons for things was an attribute only of God, an attitude which Augustine's reflections on the mysterious workings of grace in this world had strengthened. The 'certainties' of a priori argument came up against the limitations imposed by Christian belief in a God who expressed himself through time rather than in syllogisms. When logical studies re-emerged in the eleventh century, it is no accident that the status of general terms or categories became a central issue. A sense of the limits of deductive argument – its fallibility in the face of the experience of things not under human control – then contributed to a clearer distinction between 'reasons' for human action and the 'causes' of external events.

So in the midst of what have been called the 'dark ages', the church initiated a process that began to strip intentionality from the physical world – leaving it ultimately as just that, the physical world. Legislation by church councils was directed against seeing different parts of the physical world as the habitations of spirits or demigods. To be sure, the habit of interpreting events in nature, especially natural disasters, as evidence of divine 'anger' long persisted. Nor was the church always above taking advantage of that habit. Indeed, the purging of intermediate beings or demigods may have intensified the habit at first. To an extent, the cult of local saints (who might intercede with the deity) that developed so rapidly in the fifth and sixth centuries provided a substitute for polytheism. Praying over the relics of a founding 'saint' or martyr helped to meet the need for religious feelings tied to familiar local surroundings within a faith expressed in universal terms. It also helped cities to survive as centres of pilgrimage.

However, the inwardness privileged by Christian belief and its concern with intentionality did not merely help to shape the doctrines of the church and its legislation. The clergy also sought to introduce that concern into public criminal law, whenever they could. We can see such an attempt to 'pin down' intentionality – by distinguishing the intentional element in events from the involuntary – in the provisions of Visigothic legislation.

In the seventh century the clergy-dominated Council of Toledo, drawing on Roman law, tried to replace verdicts based on physical combat or oaths sworn by kinsmen with a careful search for evidence. It also sought to recalibrate the relations between crime and punishment. Law codes began to change accordingly. We can recognize in Visigothic legislation 'the efforts of an enlightened legislator to overcome the violence and want of reflection of barbarous manners'.

> The chapter, De coede et morte hominum, compared with laws corresponding thereto in other [Germanic] nations, is a very remarkable example. Elsewhere, it is the damage done which seems to constitute the crime, and the punishment is sought in the material or pecuniary reparation. Here the crime is reduced to its true, veritable and moral element, the intention. The various shades of criminality, absolutely involuntary homicide, homicide by inadvertence, homicide with or without premeditation are distinguished and defined nearly as correctly as in our codes, and the punishments vary in just proportion.[7]

Nor was that all. Moved by their belief in the equality of souls, the clergy began to reject the German custom of assigning different legal values to the lives of men.

> The only distinction which he (the legislator) kept up was that of the free man and the slave. As regards free men, the punishment varies neither according to the origin nor the rank of the deceased, but solely according to the various degrees of culpability of the murderer. With regard to slaves, although not daring to deprive the master of all right to life and death, he at least attempted to restrain it, by subjecting it to a public and regular procedure.[8]

Here we see the clergy not only borrowing from Roman law, but also developing it.

Later Roman law had already pointed towards more humane treatment of slaves. But in the language of the Visigothic code there is a new urgency:

> If no malefactor or accomplice in a crime should go unpunished, with how much more reason should we condemn those who have committed homicide lightly and maliciously! Therefore, as masters, in their pride, often put their slaves to death, without fault on their part, it is right that this licence should be entirely extirpated, and we ordain that this law should be perpetually observed by all. No master or mistress can put to death without public trial any of their male or female slaves, nor any person dependent on them.[9]

The notion of pride invoked here by the legislator suggests the impact of Christian moral intuitions. But then, as we have seen, the clergy had even greater influence with Visigothic kings than they had with the Merovingians.

However, the overthrow of the Merovingian dynasty by a leading Frankish family, a family that had shown its mettle when Charles Martel ('the Hammer') defeated the Muslim invaders at Poitiers in 733, had important consequences. The Merovingians had presided over a decentralized, even disorganized, kingdom, with the *civitates* or dioceses enjoying great autonomy. Leading Franks had often married into Roman senatorial families, who continued to dominate local affairs as counts and bishops. The new dynasty proved to be more controlling and ambitious, especially when Charles Martel's grandson, whom we know as Charlemagne, became king of the Franks in 768.

In a reign of nearly fifty years, Charlemagne not only confirmed beyond doubt the legitimacy of the new dynasty, but established Frankish control over most of Western Europe, from northern Italy to the Baltic Sea. The first decades of his reign saw him constantly on the move, campaigning against the pagan Saxons, consolidating Frankish hold over the Lombard kingdom and beginning the reconquest of Spain from the Muslims. Following the example of his father, Pepin, Charlemagne maintained close ties with the papacy. It was a mutually beneficial relationship, which culminated in Charlemagne's coronation as Western emperor by the pope in St Peter's, Rome, on Christmas Day, AD 800. There is little doubt that Charlemagne dreamed, in part, of restoring a Roman imperium that had once existed. He wanted to re-establish social order, to create defensible frontiers and to suppress barbarism. But that was not all he wanted. He wanted to establish a 'Christian empire' – to propagate 'correct' beliefs and practices.

The preconditions for order and unity seemed to be improved education and a reformed clergy reaching into rural areas. In a sense, Charlemagne revived the relationship between public power and the church that had characterized the Visigothic kingdom before it fell to Muslim invasion early in the eighth century. But there was also a difference, for now the will to reform undoubtedly came from Charlemagne himself. It was he who sought out the most gifted clergy in Europe, brought them to his court – for example, Alcuin of York, from a monastery in northern England – and initiated them in the project of reformation (*renovatio*).

During his long reign Charlemagne came to dominate the church in a way that resembled the relations between Byzantine emperors and the Eastern church. He imposed his will not only in matters of church government and clerical discipline – promoting the monastic reforms of Benedict of Aniane and insisting on improved education of the clergy, for example – but also in matters of doctrine.

That strength of will, the habit of domination joined to moral aspiration, emerges from a story about Charlemagne's reactions to the iconoclastic controversy in the eighth-century Byzantine empire. His comments are recorded in the margins of a manuscript of a report prepared for the emperor by Theodulf, a Frankish clergyman. When Theodulf argues that the Greek church was impudent to try to settle the controversy over the worship of images without consulting other churches, Charlemagne says: 'That's it.' When Theodulf then goes on to say that the primary duty of bishops is to teach the Christian people, Charlemagne adds: 'Of course!' (Brown)

His was a heady combination of power and aspiration. But it would be wrong to suppose that he succeeded in creating a 'state', as we understand the word. Charlemagne's empire remained an expression of his will, his energy. In some of its aspirations, it pointed to the future. But, in its limited ability to create a legal system and its reliance on constraint, it revealed the heavy legacy of the past. Guizot captures the precarious nature of the enterprise:

> Master of an immense territory, he (Charlemagne) felt indignant at seeing all things incoherent, anarchical and rude, and desired to alter their hideous condition. First of all he acted by means of his *missi dominici*, whom he dispatched into various parts of his territory, in order that they might observe circumstances and reform them, or give an account of them to him. He afterwards worked by means of general assemblies, which he held with much more regularity than his predecessors had done. At these assemblies he caused all the most important persons of the territory to be present. They were not free assemblies, nor did they at all resemble the kind of deliberations with which we are acquainted; they were merely a means taken by Charlemagne of being well informed of facts, and of introducing some order and unity among his disorderly populations.[10]

Charlemagne's inclination to consult others contrasted with his determination to decide by himself. But the contrast was in large part imposed by the circumstances in which he acted. For Charlemagne's achievement was not only precarious, but also ambiguous. He was moved by a vision of a society 'more extended or more regular than was compatible with the distribution of power and the condition of men's minds', as Guizot observes.

Without knowing it, Charlemagne presided over both the last gasps of antiquity and the foundation of Europe. It is that duality we must now explore.

12

The Carolingian Compromise

Charlemagne achieved less than he hoped for and more than he intended.

One way of looking at the ferment of the Carolingian period is to see it as a struggle over the meaning of lordship or *dominium*. There has been much argument over the question whether late Roman law saw the emergence of the idea of subjective rights in the form of dominium – basic rights belonging to individuals as such – rather than an objectively right 'outcome' prescribed by law. Though the question is a difficult one, I think the balance of evidence is against any such emergence of the idea of subjective rights (or the theory of justice it implics) in the late Roman empire.

In the eighth century the connotations of lordship or dominium remained those of control or power, something surviving in our word domination. The idea of lordship acted to constrain the range of public legislation – setting limits on its sphere of operation. Antecedent facts established dominium. It was not deduced from any abstract principle of equality. The function of the idea of lordship was to protect a sphere of inequality or subordination, a domestic sphere including forms of inheritance, women and children, servants and slaves. In that way lordship or dominium entrenched an aristocratic model of society, protecting wealth and paterfamilias. The Roman idea of public power – expressed as imperium – had tacitly accepted this restriction on its sphere of operation. The unit of subjection was primarily the family rather than the individual. In that sense, the two ideas of imperium and dominium complemented each other. Dominium established a range of domestic control or property outside the legitimate claims of public jurisdiction, reflecting the religious character of the family that had originally underpinned the ancient city.

Although no one was more insistent on the claims of lordship than Charlemagne, this subtle relationship between the ideas of imperium and dominium was disturbed during his reign. And the reason it was disturbed is to be found in Charlemagne's determination to recreate the Western empire and, at the same time, to ensure that it became a thoroughly 'Christian empire'. To combine those goals, Charlemagne and his advisers – the most gifted Churchmen of his day – began, in effect, to graft Christian moral intuitions onto the body of established legal concepts.

The idea of authority traditionally conveyed by imperium – with public power accepting the father as virtually unchallenged ruler over the domestic sphere – began to change. This change happened almost inadvertently. It happened because Charlemagne and his clerical advisers came to rely increasingly on what might be called the 'rhetoric of the Christian people' when addressing the relationship between rulers and the ruled. I am not suggesting that changing the meaning of imperium was a self-conscious enterprise. That would be to misread the social and intellectual circumstances of late eighth- and ninth-century Europe. What I suggest, rather, is that Charlemagne and his advisers brought to the task of rebuilding central government and restoring social order over an extended territory new intuitions about the grounds of obligation, intuitions generated by Christian beliefs.

Just how important were these moral intuitions? Here the historian has to tread warily. For it would be just as easy to exaggerate as to underestimate their importance. The question turns on a universalism inherent in Christian beliefs. Since the time of Paul, Christian thought had been directed to the status and claims of humans as such, quite apart from any roles they happened to occupy in a particular society. It is hardly too much to say that Paul's conception of deity provided the individual with a freehold in reality. It laid a normative foundation for individual conscience and its claims. In the ninth century this moral universalism began to impinge on the Carolingian conception of the proper relations between rulers and the ruled. But, just as important, it did so only within limits. To understand those limits, we must examine the 'rhetoric of the Christian people'.

Let us look first at the innovative character of this rhetoric: at its morally subversive side. The rhetoric had roots in the writings of Pope Gregory the Great, the Roman aristocrat who became a monk and then, reluctantly, bishop of Rome towards the end of the sixth century. Gregory's writings became enormously influential during the next two or three centuries. They could be found in most monastic and cathedral libraries, and diffused the rhetoric of the Christian people. Privileging the 'care of souls' and laying down a fundamental equality before God and his 'terrible judgement', the rhetoric of the Christian people helped to bring about important developments in the government of the Carolingian empire.

We are told that in AD 792 Charlemagne, wishing to secure the allegiance of his subjects and to restore a stable empire for 'the Christian people', asked for an oath of allegiance from every man. What is startling about his action is that he expected the oath to be sworn, not only by freemen, but by slaves on royal and church estates as well! Such a request would have been inconceivable in antiquity, a world in which slaves could be defined as 'living tools'. In 802 Charlemagne asked for another oath, this time requiring the oath to be taken by 'all men' over the age of twelve, apparently extending the range of self-assumed obligation. Nor was that all. The language of his later edicts at times pointed beyond gender differences, with phrases such as 'every Christian person' and 'absolutely everyone, without exception'. Charlemagne's oaths implied that slaves and women had souls as well, a moral capacity making their oaths and their loyalty worth having.

Charlemagne insisted that all people taking the oaths should be able to understand them. For those taking the oaths would, if the oaths were violated, then be liable to stern punishment for 'infidelity'. The significance of this condition should not be underestimated. 'The oaths were administered in the vernacular of each region. Those who took them could never claim that they had not understood what was spoken on that occasion. Each person was henceforth engaged by his oath to serve Charlemagne "with all my will and with what understanding God has given me".[1] That emphasis on individual will and understanding represents a momentous moral step. It opened the way to a new understanding of the foundation of social order.

A new, publicly sanctioned concern with innerness is striking. The meaning of Christian rites was reasserted, directed against pagan practices that had often become associated with them. Thus, Charlemagne himself took the lead in defending the meaning of baptism and redefining the role of godparents. In a letter written from his palace at Aachen in 802 (or 806), he described his intervention at a recent baptism:

> At Epiphany, there were many persons with us who wished (as sponsors) to lift up infants from the holy font at baptism. We commanded that each of these be carefully examined and asked if they knew and had memorized the Lord's Prayer and the Creed. There were many who had neither of the formulae memorized. We commanded them to hold back ... They were quite mortified.[2]

Charlemagne and his clergy sought to make the role of godparent a conscientious one – distinguishing it from Roman and Frankish habits of inviting others to 'lift up' their infants in order to build useful family alliances and find patrons.

In a number of ways, then, the moral norms associated with the phrase 'the Christian people' were working a revolution in minds, a revolution that foreshadowed the end of ancient slavery, even when many vestiges of it survived in the Carolingian empire. Not only did Carolingian legislation preserve the Visigothic ban on capital punishment of slaves by their masters without a public trial. It also stipulated that slaves who were married could not be separated, even if they belonged to different masters. The domestic sphere was no longer, in principle, beyond public control. The individual began to emerge as the unit of subjection, a social role as well as a moral status. The spread of rural churches and parish priests serving all believers – with the shared spaces and the shared sacraments they introduced – contributed to this still fragile development.

It is true that the emphasis on oath-taking and loyalty had Germanic as well as Christian roots. The loyalty of the members of a mobile war-band to their leader had, at least ostensibly, been based on oaths. But such oaths had created powerful groups, aristocratic enclaves, within the German tribes. There was no suggestion of universality. The farmers, women and slaves who stayed behind the German war-bands were not oath-takers. Nonetheless, this tradition of oath-taking no doubt made it easier to adopt and expand the practice within the Carolingian empire.

A message of universality or moral equality was carried by the rhetoric of the Christian people. It treated everyone as a moral agent. But at the same time that rhetoric carried limits to its own application. Outside the sway of the church and the rites of baptism, people were not considered, in a sense, fully human. They had not acquired 'souls'. When dealing with pagan Saxons on his northern frontiers and when combating Muslims to the south, Charlemagne showed himself utterly ruthless. Any appeal to 'humanity' in the treatment of foes would have been dismissed as dangerous softness – if, that is, the appeal had even been intelligible to him. Charlemagne at times relocated entire populations. And in 782 he had 4,500 Saxons beheaded outside Bremen.

Yet within his territory – and when attempting to recreate stable government and social order for 'the Christian people' – we find a different attitude. Running through his acts and legislation is an intermittent but striking respect for the role of conscience, reinforced by the urgings of at least some of his clerical advisers. Charlemagne's enforced conversions in Saxony thus drew a sharp protest from Alcuin that men can be coerced into baptism, but not into faith. 'Faith must be voluntary not coerced. Converts must be drawn to the faith not forced. A person can be compelled to be baptised yet not believe. An adult convert should answer what he truly believes and feels, and, if he lies, then he will not have true salvation.'[3] For Alcuin, this moral conviction was at the very heart of Christianity. Enforced belief, he implied, is a contradiction in terms.

It is perhaps too easy to dismiss Charlemagne's reliance on *missi dominici* (inspectors dispatched to the regions), and frequent assembling of leading figures from all parts of the realm to provide information about local conditions, as falling short of what we would call free assemblies. Yet the care Charlemagne took to keep in close touch with his notables and clergy, to carry them with him, suggests something more than mere prudence. His desire to set an example – to create a unity of will by identifying truly public interests – emerges not least from the practice of bringing the sons of leading families to his court. He sought not only to engage their loyalty but also to improve their minds. At times they acted as his secretaries. Central to his hope for the young was the presence of the learned clerics he had assembled, though he had the good sense to combine their influence with his own love of hunting!

How was the greatly extended imperial territory to be governed? Charlemagne fell back on the idea of lordship. But now it was an idea of lordship modified by German customs and Christian moral intuitions. Charlemagne did not suppose that society could be governed without a permanent governing class. The question was how that class should be related to the rest of the Christian people. As we have seen, the idea of loyalty founded on oath-taking, traditional among German war-bands, suggested itself. In the successor kingdoms, it had already shaped the practice of giving land or benefices to followers, and expecting services in return.

In practice, many such benefices had already become hereditary. And the danger of the same thing happening to public – that is, royal – lands was always present. The chief unit of administration remained the counties, which often coincided with the territory of a former *civitas*. Carolingian rulers would grant the counts appointed as governors some part of the royal domain in the county to provide for their needs – and Charlemagne at times complained that 'counts and other persons who hold benefices from us treat these as if they were their own allodial possessions'.[4] Indeed, by the end of his reign, the office of count itself was widely becoming hereditary and the land originally attached to the office a private possession.

Nonetheless, the universalizing of oath-taking – assimilating the relationship of superiors and inferiors to that of lords and their oath-bound followers – reveals the rhetoric of the Christian people modifying German habits. For it introduces, however precariously, an element of free will into general social relations, acknowledgement of a role for conscience. Charlemagne recommended that all free men should place themselves under a superior or lord, in return for benefits and protection. No doubt local circumstances often made that a practical necessity. Yet by presenting it as an act of will, he introduced a new feature into the relations between rulers and the ruled.

Charlemagne hoped to create a social structure that combined hierarchy with at least nominal consent. In his *General Capitulary* of

806 he insisted 'that every free man who has received from his lord (seigneur or senior) the value of one solidus ought not to leave him, unless the lord has attempted to kill him, strike him with a baton, dishonour his wife or daughter, or steal his property'.[5] Subordination was thus mitigated by exchange and a touch of freedom.

This attempt to stabilize the relationship between persons and property by joining the need (deemed unavoidable) for social hierarchy with at least a few claims arising from the equality of souls proclaimed by the church gives the reign of Charlemagne its originality. The combination emerges clearly in Charlemagne's *General Capitulary* for his *missi* in 802: 'all men should live a just and good life in accordance with God's commands, and should with one mind remain and abide each in his appointed place or profession: the clergy should live in full accord with the canons without concern for base gain, the monastic orders should keep their lives under diligent control, the laity and secular people should make proper use of their laws, refraining from ill-will and deceit, and all should live together in perfect love and peace.'[6]

This may seem optimistic to the point of fantasy. Nonetheless, what we can glimpse behind the developments of this period is an awkward movement between two visions of the way things should be. It was the tension between these two visions that began to give Christianity a more 'other-worldly' character. For the traditional vision of social order – rooted in the assumption of natural inequality – conjured up a fixed social hierarchy. Yet the Christian vision was of the equality of souls in the eyes of God. How could these different visions be related? The problem had begun to weigh on minds as the idea of the 'other' world became more invasive.

We have seen how torment about the fate of the individual soul on the day of judgement had by the seventh century begun to displace an earlier collective vision of the salvation of the Christian people. That more confident vision had been parasitic on an ancient corporate conception of society, reinforced in the earlier centuries by the solidarity fostered by persecution 'of the saints'. By the eighth and ninth centuries that collective confidence had gone. Dhuoda, wife of the palace chamberlain during the reign of Louis the Pious, Charlemagne's son, gives us a glimpse of the new mood in an anxious letter to her son:

Constant prayer by you and others is needed by me now. It will be more, much more needed, after my death . . . From an immense fear of what the future has in store for me, my mind is searching about everywhere. I am unsure from my merits just how I can be freed in the end. Why? Since I have sinned in thought and speech. Speech itself, if idle, leads to wicked business. Still, I shall not despair of the mercy of God . . . For me to achieve salvation at some point, I leave no other, my noble son, who might work as hard on my behalf as you.[7]

Concern for the individual soul and its fate loomed ever larger, as the high price paid for Christian emphasis on human equality and the claims of conscience.

The writings of Gregory the Great, reflecting the monastic tradition, helped to foster such concerns. They encouraged constant self-examination.

The more Christians strove for perfection, he believed, the more clearly they would see their own imperfection. For this vision of the self, Gregory uses the word horror. By this, he did not mean the fear of Hell. Rather, he referred to a nightmare sense of vertigo experienced by pious persons at the sight of the sheer tenacity, the insidiousness, and the minute particularity of their sins. The righteous were encouraged to make their own the *districtio*, the 'strict accounting', of himself. They must look at themselves as God saw them . . .[8]

That desire for transparency can, of course, be traced back further to Augustine and Paul. But in Gregory's terse prose Carolingians found a language peculiarly suited to their own time. For it encouraged them to seek a Christian identity which might bind together such a disparate empire. A new intensity of self-consciousness constantly breaks through.

These concerns help to explain Charlemagne's constant effort to propagate 'correct' beliefs and practices among the Christian people – to root out the ignorance and backsliding that stood in the way of a reformation of the *populus dei*. The duty of the clergy, Charlemagne emphasized, was 'to lead the people of God to the pastures of eternal life'. It is telling that in his later years the emperor insisted that the *missi dominici* he dispatched to inspect parts of the realm should always be two in number, one a layman, the other a cleric.

Charlemagne offers the example of a ruler trying to follow the advice of Gregory the Great. In his *Pastoral Care*, which drew on the Rule of St Benedict, Gregory had insisted that 'the care of souls' was the primary duty of those leading the Christian people. As we have seen, Gregory turned the abbot's authority over monks into a model not only for bishops but also for lay rulers. In order to achieve his goal, Gregory emphasized the importance of engaging the individual conscience. Rulers should seek to exercise moral authority and not just naked power over their subjects. That was their 'heavy responsibility'.[9]

Seventh-century Visigothic kings had been influenced by the urgings of Gregory the Great, but it was Charlemagne – with advisers such as the Anglo-Saxon monk, Alcuin of York – who turned them into an ambitious social programme. Christian humility required that rulers speak to the conscience of every person, regardless of his or her social condition. It was an ambition, as Gregory himself had acknowledged, with roots in St Paul's emphasis on innerness. For Gregory, like Paul, moral authority ought to imitate the condescension of God, seeking out and inhabiting the depths of the human condition.

In this way, the focus of justice became more egalitarian. But at a price. For a stronger sense of the self brought in its wake greater distrust of the self. Gregory the Great had acknowledged that 'the mind will often lie to itself about itself'. Consequently, his *Pastoral Care* insisted that the ideal ruler should seek to be 'intimately close to each person through compassion, and yet hover above all through contemplation'. Spiritual guidance required something like the selflessness of God.

Thus, both public order and the care of souls fell within the ruler's remit, as Charlemagne understood his Christian duty. Public order required sanctioning a diversity of law and custom within the empire, different admixtures of Roman law and German custom. But the universality of the empire was to be guaranteed by 'Christian law'. That was why correct texts and speech became so important. Such correctness provided the basis for an educated class, lay as well as clerical, to govern and minister to souls throughout the empire. Yet the purified Latin which Charlemagne and his advisers sought – with the help of a revised script, the Carolingian hand – did not yet cut them off from the vulgar forms of Latin developing among their Romanized peoples.

Rather, it was to be the guarantee of universality in a Christian empire caring for souls.

Those who see the Carolingian empire as an essentially backward-looking enterprise, driven by the dream of restoring the former Roman empire, are wrong. Carolingian leaders were confident that they were doing something original in working to promote correct beliefs in the whole Christian people. Nor did they separate promoting such beliefs from the defence of reason and learning.

The work of Agobard, who was sent from Aachen to be archbishop of Lyons in 806, illustrates this unity. In Lyons, Agobard encountered widespread belief in a world of demons inhabiting the lower atmosphere, demons who could become accomplices of human ill-will and manipulate the physical world. The work of these demons took the form of thunder, lightning and hailstorms. Agobard would have none of this. He was an unusually radical monotheist who insisted that God alone had supernatural power. No demons could control the weather. Those who attributed such events to demons were only 'half-believers'. In Agobard's eyes, underdeveloped reason was an obstacle to correct belief and individual salvation. His arguments implied that the work of conscience required the full development of reason.[10]

Growing anxiety about the individual's salvation reinforced the prestige of monastic vocations. Monks were now deemed to be part of the clergy, but a distinctive part. It had long been the view among Christians that the monastic life represented the most authentic Christian life, that it corresponded most closely to the moral demands of the faith. Did not the very simplicity of the monk's habit confirm this impression? We have seen that Western monasticism was organized in communities from the outset. The ideal that it held up was one of solitude in company, with discipline of the soul fostered by an austere life of contemplation, study and work.

The monasteries represented in principle (though, of course, not always in fact) a world in which the equality of souls became clearer – a world in which human association had a conscientious basis reflected in the practice of self-government, individually and collectively. The authority of the abbot or abbess summarized the higher self that was the goal of association. That higher self was a preparation for and a foretaste of the 'other' world.

But the election of an abbot by his monks – when local nobles did not frustrate canon law by turning monasteries into aristocratic enclaves, as had often been the case under the Merovingian dynasty – could have striking consequences in this world. In well-endowed monasteries, such an election could catapult someone, however modest his origins, into one of the commanding positions in the empire. Ruling over enormous estates, such an abbot was much less likely to be intimidated by the pretensions of the lay aristocracy. That was certainly the case with Alcuin, whom Charlemagne made abbot of the monastery of Tours in 797. Alcuin had promoted educational reform by making texts more immediately intelligible with the help of punctuation (which had been lacking in Roman manuscripts). Using monastic resources, he sought to create a clerical elite for his master's empire. But not only that. Spreading literacy and understanding to the local clergy and their congregations was also important, for it could contribute to social order and might constrain the ambitions of local lords.[11]

Reformation of the monasteries soon became part of Charlemagne's programme of *renovatio*. There were hundreds of such monasteries across his empire. In fact, monastic foundations were displacing the ancient city as the primary model of human association. The hopes and fears fostered among Christians who had lived in a pagan world were being reshaped. The contrast between the rude, often dangerous conditions of rural life and the gentle, regular routines of monastic communities – with carefully tended gardens and fields – must have made the latter seem, at times, like a glimpse of another world, of paradise. 'By the ninth century the old Merovingian custom of rewarding lay bureaucrats or loyal counts with a bishopric was unknown; most bishops ... were appointed to the episcopate from the monastery, bringing to their office a more rigorous and idealistic attitude.'[12]

The paradox is that, as Christianity became more 'other-worldly' – as it sought a clearer idea of another world – it was forging a powerful instrument for social reform. The vision of moral equality acquired a new cutting edge. What in the ninth century were still intuitions and images shaping the rhetoric of the Christian people would, two centuries later, contribute to a new sense of justice. But, even before then, that vision would be sharpened by contrast with the violence and disorder which accompanied the break-up of the Carolingian empire. That vision would make it possible for the church to embark on a remarkable course of reform in the tenth century.

We have seen how Charlemagne tried to combine two visions of the foundations of social order in his rule – lordship and 'the care of souls'. In the course of pursuing the second vision he had created a far better educated and more cohesive higher clergy, a disciplined Christian elite. It was that elite that survived the decay of his empire. In the late ninth and tenth centuries the higher clergy sought to preserve unity through its vision of the care of souls. It pursued that vision with determination, struggling against the consequences of increasingly hereditary local lordships, which were helping to destroy centralized government. The local power of lords even threatened to destroy the universality of the church itself, assimilating the secular and spiritual realms. A few bishops succumbed to the temptation. They not only went hunting, but also, in armour, led their followers into battle.

In struggling against such developments, leading clergy of the church that Charlemagne had 'corrected' began to create a new world. For it was no longer the ancient church, the urban church of Augustine, Gregory of Tours or Gregory the Great. The solidarities of an ancient and urban Christianity were making way for a faith with an increasingly individualist bias. That bias was reinforced by the changed distribution of population, the growing importance of the countryside and the fracturing of public power – by the extreme localism which developed at the end of the Carolingian empire, paving the way for what we know as feudalism.

Europe Acquires its Identity

13

Why Feudalism did not
Recreate Ancient Slavery

Charlemagne's call for a universal oath of allegiance led to the first
serious impinging of Christian moral norms on social roles, a precarious attempt to distance the self (or 'soul') from inherited statuses, in
order to give those statuses a sanction in consciences. In the century
and a half after Charlemagne's death that impinging turned into
something quite different. Instead of sanctioning inherited statuses, as
Charlemagne intended, it acquired a subversive potential.

It is usual to regard the later ninth and tenth centuries as the transition to feudalism, just as it is usual to see feudalism as the antithesis
of modern Europe – a society founded on radical social inequality,
with the ownership of land carrying with it the right to govern serfs
tied to the land. But if we look more closely at this period of transition, we discover that the moral foundations of modern Europe were
being laid, foundations which would later support the individual as
the organizing social role, the state as a distinctive form of government, and an exchange or market economy.

Why should we understand feudalism as the prelude to modernity
rather than its antithesis? To understand why, we must look at changes
in the conditions of labour that led to feudalism.

A prodigious amount has been written about feudalism. The term
itself is a problem. Some have argued that it should be abandoned,
because the social relations the term describes were not new and never
made up a complete social system. *Coloni, rustici, tributarii*: the terms
from later Roman law referring to tied labour are numerous and their
meanings hard to distinguish. Indeed, it is far from clear that there
was much consistency in their use, especially in the chaos resulting
from the Germanic invasions and the fall of the Western empire.

Yet one or two things are clear. The social condition indicated by these terms was different from that of slavery. *Servi* or slaves could be sold by their master, and, at least originally, could not marry or have property. *Coloni*, by contrast, were tied to the land but could not be sold apart from that land. They could, moreover, marry and hold some property. They could not be separated from their family nor be subject to payments in kind which were not customary.

François Guizot has provided a suggestive account of the origins of this social condition, which may have included the largest number of people working the land in fifth- and sixth-century Gaul and Italy. He denies that it was the sudden result of conquest, or that it was the result of aristocratic ambitions gradually subordinating a free rural population. Rather, he suggests that the condition of the rural population antedated not only the Germanic but also the Roman conquest of Gaul. It was the condition of rural labour characteristic of a clan or tribe, a social form primitively established among the peoples of Western Europe, whether Italic, Celtic or Germanic.[1]

Rural labourers belonging to a clan or tribe were, like Roman *coloni*, tied to the land. They had a hereditary right to cultivate the land rather than full ownership of it. They owed the chieftain of the clan rents in kind, followed him into battle when required and could not abandon their status. (In Roman law, *coloni* who absconded could be pursued and seized by their proprietor, wherever they might be found and in whatever occupation, even if they had joined the clergy.)

At first glance, the condition of *coloni* might seem little better than that of slaves. Yet there were important differences, both physical and moral. The *coloni* were not at risk of constant, arbitrary physical punishment as slaves were. Under Roman law, *coloni*, unlike slaves, could make a formal legal complaint against the proprietor – for example, if rents were suddenly increased or if a crime were committed against them. (As we have seen, the Visigothic clergy tried to alleviate the condition of slaves by extending a comparable 'right' to them.) That safeguard in Roman law meant that the *coloni* had at least a marginal public standing and protection, what might be called quasi-citizenship. They were not entirely divorced from *res publica*. That safeguard had not, of course, been available to agricultural labourers in a tribe or clan. On the other hand, such labourers had perhaps enjoyed a consolation lost by later Roman *coloni*. Their subordination was mitigated by the sense of belonging to a clannish 'family'.

Overall, the most striking thing about this condition of rural labour was its durability. Roman proprietors succeeded Gallic chieftains and, four centuries later, Germanic chieftains displaced many Gallo-Roman proprietors, without any basic change. Nor is that surprising. Germanic chieftains were used to having labourers tied to the soil, before crossing the Rhine.

Along with the important remains of ancient slavery and many small free or 'allod' holders (their extent is a matter of controversy, but varied from one region to another, with allods more common in the south), this was the condition of rural labour inherited by the Carolingians. Yet something important had happened as a result of the invasions. The Germanic invaders had no experience of large-scale rural slavery, the kind that had maintained the vast patrician estates. In the extreme disorder following the invasions – when relations between people and property were so disturbed – the new German proprietors of the soil took little notice of the difference between slaves and *coloni*. They tended to assimilate the former to the latter, the condition of rural labour they were familiar with.[2]

In this process of assimilation, the slaves gained, but the *coloni* lost advantages. What became precarious for *coloni* was the access to public justice provided under the Roman empire. Merovingian and Carolingian rulers struggled to keep a public jurisdiction alive, relying on their counts, who were supposed to be the agents of central government. But, at best, this access to public justice became more difficult. At worst, it failed almost entirely. As a result, the status of *coloni* as quasi-citizens was compromised.

Charlemagne tried to reassert the public sphere and restore easier access to justice. 'We will and order that the counts do not remit the sitting of their courts, nor abridge them unduly, in order to give themselves to the chase or to other pleasures.' The oaths Charlemagne demanded of *coloni* may, at least in part, have been an attempt to reaffirm their traditional public status – an attempt to circumscribe the powers of landed proprietors. And he had some success. But it was only temporary, a rearguard action in favour of a doomed form of quasi-citizenship.

On the other hand, the ninth and the tenth centuries saw ancient slavery virtually disappear from royal and ecclesiastical estates. Smaller-scale farming, through the settling of former slaves as well as *coloni* on family holdings, became widespread. On such estates slaves and *coloni* lived side by side, often intermarrying. The distinction between them was slowly blurred. They led similar lives. At the same time many allod-holders, to secure protection, 'recommended' their property to an ecclesiastical or lay patron, and received it back as a hereditary tenure with rents attached. By the late tenth century ancient slavery survived chiefly on the smaller estates.[3]

Medieval serfdom thus emerged from a convergence of these earlier statuses of rural labour, with the condition of many slaves and former allod-holders coming to resemble that of *coloni*. Yet there was to be a crucial difference between medieval serfs and Roman *coloni*, a difference that justifies calling the ninth and tenth centuries 'the end of antiquity'. For just as important as the decline of ancient slavery and the growth of small-scale family farming was the introduction of a new element of instability into the condition of *coloni*, a moral instability that would make medieval serfdom turbulent and relatively short-lived. What were the sources of this instability? Here we must take into account both external circumstances and new beliefs.

The most obvious change in circumstances was political. The weakening of the Carolingian empire in the later ninth century led to rapid erosion of centralized administration and, with it, any effective royal supervision of local justice. By 876 Charles the Bald was granting benefices to his men that emphasized their hereditary character, even if the principle of his imperium remained:

> We have ordered this charter to be written, through which we grant to him the estates already mentioned, in all their entirety, with lands, vineyards, forests, meadows, pastures, with the people living upon them . . . so that he for all the days of his life, and his son after him, may hold and possess them in right of benefice and usufruct.[4]

Having thus alienated so much of the royal estate, the last Carolingians did not so much dictate to their counts as negotiate with them. So the number of imperial edicts or *capitula* declined. And their aims became less ambitious. But the fragmenting of power and authority did not stop at counties. A royal right to command (called the *bannus*) which had devolved to the counts, devolved further to local landowners. By the end of the tenth century many proprietors (seigneurs or lords) had effectively become the rulers of people attached to the land – taxing, judging and punishing them. The fracturing of the empire into numerous hereditary, virtually independent fiefs was an accomplished fact.

Even if the seigneur's right to command had devolved from the royal *bannus* and was not seen simply as a property right, it increased the power in his hands. The supervision of local justice by means of *missi* or government inspectors, which had been Charlemagne's ambition, scarcely survived. And the *mallus*, a public law court presided over by the count, was rapidly losing its importance in many regions.[5] There could be only one result. Local lords began to exercise the 'rights' of high justice (matters of life or death, military service and taxation) which had previously been part of the public sphere. These new 'rights', though descended from public authority, would soon be claimed as inherent in lordship.

The change of dynasty in 987, when Hugh Capet was crowned king, is often seen as confirming the change from kingship to local lordship as the effective mode of government. Early Capetian kings had little influence outside the region of Paris. Widespread castle-building and the power of castellans (castle governors) were only the most obvious symptoms of that change. The effect of these changed circumstances must have been very disturbing. Many former slaves had been moving towards the condition of *coloni*. But at the same time the *coloni* and former allod-holders were losing their quasi-citizenship (which excluded slaves) inherited from the later Roman empire.

As the administration of justice fell into the hands of local landowners, rural labourers faced an unprecedented concentration of power. Was an arbitrary power of taxation – enjoyed, at least in theory, by Frankish monarchs as the successors to the Roman imperium – to be added to landowners' right to collect customary rents? Would there henceforth be no limits to the powers of the landowner? And if so, would the condition of rural labourers revert to something more like that of ancient slaves than of *coloni*? There was an obstacle to that happening.

As we have seen, norms associated with the rhetoric of 'the Christian people' had already invaded Carolingian public life. The language of Charlemagne's *capitula* instituting oaths of allegiance promoted a tentative moral universalism. His language conjured up the vision of a status shared equally by all 'souls'. But would the universal moral status implied in oath-taking 'by all' have the same fate as the quasi-citizenship once enjoyed by *coloni* when justice became entirely local? If so, the fracturing of power could restore a form of lordship or dominium as hard as any known to the ancient world, with labourers sinking again to the level of mere property, Aristotle's 'living tools'. Without centralized justice or any source of universal status, a new version of slavery might replace the ancient one.

The obstacle to that happening was the Christian church and its beliefs. The church adjusted to an emergent feudalism, but could not endorse it. In the late ninth century Archbishop Hincmar issued a warning to one of Charlemagne's successors:

> We bishops, consecrated as we are to God, are not like ordinary men such as lay people who can enter into a relationship such as a vassal or who can take an oath, which is forbidden to us by evangelical, apostolic and canonical authority . . . We do not fight for a terrestrial king, but on behalf of the celestial Ruler . . . for the whole people entrusted to us.[6]

To emphasize the role of the church will immediately raise hackles. For there is no doubt that in the past exorbitant claims have been made for the role of the church in the disappearance of ancient slavery. In reaction, others, like Karl Marx, have subscribed to a materialism that rules out beliefs as effective causes.

Yet it is clear that the church and its beliefs played an important part in both social and political change at the end of antiquity. But its relationship to the two levels of change was different. The church contributed to the undermining of ancient slavery and emergence of serfdom only indirectly, almost unwittingly. By contrast, the church's reaction to the dissolution of the Carolingian empire was another matter. For its reaction – sporadic and incoherent at first – gradually took the form of a new militancy, which led to a programme of reform founded on a far bolder notion of its legitimate sphere of action. But before turning to the eleventh-century reformist programme with its new doctrine of legitimacy, we must first look more closely at the church's role in influencing social change during the ninth and tenth centuries.

Just what did the church contribute to changing the conditions of rural labour? As we have seen, the institution of slavery had been weakened by the Germanic invasions and by the subsequent 'discovery' that small-scale cultivation by families carried very real advantages. Technical changes such as the use of watermills and improved rotation of crops were aspects of that discovery. Yet new moral beliefs also played a part.

Charlemagne and Louis the Pious had made an enormous effort to spread Christianity into the countryside – to cover rural areas of the empire with a network of churches, a network previously confined to cities and their neighbourhoods. The goal was to have a tolerably educated clergy serving the Christian people everywhere and reaching all social conditions. After all, the word 'pagan' had originally meant simply 'country folk'. A Merovingian abbot described the countryside as 'an area inhabited by peasants, who neither fear God nor respect any man'.[7] That was the challenge the church confronted. Not surprisingly, progress was achieved with least difficulty on royal and ecclesiastical estates.

The church laid great emphasis on marriage and the protection of the conjugal bond. In the ninth century Archbishop Hincmar was among the first to proclaim marriage a 'sacrament', a voluntary and permanent union between two individuals or 'souls' blessed by the church. Such clerical emphasis on the conjugal bond helped to diminish further the contrast between slaves and *coloni*. While slaves continued to be a source of labour on smaller estates, many others were now installed with their families on a plot of land and could reap some benefit from its yield, a step away from ancient slavery.

The ancient conception of lordship or dominium, which had made it possible to consider slaves as mere chattels, was being transformed, at least in part, out of concern for the sanctity of marriage and respect for the family. The roots of the transformation can be traced back as far as Justinian's sixth-century law code: 'Who can bear children to be separated from their parents, sisters from their brothers, wives from their husbands?' This moral revolution helps to explain why Charlemagne did not use his imperium merely to defend an unchanged lordship. He also used it to introduce a precarious element of equality. Many of his *capitula* continued to be tribal ('personal') rather than territorial ('real'). They recognized the customs and addressed the needs of the Franks, Romans, Burgundians, Saxons and Lombards. Yet other *capitula* – those concerned with political and religious matters – were universal in scope, addressed to all the inhabitants of the empire.

The degree of universality varied according to the subject of the *capitula*. 'It was especially in matters of civil and penal law that diversity according to race figures in the legislation of this period; unity is complete in religious legislation and also tends to prevail in political ("constitutional") legislation which fell under the influence of central power.' That universality had religious roots. Especially 'in matters of religion the "Christian law" was the true, universal law of Charles's empire. It was what every baptized Christian had in common with every other subject of Charles's Christian empire.'[8] This dual character of Charlemagne's laws reflected his ambitions for consolidating a diverse empire on the one hand, and for the care of souls on the other.

Can we detect the influence of the clergy, reinforcing Charlemagne's will, in his universal legislation? Some, but by no means all, of the universal legislation followed his convoking of 'national' assemblies. Other laws applying to all were issued simply on the strength of his imperium and after discussion with his closest advisers, who were often clerics. They brought a distinctive viewpoint to legal discussions. It was a viewpoint which identified the church and its rites with the defence of moral equality and the claims of the poor. 'Their sweat and their toil made you rich. The rich get their riches because of the poor. But nature submits you to the same laws. In birth and death you are alike. The same holy water blesses you; you are anointed with the same oils; the flesh and blood of the lamb (the Christ) nourishes you all together.'[9] Bishop Theodulf of Orléans did not mince his words when addressing the Carolingian elite. It would be perverse to assume that such injunctions had no effect on minds.

One measure taken was especially significant, for it began to fuse the older Roman idea of a public sphere with the new belief in the equality of souls. Charlemagne made tithing in support of local churches a legally binding obligation. The obligation to pay tithes ('a tenth part of the fruits of the earth, corn above all, wine, hay and the young of beasts') became universal. It was imposed irrespective of social status, succeeding, in a way, the old Roman capitation tax. But one of its features was new. The penalty for failure to pay the tithe was excommunication, exclusion from the sacraments and the loss of all standing among the Christian people.

As we have seen, emphasis on the equality of souls shaped other features of Charlemagne's *capitula*, beginning with his insistence that oaths should be taken by 'everyone, without exception', in order to give his rule a foundation in consciences. And to make that credible, there was growing reliance on the vernacular for oath-taking. Such an insistence on oaths that could be fully understood and were 'meaningful' – elicited from individuals rather than clans or classes – would have been inconceivable in antiquity. For it would have threatened dominium, that domestic sphere of inequality protected by religion, inheritance rules and paterfamilias.

Recognizing a distinct moral existence in 'all souls' made it difficult to sustain such attitudes inherited from antiquity. The church, for all its aberrations, struggled against them. In the cities of late antiquity, the clergy had found their followers among poorer citizens as well as those outside the pale of the citizen class. They had also welcomed slaves into the Christian community. The constituent beliefs of the church made such inclusiveness almost unavoidable. In the cities, the church had long regarded manumission as a private virtue. But the spread of the church into rural areas – providing shared spaces as well as sacraments – helped to discredit further the idea that souls could be owned.

Baptism, after all, was of individuals. Only God could 'own' souls. This new universality – the attributing of conscience and will to 'all souls' – helped to sound the death knell of ancient slavery. For, as a recent economic historian acknowledges, it 'tended to remove the moral frontier separating the free man from the slave'.[10] By the later tenth century what had once been a sharp conceptual difference between slaves and *coloni* was becoming blurred. The terms *servi* and *coloni* were used as if they were interchangeable.

If belief in moral universality was the hallmark of the faith of the clergy, it faced a formidable challenge in the century after Charlemagne's death in 814. The disintegration of centralized government, which increasingly made power local and unpredictable, obscured the universal vision carried by the rhetoric of the Christian people. As a result, it seemed that the moral unity promoted by Charlemagne and his clergy might be lost for ever. That is why the church began to forge a different role for itself. Church councils established a new ascendancy during the reign of Charlemagne's son, Louis the Pious. Charlemagne had encouraged the ambitions of the church, holding them in check through the strength of his will. But under his son the pronouncements of church councils became emphatic, even peremptory. Councils declared that secular laws had no legitimacy if they contravened the laws of God. Louis was told, moreover, that 'he did not wield power because of his ancestors, but from God'.[11]

This attitude emerges clearly in the writings of Hincmar, who as archbishop of Reims was adviser to several of Charlemagne's successors. Hincmar showed considerable political dexterity and loyalty to the Carolingians, not least because of their concern for the 'care of souls'. Yet, if the occasion demanded, Hincmar did not hesitate to call these rulers to order:

> Some so-called wise men say that the prince, being king, is not subject to the laws or judgement of anyone, if not that of God alone ... and that in the same way he must not, whatever he has done, be excommunicated by his bishops; for God alone has the right to judge him ... Such language is not that of a Catholic Christian; it is full of blasphemy and the spirit of demons. The authority of the apostles says that kings ought to be submitted to those who anoint them in the name of the Lord and who look after their souls ... The blessed Pope Gelasius wrote to the Emperor Anastasius: 'There are two principal powers by which the world is governed: pontifical authority and royal dignity; and the authority of the pontiffs is all the greater because they have to render accounts to the Lord for the souls of kings ...'

Hincmar was quite prepared to invoke the final judgement and the 'other world' to oppose princely interference in the affairs of the church.

Writing to Louis III in 881, he strikes a note not heard during the reign of Charlemagne:

> While living amidst the pomp of your ancestors at Compiègne, ask yourself where your ancestors died and now repose; so that your heart does not become puffed up in the face of him who died for you and for all of us, and who was then raised from the dead, and no more dies. And be certain that you will die; and as you do not know on what day or at what hour, you therefore have need, like all of us, to be ready for the call of the Lord ... You will pass away soon; but the holy church with its leaders, under the Christ, its sovereign leader, and according to his promise, will remain eternally.[12]

This fascinating letter contains the seeds of the future, intuitions and beliefs that led the church to lay, almost unwittingly, the foundations of a new world.

To dismiss Hincmar's arguments as examples of clerical arrogance and ambition would be to miss the point. It would miss what became the dominant passion of the higher clergy in the late ninth century: a passion for unity aroused by the fracturing of the Carolingian empire. This localizing of political power threatened to overwhelm the church, leaving it without an overarching identity or means of coordinated action.

The threat to political unity was a threat to the universality of the church's mission. That is why a 'political' will began to form within the church. Previously, it had worked in concert with secular rulers – at first to insure its own survival in the face of the invasions, and then to 'civilize' barbarian laws with the help of Roman law. These experiences had already distanced the Western church from the deferential role the Eastern church played in relation to the Byzantine emperor. But by the tenth century monastic developments in the Frankish church pointed to a different role. The universality of its moral claims made the church 'jealous' of the Carolingian empire, aghast at its dissolution and determined to save some form of unity.

What form did the defence of unity take? Insistence on the equal subjection of souls to God and his church had always been its first line of defence. And, ultimately, it was that belief which would make medieval serfdom turbulent and relatively short-lived. Christian beliefs provided grounds for an appeal against injustice that had not been available in the ancient world. The grounds of social protest began to change, even if at first not clearly or consistently. For it was not merely in defence of customary 'law' that tenth-century peasant uprisings took place. A new, more egalitarian voice can be heard in some of their protests.

Accounts of peasant uprisings in the late tenth century have a markedly different flavour from the accounts of revolts by slaves in the ancient world. Take the following description of an uprising in Normandy in 997:

> For in all the various regions of the Norman land, the peasantry assembled in numerous bodies, and unanimously resolved to live henceforth according to their own fancy [wills?], declaring that, despising what the established law had laid down touching their share of wood and water to be enjoyed by the people, they would govern themselves by their own laws; and to enact and confirm these, each troop of these persons elected two deputies, who were all to assemble at a certain place in the centre of the country, and there to pass these laws.[13]

The writer does not conceal his disdain for 'this rustic assembly', describing its forcible repression with relief. But what strikes us now is the self-respect displayed by the 'rustics'.

That is not to say that the clergy encouraged social discontent – far from it. Nonetheless, in preaching about another world in which God's justice prevailed, they inadvertently provided a basis for discontent founded not simply on desperation but on self-respect. The universalism of Christian aspiration had a subversive potential unknown to the members of Germanic tribes or to Gallo-Roman *coloni*. The new network of rural churches began to reveal this potential by internalizing Christian beliefs.

A new sense of social justice was being born. Among the clergy, it was nourished by memories of the reforming zeal of the Carolingian clerical elite. At the popular level, as we shall see, the new sense of justice at first consisted of little more than confused moral intuitions and hopes. But even though far from being coherent, its advent marked the death of an assumption, the assumption of human inequality that had underpinned the ancient world. That assumption had shaped the ancient forms of religious belief, the family and government. And so deeply was it entrenched, that it had taken centuries to displace. Yet by the tenth century the nature of both religious belief and the family had changed. Moreover, the traditional way of thinking about government was about to be challenged by the church.

14

Fostering the 'Peace of God'

During the tenth century centralized power in the Carolingian empire withered away. The fragmenting of the empire and the localizing of power led to incessant struggles between rival lords and their unruly retainers. Castle-building became a mania. A new class of armed horsemen – *milites* or knights – came into existence, obliging lords to compete for their support. These knights seem to have sprung from among the small landowners. They roamed the countryside, looking for plunder. Neither peasants nor church property were immune. Unpunished violence became almost the norm. Charles the Bald, Charlemagne's grandson, had ordered his counts to tear down many newly built castles, but with little effect.

East of the Rhine, it is true, a new German dynasty emerged which limited disorder. It sought to preserve the Carolingian ideal of a 'Christian' Roman empire, giving bishops an even more important role in government than Charlemagne had done. After the coronation of Otto I as emperor in 962, German rulers promoted ecclesiastical reform in their lands and gradually acquired considerable influence over the papacy – with dramatic, unintended consequences in the following century. But that is only half the story.

To the west, in 'Francia', the tenth century saw a struggle within the church itself to restore 'order'. While regretting the old order of the Carolingian empire, the church fell back on its beliefs – what else could it do? – when obliged to find a new foundation for order. In doing so, some monastic leaders began to innovate. During the tenth century their innovations were piecemeal. Only in the following century were they fused into a coherent doctrine by the papacy. But new attitudes towards government which would underpin that doctrine emerged during the tenth century. They took the form of appeals to defend the 'liberty' of the church.

Changes in attitude often precede and mould changes in ideas. Thanks to a struggle undertaken within the church, the assumption of moral equality began to impinge in new ways. It generated attitudes which would no longer be dominated by the radical inequality associated with ancient slavery, paterfamilias and a contempt for work. This emerging sensibility bore the impress of monasticism and it had the potential to reshape the condition of labour, the status of women and attitudes towards the poor.

The reform movement began as a response to increasingly serious threats to the church. We can only begin to understand how churchmen came to innovate – and why they felt obligated to do so – if we take into account the nature and extent of those threats.

The church was losing control of its own affairs. In Rome, the papacy had become a mere plaything of local aristocratic families. In West Francia, the princes and counts were appointing bishops and abbots (who by canon law ought to have been elected by cathedral clergy or by monks) and giving away many church properties as fiefs to their followers. Local landowners, meanwhile, regarded parish churches located on their lands as their 'property'. Sometimes they appointed their servants as priests. And monasteries were once again at risk of becoming little more than aristocratic preserves.

Is it surprising that deference to the church and the clergy declined, along with their prestige? On the one hand, bishops and abbots were often tempted to regard themselves as secular lords, indulging not only in hunting and drinking, but even, at times, leading military expeditions. On the other hand, secular lords began to claim a right to judge clerics. The principle that only ecclesiastical tribunals could try clerics – the 'lot of the lord' – was flouted.

It was not that the laity had previously been excluded from the affairs of the church, but the practice of direct 'election' of bishops by local congregations in the primitive church was now eroded. A sixth-century church council at Orléans had continued to defend it: 'No one is to be consecrated as a bishop unless the clergy and people of the diocese have been called together and have given their consent.'[1] But what had this come to mean in practice? It meant little more than that the laity 'acclaimed' the choice when the new bishop was presented to them. By contrast, the nobles customarily took part in deliberations with the clergy preceding the election. They also had the canonical right to present candidates for churches on their own domain. Yet after the fragmenting of the Carolingian empire, princes and magnates were no longer content to observe these traditional limits to their roles.

As a result, the quality of the clergy, which the first Carolingians had struggled hard to improve, was compromised. The proliferation of rural churches had led to ordination at a younger age. Now church offices, both major and minor, were sometimes simply purchased ('simony'). Many new incumbents had little or no instruction. Priests and even bishops might be married or 'living in sin'. Both simony and marriage raised a further danger, that church properties would become hereditary possessions. There was a risk that 'the bishop's office might become hereditary like that of the count'.

The apparently irresistible advance of the hereditary or 'feudal' principle in the tenth century threatened the very identity of the Frankish church. If the bishop's office became hereditary like that of the count, what would remain of the universality of the church and its mission? It had, after all, originated as a kind of revolt against the claim of the ancient family, against the empire of a domestic religion. In consecrating individual will and conscience, the church had created new moral ground. Was that now to be lost to a 'naked' hereditary principle – that is, a hereditary principle denuded of family divinities by the previous successes of the church?

In the eyes of its leaders, the threat to the church must have seemed even greater than that posed by the barbarian invasions. For the threat came from within, in what was ostensibly a Christian society. It was a threat of inward perversion, a threat to belief in the sovereignty of God.

So it is hardly surprising that, in self-defence, churchmen gave ever more emphasis to a 'moral law' derived from the sovereignty of God, a law that applied to 'all souls equally'. Hincmar had led the way in the previous century, invoking the sovereignty of God in order to set moral limits on the imperium of later Carolingian rulers and present the bishops as defenders of those limits:

When it is said that the king is not subject to the laws or the judgement of anyone, if not that of God alone, that is true provided that he is king in the proper sense of the word. He is called king because he reigns and governs; if he governs himself according to the will of God, directs others to the right path and corrects miscreants by leading them from the wrong to the right path, then he is king, and is not subject to the judgement of anyone, except that of God alone. For laws are instituted not against the just but against the unjust. But if the king is an adulterer, murderer, depraved, a rapist, then he must be judged ... by the bishops, who sit on the thrones of God.[2]

For Hincmar, not only was justice the final criterion of secular law, but the church was its spokesman. The sovereignty of God invested the church with overarching moral authority. And that, in turn, was preserved by and justified the 'liberty' of the church. The emerging issue, therefore, was the right of the church to govern itself – choosing and investing its own leaders – and to pronounce freely on moral issues.

Appeals to basic moral law reshaped the church's self-understanding. Much use was made of a mid-ninth-century collection of documents now called the *Pseudo-Isidorian Forgeries*, which drew on authentic earlier sources but 'improved' them with a view to strengthening the church's claim to be the court of final appeal. Typical was an assertion in the document attributed to 'Benedict Levita': 'The law of empires is not above the law of God, but under it.'[3] Thus the influence of the clerical elite, fostered by Charlemagne and his son, Louis the Pious, in order to 'correct' beliefs, was far from disappearing. Memories of their reforming role and their moral authority helped to rekindle sparks of reform in the tenth century. For bishops such as Agobard and Hincmar had boldly tried to bind rulers to what they considered basic Christian principles. That new boldness began to leave its marks on society at large. Not least, under the church's influence, the claims of God were slowly insinuated into the understanding of property rights.

The condition of labour emerging under feudalism – with *coloni* and slaves often assimilated – was to be marked by belief that there were limits to the rightful power of one man over another. There was an opening, however slight, for a private sphere and for freedom. It is probably no coincidence that the tenth century also saw the stirrings of a market economy. New relations of exchange grew up between the countryside and towns, which ceased to be administrative centres and became marketplaces instead – something that the dispersal and localizing of feudal power helped to make possible. In turn, that growth of 'boroughs' impacted on the countryside. New attitudes and ideas accompanied and played a part in this.

The confusion of *coloni* and slaves that might have presaged a return to the conditions of slavery, coincided instead with 'incessant revolts which, from the tenth century, characterized the relations of the rural population with their masters'. While in theory the terms 'villein' and 'serf' preserved the earlier distinction, the fact that these terms came to be used interchangeably worked to the advantage of the serfs or former slaves. What resulted? Unstable expectations – with villeins fearing loss of their former status, while slaves glimpsed a better status for themselves – fed rural resistance. In this way was forged the principle later recognized by feudal jurisprudence: 'And know well that, according to God, thou hast not full power over thy villeins. Therefore, if thou takest of his beyond the lawful rent that he owes thee, thou takest it against God, and on the peril of thy soul, and as a robbery.'[4] The sense of a God-given human status imposing limits on the exercise of power was growing. This was, in large part, a reaction to widespread uncertainty about the meaning of 'public justice'. The fact that Frankish royal authority (the *bannus*) had devolved to the local lord meant that justice was in danger of being perceived as little more than the exercise of a property right, with 'law' being hard to distinguish from the arbitrary will of that lord. The appeal to God's law filled a moral vacuum, therefore, providing a refuge for the idea of justice. And this refuge had an egalitarian potential that would prove hard to control.

Often barely literate, the rural clergy were regarded as little better than villeins by local lords, which probably made it easier for the clergy to identify with the rural poor. It would be absurd to pretend that they were consciously subversive. Were they even capable of any refined moral instruction? Nonetheless, the rudiments of the faith they served – driven home by shared sacraments, the images in churches and tales of saints' lives – conveyed a basis for self-respect and even resistance that had not been available in the ancient world.

The residual influence of the Carolingian clergy can be detected in attempts to defend a more refined conception of the nature of marriage and the status of women. Hincmar had gone so far in defence of the sanctity of marriage that, with the support of Pope Nicholas I, he rejected the attempt by Lothar, king of Lorraine, to set aside his childless wife in favour of a previous 'wife' who had borne him children. The previous union had been based on Germanic custom. The church's conception of marriage as an indissoluble union of souls based on personal volition and sanctioned by God was now advanced against the older German view of marriage as a union of bodies based on convenience.[5] Lothar's first 'wife' was declared a concubine.

The episode was piquant. But not only that. It also drew attention to the importance of moral agency, suggesting that obligations undertaken in conscience had a God-given status demanding respect. And it made the suggestion all the more powerfully as the individual affected was a woman, thus confronting ancient assumptions about her inferior nature and status. The wife was not a chattel to be disposed of at will. Within marriage, the church insisted, there was at least a core of moral equality. Hincmar had invoked the equality of souls before God in order to reject arguments based merely on custom or convenience.

It is impossible to know what impression this made on a largely illiterate laity. But at least some of the educated clergy continued to draw inspiration from such events. In order to defend the church, they insisted on the 'sovereignty' of God and his moral law ever more defiantly. If the collapse of the Carolingian empire and disappearance of centralized justice had created a moral vacuum, the clergy sought to fill it.

The disappearance of unity, which so alarmed the Frankish church, led some monastic leaders to draw on their own experience of monastic government. The roots of a rival to the Roman idea of an imperium resting on lordships and paterfamilias can be traced to this period. Monastic reform had begun under Charlemagne. He had deplored the lax practices developing in many Frankish monasteries, which were treated simply as the property of the founder's family and failed to observe the Rule of Benedict. Under Louis the Pious, another Benedict – Benedict of Aniane – was set over all monasteries, so that the Benedictine Rule (which insisted on the free election of abbots and sought to keep social distinctions at bay) might be observed with greater regularity. It was an attempt to preserve popular respect for monastic life.

The disintegration of the Carolingian empire and the growth of Viking raids frustrated that reform movement. Yet at the outset of the tenth century isolated reformers – at Abingdon in England, at Aurillac in West Francia and at Gorze in Germany – still sought to apply the Benedictine Rule scrupulously. Almost unwittingly, they contributed to a new, monastically inspired approach to government. Their piece-meal efforts prepared the way for a more ambitious movement of monastic reform during the tenth century, a movement openly determined to protect monastic 'liberty' from secular encroachments. And that determination led gradually to the recasting of relationships in government in terms of the requirements of 'souls' rather than the traditional claims of lordship (dominium) and paterfamilias.

The new vision of how 'the Christian people' should be served would prove to be far more subversive than Charlemagne's vision. For it no longer combined ancient and Christian moral impulses. Where Charlemagne and his clerical advisers had relied on aristo-cratic subordination and personal ties to promote unity in the empire and church, tenth-century Frankish reformers engaged in 'purifying' monastic life developed attitudes that would, in the next century, lead Pope Gregory VII to put forward what was virtually a constitution for Europe. Monastic reform thus generated a more aggressive, uncompromising ambition in the church, a political ambition.

We should not be surprised by this development. The emergence of a more egalitarian conception of society, inspired by monasticism, brought in its wake the need to think about government in a new way. In Germany, emperors preserved the intimate entente between church and state that had been the badge of Charlemagne's project. By now, however, the Frankish West was different. In the absence of a strong central government, some Frankish monasteries took things into their own hands and found new ways of introducing 'order' into the church. And they associated such order with independence of the church from secular rule.

The idea that the proper unit of subjection – the true subject of claims in justice – was the individual or 'soul' rather than lordships or the patriarchal family had long since gained ground among the educated clergy. It was implicit in their basic beliefs. But developments in the late tenth-century Frankish church had released it in a new form, as a concern for 'peace' and the protection of 'everyone'. Clerics influenced by the monastic reform movement initiated a series of demonstrations against the disorder and violence of the age in the name of the 'care of souls'. They did so by invoking 'God's law'.

Yet who could speak with final authority about the moral law? The first Carolingians had not only created an educated clerical elite. They had also encouraged the ambitions of the papacy. The restoration of a Western 'Roman' empire under Charlemagne had helped to revive Papal claims to a universal jurisdiction, claims which not only led to conflicts with the Byzantines, but could also be invoked to limit the authority of Frankish bishops. The mid-ninth-century pontificate of Nicholas I was a harbinger of things to come. His claims to papal sovereignty set down precedents that survived what was to be the most scandalous period of papal history.

The claim of papal sovereignty – and with it the moral authority of the church over the Christian people – would be reasserted dramatically in the eleventh century. As we have seen, the ground was prepared by German emperors who introduced reform-minded clerics into the papal court. Yet it was not so much German reformist influence but remarkable developments in Frankish monasticism that would transform the papacy in the eleventh century.

In 910, with the foundation of the abbey of Cluny, Frankish monasticism turned the corner towards enduring reform, based on stricter adherence to the Rule of Benedict. The founder, Duke William of Aquitaine, enabled the monks of Cluny to elect their abbots, free not only from interference by his own descendants but also from the local bishop. Cluny would be subordinate only to the authority of the papacy. The second abbot of Cluny, Odo, extended this reform by founding other monastic houses, which became 'priories' subject to the disciplines of Cluny. In this way a network of reformed monasteries spread throughout the Frankish domains, free from the threats of corruption assailing the Frankish episcopacy.[6]

It would be difficult to exaggerate the influence, direct and indirect, of this Cluniac reform movement. The direct influence can be found not only in the way many older monasteries rapidly submitted to the disciplines of Cluny, but also in the frequent election of monks from Cluny to bishoprics, where they began to defend the principle that the church should choose its own leaders. These bishops sought to restore order to their dioceses, attacking the sale of offices, rooting out clerical immorality and trying to recover church property that had been alienated. They met with fierce resistance from secular lords.

The indirect influence of Cluny was perhaps even more important. It restored the prestige of monasticism as representing a truly Christian life, an ordered life of personal dignity, work and self-government. It laid emphasis on learning and prayer as well as physical labour. It offered, tacitly, a challenge to the church to exert itself in a society plagued by the warfare of minor aristocrats and knights, who were profiting from the disappearance of older forms of authority. Such knights went in for banditry and, in the words of one historian, 'organising protection rackets'. Altogether, the Cluniac reform movement raised the sights of the church, inciting it to defend moral authority in a world apparently given over to mere power.

As the year 1000 approached, the fragmenting of secular power and castle-building by local lords in West Francia created an impression of anarchy – the 'dissolution of all things' – which some interpreted as the approach of the Antichrist. As a result, the Frankish church not only had an opportunity but felt an imperious need to stamp its own image on society. It alone now had a coherent conception of right rule. For the previous belief in an imperium – in an autocratic 'Roman' empire set over and regulating temporal lordships – no longer corresponded to social facts. It was up to the church to restore order. But how was it to begin?

In fact, movements sprang up almost simultaneously in a number of places towards the end of the tenth century. Stimulated by the abbot of Cluny, the clergy encouraged the expression of a new sensibility. In 975 the bishop of Le Puy convened a meeting of the knights and peasants of his diocese, eliciting from them an oath to respect the property both of the church and of paupers or the 'powerless'. In 989 a church council in Burgundy went even further. It excommunicated 'those who attacked bishop, priest, deacon or clerk, while at home or travelling; those who robbed a church; those who stole a beast from the poor or the tillers of soil.'[7] By the end of the century many other public meetings and church councils had extended this 'Peace of God', so that it included 'pilgrims, women and children, labourers and the instruments of their work, monasteries and cemeteries'. These were to be left 'undisturbed and in perpetual peace'.

Such councils had first appeared in the south of France. But they soon spread to its northern regions as well. Indeed, the movement became an irresistibly popular one. 'Peasants of every class, from the most prosperous, through the middling ranks, to the lowest of all' flocked to the councils. The power of the movement was such that by 1017 it constrained the nobles and knights to accept a 'truce of God'. They 'swore to desist from all private warfare from noon on Saturday until prime on Monday'.

> This would allow due reverence to be paid to the Lord's Day; those who broke this 'truce of God' would be cut off from the sacraments of the church and the society of the faithful in life; no priest might bury them, no man might pray for their soul. Those who swore to and observed the truce were assured of absolution from God ...[8]

The movement was at the same time religious and secular. Contemporaries greeted it with wonder and delight, almost as if it were the Second Coming. They had a sense that they were witnessing something of fundamental importance, that Christian moral beliefs were finally shaping society at large. The church was defending the defenceless. 'The movement ... depended upon and encouraged an outburst of religious fervour such as had not appeared in the written sources since the sixth century, if then.'[9]

A few decades later a Burgundian monk, Ralph Glaber, summed up the impression made by the peace movement: 'In obedience to divine goodness and mercy the heavens began to clear, to blow favourable winds and to proclaim by their peaceful society the generosity of the Creator.' Regional assemblies, convoked by bishops, became the means of expressing the new movement of opinion, opinion in which religious fervour, often accompanied by 'miracles' of healing, associated the power of God with the creation of social order on a new basis.

> A voice coming from heaven and speaking to men on the earth could not have accomplished more ... These miracles excited such enthusiasm

that the bishops lifted their crosses towards heaven and all present stretched their hands to God, crying in a single voice: 'Peace, peace, peace!' They saw in such miracles the signs of a perpetual agreement and of the obligation which bound them with God.[10]

Enveloping West Francia, the 'Peace of God' sought to protect individual souls through 'peace and security' for all. Is it fanciful to see here the glimmerings of a new notion of social justice, one with less regard for inherited status differences? It may be no accident that just at this time Odilo, abbot of Cluny from 994, introduced a new festival day for Christians, the Feast of All Souls.

Odilo had played an important part in bringing about the 'Peace of God'. By the end of the tenth century the Cluniac reform movement was sufficiently strong and confident to have hopes of reshaping the church and society at large. That strength and confidence turned on a new independence or liberty of the church, an autonomy which fostered different attitudes from the 'intimate' relations of the higher clergy and secular aristocracy under Charlemagne. In the Cluniac network of monasteries, learning, prayer and the chanting of services were joined to an earlier emphasis on agricultural labour for monks. Monastic communities were becoming harbingers of a new world. Within their confines, disciplined lives gave a dignity to labour, further dispelling the stigma of ancient slavery.

At the time of the Germanic invasions monastic life had made a deep impression on Gallo-Roman minds. But it was as the refuge from a disintegrating world that monasteries had then chiefly impressed. By the year 1000 monasteries were becoming models rather than refuges. Monastic labour would soon be engaged in reclaiming and clearing enormous tracts of land in Europe, helping to create the agricultural landscape that survives even now.

Yet it was as a model of human association that monasticism had its greatest success. For it consisted of self-governing societies founded, at least in principle, on consent, and working under a rule that recognized the moral equality of brothers. The life of willing service and self-discipline offered by monasticism at its best sharpened the contrast with the ancient model of lordship (dominium), in which some were born with the right to command and others with the duty to obey. Reformed monasticism offered to people at large a glimpse of equality.

The late tenth century became a formative moment for 'Europe'. Not only was it the moment when fragmentation of the Carolingian empire reached an extreme point. Its events also mark the sapping of attitudes about 'fate', closely associated with the assumption of natural inequality and the emergence of a new actor on the public stage: 'the people'. During the Carolingian period the people had been 'off-stage'. Now, suddenly, they appear 'onstage'. They are actors, with a purpose. Clearly, the tremendous effort made to extend the influence of parish churches throughout the countryside in the previous two hundred years had made a difference. Progress had been achieved 'with the internalising of the Christian faith'.[11]

The idea of a more 'open' future was a symptom of Christian moral beliefs affecting the population at large. The peace movement stimulated a remarkable outburst of lay piety. And the physical evidence of that outburst can still be seen. For in the decades following the peace movement – that is, well into the eleventh century – there was an extraordinary upsurge of new church building. Should we not see this building activity as the embodiment of a new hope? In the 1040s Ralph Glaber thought so. As he noted, 'simultaneously with the peace movement, and the growth of lay piety which sustained it, "a white robe of churches" began to cover the French countryside.'[12]

Suddenly, the future seemed more 'open'. For Adalbert, an aged bishop looking back on the reign of Charlemagne, it was a matter for regret: 'Changed are all the orders of society! Changed utterly are the ways of men!' Exactly what the more 'open' future would consist in remained unclear. Yet a lack of clarity did not reduce its appeal for 'the people'. Indeed, it can be argued that the lack of clarity followed from the nature of Christian beliefs.

The rejection of fate and advent of hope followed from uncertainty about the salvation of 'souls'. Such uncertainty created fears as well as hopes. We have already seen a more individualized picture of 'the other world' spreading among the Christian people. The collective sense of salvation that had sustained the persecuted 'saints' of the early church had given way to individual hopes and fears about personal salvation, to an acute perception that each soul would one day be judged according to its merits. That was unavoidable. And its unavoidability implied some freedom of choice, a moral challenge to all equally.

Not even uncertainty about whether judgement took place at the moment of death or would have to await the return of the Christ weakened the egalitarian focus of the final judgement. Indeed, by the late tenth century that focus was reshaping popular understanding of 'the other world'. Egalitarian intuitions intensified its 'otherness', the stark contrast it provided with existing social conditions. The movement of the 'Peace of God' conveyed such a message. It translated into this world a minimal respect of souls for one another, a touch of heaven on earth.

So fear of the day of judgement was balanced by hope. The biblical scenes painted on the walls of churches – especially scenes of the passion of the Christ and his resurrection – testified that the immortal soul, rather than the immortal family, was the primary constituent of reality. Is it mere chance that the doctrine of purgatory emerged at this time, with its emphasis on a period of purging individual sins? The doctrine reflected the spread from monasteries of penitential rules and the practice of individual confession. The claims of family, clan and caste were weakening.

But it was not only emphasis on the day of judgement, the new notion of purgatory and wall paintings that drove home a message of hope. Largely illiterate congregations also heard tales of saints' lives, stories which demonstrated that salvation did not depend upon social status – and that individual faith could triumph over even the most unfavourable circumstances. The Lives of the saints offered a kind of imagined mobility, a moral standing that could be achieved rather than inherited. That freeing of the imagination from inherited social status contributed to new moral intuitions. The Lives of the saints became a remarkable genre. In today's terms, they combined elements from stories of the Wild West, crime novels and science fiction with morality tales. In effect, they democratized the ancient cult of the hero, for the moral triumph they celebrated was a triumph open to everyone. It did not depend on birthright, gender, bodily strength or mere cunning. The tenacity of the saint could outdo even the cunning of Odysseus.

No wonder that the search for and reverence for relics of the saints became an obsession, almost an industry, in the tenth century – leading at times to unsavoury 'thefts' and even violent combats. After all, pilgrimages to the most important shrines, such as that of St James at Compostela, had created important economic arteries. The wealth bestowed on reliquaries is a testament to that. In retrospect, such veneration may seem distasteful, riddled with superstition and corruption. But in the tenth century such pilgrimages became the vehicle of a more democratic sociability. The physical remains of saints put believers, whatever their origins, in touch with hope, a quality of will made possible by 'God become flesh'.

The message of hope was reinforced by the recruitment of clergy. The church's emphasis on celibacy and resistance to clerical marriage prevented the clergy degenerating into a caste. The opportunity for social advancement through a career in the church, even if it was still hedged in by the privileges of birth, weakened the perception that social standing was entirely governed by 'fate'. It helped to give the church a hold over opinion, something it would badly need in the next century, when it felt obliged to free itself from secular power and feudalism.

At best, we can only recover fragments of identity from the tenth century, fragments that afford glimpses into minds beginning to be liberated from the assumptions of an ancient social order. The pieces were dispersed and disorderly. They were present in some minds far more than in others. Nonetheless, they were sufficiently widespread to prevent feudalism achieving the 'staying power' of that ancient society founded on the permanent inequalities of lordship, paterfamilias and slavery.

These fragments of identity mark the beginnings of the modern Western world. However incompletely at first, they began to make up a new picture of society and government. It was a picture that would later give the terms 'authority' and 'public' a new meaning. Government would no longer be conceived primarily as a rule over families, clans or castes. It would be conceived as rule over individuals.

15

The Papal Revolution: A Constitution for Europe?

By the end of the tenth century Christian moral intuitions were giving rise to a new sensibility. They were creating a sentiment expressed as concern for the safety and well-being of everyone, at least of all 'the Christian people'. It would be premature, however, to describe this sentiment as 'public' opinion. For its expression was localized and fostered by the clergy, who drew on the fears created by private warfare and unpunished violence, disorders which had followed the disappearance of anything like centralized justice.

Just how deep did this sensibility go as yet? To be sure, those concerned with expanding their lordships may often have feigned a sensibility that they did not really share. Nonetheless, across all social situations, attitudes inherited from antiquity and based on the assumption of natural inequality were changing. Increasing emphasis on 'protection of the poor' (the Council of Reims in 1049 decreed that 'no one should injure poor men by thefts or frauds') and insistence on the sanctity of marriage are but two examples of changing moral attitudes. The church stated that the parties to a marriage were equal before God, made divorce more difficult, worried about allowable degrees of consanguinity, and struggled to limit the authority of the paterfamilias.

So, at least in some areas and intermittently, the clergy opposed the weight of custom. The church's belief that a day of judgement for sins awaited all equally remained its most effective weapon. It pointed to the need for self-examination, pricking the skin of conscience. The day of judgement depicted in church frescos must have been imprinted on the minds of even the most sceptical churchgoers.

The basic terms of Christian belief, which accorded primacy to the soul, took little account of the 'feudal' stratification of society. That omission was important. The church's 'care of souls' encouraged a form of self-respect that had not been available in antiquity. For the most part it was minimal, and left few marks on the surface of events. Yet it could also emerge suddenly and with a vengeance. We have already seen how peasant uprisings in late tenth-century Normandy revealed a new – and almost 'democratic' – willingness to challenge old subordinations.

By the second half of the eleventh century symptoms of a new sensibility were becoming more noticeable. Indeed, Europe was – at the prodding of the church – acquiring a moral identity. The previous idea of a 'Christian empire' was receding, making way for the idea of a 'Christian Europe'. Three developments especially deserve our notice, each connected in a different way with the earlier 'peace movement'. The first was a new, idealized vision of the relations between the sexes, 'courtly love'. The second was an attempt to create a code of conduct promoting knights' 'courtesy' and 'honour' rather than brutality in their dealings. The third was a new focus for personal identity, through an appeal by the papacy to the peoples of Europe as 'Christians'. Each of these developments involved new aspirations. The all-important relationship between God and individual souls – emphasized by the clergy – can be found within each, suggesting how the church was shaping opinion. Let us look briefly at each.

The first development, the genre of 'courtly love', sprang from the south of France. It was a movement associated with the troubadours, song and poetry, celebrating an idealized pursuit of chaste love, the admiration of a courtier for 'his lady'. It was a portrayal of love as romance rather than as something merely carnal or utilitarian. And in its portrayal of love, it flattered both the admirer and the admired, conjuring up elevated, even if wistful and unfulfilled, longings. The influence of the church was not overt. But it was there.

The second development was an attempt to refine the dealings of the lords with their mounted and armoured supporters, that is, with knights. Closely connected with the widespread building of castles, knights were at first probably little more than armed thugs given to pillaging their neighbourhood. Drawn mostly from the class of small landowners, they were 'masters' rather than nobles. But the gradual creation of a code of chivalry, which insisted on the loyalty of knights to their lords as well as their duty to protect the weak and unfortunate, amounted to another attempt to moralize what at the outset had been a rather sordid role. The notion of 'chivalrous' conduct entered the world, leading to the creation of special orders of Christian knights, the *milites Christi*. 'From the Council of Clermont and the opening of the crusades, the church may be said to have undertaken, not unsuccessfully, the conversion of the feudal knighthood and its capture for the service of religion.'[1]

The third development was connected not with peace but with war. It was a development in which the papacy played a crucial part in fostering a new identity: 'Christian Europe'. The appeal by Pope Urban II for volunteers to halt the expansion of Islam – following a disastrous defeat of the Byzantines – created in Europe a new consciousness of itself. A veritable tide of enthusiasm released by the pope's appeal at Clermont in 1095 ('thousands cried with one voice: "Deus le volt!" – It is God's will!') soon led to attempts to liberate the Holy Land itself. 'Prior to the crusades, Europe had never been excited by one sentiment, or acted in one cause; there was no Europe. The crusades revealed Christian Europe.'[2]

The crusades were a truly universal event, involving all strata of the population. They revealed 'a people' with a shared identity capable of breaking through the skin of feudal stratification. In fact, it was the wildly popular character of the First Crusade which finally shamed the rulers of Europe to lead the Second and Third Crusades. 'Who were the first crusaders who put themselves in motion? Crowds of the populace, who set out under the guidance of Peter the Hermit, without preparation, without guides, and without chiefs, followed rather than guided by a few obscure knights; they traversed Germany, the Greek empire, and dispersed or perished in Asia minor.'[3] A papal summons released this new European identity, appealing to the consciences and energies of individuals regardless of their social status. It was, of course, intensified by the centuries-old conflict with Islam and no doubt benefited from the aroma of foreign adventure and loot. But the new identity also owed something to popular impatience with feudal vendetta and the yearning for 'Christian' solidarity which had emerged in the peace movement.

The statement by a church council in Narbonne in 1054 catches a new mood sweeping across feudal Europe: 'No Christian should kill another Christian, for whoever kills another Christian undoubtedly sheds the blood of Christ.'[4] The proclamation takes no notice of feudal stratification. Even more striking evidence of the emergence of 'Christian Europe' as a moral fact can be found a hundred years later. The murder of Archbishop Thomas Becket in Canterbury cathedral by courtiers of the English king, Henry II, in 1170, released powerful emotions across Europe. As he fell to the floor near the cathedral altar, Becket allegedly cried out: 'I am ready to die for my Lord, that through my blood the Church may be given peace and liberty.' Within a few years pilgrims from many countries began to make their way to the place of 'martyrdom', while representations of the 'outrage' proliferated. A notion of 'God's law' and the limits of violence was penetrating the popular mind.

But could the church harness what it was helping to create? Could this emerging European identity be given a more permanent, institutional expression? Could appeals to 'God's law' be translated into practices more durable than the 'Peace of God' and 'Truce of God'? If so, the monastic movement of reform would have to act outside the monasteries. And in order to do that, a fulcrum for action was required. There was only one fulcrum available: the papacy.

Only Rome could offer a central agency for general reform. The history of Western Europe from the mid-eleventh to the thirteenth century is the history of the papacy being recruited and transformed by the reform movement. Within a few decades the papacy became so central to the reform movement that some historians have doubted whether the Cluniac movement was as important as the 'Gregorian' reforms issuing from Rome. Cluny was not, indeed, the only source of pressure for reform. There were isolated movements for reform of the church in England, Flanders and Italy. But, as we have seen, it was from the new German empire that the first effective impetus for reform at the centre came. German emperors had renewed the Carolingian project of a 'Christian empire'. A project of moral reform was embedded in their imperial system. So in the eleventh century German emperors began to prise the papacy away from the hold of Roman aristocratic families.

This 'liberation' of the papacy had a major unintended consequence. It opened the way to the introduction of the far more
intransigent, monastically inspired reformist attitudes of Cluny into
Rome. Such attitudes contributed, in turn, to papal policies that
would put an end to the Carolingian entente of church and empire,
eventually creating bitter conflicts between the two.

It is doubtful whether comprehensive reform of the church could
have succeeded without the attitudes generated by Cluny and its
scores of affiliated monasteries. As we have seen, Cluny had provided
the means of purifying the monasteries and raising the level of the
higher clergy, who now began to act in concert with a view towards
general reform. Their efforts had already helped to foster the new
sensibility emerging at the turn of the millennium.

The eleventh century saw a number of remarkable popes – especially
the fiery, determined Hildebrand, who became Pope Gregory VII
in 1073 – draw out new implications from the moral intuitions
that had underpinned the 'Peace of God' and 'Truce of God'. As
early as mid-century Pope Leo IX gathered around him a group of
reform-minded clergy. Leo worked closely with the German emperor,
Henry III, a friend of abbot Hugh of Cluny, to promote reform by
appointing men of outstanding ability as cardinals and advisers in the
curia. Hildebrand was only one of the group – including minds as different as the legalistic Cardinal Humbert and the moralizing Peter
Damian – who developed in this monastically inspired reformist
atmosphere. Each of these cardinals had been a monk, and all shared
a discontent with the condition of the church. Their influence ushered
in a period when the popes themselves would be drawn from a monastic background. Leo IX's pontificate thus saw a first crucial, if
informal, step towards what has been called the 'papal revolution',
the creation of a clerical elite determined on systematic reform.

Leo IX convened synods in Rome to condemn abuses in the church,
while more bishops devoted to reform were appointed from Cluniac
monasteries. The practice of sending papal legates with a Cluniac background to 'enforce' reforms in France, Germany and England also
developed. Pope Leo personally led the way, travelling north of the Alps
to promote a new discipline in the church. By the end of the century a
pope, Urban II (1088–99), was recruited from the order of Cluny.

The success of the reform movement inspired a new confidence in Rome, and with it a quite new determination. That determination would, in turn, profoundly affect the relationship between the papacy and the German empire, the greatest secular power in Western Europe. Between 1050 and 1300 a fierce struggle developed between the papacy and the German empire over competing claims to jurisdiction. The significance of that struggle for the future can hardly be exaggerated. What made the struggle so pregnant with the future? It obliged both the papacy and secular rulers to reconsider fundamental questions about their identity and claims. In doing so, the struggle acquired a permanent influence on ways of thinking about society and government in Europe. In the long run, it contributed to the emergence of constitutionalism in Europe. But it also had a more immediate effect. It generated the idea of the state endowed with a 'sovereign' authority.

The struggle between papacy and empire forced the nations of Western Europe out of a tradition-bound mode of life and thought. It gradually obliged them to move beyond the ambiguities of a conception of 'law' that mingled (and confused) customary practices, legislative enactments and moral principles. The struggle led to a clearer separation of these ideas and had consequences that were not foreseen.

At first glance, the issues remained those that had inspired defenders of the 'liberty of the church' in the previous century: a dangerous stranglehold by temporal forces over the church, from the top to the bottom. German emperors were tempted to see the papal office as in their gift. Kings and leading feudatories took the same view of bishoprics, rewarding loyal followers with the office or auctioning it off. And minor feudal lords considered parish churches on their lands to be at their disposal. Altogether, lay control and sale of church offices, and immorality among the clergy (whether involving marriage or concubines) heightened a sense that the church was losing control of its own affairs. For these 'abuses' raised the possibility that the clerical offices might become hereditary and the clergy a mere caste. If so, the church would be entirely submerged in the feudal system.

The very notion of two spheres, the sacred and secular, was at risk. The prestige of the Cluniac monasteries owed something to the popular perception that, against the odds, they sustained a 'truly Christian life'. But these reformed monasteries threw the general, 'deplorable' condition of the church into even sharper relief.

Influenced by Cluny, rigorous and anxious minds gathered in Rome began to recoil from the accumulated 'abuses'. Under the direction of the new cardinals, the church came to feel an imperious need to protect and regulate itself, to define itself as a separate body, provided with its own laws and means of discipline. No longer could the church be content to be governed by Christian rulers or simply identified with the Christian people. For serious threats to the church no longer came from a pagan empire or marauding Germanic invaders. They now came from within an ostensibly Christian world.

How could the church combat these threats? There seemed to be only one way. It must develop its own legal system, a system that would make it possible to wrench control over its affairs from secular hands. The church needed its own legislation, its own system of courts, its own forms of discipline. Unfortunately, what it already possessed of these things was incoherent and unreliable, for church 'law' was a scattering of biblical citations, opinions of the early Fathers, decisions of a few universal councils and some papal letters.

The question of law thus became central. If the church was to develop a system of law, it would have to define the proper relationship between the church and lay rulers, between the sacred and the secular. In the later eleventh century the project to create coherent 'canon law' led to bitter controversy over the lay investiture of clerics, the practice whereby lay rulers appointed bishops to their office, themselves investing them with a pastoral staff and ring. Could lay rulers properly bestow the symbols of rule over souls, if that rule was the responsibility of the church, its *raison d'être*?

The struggle over lay investiture of clerics led to the most serious rethinking of the relationship between the secular and sacred since the century following the conversion of Emperor Constantine. After its adoption as the official religion of the Roman empire, Christian scripture and tradition laid the foundation for acknowledging two spheres of authority, in contrast to the unitary vision sustained by pagan civic religion. The church had, after all, grown up outside the institutions of pagan life. Long before Constantine, it had been obliged to develop its own organization, forms of discipline and self-help. It had done so comforted by Jesus' injunction 'to give to Caesar those things that are Caesar's, and to God those things that are God's'.

So from the outset the church had distinguished sacred from secular matters. Yet after Constantine, this 'duality' was overlaid by Christian feelings of gratitude and deference over support from the Roman imperium. The emperors acquired, de facto, considerable influence over the affairs of the church. Little wonder, therefore, that Augustine, while emphasizing the indispensable role of government in coping with the consequences of human sin, carefully distinguished the 'city of God' from the church.

If the popes were often submissive to imperial authority, the founding of a 'new Rome' in Constantinople and creation of a new patriarchate there saw such submissiveness become the rule in the Eastern church. However, the weakening of imperial authority in the West and papal jealousy of the pretensions of the Constantinople patriarchs began to give the Western church a new voice. Near the end of the fourth century St Ambrose insisted that 'where matters of faith are concerned it is the custom for bishops to judge Christian emperors, not for emperors to judge bishops' (and 'palaces belong to emperors, churches to the priesthood').[5]

In 390 Ambrose excommunicated Emperor Theodosius for his responsibility in ordering a massacre in Greece. This resulted in Theodosius doing penance in the cathedral of Milan, a trial of strength that was not soon forgotten in Rome. It probably contributed to the bold claim by Pope Gelasius in a letter to the Eastern emperor at the end of the fifth century: 'Two there are, august emperor, by which this world is chiefly ruled, the sacred authority of the priesthood and the royal power. Of these the responsibility of the priests is the more weighty in so far as they will answer for the kings of men themselves at the divine judgement.'[6] Yet during the following centuries of invasion and disorder in the West this claim seldom advanced beyond the threshold of memory. In their dealings with the Eastern emperors, popes – even Gregory the Great – reverted to a submissive tone, not least because they were often asking for military support against the Lombard invaders of Italy. It was chiefly in the face of repeated claims by patriarchs of Constantinople to equal status that the popes revived an earlier intransigence.

The Western church became even more closely involved in secular affairs as a result of the 'barbarian' invasions. We have seen how the bishops came to dominate municipal government, making it more difficult to distinguish the sacred from the secular. Yet they used their position not only to defend the interests of the cities, but also to impose on the imagination of the invaders that the church represented a 'law' superior to all human laws, a lawgiver whose power exceeded that of any human agency. In this way they preserved the idea of moral accountability in a world otherwise given over to brute force. This helped bishops to acquire considerable influence in the post-invasion kingdoms.

With the creation of the Carolingian empire, that pattern was reinforced. The Carolingians sought to strengthen the role of the church in order to use it as an instrument for 'correcting' government of the Christian people. They also forged a close alliance with the papacy. But the basis of this relationship between sacred and secular remained aristocratic, one of personal connections and friendships. Both parties were aware of the fragility of their control over events. So no fundamental clash of claims or doctrine resulted.

Despite a late eighth-century attempt to assert papal sovereignty over what had been the Western empire – a forgery known as the 'Donation of Constantine' – the papacy remained more an observer than a promoter of change until the mid-eleventh century. There was, it is true, a nominal hierarchy in the Western church, with archbishops receiving their 'metropolitan' pallium from Rome in return for a satisfactory profession of faith, while they in turn required a similar profession from their suffragan bishops.

> However slight the practical effects of this system might be, the principle of a supreme arbiter of the faith was maintained by this slender chain of authority at a time when papal legates were very infrequent, when there were no General Councils in the West, when papal letters seldom conveyed commands, and when papal commands anyhow could not be enforced.[7]

Though often presented as the 'memory' of better days, the idea of papal rule of the church was a mere wistful dream before the eleventh century.

The second half of the eleventh century saw dramatic change. Determined to define and defend the church as a distinct body within Christendom, and to protect its independence, popes began to make far more ambitious claims. They began to claim legal supremacy for the papacy within the church, what within a few decades would be described as the pope's *plenitudo potestatis*, his plenitude of power. But how could this become more than a mere claim? How could the papacy become a truly effective agency of government? What would be required for church 'canons' to become law properly so called?

The only way forward was to remove all doubt about the source of law and to secure its autonomy, taking what we would now call 'constitutional' steps. Two such steps were needed. The first was procedural, a way of identifying the legitimate holder of supreme legal authority. The second was a matter of substance, of clarifying the nature of that supreme authority. Each was indispensable if the church was to become an autonomous legal body. In taking these constitutional steps, the reformers no doubt had in mind the Roman law notion of imperium. The emperor's final legal authority had, in an unsystematic way, shaped papal ambitions from the time of Constantine, emerging as a claim to universal rule over the church. But the reformers were probably also aware of the lack of any reliable procedure for choosing Roman emperors. For the papacy suffered from the same problem.

The first step taken by papal reformers was to secure the independence of the papacy itself. The Cluniacs had always defended papal primacy, in part because it provided the guarantee of their own independence from local secular influence. But events of the tenth century (when the papal office had been virtually auctioned off between leading Roman families) had shown only too vividly how the papacy itself could be corrupted by secular powers. So in 1059 the procedure for papal elections was reformed, with the creation of a college of cardinals as electors, intended to be free from external constraint.

It was enacted in the sight of God that the election of the Roman pontiff should be in the power of the cardinal bishops, so that anyone who is enthroned without their previous agreement and canonical election and without the subsequent consent of the other orders of clergy and of the people shall not be held for a pope and apostle but rather for an apostate.[8]

German emperors had acquired the habit of imposing their own candidates as popes, denying any significant role to the Roman clergy and people. The decree of 1059 was thus, in the words of an eminent medievalist, a 'declaration of independence'.

It was a declaration that marked the emergence of constitutional order in the church, providing it with a rule that could underpin its self-government and enable it to act as an independent body within Christendom. That rule would make it possible, as a second step, to claim, unequivocally, supreme legislative authority for the papacy, a plenitude of power. That was the step taken by Gregory VII, the fiery former monk Hildebrand.

The pontificate of Gregory VII is usually taken to mark the high point of the struggle over investitures between the papacy and the German emperors. Yet the war of words had begun before the reign of Gregory VII. Cardinal Humbert had led the struggle in the 1050s, by insisting on the moral superiority of the church as the justification of its independence and authority:

> Anyone then who wishes to compare the priestly and royal dignities in a useful and blameless fashion may say that, in the existing church, the priesthood is analogous to the the soul and the kingship to the body, for they cleave to one another and need one another and each in turn demands services and renders them one to another. It follows from this that, just as the soul excels the body and commands it, so too the priestly dignity excels the royal or, we may say, the heavenly dignity the earthly.[9]

Might it follow that not only could emperors not appoint popes, but that popes had the right to depose emperors in some circumstances? Certainly, it was finally his excommunication by Gregory VII that obliged a bare-footed European Henry IV to seek pardon from the pope in the snow-covered courtyard at Canossa.

In the face of German refusals to abandon the lay investiture of bishops – not to mention claims that the emperor had the right to choose and even depose popes – Cardinal Humbert pushed his opposition to simony or the sale of offices to an extreme point. He went so far as to reject attempts to distinguish investiture as a grant of property from the conferring of a spiritual office (the 'compromise' which in fact prevailed between the church and secular rulers in the next century). Humbert 'denounced the practice of lay investiture as a usurpation of sacramental functions by an unqualified lay ruler, and he also insisted that a cleric who was elevated to the episcopate without due canonical election could not be regarded as a true bishop at all'.

Hildebrand, when he became Pope Gregory VII, completed the constitutional revolution by boldly setting out the sphere of papal jurisdiction. Even before coming into conflict with the young Emperor Henry IV (who did not share his father's sympathy for the reform movement), Gregory VII laid down his conception of the church in the *Dictatus Papae*. This is a fascinating document. It takes us into a new world, a world in which papal sovereignty is asserted to be the fulcrum of Christian civilization. The church is presented as a self-contained legal order, with the papacy as the supreme source and final judge of what is lawful.

In the *Dictatus Papae*, Gregory puts forward a dramatically unitary vision of authority within the Church, which begins and ends with the papacy, due to its God-given (given, that is, to St Peter and his successors) responsibility for the care of souls. Even a short selection from Gregory's propositions reveals the radical character of the document:

That the Roman Pontiff alone is rightly to be called universal.

That he alone can depose and reinstate bishops.

That his legate, even if of lower grade, takes precedence in a council.

That we . . . ought not to stay in the same house as those excommunicated by him.

That for him alone it is lawful to enact new laws according to the needs of the time.

That he may depose Emperors.

That no synod may be called a general one without his order.

That to this See the more important cases of every church should be submitted.

> That he should not be considered as Catholic who is not in conformity
> with the Roman Church.
> That the Pope may absolve subjects of unjust men of their fealty.[10]

Gregory was more original than he may have realized. For in the *Dictatus Papae* he merged the Roman law conception of imperium, or supreme legal authority, with the church's 'care of souls'. In consequence, the basic unit of subjection to a legal order became the individual.

Gregory's claims tie the church as a legal system to an individualized model of society. Nor was this accidental. Gregory's vision of papal authority over individuals followed directly from the Christian idea of the sovereignty of God over souls. Therefore, in putting forward his vision of the church as a legal order, Gregory VII did not merely defend the liberty of the church. He also insisted on its moral primacy, a primacy that he understood as having important secular implications.

Gregory's opponents – especially the German Emperor Henry IV – seized on his 'innovation', in order to condemn Gregory as an over-ambitious 'usurper' and apostate. 'Without God's knowledge he has usurped for himself the kingship and the priesthood. In this deed he held in contempt the pious ordinance of God, which especially commanded these two – namely, the kingship and the priesthood – should remain, not as one entity, but as two.'[11] These criticisms were not entirely off the mark. In some of his pronouncements Gregory did seem to reduce temporal government to merely an instrument of papal supremacy. He moved beyond excommunication as an indirect way of undermining royal power by encouraging subjects to withhold their obedience. In 1080, when excommunicating Henry IV for the second time, Gregory's strong language ('I forbid all Christians to obey him as king') conjured up the vision – or nightmare – of a papal theocracy in Europe.

Yet, on closer inspection of his writings, we find that this was hardly his goal. Gregory's claims fell far short of a complete theocratic programme. 'Although he asserted a right to depose Henry he never suggested that the king's authority was in principle delegated to him by the pope; nor did he claim in practice the right to choose anyone he wished as king, but rather acknowledged that the right of election belonged primarily to the princes.'[12] Still less did Gregory himself seek to assume the imperial mantle. What Gregory did seek was a kind of moral supervision of secular rulers, through his access to and authority over the consciences of their subjects.

That moral supervision was claimed at times in the name of 'justice'. But what did Gregory understand by that word? A fundamental reversal of assumptions had taken place. Justice was no longer understood in terms of natural inequality, but rather of natural equality. The emphasis on the moral equality of humans running through Gregory's pronouncements is remarkable. It followed directly, in his mind, from acknowledging the sovereignty of God.

Gregory's assertion of papal sovereignty transformed the notion of government inherited from ancient Rome, the idea of imperium.

Gregory touched on the difference between the pagan notion of imperium and Christian 'sovereignty' in a letter to Bishop Hermanus of Metz, written in 1081 and defending his policies towards the German emperor. Claims derived from the imperium of ancient Rome have to be reviewed, he implies, in the light of Christian beliefs. 'Is not a sovereignty invented by men of this world who were ignorant of God subject to that which the providence of almighty God established for his own glory and graciously bestowed on the world?'[13] For Gregory, the latter had a superior moral foundation. It rested on the care of souls.

The 'fear of God' figures in Gregory's letters as the threshold to a proper sense of justice:

> All kings and princes of this earth who live not piously and in their deeds show not a becoming fear of God are ruled by demons and sunk in miserable slavery. Such men desire to rule, not guided by the love of God, as priests are, for the glory of God and the profit of human souls, but to display their intolerable pride and to satisfy the lusts of their mind.[14]

Gregory's egalitarianism even led him into an astonishing inversion of social roles: 'All good Christians, whosoever they may be, are more properly to be called kings than are evil princes; for the former, seeking the glory of God, rule themselves rigorously; but the latter, seeking their own rather than the things that are of God, being enemies to themselves, oppress others tyrannically.'[15] The pope did not feel he was innovating. Rather, he was drawing out the deepest moral intuitions of the church.

To buttress his case, Gregory drew on Paul, Augustine, and his predecessor, Gregory the Great. From Augustine's book on Christian doctrine, he cited a judgement about the uncontrolled ambition of rulers: 'He who tries to rule over men – who are by nature equal to him – acts with intolerable pride.' From Gregory the Great, he cited something equally emphatic: 'When a man disdains to be the equal of his fellow men, he becomes like an apostate angel.'[16] For Gregory VII, the beliefs of the church suggested a different basis for government. Humility and service rather than pride are the keys to right government. Here nothing less than the support of the Gospels would do. 'He who would be the first among you, let him be the servant of all' (Mark 10: 44).

The argument was clear. God would judge rulers according to what they have done for 'all souls', irrespective of social standing.

> They shall render unto God an account for all men subject to their rule. But if it is no small labour for the pious individual to guard his own soul, what a task is laid on princes in the care of so many thousands of souls! And if Holy Church imposes a heavy penalty on him who takes a single human life, what shall be done to those who send many thousands to death for the glory of this world?[17]

This was a bold inversion of ancient pagan values, which had identified morality with the strength and glory of the polis, and with the fortunes of a privileged citizen class. By contrast, Gregory's monastic vision subordinates the secular sphere, and with it the nature of government itself, to the requirements of morality, understood as the care of individual souls. His vision subordinates government to fundamental moral claims.

In making that move, Gregory swept away the remains of a vision of society and government that had survived the Roman empire, the notion of an imperium resting on lordships and paterfamilias. Human inequality had been its underlying assumption. Now, moved by moral intuitions generated by Christianity, Gregory was introducing a new model for society and government, whether he fully realized it or not.

The process of turning the church into a unified legal system did not take place overnight. Its complete development awaited the thirteenth century. Yet its implications would prove to be revolutionary. For although it was the popes who first claimed a 'sovereign' authority within their sphere, it was not long before secular rulers came to understand their authority in the same way. The example of the church as a unified legal system founded on the equal subjection of individuals thus gave birth to the idea of the modern state.

16

Natural Law and Natural Rights

Gregory VII's vision had monastic origins. By the eleventh century the communal character of Western monasticism – which had merged the ideals of a solitary, contemplative life and a life of social responsibility – was being translated onto a wider stage. Augustine had shown the way. He had rejected the sharp contrast in early Eastern monasticism between life in 'the desert' and life in 'the city'. The Cluniac reform movement raised the possibility that greater self-discipline might be extended to society at large. It contained the seeds of a social revolution.

Gregory's vision of a social order founded on individual morality and self-discipline, rather than on brute force and mere deference, had taken centuries to prepare. But it required the vocation of the reformed monasteries to give that vision a confidence and sweep which began to create a new world. From the eleventh to the thirteenth century the church sought – in a high-handed, even arrogant way – to constrain secular rulers by means of this new framework of ideas. The struggle between the empire and the papacy over investiture went on for decades. We have no need to follow all the episodes of the struggle. Secular rulers – for whom richly endowed and influential bishoprics were important instruments of government – proved unwilling to divest themselves entirely of a role in investiture. Nor did the papacy have the means of excluding them. So, in the course of the twelfth century, a compromise emerged, drawing on traditional dualist thinking.

It was in England, perhaps because of the relative power of the Anglo-Norman crown, that the compromise first appeared. In slightly different forms, the compromise soon took root in Germany and France as well. The Concordat of Worms (1122) came to symbolize it.

The compromise involved the sharp separation of spiritual office from temporal possessions. The bishop as a feudal lord holding lands from the king had a different persona from the bishop as part of a sacramental order, the church. Canonical election of bishops was protected. However, the king's role in investing the bishop after election with his temporal possessions, whether properties or jurisdictions, could be distinguished from the church's role in investing a bishop with his spiritual office. The latter took the form of an archbishop, representing Rome, bestowing the pastoral staff and ring, symbols of the 'care of souls'.

Kings retained very considerable influence. But, in abandoning the right to confer the symbols of spiritual office, they in effect acknowledged the autonomy of the church and of the moral sphere. Were they also acquiescing in the emergence of a kind of constitutional order in Europe, an order giving the papacy a unique role? That now became the question.

The papacy stood out against any claim by secular rulers to be the sole source of law. It presented itself as the court of final appeal for Western Europe. In that sense it sought to create a constitution for Europe, although, of course, such a constitution was never written or fully accepted. Whatever their other disagreements and struggles, the feudal nobility, national monarchies and independent communes of medieval Europe were united by a distrust of papal ambitions – by the attempts of some popes to make systematic a set of norms which would have formalized the papacy's role as the court of final appeal in a European *Rechtsstaat*. Yet that is certainly how the most lucid and ambitious medieval popes understood their calling.

What are often described as the theocratic pretensions of Innocent III (1198–1216) can be seen as such an attempt to create a legitimate pan-European order, an order which recognized and protected certain ecclesiastical and moral claims against secular powers, of whatever kind. The public response across Europe to the 'martyrdom' of Thomas Becket, murdered in his cathedral by 'agents' of the English king, suggests that the papacy had made headway in shaping opinion. On the other hand, the claim to a universal jurisdiction by Innocent III and Innocent IV (1243–54) was also seen as threatening an unprecedented subordination of the secular sphere, with the 'sword' of secular power, in the form of the empire, merely delegated by the papacy.

So the focus of disputes over the relationship of sacred and secular powers shifted from the issue of investiture during the twelfth century. Instead, the 'constitutional' issue of the rights of the papacy vis-à-vis the empire became central. Ever since the coronation of Charlemagne as emperor by the pope in the year 800, the papacy had at its disposal an historical precedent for claiming overlordship of the Western empire. By the end of the twelfth century it was asserting that claim strenuously.

In making claims for papal 'sovereignty', Innocent III and Innocent IV were doing more than protecting the papacy from the efforts of emperors of the new Hohenstaufen dynasty (notably Frederick Barbarossa and Frederick II) to establish control over Italy as well as Germany. They were not merely intent on preventing renewed secular domination over the affairs of the church. They were also claiming an overarching moral authority over secular affairs. In doing so, they moved beyond the traditional argument that spiritual authority was inherently superior to secular power because 'the soul ought to govern the body'.

An intellectual revolution was making that analogy seem simplistic. The attempt to create a regular government of the church directed from Rome drew on ideas that led Innocent III and Innocent IV to become innovators, almost despite themselves. These popes put forward a model for a properly governed Christian society, a model that was to be of crucial importance for the emergence of a new form of secular government, the state. What were the sources of this development? They were twofold: the egalitarian moral intuitions long since generated by Christianity were being joined to far greater knowledge of Roman law. Roman law had helped to shape the law codes of the post-invasion Germanic kingdoms, but from the late eleventh century it acquired a radically new importance.

Here we must be careful. For at times it has been suggested that the revival of Roman law was the real source of the papal reform movement or 'revolution'. But that is putting the cart before the horse. We have seen how important the austere moral attitudes generated by the monastic reform movement were for the papacy. The perceived need to protect and reform the church by creating an autonomous system of canon law was the real catalyst for the revival of interest in Roman law.

It is no accident that the revival can be traced to the final decades of the eleventh century. Gregory VII may have encouraged the Countess Matilda of Tuscany to establish law lectures at Bologna, in order to promote the study of Roman law. Within a few decades this school of law acquired a remarkable reputation. It began to attract students from across Europe. By the end of the century a jurist, Irnerius, was lecturing at Bologna on the body of Roman law, the *Corpus Juris Civilis* of Justinian. Irnerius and other jurists did not merely discover in Roman law a rich, sophisticated collection of rules relating to different conditions of life and society. Their encounter with Roman law stimulated reflections on the nature and requirements of a legal system, a kind of jurisprudence. For them, Roman law conjured up the vision of an autonomous, self-contained legal system.

Such a vision inevitably prompted comparison with the rules or canons supposedly governing the life of the church. These seemed painfully inadequate when compared to the elaborate, articulated structure of Justinian's *Corpus*. There had, it is true, been earlier collections of canons that brought together the decisions of 'universal' church councils, papal decrees and the opinions of church Fathers such as Augustine and Gregory the Great. But these collections were centuries-old and incomplete, often incoherent or inconclusive. The new Roman lawyers or 'civilians' viewed them with some contempt.

What was needed to introduce order and unity into the laws of the church? What were the logical and practical prerequisites of a legal system? Justinian's *Corpus Juris Civilis* suggested a clear answer: 'The emperor is not bound by statutes.' Supreme authority had to be invested in a single agency that would itself be above the law. Just as the emperor's imperium had become the final source of Roman law, the laws of the church required a source that was not itself bound by law and so was able to prevent contradictions or anomalies developing within the system. Such a source for law also provided the means of abrogating undesirable customs.

The revival of the study of Roman law from the later eleventh century provided a new and sophisticated model for legal argument in the church, making it far more than merely a competition in quotations from the Old and the New Testaments. The revival had its first impact through the refashioning of papal claims. It reinforced the ambition of the reforming papacy, leading the popes to insist that an unquestioned source of validity and a court of final appeal were indispensable, if the church was to develop a coherent legal system.

During the twelfth century a new breed of lawyers, the canonists, set about creating such a system for the church. Within a few decades they achieved a sophistication that made them the equals of the civil lawyers. Indeed, the canonists enjoyed certain advantages over the 'civilians'. Instead of merely commenting on a 'complete' or ideal system of Roman law, they were involved in creating a new system, one which would be in daily use throughout the rapidly expanding network of church courts. Whereas in most of Western Europe Roman law was introduced only when local or customary law proved insufficient, canon law was applied in the first instance in all ecclesiastical jurisdictions.

There was a deep excitement attached to the creation of canon law. It derived from the need to sift through the rules of Roman law to establish which were compatible with Christian beliefs. As Ivo of Chartres insisted at the end of the eleventh century, only those parts of Roman law acceptable to the church should be adopted. Yet before long the areas invaded by canon lawyers included important parts of both private and criminal law, for the church took a close interest in matters such as marriage, testaments, adultery, divorce, perjury, usury and homicide. Little wonder that at times civil lawyers felt their domain was under threat.

The papacy was the fulcrum of the system canon lawyers were creating. Theirs was an audacious enterprise, for the attempt to invest one agency with a monopoly of final legal authority flew in the face of the habits and attitudes of a feudal society, with its radical decentralization, multiple jurisdictions and emphasis on custom. Changes in language – the infiltration of legal terms – soon reflected this attempt to identify the legitimate claims of the papacy as what we would call 'sovereign' claims. By the later eleventh century, as we have seen, papal authority was more and more often referred to in terms of a plenitude of power, *plenitudo potestatis*. This term became a virtual synonym for legislative sovereignty.

There was a closely linked emphasis on the role of the papacy as a court of final appeal. In the 1080s, Manegold of Lautenbach argued that 'according to the harmonious witness of the holy fathers, no one is permitted to judge its [the Roman church's] judgements or reverse its sentences and no one may rightfully have the will or power to disobey its decrees . . . and whatever is done against its discipline can in no wise be held lawful'.[1] Drawing on Roman law, new procedures for appealing to the papacy were introduced, bringing in their wake the rapid expansion of papal bureaucracy.

By the 1140s the impact of Roman law on the thought and practice of the papacy reached a point where Bernard of Clairvaux, a famous ascetic and Cistercian monk, felt compelled to warn one of his former followers who had become pope:

> What slavery can be more degrading and more unworthy of the Sovereign Pontiff than to be kept thus busily employed, I do not say every day, but every hour of every day, in furthering the sordid designs of greed and ambition? What leisure hast thou left for prayer? What time remains over to thee for instructing people, for edifying the church, for meditating on the law? True, thy palace is made to resound daily with noisy discussions relating to law, but it is not the law of the Lord, but the law of Justinian.[2]

Bernard was not entirely fair, for he failed to take account of the Christian modifications of Roman law involved in the creation of canon law. But his stinging rebukes do conjure up the extent of the intellectual revolution under way.

In developing a distinctively Christian legal system, popes and canonists based their arguments on the equality of souls in the eyes of God, with its implications for the claims of morality. They sought to establish that there is a moral law ('natural' law) superior to all human laws, and, consequently, that the spiritual realm cannot be made subject to the secular sphere. The claims of public power cannot obliterate the claims of conscience, when the latter are properly understood. It is true that the popes and canonists also assumed – more questionably – that the church uniquely represented these claims of conscience. In their eyes, Paul's idea of 'Christian liberty' and the liberty of the church were necessarily joined. Nonetheless, they laid down principles that could, one day, be turned against the church as well as against secular rulers.

The revolution under way was greatly reinforced by the appearance in about 1140 of a systematic study of canon law, Gratian's *Decretum*, a work which, in its own way, could bear comparison with Justinian's *Corpus* and was rapidly accepted as authoritative. A monk of Bologna, Gratian presented his study by examining texts and arguments on both sides of disputed questions in canon law. Typically, he sought to reconcile such differences. But where that was not possible, he often rendered his own verdict. The existence of such a synthesis of church law had a major impact on minds and practices throughout Western Europe. During the rest of the twelfth century hundreds of commentaries on the *Decretum* were written across Europe. They testified to an extraordinary outburst of intellectual activity. As Brian Tierney has observed, 'the works of these Decretists, most of them unpublished so far, contain the most sophisticated thought of the age on problems of church and state'.

Discussions about the proper relationship between the papacy and the empire rapidly gained in subtlety and precision.

> Supporters of popes and princes were no longer content to ask whether the Scriptures and the Fathers had attributed a higher authority to the priests or to kings. They also tried to define what precise classes of legal cases could be judged by a pope, what were the limits (if any) to his legislative authority, what legal sanctions he could use in his dealings with temporal rulers, and whether he could hear appeals from their courts.[3]

In turn, papal legislation or decretals, influenced by the arguments of the canon lawyers, accumulated so rapidly that by 1234 a new compilation of canon law, called the *Decretales*, was needed. Lawyer-popes, whose outlook had been shaped by canon law, were thus able to influence its further development by means of their decretals. Theory and practice were joined.

During the later twelfth and the thirteenth century nearly all the leading popes were not only theologians but also canon lawyers. They drew on Roman law to create a more systematic legal system for the church. Some of these popes had lectured in a university before being called to the papacy, for legal studies flourished in the new universities of Bologna, Paris and Oxford. Not only had Innocent IV, for example, lectured on canon law at Bologna before becoming pope, he managed to write a major commentary on the *Decretales* during his pontificate.

The papal claim to a 'sovereign' authority reached its climax under the pontificates of Innocent III and Innocent IV. Innocent III, in particular, did not mince his words when describing the pope's status and role: 'You see then who is this servant set over the household, truly the vicar of Jesus Christ, anointed of the lord . . . set between God and man, lower than God but higher than man, who judges all and is judged by no one . . .'[4] Innocent III did not contest the ordinary jurisdiction of secular courts. But he did assert the right of the papacy to act as the court of final appeal for all cases, whether ecclesiastical or civil, when the 'matter is difficult and ambiguous', 'when the judge is suspect', or 'when there is no superior judge'. This appellate jurisdiction, he argued, was founded on the authority conferred on Peter and his successors by the Christ – the right to defend moral law (*ratione peccati*) central to the mind of a pope who was both theologian and lawyer.

> Paul, when writing to the Corinthians to explain the plenitude of power, said, Know you not that we shall judge angels? How much more the things of this world? (1 Corinthians 6.3) Accordingly (the papacy) is accustomed to exercise the office of secular power sometimes and in some things by itself, sometimes and in some things through others.[5]

Sovereignty, the plenitude of power, was henceforth deemed to be intrinsic to the jurisdiction of the papacy.

Yet 'plenitude of power' was not the only innovation in the language deployed by popes that revealed the intellectual revolution under way. For centuries popes had described themselves as the 'vicars of St Peter', a description that confirmed their special status by relating it to the tomb and body of the apostle in Rome, where his presence attracted thousands of pilgrims each year (even in 'dark' centuries when the hazards of travel abounded). This physical connection with the 'founder' of the Roman church had not only fostered acts of private devotion but also facilitated political agreements sworn 'in the presence of the apostle'. Altogether, the papacy's role as guardian of Peter's tomb had helped to preserve for Rome its dominant place in the imagination of Western Christians. During the twelfth century, however, that self-description of the popes gave way to another. Rather than styling themselves as the 'vicars of St Peter', popes increasingly referred to themselves as the 'vicars of Christ'.[6]

What lay behind this change? The development of the papacy as an effective agency of government – and the impact of more abstract thinking stimulated by Roman law – led to a downgrading of the physical connection with the apostle and an emphasis instead on the legal jurisdiction conferred by his divine master. The claim by Rome to possess universal jurisdiction drew attention to its ultimate source, the Christ.

This symptom of more legalistic thinking in the interests of creating effective papal government completed a process that had begun under the Carolingians. The rhetoric of the 'care of souls' had reshaped the language of government and administration. There was no longer any equivocation about the unit of legal subjection. Papal sovereignty was tied to 'equal subjection'. It was tied – through the care of souls – to the government of individuals, whose moral status as children of God gave them an equal claim to concern and respect.

In this way canon law developed around a new theory of justice, a theory resting on the assumption of moral equality. To find it, we have only to look at the opening words of Gratian's famous *Decretum*: 'Natural law [*jus*] is what is contained in the Law and the Gospel by which each is to do to another what he wants done to himself and forbidden to do to another what he does not want done to himself.' Here the biblical 'golden rule' has been imposed on the ancient theory of natural law, so that equality and reciprocity are made the mainsprings of justice. Without, perhaps, fully realizing the novelty of his move, Gratian fused Christian moral intuitions with a concept inherited from Greek philosophy and Roman law. Relations of equality and reciprocity are now understood as antecedent to both positive and customary law. They provide ultimate standards for judging the contents of each. By identifying natural law with biblical revelation and Christian morality, Gratian gave it an egalitarian bias – and a subversive potential – utterly foreign to the ancient world's understanding of natural law as 'everything in its place'.

This new theory of justice, developing within canon law, would have far-reaching consequences. For it marked a departure from the assumptions about status embedded in Roman law since antiquity. For example, the second-century jurist Gaius had relied on three tests to establish personal status:

Is the person free or unfree?
Is the person a citizen or foreign born?
Is the person a paterfamilias or in the power of an ancestor?

Evidently, Gaius did not assume an underlying equality of moral status. His use of 'person' was purely descriptive and physical. It carried no moral implications. The church, following Constantine's conversion, had accepted much Roman private law, modelling its courts and procedures on that law. But when knowledge and practice of Roman law declined after the fall of the Western empire, the overriding concern of the clergy was to save as much as possible, by helping Germanic rulers to create law codes for their new kingdoms and trying to protect their Romanized subjects. The understanding of Roman legal terms became fragile. For centuries there was neither leisure nor the ability to review basic assumptions about status in Roman law.

Gratian's interpretation of the requirements of natural law amounted, however, to just such a review. It amounted to a reversal of assumptions in favour of human equality. For, in effect, it stipulated that all 'persons' should be considered as 'individuals', in that they share an underlying equality of status as the children of God. Instead of traditional social inequalities being deemed natural – and therefore not needing justification – an underlying moral equality was now deemed natural. This reversal of assumptions meant that paterfamilias and lordship were no longer 'brute' facts that stood outside and constrained the claims of justice. They too were now subject to the scrutiny of justice.

Papal insistence on 'equal subjection' to its rule carried this reversal of assumptions, with its potential for subverting paterfamilias and traditional lordships. The first prohibition of lay investiture by Pope Nicholas II in 1059 stressed the nature of the papacy's universal authority: 'We must be diligently solicitous for all men with the vigilance that pertains to our universal rule, taking heed for your (individual) salvation.' And Gregory VII had reinforced that language: 'By thy favour, not by any works of mine, I believe it is and has been thy will, that the Christian people especially committed to thee should render obedience to me thy specially constituted representative. To me is given by thy grace the power of binding and loosing (souls) in Heaven and upon earth.' There was to be no exception of persons, emphasized Innocent III: 'but it may be said that kings are to be treated differently from others. We, however, know that it is written in the divine law, "You shall judge the great as well as the little and there shall be no difference of persons".'[7] The ancient formula defining justice as 'the set and constant purpose to give every man his due' – a formula adopted by canon lawyers from Justinian's *Institutes* – was thus shorn of any remaining belief (as in Aristotle) that unequal birthrights constitute a morally relevant ground for treating people differently.

Of course, the canonists did not foresee all the implications of this reversal of moral assumptions. They were not social revolutionaries. But the fact remains that they laid the foundation for a move away from an aristocratic society to a 'democratic' society. Such a reversal of assumptions not only foreshadowed a fundamental change in the structure of society. It also freed the human mind, giving a far wider scope and a more critical edge to the role of analysis. It made possible what might be called the 'take off' of the Western mind.

While the recovery of much Greek philosophy in the twelfth century (often translated in Spain from Arabic texts) held up a powerful example of abstract thinking to the medieval West, the assumption of moral equality in canon law created a new habit of generalization. Canonists habitually considered how any rule of law or practice would affect 'all souls'. Their concern, unknown to antiquity, was with the experience of 'all equally'. In that way, belief in a human agency prior to established social roles – the distinction between individuals and the social roles they occupy – cut through a compartmentalized view of the world. Where the older corporate conception of society had inhibited any temptation to generalize, it was experience of human agents as such that dominated the writings of the canonists. And by distancing human agency from particular social roles, it made possible a sharper distinction between 'is' and 'ought' – statements of observable facts and moral prescriptions.

This change gave a tremendous impetus to logical speculation. For it immediately called into question the status of terms which had sustained a corporate conception of society. Instead of terms designating classes of phenomena being deemed to have a substance or reality in their own right, terms began to be seen as mental constructions, as what we now call concepts. From Abelard in the twelfth century to Ockham in the fourteenth, that contributed to a debate between 'realists', who defended the objective, extra-mental reality of general terms or concepts, and 'nominalists' who insisted that 'a universal thing does not exist, except in individual things and through individual things'. This latter view rapidly gained ground.[8]

We can see the impact of this intellectual revolution on thinking about political authority. The canonists were greatly influenced by the notion of imperium in Roman law. Yet their translation of imperium into the papal claim of sovereignty changed its meaning. Individuals rather than established social categories or classes became the focus of legal jurisdiction. Individuals or 'souls' provided the underlying unit of subjection in the eyes of the church, the unit that counted for more than anything else. In effect, canon lawyers purged Roman law of hierarchical assumptions surviving from the social structure of the ancient world.

This shift away from the assumptions of the ancient world gave birth to the idea of sovereignty. By making the individual the unit of legal subjection – through the stipulation of 'equal subjection' – the papal claim of sovereignty prepared the way for the emergence of the state as a distinctive form of government. But if we look closely, the papal claim introduced equality both as a foundation and as a consequence. While 'equal subjection' is a necessary condition for the state and sovereignty, moral equality also provides the basis for limiting the power of the state and its sovereign authority. The intellectual sword raised by the papacy was thus two-edged.

The papal claim of sovereignty initiated the translation of a moral status into an organizing social role. As we have seen, this required the definition of a primary or meta-role ('the individual') shared equally by all persons. Other social roles became secondary in relation to that primary role. To that primary role, an indefinite number of other roles might be added as the attributes of a subject. But they no longer exhausted the subject's identity. Being a 'seigneur', 'serf' or 'burgher' might be added to or subtracted from an individual's identity, but the individual or 'soul' remained. That had not been the case in ancient societies.

The idea of sovereignty thus provided the keystone for the new conception of society. For only through equal subjection to a sovereign could there be a primary or meta-role in a society, and therefore 'individuals' sharing equally a fundamental, moral status. That is how the papal claim of sovereignty or *plenitudo potestatis* transformed the meaning of ancient imperium. And before long that change of meaning had repercussions in the secular sphere.

The investiture controversy had taken a heavy toll of the idea of sacral kingship. Before the controversy, both the church and secular rulers had used the idea to claim a pre-eminence. It was invoked by kings to insist on their right to govern the church and by the church to assert a God-given duty to regulate secular affairs. Yet the repeated attempts to resolve the investiture controversy, and the compromise that slowly emerged, led to a remarkable 'moral' transaction.

On the one hand, kings ceased to be regarded, as in the tenth century, as the 'vicars of Christ' – almost as high priests. Their thrones were still surrounded by religious symbolism. But they were no longer the direct agents of spiritual government. The dualist tradition had triumphed over royal theocracy. Kings acknowledged, at least tacitly, the moral claims of an independent spiritual order, liberties of the church that lay outside their jurisdiction and constrained it. But at the same time the papacy acknowledged the autonomous jurisdiction of temporal powers. So there was a stand-off. Two structures of authority were acknowledged, and, in the gap between them, an important part of the future of European liberty would be lodged.

Yet there was more to the compromise than might at first appear. Despite the apparent stand-off, a new common denominator emerged. Secular rulers learned much from the papal revolution. They were not simply losers. However distrustful of papal pretensions many rulers remained, the papal claim to sovereignty began to ease them into the conception of society that now shaped papal ambitions, a conception that stood in sharp contrast to the elaborate hierarchies of feudalism.

In accepting the church's claim to a jurisdiction founded on the care for souls, rulers were themselves encouraged to think of society in a less hierarchical, more individualized way. They were not immune to a theory of justice resting on the moral intuitions generated by Christian beliefs, even if, at times, they manipulated those beliefs. So the papal claim to possess a sovereign authority began to transform secular thinking about social relations. The example of the church as a unified legal system, founded on the subjection of individuals, gave birth to the project of creating states. And this development doomed feudalism.

The model of a government claiming 'sovereign' authority suggested to secular rulers a means of extending their jurisdiction. By recognizing the claims of the individual or 'soul' as primary, they might establish their authority as rulers directly over individuals rather than having to reach persons indirectly, as members of groups, whether families, castes or corporations. 'Sovereigns' might break out of the limits of feudal kingship and found what we have learned to call the 'nation-state'. The papal claim to a sovereign authority thus awakened new ambitions in secular rulers. It initiated the process that led to the creation of European nation-states. Of course, that process would prove to be fitful, difficult and slow. But, in the end, it dealt a death blow to the corporate conception of society inherited from antiquity.

So the apparent triumph of feudalism in Europe – with the extreme parcelling out of public authority and the spread of a new form of subjection, serfdom – coincided with developments that doomed it. Feudalism could not resuscitate the assumption of natural inequality. For the 'moral transaction' I have described meant that feudalism could not establish itself in the durable way that ancient slavery had done. Feudalism ran up against moral intuitions and a conception of society in which the self-interest of both the church and secular kings became engaged.

The lawyer-popes did not succeed in establishing a papal constitution for Europe. But in the course of failing to do so, they laid the foundations of modern Europe.

A New Model of
Government

17

Centralization and the New Sense of Justice

We are now in a position to identify the opposing tendencies at work in the eleventh and twelfth centuries. The extreme parcelling out of public authority that was a feature of early feudalism, so that the idea of a public jurisdiction almost disappeared into a property right, opened the way for a redefinition of the nature and grounds of public authority. It enabled the church, under the papacy, to insist that the primary unit of concern and subjection was no longer the family, tribe or caste, but the individual.

With the dismemberment of the Carolingian empire and localizing of political power in the Frankish West, the experience of centralized control – and the confidence bred by exercising it – passed from the secular sphere to the church. That was the larger significance of the monastic reform movement emanating from Cluny. By freeing monasteries from local secular influences and disciplining its affiliates, Cluny rehabilitated the idea of centralized government, though now within the confines of the church. It created a new ambition as well as new confidence among monastic leaders.

We have seen that, in order to act on that ambition and with that confidence, three things had proved to be necessary. The first was the recruiting of a reformist elite at the centre of the church in Rome during the pontificate of Leo IX. The second thing that proved necessary was an unequivocal assertion by Gregory VII of the pope's legislative supremacy, in the form of papal decrees (decretals). The third involved the creation of a far more systematic body of canon law, which both drew on and transformed Roman civil law. These changes began to reshape the structure of European society and government. They lay behind the shift in meaning from ancient imperium to papal 'sovereignty'. And the impetus for that change came from monasteries. Remarkably, the papacy itself was occupied by a series of former monks, starting with Hildebrand, from 1073 to 1119. Only later did the 'monkish popes' make way for 'lawyer-popes'.

The development of papal government and administration turned the papacy from a passive authority into an active power in the period from 1050 to 1300. And this papal activity soon impinged on life at every level of society in Western Europe. The elaboration of canon law was central to this process. Canon law became, in that way, the original vehicle of modernity. Harold Berman is right to describe it as 'the first modern Western legal system' and to argue that 'the papal revolution' is an apt description of what resulted.[1]

How were the popes able to promote legal reform so rapidly? They had several means: by calling and presiding over general councils of the church; through papal decrees and settling disputes, acting both as legislator and supreme court of appeal; and by supplementing bishops' courts with legates who supervised the local enforcement of the decisions of councils as well as papal decrees.

The Oxford medievalist Richard Southern has provided impressive statistical evidence of the growth of papal activity in these fields after 1050. Whereas in the five centuries before 1123 there had been only three councils recognized as general or ecumenical (and they had all been held in the Byzantine empire, with only a papal representative present), from 1123 to 1312 there were seven such councils, all of them called by and presided over by a pope. They pursued an ambitious programme touching both doctrine and government. There was a similar growth in the use of papal legates, who often convened local councils to carry out their missions. In England there had been only one such council (in 786) before the later eleventh century, whereas between 1070 and 1312 there were more than twenty councils.

But it is the growth of papal correspondence that is most revealing. Only one letter a year survives from the pontificate of Benedict IX (1032–46). That rises under the reformist Leo IX (1049–54) to thirty-five a year. But after 1130 the acceleration is truly remarkable, according to Southern. Under Innocent II (1130–43) the annual average rises to seventy-two; under Adrian IV (1154–9) to one hundred and thirty; under Alexander III (1159–81) to one hundred and seventy-nine; under

Innocent III (1198–1215) to two hundred and eighty; under Innocent IV (1243–54) to seven hundred and thirty; and under John XXII (1316–34) to three thousand six hundred and forty-six![2]

Reformist popes did not anticipate the extent to which active papal government and church courts would draw business to Rome. Yet this happened so rapidly that the papal office itself was transformed. Legal reform and the growth of bureaucracy went hand in hand. It is worth quoting again from St Bernard's admonishing letter to his protégé Eugenius III in 1150: 'I will speak to you as Jethro spoke to Moses and say, "What is this thing you are doing to the people? Why do you sit from morning to evening listening to litigants?" What fruit is there in these things? They can only create cobwebs.' It is no accident that by the later twelfth century nearly all the popes were lawyers as well as theologians. They could hardly have dealt with the matters that came to them otherwise.

Why could the popes not govern without being overwhelmed by litigation? The development of canon law and a hierarchy of courts administering it – with the papacy at the apex – created a system that offered litigants coherence, relative predictability and other benefits. It was a system that stood in contrast to the secular courts, in which the application of customary and feudal law allowed recourse to Roman law only intermittently. But that was not all. The prospect of freedom from the pressure of local interests and magnates (whether secular lords or bishops) created an incentive to take advantage of a system of written law operating in a wider sphere. Altogether, the appeal of a legal system that was more coherent, predictable and centralized favoured the rapid growth of litigation.

We can see this in the first wave of litigation reaching the papacy after 1050. Monasteries and convents rushed in, seeking confirmation of their charters and privileges, not least, their freedom from the interference of local bishops. To be sure, their requests were often accompanied by generous gifts to the papacy, monetary and otherwise. Thus, monastic benefices more often went to papal nominees as a result. In that way an incentive was also created at the centre to entertain petitions from litigants. However, the attraction for Rome was not simply pecuniary. Tacit admissions of its claim to a plenitude of power strengthened its authority.

The habit of looking to Rome for the settlement of grievances and conferring of benefits grew apace. By the mid-twelfth century the consequence was clear. The papacy was becoming not merely the court of final appeal, but even a court of first instance for some types of litigation. Southern gives a piquant example of this judicial activism, an example that flies in the face of preconceptions about the feudal period as one marked by extreme localism. It is the example of a mid-twelfth-century dispute about rights over an English church located in the diocese of Lichfield. Did the rights of presentation to its living still belong to the canons of Evreux in Normandy? They alleged that 'their' vicar had been expelled by the earl of Worcester, who had then 'sold' on the rights of presentation to the archdeacon of Chester! In 1144 Pope Lucius II wrote to the bishop of Worcester, instructing him to take as his fellow judge the bishop of Hereford, and decide the matter:

> By the time we hear of it the case had already travelled from Normandy to Rome and from Rome to England, and now two English bishops were required to summon representatives of an earl, an archdeacon, a cathedral chapter, and two or three vicars or ex-vicars from both sides of the Channel, and settle the affair on papal authority. If we reflect on this it is very remarkable. At a time when England was in a state of acute civil war, when relations with Normandy were severed, and local powers were everywhere supreme, the pope could expect his orders to be carried out two thousand miles from Rome, in a dispute about a property worth perhaps £10 a year.[3]

At first popes made little attempt to stem the tide of litigation to Rome, even when it was at the expense of bishops' and archbishops' courts. As we have seen, the tide reinforced papal claims to a supreme legislative and judicial authority. By the thirteenth century those claims had reshaped attitudes and habits across Europe. The curia was then able to establish more graduated procedures under papal supervision.

The union of papal supremacy with canon law helped to introduce order not only into the affairs of the church but into secular life as well. Canon lawyers continued to invade the sphere of civil lawyers. It could hardly have been otherwise, for the church was interested in all the principal moments of life, from birth to burial. Through its involvement at these crucial moments of life, it left a permanent mark on the social order emerging in Europe.

Canon law helped to give a new direction to the European mind. Its systematic character and the procedures required for administering it stimulated an analytical frame of mind, leading, inexorably, to the emergence of philosophy as a discipline distinct from theology. It was not just that new standards of precise argument were encouraged. The egalitarian foundation of canon law raised questions which led to challenges to assumptions inherited from the corporate society of antiquity.

Logical studies developed with astonishing rapidity during the twelfth century. The egalitarian foundation of canon law immediately raised the question of how general terms are related to the experience of individuals, and it engendered a debate which raged for two or three centuries, the debate between 'realists' and 'nominalists'. Did general terms correspond to something with an independent existence or were they merely convenient ways of bringing together individual experiences, giving them a linguistic unity? Increasingly, general terms ceased to be understood on the model of Platonic ideas, as having a reality superior to that of mundane experience. The underpinnings of a corporate society were being removed. So it is not too much to claim that the church presided over Europe in its formative period, something that secular rulers envied, resented and learned from.

What did secular rulers learn? They learned that a system of centralized justice favoured the transition from law understood chiefly as custom (the 'discovery' or clarification of something that already exists) to law understood as the expression of a sovereign will. They learned that the concept of sovereignty offered them a means of centralizing not only authority but also power in their kingdoms, a basis for undermining 'feudal' jurisdictions. It was an irresistible offer.

But that was not all. Something else lay behind the extraordinary impact of canon law, something with less immediate appeal for secular rulers, but which had long-term consequences for their rule. Canon law introduced a new standard for legal comparison, a 'rational' basis for comparison that cast the norms of customary and feudal law into unfavourable light.

If we are to appreciate this deeper impact of canon law, we must put aside prejudices surviving from eighteenth-century anti-clericalism. To a large extent, the standards introduced into social life by canon law were more humane and equitable than those that had preceded them. For the church, the care of souls meant that attaching different values to human life, according to social status, did not govern the consideration of cases. Whether it was a question of the standards of proof required to win a case or the penalties inflicted on those who lost, canon law also moved beyond the norms preserved in customary and feudal law.

There was no question of innocence or guilt being established by the outcome of 'ordeals' – such as surviving hand-to-hand combat and submergence in water – or by the sheer weight of numbers of family and friends testifying on behalf of the plaintiff or the accused. Instead, 'rational' proof required the sifting of evidence, the probing of witnesses and written records. In this way, the roots of tribal practices that had survived from the Germanic invasions of the Roman empire were cut. The fourth Lateran Council of 1215 effectively abolished trial by ordeal by forbidding clergy to take part in them.

The church, drawing on the inheritance of Roman law, had struggled against such 'barbarous' practices since the fall of the Western empire. It had made headway as early as the Visigothic law codes, when it had distinguished the truly moral element in crime – that is, intention – from its physical aspects. But political disorders and educational decline took a heavy toll of the church itself in succeeding centuries. Only with the development of canon law in the twelfth century can we see the full extent of the church's potential for changing social attitudes and habits. Thus, basic forms of legal procedure for both civil and criminal cases were invented by canon lawyers – drawing on Roman precedents – and applied in church courts, before being adopted by secular courts in the late thirteenth century. This Romano-canonical procedure, which involved judges investigating disputed facts and required recording of evidence in writing, contributed to the emergence of what by the fourteenth century was virtually a new common law for Western Europe: a *jus commune* which fused elements of civil, canon and customary law.[4]

Not only formal legal procedures but also informal attitudes changed.

These attitudes reflect the direction given to legal change by the moral intuitions inspired by Christian beliefs. Early canonists even discussed whether the biblical injunctions in favour of equality, reciprocity and humility permitted *anyone* to act as a judge of another human being! Nothing testifies more clearly to the extent of moral change.

A late eleventh-century tract, *Concerning True and False Penance*, prescribes the proper attitudes for a judge. The judge must take the golden rule seriously, and put himself in the place of the person being examined, for attempting to understand a person's motives is also the best way of taking account of the context of action, inducing humility as well as understanding.

> For one who judges another ... condemns himself. Let him therefore know himself and purge himself of what he sees offends others ... Let him who is without sin cast the first stone (John 8.7) ... for no one is without sin in that all have been guilty of crime. Let the spiritual (that is, ecclesiastical) judge beware lest he fail to fortify himself with knowledge and thereby commit the crime of injustice. It is fitting that he should know to recognize what he is to judge.[5]

Evidently, relations of equality and reciprocity were setting a new standard of ambition. This moral vantage point fostered a mildness in canon law which distinguished it not only from customary and feudal law but also from Roman civil law.

New ideas of punishment emerged. The most striking thing about them is the extent to which they separate the need for punishment from the desire for retaliation or retribution. Instead, there is constant emphasis on penance and deterrence, an emphasis taken over from earlier monastic penitential practice. The aim of the church is to reach and stir the conscience of the offender, as well as to influence the will of others who might consider offending. 'If you study the nature of the punishments of the church, and the public penances which were its principal mode of chastisement, you will see that the chief object is to excite repentance in the soul of the culprit, and moral terror in the beholders, by example'.[6] The analogy with what are usually considered to be essentially modern, secular ideas about penal reform – conveyed by the term a 'penitentiary system' – is striking.

Another consequence of the developing system of church law and courts was more careful consideration of the difference between sin and crime.

> In the late eleventh and the twelfth centuries a sharp procedural distinction was made for the first time, between sin and crime. This happened partly because the ecclesiastical hierarchy succeeded in withdrawing from secular authorities jurisdiction over sins – thereby, incidentally, giving the word 'secular' a new meaning. Any act punishable by royal or other 'lay' officials was henceforth to be punished as a violation of secular law and not as a sin, that is, not as a violation of a law of God. When the secular authority punished for robbery, for example, it was to punish for the breach of the peace, for the protection of property, for the offence against society. In this world, it began to be said, only the church has the jurisdiction to punish for sins – thereby, incidentally, giving the word 'church' a new meaning . . .[7]

Just as intentions had scarcely been distinguished from actions in 'barbarian' justice, so the ideas of crime and sin had scarcely been separated, making it difficult, if not impossible, to distinguish social claims from religious duties.

Such distinctions made by canon lawyers began to reshape social attitudes. The claim of papal sovereignty over the church had already made it possible to create a 'spiritual' jurisdiction apart from the 'secular'. Yet the canonists soon found that they had to distinguish between two types of authority over sin. All the church could offer in the case of 'internal' sins – thoughts and desires contrary to God's will – was the consolation of its sacraments, confession, penance and absolution. By contrast, 'external sins' were those that offended against both God and the discipline of the church as a corporate body. Such sins fell under the jurisdiction of church courts applying ecclesiastical law.

In the twelfth century the philosopher Peter Abelard reinforced such canonist thinking about a sphere of conscience. Abelard's arguments reveal how the development of canon law can scarcely be separated from that of theology. He distinguished between a 'heavenly forum' of judgement – for God alone can see into hearts and minds – and the 'earthly forum' provided by ecclesiastical courts. The latter could only judge external actions. Indeed, as Berman reminds us, that conclusion rapidly became a principle of canon law: 'the church does not adjudicate matters that are hidden.' (Abelard even doubted whether the preparation of a crime that was not executed should be punished.) The canonists protected the sphere of intentions by forbidding all legal actions if they were not founded on a pre-existing law. Peter Lombard, a pupil of Abelard's who wrote *The Book of Sentences* (*circa* 1150), which became the standard theological text for centuries, formulated the underlying principle: 'there is no sin if there was no prohibition.'[8]

The concern of canon lawyers to identify and protect the role of intentions is striking. That concern is the key to a host of legal developments in the twelfth century.

> In marriage law, by the end of the twelfth century, the simple consent of two parties, without any formalities, could constitute a valid, sacramental marriage. In contract law, a mere promise could create a binding obligation – it was the intention of the promisor that counted. In criminal law, the degree of guilt and punishment was again related to the intention of the individual defendant, and this led, as in modern legal systems, to complex considerations about negligence and diminished responsibility.[9]

Canon lawyers were redefining the sphere of personal responsibility – and, at the same time, creating a sphere of personal autonomy. Choice and responsibility were being closely joined.

Take, for example, issues about marriage, the status of women and natural children. The fourth Lateran Council adopted measures to ensure that marriage was based on consent rather than coercion. In combating family pressures, canon law became far more restrictive about the degrees of cousinhood permitted to couples wishing to marry. Divorce, in turn, became more difficult. The status of women as wives and mothers gained from the protection of the church. It became more difficult for fathers to turn natural children into legitimate heirs. (When the last count of Montpellier in 1202 sought a dispensation to legitimate a natural son, so that he might inherit, Pope Innocent III denied the request.)

Just as canon lawyers cleared a new path when exploring the sphere of intentions and personal responsibility, so they became innovators when they considered the nature and grounds of association.

We have seen how, at the end of the Western empire, the role of bishops as leaders of their cities undermined the hereditary basis of civic offices. Members of the curia began to be understood as the representatives of the urban populations rather than as their masters. But while this change had some impact on late Roman law, that impact was limited by the collapse of the empire, the withering of urban life, and the importance of customary law in the new Germanic kingdoms. It was only with the papal revolution that the legal overthrow of the aristocratic basis of association and its replacement by a democratic basis was confirmed and extended. By declaring the independence of the church from secular authorities, and creating a legal system founded on belief in moral equality, canon lawyers transformed the meaning of a 'corporate' body.

Four fundamental changes in corporation law were introduced by the canonists, changes in the principles that had governed corporations in Justinian's *Corpus Juris Civilis*. Yet simply noticing these changes is not enough. What was their source? These changes followed directly from substituting the belief in moral equality for the ancient belief in natural inequality. That substitution generated the four changes. First, canonists rejected the view that only associations recognized by public authority could possess 'the privileges and liberties of corporations'. In canon law, by contrast, any group of persons organizing themselves to pursue a shared goal – whether as a guild, hospital or university – could constitute a legitimate corporation. This model of voluntary association, of association based on the individual will, can be traced back to the way monastic communities had been created. Implicit is the assumption that authority flows upwards rather than from the top down.

Secondly, the Roman view that only a public authority 'could create new law for its members and exercise judicial authority over them' was replaced by the view that any corporation 'could have legislative and judicial jurisdiction over its members'. That is, by becoming members of a corporation individuals could be deemed to have accepted its rules. The monastic model impinged here too. For the model of voluntary association was joined to the idea of self-government, the principle of electing superiors (just as monks elected their abbot) as the representatives of the community. The authority of superiors thus became a delegated authority. Authority is again understood as flowing upwards.

The third change reveals that reversal in the lines of authority even more dramatically. The canonists 'rejected the Roman view that a corporation could only act through its representatives and not through the ensemble of its members'. Instead, canonists insisted that in making some decisions corporations were bound to seek the consent of their members. But here speaking of 'representatives', when referring to the maxim in Roman law, confuses the issue. For the reference is to officers whose authority was not delegated by members of the corporation; rather, it was a birthright or bestowed by imperial authority. Such officers were *not* representatives.

The reaction to that aristocratic view of the nature of a corporation – as constituted from above – also explains the fourth change made by canonists. They rejected the maxim in Roman law that 'what pertains to a corporation does not pertain to its members'. By contrast, canon lawyers took the view that the property of a corporation was the 'common property' of its members, with both the advantages and liabilities that entailed for each member; it did not belong to its officers, to dispose of as they saw fit.[10]

The overturning of these Roman law maxims provides the clearest possible evidence of the way canon lawyers rejected the aristocratic assumptions underlying Roman law. It reveals how creative they were. At times a majority principle for decision-making seems to be emerging. Canon law was not simply parasitic on Roman law. Canonists promoted an understanding of the corporation as a voluntary association of individuals who remain the source of its authority, rather than as a body constituted by superior authority and wholly dependent on that authority for its identity.

It was a model of association that presaged a new world. Altogether, canon law gave a new direction to the European mind. The systematic character of canon law and the procedures required for administering it stimulated philosophical thought, contributing to its separation from theology. Not only did canonist argument encourage new standards of precision. The egalitarian foundation of canon law suggested questions which led to challenges to terms and assumptions inherited from the corporate society of the ancient world.

We should not underestimate the significance of the philosophical debate which would rage for three centuries between 'realists' and 'nominalists'. What was at issue – the status of general terms – had profound social implications. Did general categories correspond to a superior reality on the model of Platonic ideas or were they effectively human constructions and tools? Were humans meant to be governed by Plato's 'guardians' or by themselves? Under the banner of 'nominalism', the assumption of moral equality was advancing.

18

The Democratizing of Reason

Changes initiated by the papacy from 1000 to 1300 laid the foundation for a new type of society. They were revolutionary changes. Yet it has taken a long time to recognize them as such. Why were they so long underestimated?

They used to be described as the 'Gregorian reforms'. Yet that description can be misleading, by giving too much credit to one pope, and failing to make clear that the reform movement began before Gregory became pope and continued long after his pontificate. It also fails to make clear the profound impact of these reforms outside the church, their impact on secular government. A more recent description – the 'twelfth-century renaissance' – can also miss the full nature of the changes under way. Often it focuses on cultural developments at the expense of institutional changes. Moreover, describing these developments as a 'rebirth' misses their originality. It gives too much credit to classical sources and underestimates the role of the church.

There is much to be said for another description, the 'papal revolution', introduced by Harvard's Harold Berman. Yet even that does not quite get to the heart of the matter. For what made the papal revolution so dynamic that it began to transform secular government as well? What was it about the legal system created by the church and founded on theology that gave it such subversive potential? The deeper source was the invention of the individual, the introduction of a primary social role which began to undercut the radical differences of status and treatment 'carried' by traditional social roles. The equality of status defined into that new role sent Europe along a road which no human society had previously followed.

Under way was nothing less than a reconstruction of the self, along lines more consistent with Christian moral intuitions. For the new sense of justice – introduced first into canon law and later into civil law – privileged equality and reciprocity. In that way, the 'golden rule' began to transform the socializing process. It threatened the social stratification we know as feudalism almost from its outset. What ultimately superseded feudalism was a new social role shared by all equally, the individual.

Promoted by papal reforms, the translation of a moral status (the 'soul') into a social role recast the basis of thought and action in Europe. As that translation spread from the church into the secular sphere – with the first steps that would lead to the creation of nation-states – it changed the relations of Europeans with themselves. It gave thought and action a character that they did not and could not possess in traditional societies. Translating a moral status into a social role created a new image of society as an association of individuals rather than of families, tribes or castes. The claim of papal 'sovereignty' made that translation possible. For the claim of equal subjection to a sovereign authority has a remarkable implication. No subject of a sovereign has an intrinsic obligation to obey any other person as such. So the right to command or duty to obey is no longer written into separate hereditary or customary roles. The appearance of a sovereign authority distances agents from other roles they happen to occupy. It turns them into role-bearers, agents whose identity is not exhausted by their other roles. They are invited to develop wills of their own and become individuals.

Papal sovereignty thus promoted an identity at odds with the roles associated with feudalism, sowing the seeds for an eventual conflict of identity. By introducing an attribute shared by all equally, papal sovereignty and canon law allowed a general presumption in favour of equality to enter. They weakened – in the event, fatally – the ancient presumption that inequalities of status and treatment need no justification, for they are 'natural' and unavoidable.

Such a reversal of assumptions opened the prospect of a new transparency in social relations. The substitution of moral equality for natural inequality paved the way for new forms of comparison, comparisons that Christian thought had hitherto confined to the afterlife, to the ultimate fate of souls. As we have seen in the advice given to judges, this substitution encouraged people to understand themselves through others and others through themselves. Once legitimated, the process of comparison became an almost irresistible source of social change, breeding both hope and resentment, ambition and insecurity. It provided the recipe for a new type of society, a society that would be restless and progressive – a society that would one day challenge the 'privileges' of the church itself. The pontiffs and canon lawyers who promoted the papal revolution are unlikely to have foreseen all the implications of their reforms.

In societies resting on the assumption of natural inequality, the process of comparison is inhibited. For that assumption raises impervious shields around unequal assigned identities; it does not introduce the claims of a common humanity or, with them, the pursuit of moral transparency. Canon law, by contrast, promoted such transparency through provisions for marriage, property and inheritance. Consent and free will provided the basis for rules in each area. In the case of marriage, consent was required at every step: for betrothal, for the formalities of marriage and for its physical consummation. The church made careful provision for annulment, if marriage was founded on mistaken identity, fraud or coercion. It sought to protect the married woman. 'Before God the two parties to marriage were equal and this doctrine of equality was first taught by Christianity. In practice it meant, above all, that obligations, especially that of fidelity, were mutual.'[1] Nor was that all. Feudal magnates who looked on their wards merely as valuable property to be disposed of, came up against the church's insistence on consent. And in the case of the rules governing inheritance, an overriding concern in Germanic custom and Roman law to perpetuate the family as a unit was modified to respect the individual testator's wishes, for the 'protection of his soul'. As a consequence, the 'testament' became a 'will', a term evoking the individual.[2]

Such rules projected and privileged the image of society as an association of individuals, each endowed with conscience and free will. By creating 'universal' claims and thus fostering the habit of comparison, canon law also provided a model for the growth of secular authorities able and willing to promote such claims.

Popes were well aware of the depth of moral change they were promoting, even if they did not foresee many of its consequences. By the thirteenth century Innocent III could marvel at the rapidity of change. 'How jurisdiction first began I do not know unless perhaps God assigned to some person or persons to do justice to criminals or unless in the beginning the father of a family had complete jurisdiction over his family by the law of nature, though now he has it only in a few minor matters.' Thanks to the doctrine of papal sovereignty, the connotations of 'nature' were changing. Appeals to 'nature' were increasingly associated with equality, that is, with the basic claims of individuals. 'But it may be said, that kings are to be treated differently from others. We, however, know that it is written in the divine law, "You shall judge the great as well as the little and there shall be no difference of persons".'[3]

Through the impress of Christian beliefs on canon law, differences of status no longer seemed to reflect an objective natural order. In church courts, such differences seemed less important than the everyday reality of choice and human sin, matters that in local churches were constantly called to mind by homilies about the Last Judgement. Invoking a day of judgement testified to the reality of human freedom (something also implied by the church's constant struggle against vulgar forms of determinism such as belief in astrology, the stars' control over human destiny). That emphasis on the judgement of individual souls generated – during the twelfth and the thirteenth centuries – a new belief in the 'purging' of individual sins during a transitional period after death ('purgatory') but before the apocalyptic Last Judgement. A touch of freedom thus invaded even the afterlife.[4]

The undermining of traditional identities and practices went very deep. Drawing on the vision of a better world (where the equality of souls prevailed and virtuous choice would gather its proper reward), canon law helped to transform thought itself. Evidence of this transformation in the twelfth and thirteenth centuries is abundant and startling. As we have seen, generalization became both interesting and plausible, in a way that was scarcely possible in societies founded on the belief in natural inequality. The image of society as an association of individuals made shared traits, actual or potential, a far more important subject for speculation. The habit of generalizing helped to strengthen, in turn, the faculty of abstraction, of searching out, bringing together and labelling common attributes.

We can see this if we look at the changes in Roman law introduced by twelfth-century canonists. Berman has emphasized how Roman law was distrustful of and, indeed, avoided abstractions. It was radically case-bound, and sought only to find the right answer to particular legal questions. It derived particular rules from cases, but not general principles. The habitual turn of the canonist mind was different. It sought to identify the shared features of particular legal decisions and raise them to the level of a concept. Behind the rules it sought to identify principles. This urge for abstraction was generated by the new image of society promoted by the doctrine of papal sovereignty. It meant that canon lawyers brought to bear not just legal techniques they acquired from the study of Roman law, but a 'democratized' interest in generalization and abstraction, an interest combining knowledge of Aristotelian logic with Christian moral intuitions.[5]

Ancient Roman jurists had gradually adopted Greek methods of classification but had restricted them to a particular context – quoting the jurist Paul who insisted that 'by means of a rule a short account of matters is passed on and . . . if it is inaccurate in any respect, it loses its effect'. Such rules were therefore not general. Roman lawyers resisted attempts to make logical consistency the basis of a jurisprudential system. It is easy to understand why Roman lawyers resisted as they did. Their conception of society – which took radical differences of status for granted – impeded the process of generalizing, making it seem almost pointless.

From the late eleventh century onwards, however, the students of rediscovered Roman law brought a new attitude of mind to bear.

> The western European jurists of the eleventh and twelfth centuries carried the Greek dialectic to a much higher level of abstraction. They attempted to systematize the rules into an integrated whole – not merely to define elements common to a particular species of cases but also to synthesize the rules into principles and the principles themselves into an entire system, a body of law . . .[6]

The difference sprang from the new concern that law should be understood as applying to 'all (souls) equally'. Hence it needed to be systematic.

Formal equality of status made generalizing and abstraction seem 'natural'.

Theology led the way. Both directly and indirectly through its influence on canon law, theology shaped dialectical reasoning in the twelfth century. Early in the twelfth century Abelard's *Sic et Non* (*Yes and No*) suggested a framework for analysis, soon to be reinforced by Peter Lombard's *Sentences*, the standard textbook for systematic theology. Both promoted a 'dialectical' form of reasoning, comparing the arguments for and against particular propositions.

Theological argument and legal argument interacted and created a common discipline. The habit of generalizing, from the bottom up, into a system of coherent propositions or principles – and then applying those principles, from the top down, to examples or cases – began to create a distinctive mind-set. It involved the analysis of logical and textual inconsistencies, while fostering attempts at synthesis. The full title of Gratian's *Decretum – A Concordance of Discordant Canons* – perfectly illustrates this new problem-solving approach.

Thinking about basic Christian doctrine lent itself to this model of argument. For if faith was the result of revelation and therefore 'given', the task of reason was to explore it and try to understand it, not to dictate its content. Thinkers became much less inclined than in the ancient world to assume that reason, merely from its own resources, could dictate conclusions about the nature of things. Instead, those results had to be compared with the contents of faith in order to root out anomalies and inconsistencies, as in Abelard's *Sic et Non*. This form of dialectical reasoning in theology helped, in turn, to shape legal argument.

If the constraint of faith contributed to a more experimental understanding of the role of reason, that new understanding was soon extended to other matters. For twelfth-century canonists had to balance their Christian moral intuitions with a complex and often conflicting inheritance of Germanic customs, Roman law and Greek philosophy. Little could be taken for granted in the face of such diverse beliefs and the practices they sustained. Yet creating a legal system for the church made finding such a common ground indispensable. Aristocratic, theocratic and imperial traditions had to be 'tamed' and reconciled with the moral intuitions generated by Christian beliefs. In order to find common ground for discussion, lawyers, both civil and canon, paid careful attention to assumptions and definitions. For specifying such assumptions and definitions helped to make possible a more widely shared conversation across Europe. During the twelfth century that conversation acquired an institutional nexus, with the emergence of universities at Bologna, Paris, Montpellier and Oxford. Theological and legal argument thus shaped each other, giving rise to what later came to be described as the 'scholastic method' – a method that made reasoning more precise yet also more tentative, gathering evidence in order to test the validity of arguments and generalize the results.

What we are encountering is a decisive transition. 'Reason' (understood as a faculty commanding reality and very unequally distributed in society) was giving way to 'reason' (understood as an attribute of individuals who are equally moral agents). In the twelfth century, reason began to lose the ontologically privileged position it had been accorded by an aristocratic society. Its propositions were open, at least in principle, to equal scrutiny, grounded in a shared faith. (Did not St Bernard complain that under Abelard's influence matters of the faith were being discussed at the crossroads?) The role of reason was being democratized. Reason ceased to be something that used people, and became something people used.

This democratizing of reason was a stupendous achievement – and it rested on that understanding of society as an association of individuals 'carried' by the papal revolution. That becomes clear if we look at three questions widely debated in the course of the twelfth century: the meaning of natural law, the grounds of political obligation and the status of abstract ideas. The debates developing around each of these three questions reveal the development of a more analytical, less status-governed intelligence in Europe.

Appealing to 'nature' or natural law (*jus naturale*) as the foundation of justice rapidly became standard for the canonists. For example, they defended the new forms of legal procedure designed to permit a fair trial in those terms, as something that was required by 'nature' rather than merely by custom or positive law. But this was no longer 'nature' as understood by the ancient Stoics. The canonists' egalitarian concern for individual conscience and free will led them gradually to recast natural law as a system of natural rights: pre-social or moral rights inhering in the individual. In that way, the canonists converted the primordial Christian concern with 'innerness' into the language of law.

That conversion laid the foundation of modern liberalism.

When the canonists drew on the Stoic doctrine of natural law, they adapted a language that had been a means of speculation about social conventions rather than an instrument of moral reformation. By contrast, canonists invested this language with urgent moral content. Almost instinctively, they introduced into it a strong distributive principle, the golden rule. As we have seen in Gratian's *Decretum*, equality and reciprocity – the claims of individuals – were its hallmarks.

The assumption of moral equality gave rise, in turn, to the claim for equal liberty. For if humans have an equal moral standing, then it follows that there must be an area in which their choices ought to be respected. Otherwise, what is the point of having a moral capacity?[7] Canonists commenting on the *Decretum* – the Decretists – perceived a connection between Gratian's concern for the role of conscience and St Paul's emphasis on 'Christian liberty'. Did not Gratian insist that the rights of liberty could never be renounced, even if a man were enslaved?

Gratian and the Decretists began to argue that all humans have an intrinsic moral nature, which confers on each person licit pre-social claims, claims prior to custom and positive law. So the canonists moved away from the idea of a preordained external ordering of things – with its implicit emphasis on 'fate' – to the assertion of subjective right, the right of individuals. Instead of associating 'nature' with an objective and harmonious hierarchy ('everything in its place'), they interpreted it as a force or power inherent in human personality. The result was a conception of natural right that privileged human freedom.

The idea of natural right formalized in legal terms the egalitarian moral vision that had shaped Paul's conception of the Christ and had been elaborated by Augustine, leading the latter to reject the hierarchical assumptions underpinning ancient thought, temptations of pride which he considered to be subversive of the 'city of God'. Paul and Augustine had drawn on Jewish tradition, with its emphasis on the commands of God (the Torah), to revise the ancient association of rationality with inequality. For them, God's will was to be discovered 'within' each and every self, demanding and making possible a conscientious response, a moralized will. By associating 'right reason' with individual will, Paul and Augustine put forward a 'democratic' vision of rationality. Rationality lost its association with hierarchy. Instead, through its association with the conscience and will of the individual, rationality gave a new dignity to the human self, the gift and burden of freedom.

Paul and Augustine transformed Jewish belief in a divine will directed at a 'chosen' people. They universalized the claims of that will and internalized it, making it available to all of humanity. In doing so, they created the potential for 'Christian liberty', a rightful power for individuals. By combining the assumption of human equality with the need to discover the divine will, a new relationship with deity became possible, one that was personal rather than tribal. Yet if Paul and Augustine conjured up a vision of moral freedom, it was the twelfth-century canonists who converted that vision into a formal legal system founded on natural rights.

It is only recently that the origins of the idea of natural rights have been traced to twelfth-century canon law. Previously, those origins were assigned to the later middle ages or the early modern period. But Brian Tierney has demonstrated that twelfth-century canonists were the originators. The story he tells is fascinating.[8]

Arguments about the meaning of natural law (*jus naturale*) developed rapidly among Gratian's commentators, for they noticed the confusions resulting from different uses of the term. They soon moved away from the Stoic sense of an objective, external order. But they also became dissatisfied with Gratian's definition of natural law as a set of moral precepts, founded on scripture but discernible by reason. They were anxious to anchor natural law, unequivocally, in individual agency. So they began to use the term to refer to a subjective force or power intrinsic to man, and to a corresponding sphere of freedom, where action is neither commanded nor forbidden by 'nature'.

In about 1160 the canonist Rufinus elaborated this new and important version of jus naturale as rightful power. 'Natural jus is a certain force instilled in every creature by nature to do good.'[9] That rightful power implied, in turn, an area of individual liberty. So Rufinus distinguished the commands and prohibitions of nature from an area of variability ('demonstrations'), where appeal to the idea of nature did not rule out different conclusions (for example, property to be held 'in common' or privately). This new category staked out and protected an area of liberty. 'Natural jus consists in three things, commands, prohibitions and demonstrations. It cannot be detracted from at all as regards the commands and prohibitions . . . but it can be as regards the demonstrations, which nature does not command or forbid . . .'[10] Understood in that way, natural law or jus ceased to be a relatively simple set of 'dos and don'ts'. It was a crucial innovation, for it created a sphere where choice was authorized. Authorizing a range of choices created 'an area of permissiveness where rights could licitly be exercised'. The idea of a right entailed such an area of choice.

Increasingly, the canonists insisted on the role of choice. Odo of Dover commented in about 1170 that 'natural jus is a certain force divinely inspired in man by which he is led to choose what is right and equitable'. And in the English *In nomine*, we find that 'natural jus is a certain ability by which man is able to discern between good and evil, and in this sense natural jus is a faculty . . . and this is free will'.[11]

By the 1180s the sphere of freedom was identified as a sphere where the rightful claims of the individual could be exercised or not:

> Jus naturale . . . licit and approved, neither commanded nor forbidden by the Lord or any statute . . . as for instance to reclaim one's own or not, to eat something or not to eat it, to put away an unfaithful wife or not to put her away . . . whence, upon the words of the Apostle, 'All things are licit for me', Ambrose commented, 'by the law of nature' [*lege naturae*].[12]

The trend was clear. Individual agency was becoming the ground of natural law.

By the later twelfth century some commentators had moved a long way from Gratian.

> Many Decretists included a definition of jus naturale as a kind of subjective force or power inherent in human personality, along with many other definitions. But the greatest of them all, Huguccio, was unusual in insisting that this was the one primary and proper meaning of the term. According to his definition, 'natural jus is called reason, namely

a natural force of the soul . . .' Huguccio added that, in a second sense, the term could be used to refer to the moral laws known through reason, which could be summed up in the scriptural rule 'Do not do to others what you do not want done to yourself'.[13]

What is truly remarkable is the way that Huguccio then turns his argument against Gratian. For it reveals how the assumption of moral equality was leading canonists to anchor reason in individual agency rather than in the external world. Huguccio argues that the second sense – moral laws or precepts – is *not* really a proper definition of natural *jus*. 'We ought to say that moral precepts are effects of natural jus or derive from natural jus rather than that they are natural jus.'[14]

What lay behind this dramatic move? The ancient doctrine of natural law was being revised to take account of belief in the incarnation, the idea that 'God is with us'. For that belief removed the previous radical divide between divine agency (whether in the form of the 'gods' of polytheism or the Old Testament's Yahweh) and human agency. The idea of the incarnation is the root of Christian egalitarianism. It lies behind the transformation of the ancient doctrine of natural law into a theory of natural rights. For the idea of the incarnation suggested that deity is not something remote from human agency but rather something intrinsic to its rightful exercise. The fourteenth-century theologian Jean Gerson summarized this development: '*Natural Dominium* is a gift of God by which a creature has the right [*jus*] immediately from God to take inferior things for his use and preservation.'[15] The divine logos or 'word' ceased to be an external constraint and became instead the means of human liberation.

If insisting on a sphere of permissiveness – where the agent is free to choose responsibly – was the first step taken by the canonists, the second was to identify specific natural rights. This did not happen overnight. Nor were their arguments always consistent. In particular, there was ambiguity about the consequences of conflicts between human laws and natural rights. Although Gratian had asserted that if human laws conflict with natural jus they are invalid, he had not really worked out the implications. Yet Tierney is able to say that by 1300 a number of particular rights were regularly defended in terms of natural *jus*. 'They would include rights to property, rights of consent to government, rights of self-defence, rights of infidels, marriage rights, procedural rights.' Moreover, the first steps were taken to give those rights teeth, by making them enforceable against positive law.

How did a form of 'judicial review' emerge? The canonists defined as fundamental the right of self-preservation, a right that could be defended even against ordinary property rights. And they developed the idea by focusing on the role of intention. Huguccio led the way, redefining 'theft' so that a poor man was not guilty of theft if he took something from its owner believing that the owner would accept his genuine 'need' for it. But Huguccio went much further. He rejected the conventional view that the 'common ownership' held up as good by a 'demonstration' of natural *jus* referred to a primitive condition that had been superseded by human law and divine commandments permitting private property (for example, 'thou shall not steal'):

> When it is said that by natural jus all things are common ... this is the meaning. By natural jus, that is, in accordance with the judgement of reason, all things are common, that is they are to be shared with the poor in time of need. For reason naturally leads us to suppose that we should keep only what is necessary and distribute what is left to the needy.[16]

So Huguccio redefined the word 'common' to mean 'common ... that is ... to be shared'. Tierney concludes, rightly, that the canonists were coming to understand property as a social institution that was both private and public, creating individual entitlements but also carrying an obligation to share with others 'in time of need'. One of the Decretists would even go so far as to argue that a man in need could 'declare his right for himself'!

But declaration is one thing, enforcement quite another. Could such rightful claims be enforced? Even Huguccio doubted that they could. In his view, 'many things are owed that cannot be sought by judicial procedure, such as dignities, dispensations and alms ... but they can be sought as something due mercifully for the sake of God and piety'.[17] Yet his successors were more determined. In the thirteenth century canonists created a legal procedure for making such claims enforceable. The bishop's court was invested with the right to intervene through a process called 'evangelical denunciation', a process enabling a person in extreme need to appeal for help as his 'natural right' to the bishop's jurisdiction. The bishop could then require the rich to give alms, on pain of excommunication. By incorporating this procedure into the standard textbook on the *Decretum*, 'a judicial sanction for the rights of the poor' emerged.[18]

The development of such natural rights claims both reflected and reinforced the new view of reason, a view associating it with human agency, with choice and upright intentions, and providing a basis for social intervention that makes it the ancestor of the modern welfare state. The same 'modern' associations can be glimpsed in two other areas of twelfth-century debate.

It is hardly accidental that one of the earliest examples of a contractual model for understanding the proper relationship between rulers and ruled – what in later centuries would be called social contract theory – had emerged by the late eleventh century. Once the focus of obligation was the soul or individual conscience, it seemed to follow that political obligation presupposed an element of choice or election. Writing to defend Pope Gregory VII's deposition of Emperor Henry IV, Manegold of Lautenbach argued that the authority of a king was conditional:

> For the people do not exalt him above themselves so as to concede to him an unlimited power of tyrannizing over them, but to defend themselves against the tyranny and wickedness of others. However, when he who is chosen to repress evil-doers and defend the just begins to cherish evil in himself, to oppress good men, to exercise over his subjects the cruel tyranny that he ought to ward off from them, is it not clear that he deservedly falls from the dignity conceded to him and that the people are free from his lordship and from subjection to him since it is evident that he first broke the compact by virtue of which he was appointed?[19]

Here the 'compact' being broken was not a feudal one. It was not the betrayal of the reciprocal obligations created by vassalage. Rather, Manegold is concerned with a ruler's obligations to the generality of his subjects – 'the people' – even while he assumed that magnates would play an important role in enforcement. If Manegold's inspiration came from any contemporary practice, it is likely to have come from the monastic practice of electing an abbot who was expected to act as both a father and the servant of his monks. In any case, one thing about such an early example of a contractual model for political obligation is clear. It reveals how the image of society as an association of individuals was acquiring increasing influence over minds.

Another, third area in which the new image of society and its impact on rationality can be glimpsed by the early twelfth century is philosophical argument, for this period sees philosophy growing out of the tutelage of theology. The dominant figure was the brilliant, combative logician Peter Abelard. His insistence that all knowledge is open to re-examination expanded the new analytical approach shaping civil and canon law. 'By collecting contrasting divergent opinion, I hope to provoke young readers to push themselves to the limit in the search for truth, so that their wits may be sharpened by their investigation. It is by doubting that we come to investigate, and by investigating that we recognize the truth.'[20] Abelard liked to provoke conventional minds by insisting that 'the Lord (Jesus) said "I am truth", not "I am custom"!'

Abelard especially began to probe the relations between words and things. His thinking was stimulated by the canonists' attempt to derive principles or maxims from different types of legal decision, in order to create a system of law. He began to worry about the status of such maxims, learning from Aristotle (by way of the writings of Boethius) that maxims were maximum or 'universal' propositions from which the conclusions of syllogisms could be drawn. Such statements of logical entailment differ from statements of fact. In the former, as Abelard put it, 'the truth of the antecedent requires the truth of the consequent'.

But did universal propositions merely summarize meanings of propositions they implied or were they 'real' in their own right? Was 'a universal term' (*nomen*) also 'an individual thing' (*res*)? Abelard contributed to the growing attack on the 'realist' interpretation, refusing to attribute an external reality to classes defined by shared characteristics. Instead, Abelard insisted that 'universals are names (*nomina*) invented by the mind to express the similarities or relationships among individual things belonging to a class'.[21] Abelard did not doubt the reality of things. But he emphasized that the process of abstraction simplifies the complex world of things. The relations between things are concepts. 'When I hear *man* a certain figure arises in my mind which is so related to individual men that it is common to all and proper to none.' Thus, general terms or concepts abridge the world of things. They do not exist as one thing among others.

This preoccupation with the difference between 'words' and 'things' was no mere accident. The Christian preoccupation with 'innerness' and human agency – an intensified awareness of the difference between 'inner' and 'outer' experience, between the will and the senses – contributed to a veritable outburst of logical studies in the twelfth and the thirteenth centuries. It reflected a growing distrust of the coercive potential of general terms or concepts, if an extra-mental reality is attributed to them. Distinguishing the constructive role of the human mind from information provided by the senses gave nascent European philosophy a quite different flavour from ancient philosophy. The movement it eventually generated – 'nominalism' – would exemplify the more analytical, less status-governed intelligence released by the papal revolution.

Classes or categories were deemed to organize the experience of individual minds, to give them a 'handle' on the world. This was a far cry from the ultra-realist position associated with Plato's doctrine of 'forms' deemed to be more real than mere sense experience, a view which early medieval thinkers often associated (less fairly) with Aristotle too. Yet Abelard distanced himself from Aristotle too. For it is hardly too much to say that, through his analysis of the relationship between words and things, Abelard initiated a process which would ultimately lead to the purging of explanations in terms of intentions ('final causes') from our understanding of the physical, non-human world. The claims of reason were being redrawn.

In refusing to give classes or categories a higher status than individual, discrete experiences of things – by making classes abridgements rather than coercive – Abelard helped to shape the outlook of his contemporaries. In his work, we can see the image of society as an association of individuals contributing to a new philosophical departure: definitions imposed by reason create concepts and logical entailment, whereas knowledge of the external world is contingent, based on the experience of individual things. Abelard's account of knowledge had an important future ahead of it, one that would reinforce the democratizing of reason.

19

Steps towards the Creation of
Nation-States

The papal revolution turned the church into a self-governing corporation, a quasi-state. And this had remarkable consequences. It is now time to look more carefully at the impact of the system of canon law on other forms of government.

We have seen how fearful the church had become about losing its independence and even its identity, as a result of what were deemed to be the encroachments of dukes, counts and other feudal magnates – rulers who treated church property and positions as part of their own domains. By turning itself into a distinct corporate body governed by its own laws, the church had sought to identify and protect its 'rightful' domain, the government of souls. This, in turn, led the papacy into conflict with German emperors who had preserved a Carolingian entente between secular and sacred claims. But in asserting and defending its own exclusive domain, the papacy helped to define another domain.

By claiming a monopoly of authority over spiritual matters, the church withdrew central religious responsibility from other forms of government. It redefined their role, withdrawing their right to govern the sacred. Instead, their central role became that of keeping the peace and protecting property rights. In that way, the difference between secular and spiritual spheres – implicit in Christian thinking from the outset – became explicit and practical. Through the creation of a legal system for the church, it acquired teeth. Christian dualism no longer referred simply to the difference between the moral claims of 'this' world and the 'next': it became anchored in the institutions of this world. The development of canon law led to the creation of an administration centralized in the papacy and a hierarchical system of church courts.

The contrast between this centralization in the church and the localized, incoherent pattern of secular governments began to create new ambitions in secular rulers, who were, after all, often advised by clerics trained in the new canon law and able to draw on direct experience of centralized papal government. The increasing coherence of church government came to pose a challenge to secular rulers. Should they not strive to achieve something like the same coherence, by centralizing authority in their governments? A desire to emulate papal centralization became nothing less than a passion in many secular rulers during the twelfth and thirteenth centuries. It is the consequences of that passion that we must explore. But, first, we must notice the predicament of the secular sphere when compared to that of the church.

The Cluniac reforms and the papal revolution had been able to draw on a deep, if only latent, sense of unity in the church. By contrast, there was little if any sense of unity in the secular sphere. For in that sphere pluralism was the outstanding, recalcitrant fact. That pluralism emerged, not least, in disagreements about the meaning of 'law'. Until the papal revolution, the idea of 'law' in Western Europe covered a very unstable mixture of moral precept, custom and legal innovation. But now the papal claim of a sovereign authority, underpinning the new system of canon law, began to force clearer distinctions on both thought and action. The traditional phrases borrowed from Pope Gelasius contrasting 'papal authority' with 'royal power' – as well as references to the need for 'two swords' from the Gospel of Luke – suddenly seemed little better than clichés.

For, despite these traditional phrases and the moral intuitions behind them, the truth was that before the papal revolution spiritual and temporal authority in Europe had been so mixed as to be difficult to separate. Kings had come to understand their role in sacral terms, while emperors had often made and unmade popes. The papal revolution changed that. It pointed towards the de-sacralizing of kingship and of all secular government. It was in that sense that the church created the secular realm.

But could the secular realm imitate the legal and administrative reforms conjured up by the papal revolution? It was far from clear that it could, for the secular sphere included utterly divergent forms of government and law. It included kingship (which often looked back with nostalgia on the Roman claim of imperium), feudal magnates both great and minor whose claims were based on custom and force, manorial practices with a similar basis, new towns or boroughs with a form of self-government more oligarchic than democratic, and, finally, rules governing trade, a mixture of custom and urban legislation.

The diversity was dizzying rather than dazzling. It posed a formidable challenge to rulers who wished to emulate the papal revolution. Incoherence, disorder, recourse to violence: by the twelfth century all of these things betrayed the inability of Western European feudalism to organize itself into a unified legal system. Nonetheless, if unity on the model of papal government of the church was to be created, the only plausible contenders were kings. For their traditional identity was by far the most inclusive. It embraced memories of Roman imperium, the Carolingian empire, at least nominal feudal overlordship and, frequently, patronage of the new boroughs or towns.

The legal and administrative model held up by the church rapidly became a matter of both 'emulation and competition' for kings. In the long run, that emulation and competition led to the creation of the European nation-state. It led to kings claiming a 'sovereign' authority modelled on that claimed by the popes. But this did not happen suddenly or easily. Would-be sovereigns had to overcome major obstacles, both practical and intellectual.

Feudalism had reduced kingship in France (the German emperors, too, were losing power) to hardly more than a symbol, while the effective reins of government were in the hands of feudal magnates related, through vassalage and homage, in such a complex web of privileges and obligations that it could hardly be called a 'system'. Even in England, where a more centralized form of feudalism emerged after the Norman Conquest, the power of the crown was soon constrained by the alliance of feudatories. Nor were kings and feudal magnates the only rivals. The growth of urban centres and trade led to a kind of insurrection across Western Europe of 'burgs' or 'boroughs' seeking the right of self-government from their local lords, whether bishops or feudal. Urban autonomy served, in turn, to draw serfs seeking enfranchisement away from the countryside. It stimulated the growth of conventions governing trade at a distance and, locally, often had a subversive impact on the government of manors.

All these contending institutions claimed legitimacy in the name of 'the law'. Yet their conception of law was still rooted more in custom rather than in anything like legislative enactment, so assimilating their customs and pretensions to the model of a unified legal system posed enormous problems. For, as we have seen, the papal model represented an intellectual revolution, a conception of jurisdiction over individuals rather than groups. Administrative hierarchy developed at the expense of social hierarchy. Nor was that all. The papal model presented the sovereign as essentially a lawmaker. Law, that is, became the expression of a sovereign will (even if that will was assumed to be subordinate to natural and divine law). Legislative enactment or 'fiat' overturned 'custom' – traditional social practices – as the criterion of law 'properly so-called'. Thus, legal innovation no longer had to masquerade as the 'rediscovery' of neglected custom. Rather, it became the crux of government, the heart of a sovereign authority.

Applying the papal model to secular government had another striking consequence. It gave kingship a more territorial basis. At the risk of oversimplifying, the 'king of the Franks' became the 'king of France'. In the past, kings had been related only indirectly to their peoples. They had governed through a series of lordships and status differences, that is, through intermediaries (whether feudal, ecclesiastical, tribal or paternal). Indeed, that chain of intermediaries defined the kingdom. But applying the papal model broke the chain. 'The king was no longer primarily chief warrior of the clan (or federation of clans) and chief baron in the feudal hierarchy.'[1] He became a sovereign over a well-defined territory inhabited by his subjects, individuals.

The development of the French monarchy in the twelfth and thirteenth centuries illustrates this. From its near eclipse under the first Capetian kings at the turn of the millennium, royal power spread from a restricted area in the Île de France across an ever-increasing area of what became France. By the reign of Louis VII it was clear that royal jurisdiction was growing on the basis of a new title and claim. No longer was it the elected military kingship of the Germanic tribes. Nor did it hark back to Roman imperium or theocratic royalty. Rather, Capetian kings increased their sway by acting as intermediaries and defenders of the 'public weal', at times playing off the claims of feudatories against each other, at other times sponsoring new urban insurrections against feudal 'oppressors', and at most times seeking to create and extend a sphere of general legislation. The cause of justice with which Capetian kings identified themselves had thus a distinctly new, individuated flavour.

That is how the model of authority inspired by the papal revolution undermined a corporate conception of society. It fed a desire in rulers to overcome difficult, often uncontrollable intermediaries. Yet the pluralism of European society posed a formidable obstacle to realizing such an ambition. Imposing a common measure on that pluralism was no easy matter for would-be sovereigns. They could only set limits on traditional attitudes and jurisdictions in a step-by-step process, a process which amounted to presenting themselves as arbiters, which is why Guizot described them as 'justices of the peace'. They profited from the new egalitarian sense of justice lurking in the papal model of a unified legal system, providing its ultimate basis of coherence. So in emulating that model, would-be sovereigns also helped to propagate the new sense of justice. This explains not only how kings came to redefine their own role, but also how the different mentalities associated with the pluralism of European society began to be fused.

It is difficult for us to re-enter a social world where so little was shared. It is true that, at least ostensibly, Christian beliefs provided a common denominator. But beyond that, what? In the twelfth century each group – whether of feudatories, serfs or townspeople – was a world unto itself. People did not locate themselves in a world of commonality. That provided the deepest challenge to the moral revolution 'carried' by canon law and the papal revolution.

Thus, the first step would-be sovereigns had to take was intellectual. They had to come to terms with the nature of papal pretensions. While the papacy was helping to define the secular sphere by asserting a monopoly of authority over spiritual matters, the popes – encouraged by their location at the original centre of the Roman empire – also claimed a 'universal' jurisdiction. What did this mean? Could it be reconciled with a claim by secular kings to be 'sovereigns' in their own right, the claim increasingly recognized and defended, not least by the influential thirteenth-century theologian Thomas Aquinas?

The bishops of Rome were now obliged to consider the meaning of their claim to a universal jurisdiction far more carefully.

We can see that if we examine the thinking of the formidable canon lawyer turned pope, Innocent IV. For this pope helped to resolve an issue that had lain dormant for centuries, an issue that had not really been faced by those who relied on the rhetoric of the 'care of souls' from the time of Gregory the Great, through Carolingian times and into the eleventh century. Did only Christians have souls? Were moral claims generated by belief in the equality of souls in God's eyes restricted to those who have been baptized in the Christian faith and entered the church? Christian rulers had often seemed to work on that assumption. Charlemagne's furious massacre of Saxon 'heathens' had not, apparently, troubled his conscience. As both lawyer and pope, Innocent IV approached the issue through a particular question. How do infidels stand in relation to the papal claim of a universal jurisdiction?

Innocent reached his conclusion by relying on the language of natural law, but in its revised form as a theory of natural rights. His conclusion encapsulates the fine mixture of Greek philosophy and Christian moral intuition that had permeated canonist thinking. For he argues that all humans, by their nature, have some natural rights or liberties.

> I maintain ... that lordship, possession and jurisdiction can belong to infidels, licitly and without sin, for these things were not only for the faithful but for every rational creature, as has been said. 'For he makes his sun to rise on the just and the wicked and he feeds the birds of the air' (Matthew, 5.6). Accordingly, we say that it is not licit for the pope or the faithful to take away from infidels their belongings or their ... jurisdictions ...

At first glance Innocent's argument might seem to undermine the papal claim to a universal jurisdiction. But he quickly dispels that impression, by refining the nature of that claim:

> Nevertheless, we do certainly believe that the pope, who is the vicar of Jesus Christ, has power not only over Christians but also over all infidels, for Christ had power over all ... and he would not seem to have

been a careful father unless he had committed full power over all to his vicar whom he left on earth ... But all men, faithful and unfaithful alike, are Christ's sheep by creation even though they are not of the fold of the church and thus from the foregoing it is clear that the pope has jurisdiction and power over all de jure though not de facto.[2]

By making that distinction, Innocent IV identified the papal claim to sovereignty with the universal claims of justice, understood in terms of equality and reciprocity. It was the claim to speak with unlimited authority over issues to do with morality and conscience, a claim from which revelation allowed neither retreat nor concession.

This passage illustrates how the new habits of thought were making possible a clearer separation of the claims of justice from prevailing social facts. In traditional societies, norms and facts, laws and customs were not clearly separable ideas. It required the emergence of a sovereign agency – with its claim to rest on and have authority over individuals – to make such distinctions fully intelligible. For the claim of a sovereign authority separated the idea of human agency – with all its potential revealed in the Christ – from established social practices. It was that claim which made possible the emergence of the idea of natural rights.

But if the idea of natural rights could be used to protect the possessions and jurisdictions of infidels outside the Christian fold, could it not also be invoked to protect non-believers and dissenters within Christian societies? This was far from being Innocent IV's intention. Yet such respect for the rights of conscience may be lurking in his arguments. For they relied on a conception of moral claims founded on a 'proper' understanding of human agency, an understanding championed by canon lawyers that could and would be turned against legal privileges for the church.

Did kings and would-be kings glimpse such a possible development of the idea of secularism? It is a tantalizing question. But it is difficult, probably impossible to answer. Certainly the monarchies, feudal nobilities and independent communes of medieval Europe shared a deep distrust of papal pretensions, to the extent that they were never reconciled to the attempts of popes such as Innocent IV to make explicit and systematic norms presenting the papacy as the final court of appeal in Europe. Yet despite their continuing struggle against papal pretensions, secular rulers carried two things away from the conflict. The first was papal acceptance that secular jurisdictions had their own origin and validity. The second was a gradual disengagement from a corporate conception of society. This made the relationship of secular rulers to the papal revolution one of emulation as well as competition.

Accepting the model of authority promoted by the papal revolution to that extent was useful for the kings in pursuing their ambitions. By confirming the individual as the basic unit of legal subjection, it became a part of the arsenal they deployed when asserting their 'sovereign' rights. The salient part of that arsenal remained the image of a legal system projected by canon law. Beneath its strong emphasis on uniformity and coherence lay the assumption of moral equality. Canon law and civil law increasingly influenced each other. They held what amounted to a conversation. When canon law was silent on some question, canonists had recourse to Roman civil law. On the other hand, understanding innovations in canon law, which sprang from the church applying its moral beliefs to a society so different from that of ancient Rome, helped to turn students of civil law into something more than antiquarians. When there was a conflict between civil and canon law over a question, resolving that conflict made both types of lawyer more self-conscious about the values involved. For example, the question of whether an oath never to change the contents of a will could override freedom of testament saw canonists emphasize the moral obligation created by the oath, while civilians usually defended testamentary freedom.[3]

The interaction between canon and civil law helped to develop and strengthen the new sense of justice. Increasingly, lawyers were trained in both systems. Many canon lawyers were, in fact, laymen. Nothing illustrates better the interaction of the two legal systems – and the new sense of justice – than the way canonists turned a maxim of private law into a principle of public law: 'what touches all should be approved by all', a principle that would later have profound political consequences.

Of course, what secular rulers first appreciated in these legal developments was not so much their humane potential as their potential for a more efficient organization of government. The example of the papal bureaucracy was not lost on them.

As a result of the Gregorian reforms the papal curia had become divided into separate sections dealing with legislation, judicial decisions, and administration. The sight of administrators relying on careful written records to spread their sway over remote localities, the example of lawyers and courts using the papal claim to a plenitude of power to bring archbishops and bishops within a single hierarchical organization, the impact locally of papal delegates dispatched to carry out the will of the curia, the successful raising of revenues: these things did not fail to make an impression on secular rulers struggling to impose their authority over powerful feudal vassals.

The efficiency and coherence of papal government made such an impression on lawyers themselves that they began to distinguish 'authority' from 'administration'. If authority was 'the inherent right to direct affairs, administration was the actual exercise of power'.[4] Thus, it was the pope's ability to govern the far-flung church that secular rulers first wished to emulate. And, not surprisingly, they associated such ability with an enhanced role for lawyers. So emperors and kings began to consult lawyers, employ them and even found schools of law. After all, both civil and canon law offered such rulers the tantalizing prospect of a primacy which feudal institutions denied them. That is why the new idea of a legal system led to such revolutionary changes in European government.

In the twelfth and thirteenth centuries a distinct pattern emerged. Feudal kingship gave way to a new form of kingship, a form involving centralization of authority and the growth of bureaucracy. Royal councils, traditionally composed of tribal chiefs or feudal magnates, were reformed along the model of the papal curia. The names given to new, separate agencies varied. But the pattern involved separating legislative, administrative and judicial functions, and giving each into the hands of people with some appropriate training. Often these were 'new' men rather than leading feudatories. In this way a wider pool of talent became available, men whose modest origins also made them more amenable to discipline. (Once again, kings learned from the church, which had opposed marriage of the clergy at least partly on the grounds that it might make church offices hereditary and turn the clergy into a caste.)

These changes can be observed in southern Italy and in Sicily, the principality put together by Norman invaders from the later eleventh century. Two things may help to explain why its rulers created the 'first modern system of royal law'. The first was the fact of proximity to Rome and constant contact with papal government. But the second and more important was their need for a legitimacy that the papacy could bestow. These Norman 'intruders' wished to become kings properly so called (a wish which also led Duke William of Normandy to cultivate relations with the papacy, before invading England in 1066).

What institutions did the Norman rulers create? They created 'a system of civil service examinations' which provided officials to staff new central agencies, a chancery which prepared and issued royal decrees, a treasury (the *dogana*) which organized and directed an efficient system of taxation, and a high court claiming direct jurisdiction over the most serious cases and providing itinerant judges to deal with lesser cases outside the capital of Palermo. Altogether, the pattern strongly resembled that of the reformed Roman curia.

But Norman innovations did not stop there. These rulers inherited a peculiarly complex set of 'legal' traditions, the result of Sicily and southern Italy having been subject, at various times, to Byzantine, papal and Arab rule. The consequent absence of anything like coherent customary law made it easier for the Norman rulers to assert themselves. Early in the twelfth century a shrewd, determined ruler who styled himself King Roger II did just that. 'He carved out of the legal universe a separate jurisdiction, that of the king of Sicily in matters of high justice, and then he defined that jurisdiction by a set of interlocking principles and rules that created a unified ... body of law.' Roger did not hesitate to claim a sovereign right for himself.

Roger II declared that the king is a 'maker of laws' (conditor legum). Indeed, Roger promulgated the first modern code of royal law in ... the Assizes of Ariano. This is called a modern code and the first of its kind in the West because it did not purport to be merely a collection of rules and principles, but instead was a systematic presentation of what were thought to be basic features of the legal system ... It was presented as positive law, enacted by the king as legislator. It drew, to be sure, on customary law, natural law and divine law, and it fused many diverse features of the Byzantine, Moslem, Lombard, Norman and Romano-canonical legal traditions, but it recast those sources in the form of a new and comprehensive legislative act.[5]

The Assizes of Ariano deserve such a description because of their unequivocal character. They set out Roger's claim to legal supremacy not only over the feudal nobility, urban communes and the population at large, but also, in some respects, over the church as well.

In the next century the most brilliant of Roger's successors, the ambitious Frederick II, carried these changes further, intending, probably, to apply to the whole of Italy the institutions of his kingdom of Sicily. How did Frederick go about this? He strengthened the central bureaucracy, insisted on legal training and laid even greater emphasis on written records and consistency in administration. Whenever possible, he avoided making feudal magnates the agents of local government. They were often obstinate and under-educated. Instead, he recruited 'new men' to act both as his 'vicars' for the government of provinces and as his *potestates* for the government of cities.

Frederick II issued a revised and even more ambitious code of laws for Sicily. When introducing his new code, he borrowed Roman law texts to establish his lawmaking supremacy and proper rules for procedure in his courts. He was especially careful to insist that whenever judges faced competing rules drawn from royal legislation and feudal or customary law, their first obligation was to apply royal legislation. Only if there was nothing relevant to the case in royal legislation, could the judge turn to the rules of feudal or customary law.[6]

France in the twelfth and thirteenth centuries exhibits similar institutional changes, though with one noticeable difference. In France, the extension of royal jurisdiction and centralization gained especially from the tacit alliance between the crown and newly important boroughs directed against the local powers of bishops and secular lords. Supporting urban uprisings – 'swearing the commune' – became an important instrument of policy for Louis IX and Philip Augustus.

They too changed the composition of the royal council in favour of 'new men', while creating separate bodies to extend their fiscal reach and superintend legal decisions (the parlement of Paris). The power of the French crown grew from 'listening to complaints' and then intervening as an arbiter.

The extent to which the new model of kingship was tied to a burgeoning class of lawyers soon became a matter for anecdote. There is a story about how one of Frederick's predecessors, the emperor Frederick Barbarossa, sought confirmation of the extent of his 'sovereign' powers from the leading lawyers at Bologna. When Barbarossa asked two famous jurists, Bulgarus and Martinus, whether he was 'lord of the world', Bulgarus said that his power was limited by private property, while Martinus said that his power had no limits. As a reward, Martinus was given a horse by the emperor, while Bulgarus went away empty-handed ... The story shows how the question of sovereign right was a live one.

It was no accident that royal patronage of law schools in the new universities became widespread. These law schools taught only civil and canon law. They had no place in their curriculum for the study of feudal or customary law. In this way, the law schools came to supply advisers to rulers who were seeking to overcome the diversity of customary law in their kingdoms, with the help of the new concept of a sovereign right.

England and Castile all provided variations on the same pattern. Thus, Edward I of England (1272–1307), whose interest in legal reform led to him being described as 'the English Justinian', recruited the son of the great Bolognese jurist Accursius to advise him. In thirteenth-century Castile, Alfonso the Wise came to Roman law under the influence of his tutor, who had studied at Bologna.[7] In Paris, meanwhile, interest in legal studies developed so rapidly that a pope attempted to forbid its study on the grounds that it was undermining interest in theology!

Little wonder that a Byzantine visitor to Western Europe in the early fourteenth century was impressed by one thing more than anything else: the omnipresence of litigation, courts and lawyers.[8] He was not prepared for it. It had no counterpart further east. He was, in fact, encountering the attempt to create the rule of law on a new, individualist basis, spreading from the church into the secular sphere. To be sure, papal sovereignty, which had opened the way to an ambitious legislative programme and the centralizing of justice in the church, encountered fewer obstacles than attempts by secular rulers to assert the same prerogative. Those rulers' use of Roman and canon law was circumscribed by entrenched local custom, the nobility's defence of feudal law as well as by the 'liberties' of municipalities.[9]

Yet if progress towards the rule of law in the secular sphere was halting, a popular culture favourable to it began to develop and with it a new genre of writing. A strange, vernacular fusion of religion and law can be seen in the popularity of fourteenth-century tracts recounting the so-called 'trial of Satan': Christ presides over the court. Satan appears before it, and brings an action against mankind. Through a series of legal moves, Satan claims possession of humanity for its sins, moving from procedural devices (such as the failure of mankind, the accused, to appear before the court) to substantive claims about 'his' property since the Fall. Eventually the Virgin Mary appears as an advocate for the defence. She argues that as Satan was the cause of the fall of mankind, he should not be able to benefit from his own crime. Unsurprisingly, Satan loses the case.

Such tracts are not just amusing or bizarre. Their popularity reveals how religion and law were being fused to create something new in Western Europe. For these tracts did not only help to instruct people in basic features of legal procedure. They conveyed a sense that the moral guarantees offered by the Christian faith could and should become a matter of social justice as well as of grace.

That sense would provide one of the foundations of modern secularism.

20

Urban Insurrections

Kings were the first to recognize the advantages of the new idea of sovereignty, with the prospect of a jurisdiction over individuals that it offered. The vision of a society freed from the constraints imposed on feudal kingship touched their self-interest directly. It was a vision of greater power. But that vision also drew on the moral intuitions of clerics who, trained in canon law, often acted as royal advisers.

To be sure, these moral intuitions had been present in the Christian church from its outset. But the development of the church into a self-governing corporation, with a legal system founded on the assumption of moral equality, gave those intuitions a new potency and reach. It gave them access to the less privileged reaches of society, where they could become agents of further change.

We can see this if we look at a revolution contemporary with the papal revolution: the insurrection and enfranchisement of the towns or 'boroughs'. Along with the papal revolution and the new ambitions of kingship, the revival of urban life is one of the remarkable features of eleventh- and twelfth-century Europe.

What had become of the ancient city? However much cities had suffered from the Germanic invasions, they did not disappear. Approximations of Roman urban life survived, especially in Italy, southern France and Catalonia. We have seen how, in the aftermath of the invasions, bishops (many drawn from the old senatorial class) became the de facto leaders of cities. Yet the disappearance of ancient social classifications meant that civic magistrates were no longer deemed to have a hereditary claim. They were understood as representatives of the people. Other forms of ancient civic life, however, at first survived the invasions unchanged.

One meets at this epoch ... with frequent convocations of the curia; there is mention made of public assemblies and municipal magistrates. The affairs of the civil order, wills, grants and a multitude of acts of civil life, were legalized in the curia by its magistrates, as was the case in the Roman municipality. The remains of urban activity and liberty, it is true, gradually disappeared. Barbarism, disorder and always increasing misfortunes, accelerated the depopulation. The establishment of the masters of the land in the rural districts, and the growing preponderance of agricultural life, were new causes of decay to the towns. The bishops themselves, when they had entered the frame of feudalism, placed less importance on their municipal existence. Finally, when feudalism had completely triumphed, the towns, without falling into the servitude of serfs, found themselves entirely in the hands of a lord, enclosed within some fief, and robbed of all the independence which had been left them ... in the first ages of the invasion.[1]

The condition of towns by the ninth and tenth centuries cannot be described either as one of freedom or of servitude. Rather it was a marginal, insecure and unregulated condition. Apart from servants of the local bishop or count, most of the inhabitants of towns farmed to survive.

Yet feudalism, which at first took such a toll of urban independence, soon gave the cities a new lease of life. From the tenth century urban population grew rapidly. Why? When urban life began to revive, the towns no longer conformed to Greek or Roman models. They were not fully independent city-states. Nor were they administrative centres, where a hereditary elite extracted an agricultural surplus from country estates worked by slaves, for the benefit of a distant imperial government. Serfdom and the extreme localism that resulted from the dissolution of the Carolingian empire – with relatively small fiefs governed by lords from their castles – began to create a different relationship between towns and their surrounding countryside. A new interdependence between town and countryside developed. The agricultural surplus created by serfs attached to plots of land on a lord's domain created a demand for other goods, which artisans and merchants located in a nearby town could exploit.

That is why the reviving cities and towns ceased to be administrative centres or places for leisure. They became marketplaces instead. They catered for new needs felt by a feudal class that was more sedentary. So the growing urban population consisted chiefly not of clergy or notables, but of artisans and merchants. In that way, the seeds of a new social class – devoted to commerce rather than the pursuits of war and the chase – developed in the midst of feudalism. This new class consisted of people who wanted the freedom to move about, buy and sell: the creation of a jurisdiction and 'peace' that would provide security needed for trading.

In retrospect, it was more than a new social class being born. For that class would, eventually, provide the model for a new type of society. So we must ask what attitudes and habits the refugees from the countryside and from the feudal system brought with them into their new circumstances. How did the contours of their minds – their *mores* – begin to shape urban institutions?

If we compare these refugees with the founders of ancient cities, we notice one difference above all. For these refugees, the religious question was already settled. There existed a priesthood and a corporation called the church, governed by its own laws. There was no need or temptation to create new beliefs as well as new institutions. The church, after all, claimed a monopoly of religious authority. The urban associations that were being formed had, therefore, no inclination to claim such authority. They were prepared to acknowledge a religious authority external to their own affairs, an authority which laid down a basic moral framework for their transactions, exemplified in the oaths for mutual assistance and solidarity ('swearing the commune') that provided the earliest form of new urban governments. That appeal to individual conscience drew on moral intuitions fostered by the church. Yet the church did not seek to govern the new urban centres directly.

The 'sacred' sphere now possessed its own form of government. So the affairs of the rapidly growing urban settlements could – within limits imposed by Christian beliefs – be left to their inhabitants. And so it was. They began to govern themselves. These towns or boroughs became the first secular governments – governments that, freed from quasi-religious ideas of lordship and paterfamilias, acknowledged an underlying equality in their inhabitants and the freedom this implied.

Kings might have begun to see the advantages of such a presumption in favour of liberty, but kingship was still tainted with its earlier theocratic claims. Feudalism might rest on a form of servitude more equivocal than ancient slavery, but inequality remained its defining characteristic. By contrast, with a kind of innocence, townspeople were creating a new form of society.

Only later did townspeople relate their new liberty to the moral equality proclaimed by Christian beliefs. Yet that relationship emerged almost immediately in the language they adopted when 'swearing the commune' and defending its interests. It was the language of brotherhood. Thus, a twelfth-century Flemish borough charter prescribed: 'let each help the other like a brother'. This language of equality and reciprocity – of moral transparency – was not the language of the ancient polis, but rather that of St Paul. Its adoption by eleventh- and twelfth-century burghers gave their struggle for concessions from feudal lords the advantage that follows when conviction is added to interest.

As and when that happened, urban egalitarianism was reinforced. Burghers were not, of course, relying on anything like the idea of natural rights being developed by canon lawyers. Theirs was an instinct rather than a theory. If Christianity declared all men equal in the sight of God, should not they be equal in the sight of the law? However indistinctly at first, that was the novel idea 'carried' by the rapidly growing boroughs. Unlike in the ancient city, liberty was being claimed, not merely for the borough, but also for the individuals who lived and worked in it. It was the agitated, inchoate birth of the ideal of equal liberty. For personal liberty rapidly became identified with the very meaning of 'burgher'. To struggle for the freedom or 'franchise' of a borough was also to struggle for a new personal status. 'It is to Jesus Christ that we owe the development of the laws and advantages of our city,' proclaimed the citizens of Marseilles in 1219.[2]

Thus the church was both present and absent at the birth of a new form of society, something that has confused discussions of the nature of secularism ever since. Christian beliefs provided a sanction for the individual as the fundamental social role, an egalitarian understanding of justice. But in most other respects, the church did not seek to shape urban institutions directly. Its influence remained indirect. The medieval borough developed as an association of individuals rather than as an association of families. The family was no longer itself a religious cult and form of worship. And, unlike ancient cities, the governments of towns or boroughs did not claim religious authority. They did not perform religious rites or administer religious rules.

The contrast with ancient cities could hardly be greater. As we have seen, their formation had been an avowedly religious act. It involved the creation of a new cult, an association of family and tribal cults through civic magistrates who at the same time acted as priests. The ancient city fused religious and political functions. And its mould was aristocratic. From the outset, it conferred on the heads of certain families a hereditary right to officiate and govern. Neither ancient lordship nor paterfamilias shaped the new urban centres. Instead, the gradual enfranchisement of the boroughs created a class of people who were formally equal and free to move about, buy and sell. They were no longer slaves or serfs attached to the land. For burghers, land itself became a commodity rather than the source of permanent privilege or subjection. Burghers had already formed self-governing trade associations such as guilds or *hanses*. In due course, they were also acknowledged to have the right to manage the affairs of their boroughs, to legislate, impose taxes and even make war. A German proverb expressed the new social reality: 'the air of the city makes free'.

The process of enfranchisement did not happen overnight. Often it involved repeated struggles against feudal overlords and bloody defeats. At first the bishops, who lived in the cities, proved more reluctant than secular lords to forgo their traditional dominance of urban affairs. But they did so as feudal lords rather than as spokesmen of a church disentangling itself from secular jurisdictions with the help of canon law. Indeed, it was not unknown for some churchmen – monastic authorities and the lower clergy – to support an urban population against the feudal pretensions of a bishop, if only to defend papal authority.

Urban uprisings against feudal lords spread like wildfire across Western Europe in the eleventh and twelfth centuries. They were not coordinated uprisings, though travellers' tales of successful uprisings elsewhere no doubt offered much-needed encouragement to other burghers at times. Deeper causes were at work. Similar circumstances were leading to similar outcomes. What exactly were the circumstances and the outcomes? And what role did the church play at each stage in these unprecedented social developments?

To find out, we must examine several steps in the development of the boroughs. First we must look more closely at the process of their formation, then at the 'charters' that symbolized and consolidated their enfranchisement, and, finally, at social developments within the boroughs following their enfranchisement. The church's influence on each step was indirect, but it was nonetheless important.

A long if ill-defined tradition – which identified the churches as places of refuge – gave birth to the convention that any serf who lived in a town for more than a year could not be forcibly removed by his former master. The traditional 'right' of sanctuary in a church thus contributed to the growth of urban populations.

> Before the boroughs had established themselves, before their strength and their ramparts enabled them to offer an asylum to the afflicted population of the country, when they as yet had no safety but that afforded by the church, this sufficed to draw into the towns many unhappy fugitives. They came to shelter themselves in or around the church; and it was the case not only with the inferior class, with serfs and boors, who sought safety, but often with men of importance, rich outlaws.[3]

Such 'outlaws' introduced a less servile attitude, and contributed to a new recalcitrance in the towns. Even more important was the success of merchants who had learned to band together in guilds or *hanses*, in order to trade at a distance with greater security. These would provide the nucleus of a new urban government.

If the towns grew with the arrival of refugees from the countryside, they prospered with the rebirth of trade. They became centres of and for work, centres where no superior class cast work in an inferior light. But as the prosperity of merchants and artisans grew, so did their insecurity. As trade increased, the wealth of the urban centres attracted the attention of local lords, who soon attempted to appropriate that wealth through tolls, taxes and outright confiscations. Now settled within their fiefs, such lords had not lost the avidity of bandits. 'Instead of going to pillage at a distance, they pillaged at home.'

By the late eleventh century this created such fury among townsmen that they rose against their local feudal oppressors.

This reaction of townsmen runs against an assumption inherited from ancient political rhetoric that commerce leads to the 'corruption' of manners, installing weakness and effeminacy in the place of warlike 'virtue'. The experience of social equality in boroughs led to a different result. Townsmen became fighters. 'Nothing can irritate a man more than being interfered with in his work, and despoiled of the fruits which he had promised himself from it . . . There is in the progressive movement towards fortune of a man or a population a principle of resistance against injustice and violence far more energetic than in any other situation.'[4] Responding to the threats to their livelihoods, townspeople banded together and formed militias. They created virtual corporations that existed in fact before their rights were recognized. These took the form of all the inhabitants swearing an oath of mutual aid and solidarity. Assemblies of the people, who were summoned by the bells of the church or criers, began to make their own decisions. They began to exercise many sovereign rights. Feudalism itself contributed to this outcome. For in the relations of vassals to their suzerain, the right to which feudalism constantly appealed was the right of resistance. In this respect, the townspeople can be said to have learned from their 'betters'.

The medieval borough acquired its identity through an insurrection which, though not at all coordinated, became general.

> The enfranchisement of the commons in the eleventh century was the fruit of a . . . veritable war, a war declared by the population of the towns against their lords. The first fact which is always met with in such histories is the rising of the burgesses who arm themselves with the first thing that comes to hand; the expulsion of the followers of the lord who have come to put in force some extortion; or it is an enterprise against the castle . . . If the insurrection fails, what is done by the conqueror? He orders the destruction of the fortifications raised, not only round the town but round each house. One sees at the time of the confederation, after having promised to act in common, and after taking the oath of mutual aid, the first act of the citizen is to fortify himself within his house.[5]

Insurrections often did fail – at first. But the towns became ever more militant and the houses of townspeople ever more like small fortresses. So after sometimes prolonged struggles, many boroughs achieved what they sought, liberties and immunities giving them a large degree of self-government. They were often supported by kings (especially in France) who saw these urban uprisings as a way of reducing the power of feudal lords.

Let us now look more closely at the 'charters' created when an insurrection succeeded. This will involve constructing an ideal type of the charters, for, not surprisingly, there was a great variety in their terms. These terms reflected differences between the more centralized feudalism of England and weaker royal power in France, between European regions where a secular lord or the church retained the upper hand and those (as in Flanders) where the wealth and size of the boroughs gave them greater bargaining power. Nonetheless, a number of features were widely shared.

Charters turned citizens de facto into citizens de jure. The early twelfth-century charter of Beauvais was typical. It stipulated that 'all men within the walls of the city and in the suburb shall swear the commune', before setting out the rights and privileges of burghers. Charters were 'peace treaties' at the end of a war. But they were also more than that. They created new legal entities. They created the boroughs as self-governing corporations, with their own jurisdiction. The charter gave an urban corporation its own sphere of competences and defined its relations with a local lord or king. It created the basis for a new legal system.[6]

It would be an exaggeration to say that the boroughs achieved complete sovereignty. For limits on their rights remained. Kings usually reserved the rights of 'high justice' over capital offences. Local lords or bishops often reserved the right to appoint judges or collect a particular tax from the borough. Nonetheless, the charters set limits on such claims over the boroughs, giving the boroughs immunity from the full range of royal and feudal impositions. They firmly excluded new, arbitrary claims on the boroughs. This was a crucial principle. For apart from pre-established claims, the boroughs acquired a sovereign right, the right to govern their own affairs – which is not to say that kings and local lords did not sometimes regret the concessions they had made and threaten the 'liberties' of a borough. But the claim of a right could survive such facts.

Thus, the model of a legal system – of a self-governing corporation – shaped the enfranchisement of the boroughs. That model, with its roots in the church and canon law, promoted egalitarianism by reinforcing the notion that the individual was the fundamental unit of legal subjection. Such a development in urban centres should not be taken for granted, as something 'natural' or unavoidable. There was a major difference between European and Islamic cities in that respect. Islamic cities developed, but they were never legally constituted. They grew, but they were never founded as autonomous legal entities.

By contrast, some eleventh- and twelfth-century charters became models widely copied by other boroughs founding themselves, for example, that of London by other English cities and that of Magdeburg by German-speaking cities further east. Such charters established a clear difference between urban law and both feudal and canon law. Urban law developed as a mixture of local custom, improvisation and, especially, rules of commerce developed by merchant guilds trading at a distance and recognizing the importance of reciprocal rights for protecting profits from trade. It is certainly no accident that borough charters devoted a great deal of attention to protecting the claims of 'foreign' merchants. Equality and reciprocity shaped dispositions in borough charters. It was an inheritance of canon law, although now these principles were applied to keep temporal peace and serve justice rather than to promote the faith as such.

Here, once again, we meet the paradox of the papal revolution. By proclaiming the church's independence from 'secular' government, it helped to create the latter. The de-sacralizing of kingship was under way, but would take far longer to accomplish. So enfranchised boroughs (even when churches played an important role in the local economy) provide the first examples of secularism. 'They were wholly separate from the church, and in that sense they were the first secular states of Europe.'[7]

Let us now look at developments within the boroughs after their enfranchisement. If we look closely at these developments, we can learn other things about secularism. The first is the connection between secularism and constitutionalism, a connection that became explicit in the charters organizing the boroughs, defining their immunities and specifying citizens' rights. Were they 'the first modern written constitutions'? That is going too far, for they did not attempt to provide an entire framework for government, leaving much to be settled. What is closer to the truth is that the charters were one of the sources from which modern social contract theory would develop. For the borough charters were more like an original social contract than a full-blown constitution. Yet they certainly had constitutional features.

The new idea of a sovereign authority exercised directly over moral equals – that is, over individuals – presupposed a rule locating the sovereign. Thus, the claim of papal authority over the church was grounded in belief that the Christ had made Peter and his successors the representatives of God's moral authority over souls on earth. Yet the definitive assertion of papal sovereignty by Gregory VII was preceded by a 'constitutional' measure to free papal elections from interference by secular rulers, to ensure that the church was self-governing.

The first feature of the borough charters was to secure self-government by lodging final authority in the assembly of all citizens. Secularism introduced a formal equality of status for citizens, who had the right to take part in the assemblies. Popular assemblies had the right to legislate, levy taxes and make war. As we have seen, certain rights reserved by the king or a local lord might limit the sovereignty of newly enfranchised boroughs. But in other respects they were free. Boroughs were usually exempt from feudal services and dues, as well as from royal taxes, except those that had been agreed in advance. Their independence emerges especially in the absence of obligation except by prior agreement.

In the boroughs, as in the church, the exercise of a sovereign authority before long raised difficult questions about the distribution of authority and representation. Such questions followed directly from the assumption of moral equality. For the right to govern and the duty to obey were no longer allocated by inherited differences of status, by assuming inequality to be natural. Were there, in consequence, moral limits to legal subjection to a sovereign authority? Could sovereign authority be shared or delegated? And what was the status of intermediate or partial associations, associations composed of only some subjects of the sovereign body?

In the church, these problems emerged in arguments about the relationship between papal authority and general councils of the church, as well as in arguments about whether a heretical pope could be deposed. Did not the pope's 'plenitude of power' have to respect divine and natural law, in order to command the consciences of believers? And what autonomy did this plenitude of power leave to archbishops, bishops and monastic orders?

In the boroughs, lodging a monopoly of power in an assembly of the citizens gave rise to analogous questions. Were popular assemblies able to formulate coherent policies or deal justly with individual dissent? How much authority should such assemblies confer on magistrates? How could magistrates be held to account? Did self-government require the creation of a more permanent body deemed to represent all the citizens? In the first phase of their history – during insurrections and the immediate aftermaths – the boroughs were the scenes of an almost unlimited, even anarchical democracy. It is true that there were urban magistrates, but they were elected annually and were subject to one overriding control, the ever-present threat of popular rioting. This volatile internal situation drastically limited the ability of the boroughs to deal confidently with local lords and kings, often providing the latter with pretexts for intervention.

The need for more stable government brought change. The development of trade and the importance of guilds or *hanses* – 'industrial corporations' – had created a set of richer merchants in the boroughs. Their influence on the organization of work was increasingly reflected in the arrangements of urban government, which became far more oligarchic. This involved the emergence of a council or senate deemed to represent the community as a whole. This body was invested with the right to choose the leading magistrates, often from within its own members. At first such councils were elected for a fixed period, but later they acquired the right to renew their own membership. Assemblies of the citizens became rare, though the right was never extinguished. References in municipal documents to 'the leading citizens' became more frequent.

But that was not the only constitutional development. A form of separation of powers also began to emerge. A more permanent judiciary – with professional judges – was created, in place of judges who had at first been elected by the popular assembly for a term so short that it allowed them little independence. And the publication of laws rather than appeals to custom (which often meant the opinion of elders) became the usual basis for judicial decisions.

The protection for individual rights also became more explicit and systematic – and here again the influence of canon law is perceptible.

> The civil rights granted by urban law ... included a rational trial procedure, with judgement by peers rather than proof by ordeal or trial by combat. There were to be no arbitrary arrests and no imprisonment without legal process. Body attachment for debt was prohibited. Types of punishment were limited. In theory, rich and poor were to be judged alike. Citizens had the right to bear arms. They had the right to vote. Immigrants were to be granted the same rights as citizens after residence for a year and a day. Merchant strangers were to have rights equal to those of merchant citizens.[8]

This account may be rather idealized. But it remains true that urban government contained the seeds of a modern constitutional order.

Through their legal innovations, medieval boroughs gave birth to a new social class, a class intermediate between the original castes of feudal society, the nobles and serfs. This class is what we have come to call the 'middle' class or bourgeoisie. And it is no accident that we call it a class rather than a caste. Formal recognition of a fundamental equality of status – the status of citizens – distinguished this class from feudal castes, which preserved more of the ancient assumption of natural inequality. Despite oligarchic trends in the government of boroughs, the equality of citizenship remained a counterpoise to de facto inequalities of wealth, status and power. This fundamental equality proved to be deeply subversive. Over the coming centuries it would lead to the collapse of the original feudal castes into this 'middling' social condition, with the emergence of nation-states.

We must be careful, however, not to project back into the twelfth century the class that took possession of society during the early modern period. In its origins it was comprised largely of artisans and merchants. Even after the enfranchisement of the boroughs it retained a sense of social inferiority, preventing it from assuming any great role in the public life of Europe. In their dealings with royalty and the

feudal nobility, the burghers remained humble and even submissive –
except when it was a question of defending the immunities of their
boroughs! It was only when lawyers, wealthy bankers, physicians and
scholars were added to their ranks that they became fully conscious
of themselves as a class.[9] Only then did they begin to acquire a will to
fashion society as a whole after their own model.

Such a will – what François Guizot describes as a truly political
will – had previously depended on a sense of social superiority, on
aristocracy. The challenge facing the new middle class was to create a
'democratic' will on the basis of equal rights, that is, on civil and political liberty.

The Birth Pangs of
Modern Liberty

21

Popular Aspirations and the Friars

Egalitarian moral intuitions generated by Christianity have played a crucial part in our story. They can be traced back to Paul's mystical vision of believers becoming 'as one' in the Christ, the vision of an utter transparency of mind and will. But in a simpler form, the biblical 'golden rule' conveyed these egalitarian intuitions, making them easily accessible.

We have just seen how these intuitions helped to shape new urban institutions. Refugees from the countryside, most of them former serfs, were the major source of growing urban populations. Typically, they were poor and illiterate. But that did not prevent them already having some inkling of the meaning of 'the equality of souls'. Were they not told in sermons that they had a will and a conscience, and that they would be held to account for their thoughts and actions on the day of judgement? This was not the language in which ancient slaves had been addressed. Nor did it escape the notice of serfs that their feudal lords accepted, if only tacitly, the language of the church.

This, of course, is surmise. How can we find firm evidence of the spread of egalitarian moral intuitions among the poor and illiterate? What exactly should we be looking at? The answer can be found, I think, by looking at the role of comparison. For a process of comparison is unleashed by the assumption of equality, a process forestalled in cultures resting on the contrary assumption of natural inequality.

Popular movements in the medieval countryside – rural radicalism – betray this substitution of one assumption for another. They betray something more than the mere desperation of the slaves who, under Spartacus, revolted against Roman power in the first century BC. They betray conviction, the vision of a social order transformed along

Christian lines. This was imagined as a return to an 'original' Christianity, a condition of simplicity, brotherhood and sharing.[1] If we are to disentangle that vision – and neither overestimate nor underestimate its importance – we must be careful. For the vision was joined to a bewildering variety of other beliefs and attitudes: belief in the millennium, a form of dualism so exaggerated that good and evil scarcely touched, 'superstitious' credence in omens and portents, the cult of saints and their relics, the excitement of joining a popular movement and taking up a wandering life, and, not least, the distrust of clerical authority. So we must ask difficult questions about the moral condition of the rural poor. To what extent had the church really touched them? And if the rural poor had acquired egalitarian intuitions, how were they expressed?

In contrast to the bourgeoisie, who acquired a consciousness of themselves as a class through struggling against their feudal oppressors, the rural poor did not acquire such a consciousness. How could they? Dispersed and ignorant, with imaginations limited by confined lives, serfs in the eleventh century could not have understood notions like 'country' or 'nation'. In some ways they must still have considered their own condition as a thing fated, their 'nature' or 'lot' in life. And yet there was the church in their midst. And the church did not speak of fate, but rather of salvation or damnation, and so of a soul at risk in every person, of crucial choices open to each. Taking Christianity into the countryside, with the creation of rural parishes during the Carolingian period, may already have contributed to the emergence of serfdom as a status quite distinct from ancient slavery. But the influence of the church did not stop there.

We have seen how the monastic reform movement stimulated the papal revolution and helped to shape new urban institutions. What was its impact in the countryside?

From the beginnings of monasticism in Western Europe monks had enjoyed a special standing among the poor. They aroused respect and even affection because they were understood as representing the Christian life more fully than any other group, including – perhaps especially – the secular clergy. Evidently the austere, communal life of monasteries that observed the Benedictine Rule carried resonance for the poor. Not only was it a life requiring chastity, prayer and obedience, but it did not hold labour in contempt. By the tenth century the sharp contrast with bishops who bought their offices and adopted the ways of feudal lords, with priests living openly with concubines and promoting the interests of 'natural' children, was threatening to bring the church into disrepute among the poor.

Apart from the monastic life, what claim did the church have to represent another, more spiritual world? This question had generated the Cluniac reform programme, a programme that created a new image in the countryside of what the entire church ought to be. For Cluniac reformers held up the image of a radically purified church – a church free of both simony and clerical immorality. They attacked members of the secular clergy for wantonness, drunkenness, greed, theft, fighting and even sacrilege. They conjured up a church so rotten that it was in danger of merging completely with the secular world.

Nor was that all. Cluniac reformers began to ask questions that disturbed the laity, especially the rural poor, whose approach to the church was largely uncritical. Were the sacraments offered in village churches by simoniac or immoral priests really valid? Was the tithe a form of exploitation rather than an indispensable support for the true church? Did members of the church hierarchy who had purchased their office – including perhaps the local bishop – have any legitimate authority? Why should any Christian submit to those whose life was so contrary to the life of the Christ?

The development of a radical and simplified – doubtless an oversimplified – model of what the church ought to be had far-reaching if unintended consequences in rural areas. It created what might be called a thirst for legitimacy, for a purer form of the church. And that thirst, in turn, developed out of egalitarian moral intuitions. We can get a taste of what satisfied that thirst by looking at the leadership of some radical movements in the twelfth and the thirteenth centuries.

An instructive early example is the preaching of a former monk called Henry, who became an itinerant preacher. When he arrived in Le Mans in 1116, preceded by his 'disciples', he was at first tolerated by the local bishop. But when the bishop left for Rome, Henry's real message emerged. With a powerful voice and wearing only a hair shirt, he denounced the corruption of the local clergy. 'After a short course of Henry's preaching the populace was beating priests in the streets and rolling them in the mud.' When Henry later moved into the countryside of southern France and Italy, his message became more extreme:

> Baptism, he taught, should be given only as an external sign of belief. Church buildings and all the trappings of official religion were useless; a man could pray anywhere as well as he could in a church. The true church consisted of those who followed the apostolic life, in poverty and simplicity; love of one's neighbour was the essence of true religion.[2]

Here it is not difficult to see the belief in equality and reciprocity shaping moral intuitions.

The pattern of religious radicalism in the villages of the countryside was fairly constant. An obscure man – with varying rumours about his origins as 'a monk' or perhaps even 'a noble' – suddenly emerges from the forests, often claiming to have become a holy man through a period of solitary withdrawal and profound meditation. He begins to preach, and his preaching is eloquent, far more so than that of village priests. The number of his followers grows rapidly, and with them his confidence and his pretensions increase.

The career of a certain Tanchelm, who acquired so many followers in Flanders and the southern Netherlands early in the twelfth century that the cathedral chapter of Utrecht became extremely anxious, illustrates the pattern. According to a report of the chapter,

> Tanchelm began his preaching in the open fields, dressed as a monk. We are told that his eloquence was extraordinary and that multitudes listened to him as to an angel of the Lord. He appeared to be a holy man – the Chapter of Utrecht complained that like his master the Devil he had all the appearance of an angel of light. Like so many other wandering preachers, he started by condemning unworthy clerics – such as the priest at Antwerp . . . who was living in open concubinage – and then broadened his attack to cover the church as a whole. He taught not merely that sacraments were invalid if administered by unworthy hands but also that . . . holy orders had lost all meaning, sacraments were no better than pollutions, and churches no better than brothels. This propaganda proved so effective that people soon stopped partaking of the Eucharist and going to church. And in general, as the Chapter

ruefully remarked, things came to such a pass that the more one despised the church the holier one was held to be.[3]

Increasingly Tanchelm claimed a Christ-like status for himself – going so far as to betroth himself to the Virgin Mary! Far from being dismayed by such a development, his followers welcomed it. One group even bound themselves together as his twelve 'apostles'.

None of this was entirely new. There had been the occasional prophet or messiah in previous centuries. But the frequency and scale of messianic movements increased dramatically from the late eleventh century onwards, and their following was overwhelmingly the rural and urban poor. These movements were rooted in moral conviction and difficult to extirpate. The chapter of Utrecht argued that the whole diocese was in danger of being lost to the church 'for ever' if Tanchelm went his way unhindered.

The slide from someone preaching an apostolic way of life to his claiming to be not just an apostle, but a living saint and vessel of the holy spirit, took place with some regularity. In the mid-twelfth century a Breton called Eon (or Eudes de l'etoile) led a movement that challenged the established church in Brittany. Although a layman, he celebrated mass for his followers and, apparently, claimed to be the son of God. 'In the end he organized his followers in a new church, with archbishops and bishops whom he called by such names as Wisdom, Knowledge, Judgement and by the names of the original apostles.'[4]

Such movements revealed and ministered to the new thirst for legitimacy. It is hardly surprising that they caused great alarm among church leaders. How well did these leaders understand the nature of the challenge? It is fair to say that they did not underestimate it. By the twelfth century many leading churchmen had been shaped by the movement of reform. When some of Eon's followers became little better than brigands, looting and burning churches, the archbishop of Rouen felt able to have Eon captured by force. But his estimation of the nature of the challenge Eon represented emerges from the status of Eon's 'trial'. He was summoned before a special synod in Reims cathedral by no less than the pope, Eugenius.

At first church authorities responded to such threats in a piecemeal way. They countered would-be messiahs with some of their own most gifted and 'orthodox' preachers. But within half a century or so there developed a more permanent – though at first extremely controversial – remedy: the mendicant orders, the Franciscans and Dominicans. The sudden growth of these two orders amounted to an almost revolutionary development. They discarded the pomp of the established church, and reached out to the poor through preaching and charitable acts, while themselves depending upon the giving of alms in urban centres. In a dramatic way, they both responded to the new sensibility among the poor and strengthened it. The evidence for that is the astonishing speed with which the Franciscans and Dominicans developed during the thirteenth century.

Both orders responded to the new sensibility. Yet on closer inspection they were very different in inspiration. For the characters of their founders, Dominic and Francis, left a distinctive mark on each. In their approach to church order and belief, it was the difference between reform 'from above' and 'from below', between an emphasis on refuting heresy with correct doctrine and an urge to adopt a Christ-like life of poverty and humility. So let us explore the difference.

Dominic was an educated Spanish canon who, returning by way of the Languedoc from a visit to Rome, was struck by the threat posed by a heresy called Catharism. Allegedly Catharism had spread from eastern Europe into Italy and southern France, though it probably had domestic roots which were just as important: a reaction against church rituals and clerical privilege in favour of a more austere spiritual life, even a quest for personal perfection. Led by *perfecti* who had 'liberated' themselves from the material world, the Cathars displayed contempt for the established church. Their name for themselves was 'the good Christians'.

Dominic concluded that Catharism constituted a grave threat to the church, and that the only effective remedy was for those preaching 'true' doctrine to adopt an 'apostolic' way of life, shunning all privileges and display in favour of austerity. Dominic also saw education as crucial to effective preaching against heresy. His followers soon established relations with the new universities at Paris and Bologna. But, most important of all, Dominic had papal approval and support for his mission. By the time of his death, in 1221, the Dominicans were formally established as a new order in the church. Their close ties with the papacy – and their obedience to it – would make possible the spread of Dominican 'houses' throughout Western Europe.

Rome had always been concerned to root out heresy. In its own eyes, it was the crucial instrument for defining 'orthodoxy'. Yet for centuries its means of action were limited. Often it had to rely on provincial church councils to pursue dissent and tolerate protracted debate. For it did not then have the means to impose its will on the Western church. By the thirteenth century, however, the papal reform movement, inspired by Cluny, had changed all that. The papacy was far stronger and more confident. Administrative and legal changes had turned the papacy into a powerful centralized government. The papacy had become almost 'imperial'.

Dominican preaching became part of a virtual war waged by the papacy against the Cathar heresy. The Cathars were accused of reinventing the Manichaean heresy, of adopting a dualism so extreme that the idea of the incarnation itself was at risk, and of embracing a kind of spiritual elitism, led by the *perfecti*. Since our knowledge of Cathar beliefs, apart from their rejection of the sacraments, derives almost entirely from opponents, it is difficult to reconstruct them with confidence. But that Cathars shared the new sensibility, deploring the ostentation and worldliness of many clergy as an 'affront to true religion', is clear.

The new confidence of the papacy had already led it to sponsor crusades to counter the spread of Islam and recover the holy sites in Palestine. Now it also sponsored a crusade of northern feudatories led by Simon de Montfort against Cathars in the Languedoc, a crusade which led to the infamous massacre of nearly twenty thousand inhabitants of Béziers. In theory, the papacy only 'borrowed' the secular arm to pursue heresy. But the episode revealed how the principle of equal subjection defined into the idea of papal sovereignty could lead to the coercion of belief, despite the fact that leading canon lawyers were developing a theory of natural rights.

Could belief really be enforced? Or was enforced belief a contradiction in terms? For the moment, the papal and Dominican concern for 'correct' belief ignored such doubts. Yet such doubts had played an important part in Christian thinking about the role of conscience from the outset. Was the reformed papacy in danger of denying the moral intuitions which had helped to create the reform movement? Just as some popes had been tempted to override the distinction between secular and spiritual powers in their struggles with the German emperors – despite the fact that the distinction provided the principal weapon of the reform movement – so the papacy now ignored the claims of conscience underpinning that distinction in order to extirpate heresy.

A papal court of enquiry, the Inquisition, was created by Gregory IX, extending (and tending to replace) a right of enquiry into threats to 'the purity of the faith' which the bishops had long exercised. Even writers well disposed to the papacy concede that 'the juristic principles which the procedure embodied bore hardly any resemblance to those which were commonly accepted and consistently advocated by the papacy itself'.[5]

Is it a mere accident that contemporary canon lawyers tended to elaborate a series of natural rights, rather than emphasize a general right to freedom? They were perhaps being cautious. Yet during the thirteenth century the exercise of papal sovereignty (not only in dealings with the Cathar heresy) did begin to prompt new questions about the limits of its sovereign authority. If the sovereignty of German emperors and other secular rulers was limited by the natural rights of their subjects – rights which helped to define the spiritual sphere defended by the church – were there not also limits on the pope's authority? In conferring a so-called 'plenitude of power' on the successors of Peter, did not God restrict its exercise by conferring rights on individuals? Were not certain individual rights an expression of divine will, formulated in natural law?

The language of natural rights was beginning to impinge on public argument. And in an unexpected way, this development was forwarded by the other great order that emerged in the thirteenth century, the Franciscans.

Francis was an extraordinary person. He was consumed by the desire to imitate the life of the Christ. The son of a well-to-do merchant of Assisi, the young Francis abandoned a life of pleasure when, after stumbling on an abandoned chapel, he felt an imperative and radical need to live according to the model of the Gospel, 'selling everything, giving everything to the poor, giving up every form of worldly glory, wealth, aid, comfort, organization, everything'.[6] The life he embraced stood out against the increasingly acquisitive mercantile life of the Italian cities. Yet it soon brought him followers – so many, indeed, that he was at times almost alarmed by them. The gentle life and character of Francis made a powerful impression on his contemporaries. It was almost as if the Christ was in their midst again.

The idealizing of renunciation and poverty struck a deep popular chord. Within a few years Francis and eleven of his followers were in Rome, giving an account of their movement, the aims of which had far more to do with 'the spirit' than 'the letter'. Consequently, Francis' relations with the papacy were more complex and uneasy than those of Dominic. For one thing, with their 'grass-roots' appeal, the Franciscans already had thousands of followers across Europe. With an unregulated, almost mass following they resembled some of the heretical movements of the previous century more than the carefully regulated Dominicans, which meant that they were less amenable to papal direction and control.

If the subtext of the Dominicans was the importance of 'equal submission', the spontaneous growth of the Franciscans pointed rather in the direction of 'equal liberty'. The Dominicans and Franciscans did learn from each other, with the Franciscans eventually adopting some of the organization of the Dominicans. Yet at first the contrast in their popular appeal was dramatic. 'When the two leaders met in Rome in 1218, Dominic was still the leader of only a handful of preachers, while Francis was the reluctant head of an organization with branches in nearly every country in Western Europe.'[7] The popular – it is tempting to say democratic – roots of the Franciscan movement and its resistance to hierarchy help to explain one of its most surprising consequences: the development of argument about natural rights. Why did a movement, practising poverty, humility and charity, lead to a new emphasis on natural rights? It is a remarkable story.

An important 'exchange' took place in early Franciscan thinking. Francis set out to imitate the life of the Christ. But it was soon assumed by his contemporaries that 'the Franciscan way of practising poverty . . . showed how Christ and the apostles must have lived'. Francis himself had little or no interest in the law. In the course of the thirteenth century, however, his followers drew on the distinctions of civil and canon law in order to define the Franciscan way of life. They then projected these distinctions back onto the world of the Gospels. 'The Franciscans came to believe wholeheartedly that Christ and the apostles, like good Franciscans, had renounced all "property, possessions, usufruct and right of use", retaining for themselves only a simple "use of fact".'[8] Thus, it was the Franciscan emphasis on the renunciation of property that led the order to stimulate important developments in the language of rights.

Bonagratio of Bergamo helped to initiate what became a formidable argument within the early fourteenth-century church. He argued that, following the example of the Christ, Francis had sought to renew the 'state of innocence' (that is, before Adam's sin and fall from grace). The crucial fact about the state of innocence, Bonagratio argued, was that there had been no property rights, no 'mine' or 'yours'; instead the use of all things was to be common to all. 'If blessed Francis vowed and promised to observe the gospel, living without property singly or in common, it follows that such was the teaching and the rule of the gospel and consequently Christ had nothing, singly or in common.'[9] The Christ had only what the Franciscans called a 'simple use of fact'.

The obvious retort by critics was that consumption itself was a kind of ownership, inseparable from use. Bonagratio met that criticism by arguing that natural law prescribed that every living creature should seek to preserve its own life, and that such a 'natural' instinct underpinned the human use of consumables such as food, clothing and shelter. This natural instinct was different from the rights governing the ownership and use of property established by human laws. Such rights, insisted Bonagratio, could be renounced voluntarily. Yet by insisting that legal rights and entitlements could be renounced in this way, Bonagratio laid down – at least in effect – a more fundamental natural right, the right to freedom. The claim of that right, with its egalitarian implications, led to a vigorous response from the papacy.

The Franciscan position was judged to be potentially subversive of order, both in church and state. It had been almost a cliché of natural law theory that in the 'state of nature' all things were held in common. 'But none of the many canonists who had commented on that text had interpreted it as meaning that the fruit Adam ate did not become his own, or that he had no right of use or usufruct in the things he actually did use.'[10] By the late 1320s Pope John XXII decided that the Franciscan arguments had to be opposed and discredited.

John XXII's counter-argument is fascinating and paradoxical. In order to reject the view that no property rights were present in the state of nature or 'innocence', he fell back on a position just as indi-vidualist as the claim of a general right to freedom. He wished to reinstate property into the state of innocence. His argument had two steps. First, he insisted that the division of property after the advent of sin by Adam and Eve implied that there had been common property before. So the Franciscan argument that there had been only a 'simple factual use of things without individual or common ownership' failed. The second step in John's critique was far more radical. Before the creation of Eve, property could not have been held 'in common'. So when God gave Adam dominion over the earth and its creatures, he made Adam – as an individual – the owner of the earth. Therefore, 'what God established at the very beginning of things in an ideal state of nature was not common possession but individual property'. Indi-vidual ownership was traced back to the beginning of things and the will of God as creator. Property was not a mere creation of human laws, and could not, as the Franciscans claimed, be renounced, for even the act of consuming things created property. Property and human agency were intimately joined.

What is striking about this debate is not so much an area of disagreement – that is, whether the right of property could be renounced – as the larger area of agreement. For both arguments work within a radically individualist framework. Both turn on individual claims, whether they are inalienable God-given rights of ownership or the natural right of renouncing property entitlements created by human laws. In that way, the assumption of moral equality set the stage for both positions in the debate.

Both positions were markedly voluntarist, and stressed the role of the individual will. At the very outset of the debate, a Dominican, John of Paris, rejected the theocratic view that all dominium – whether the ownership of property or the authority of the rulers – belonged ultimately to the pope. Such a view seemed to ignore the claims of individual agency, even in the eyes of the member of the order which owed so much to the papacy. John of Paris insisted that 'individuals as individuals have right and power and true dominion': 'They acquired this right, not from any ruler, either pope or king, but by their own "skill, labour and industry". The pope was only an administrator of property that belonged to the church, the king only a judge who could settle disputes about lay possessions. Neither was the source of the individual's right to property.'[11] This summary of John's argument catches the individualist turn of thinking taking place in mendicant orders devoted both to reaching the poor and to keeping them within the bounds of orthodoxy. God-given natural rights were coming to the fore.

Should we not conclude that their wish to adopt 'the apostolic life' had an important effect on the mendicant way of thinking? By recognizing mendicant orders in order to reach the poor and preserve orthodoxy, the reformed papacy achieved only a partial success. The development of the orders, especially the Franciscans, had a major unintended consequence: it laid the foundation for a radical critique of the role of the church in society, a critique which, drawing on the language of natural rights, began to emerge in the fourteenth and fifteenth centuries.

Through the idea of natural rights, Paul's emphasis on 'Christian liberty' acquired renewed life and potency. This was a moment of the greatest importance. For it was the moment when the egalitarian moral intuitions generated by the church began to be turned against the church itself, creating misgivings that eventually led to a principled rejection of any coercive or 'privileged' role for the church. In this way, these moral intuitions provided the basis for what would become the central project of secularism: the identification of a sphere resting on the 'rightful' claims of individual conscience and choice, a sphere of individual freedom protected by law. A commitment to 'equal liberty' was emerging from Christian moral intuitions.

22

The Defence of Egalitarian
Moral Intuitions

We have just seen how Franciscan-inspired debate about the origin of property rights became focused on the individual and his rights. This was no isolated development. What stands out from fourteenth-century writings about both church and government is the extent to which the image of society as an association of individuals was gaining ground. It was becoming the shared basis for argument. This image of society had spread from the rhetoric of the 'care of souls' into canon and civil law, shaping first of all the claim of papal sovereignty and then the claims of secular rulers to a sovereign authority. By the fourteenth century it was also shaping arguments about the origin and nature of authority as such. The primary unit of subjection to authority was identified as the individual. A corporate conception of society was rapidly waning.

One symptom of the change was the reinterpretation of terms inherited from antiquity. This had already been noticeable in the new meanings which canon lawyers were giving to the term 'natural law', meanings which moved away from duty-imposing rules (such as 'thou shalt not lie') towards subjective rights. This move reflected the need to recast thinking on a ground which acknowledged all humans as moral agents, as free choosers. Franciscan use of the 'state of nature' convention to establish a natural right to renounce all property was but one example of such reinterpretation. New distinctions were also made when discussing 'liberty' and dominium. These distinctions added to the conceptual groundwork for separating a private sphere from the public sphere, what would later be called 'civil society' from 'the state'.

We can see this process under way in the thinking of the Franciscan theologian and philosopher, John Duns Scotus, at the end of the thirteenth century. His analysis of the nature of moral obligation is striking.

Duns Scotus lays it down that 'an act is neither praiseworthy nor blameworthy unless it proceeds from the free will'.[1] For him, freedom is a prerequisite for moral conduct.

Why is this important? In effect, Duns Scotus separates two elements in St Paul's vision of 'Christian liberty'. When rejecting reliance on the Jewish law, Paul had held up the quality of the will – love of the Christ – as a liberation from mere rule-bound behaviour, and offered a moralized conception of liberty. For him, aligning the will with the Christ meant freely choosing the injunctions of brotherly love, the claims of human equality and reciprocity. To be 'truly' free was to love God in that sense.

Duns Scotus disentangles two things from Paul's vision. He identifies freedom as a necessary condition of moral conduct. But he does not believe that it is a sufficient condition. He does not identify it wholly with morality. Freedom may result in 'blameworthy' as well as 'praiseworthy' choices. For the latter to be the case, human choices must conform to justice, what Duns Scotus calls 'right reason': 'To attribute moral goodness is to attribute conformity to right reason.'

> Every morally good act must be objectively good, in the sense of having an object conformable to right reason; but no act is good on this count alone . . . 'the goodness of the will does not depend on the object alone, but on all the other circumstances . . .' But though the end holds the primary place among the circumstances of the act, an act is not morally good merely because the end is good: the end does not justify the means.[2]

Freedom emerges as a necessary but not a sufficient condition for morality:

> 'It is necessary that all the requisite circumstances should occur together in any moral act, for it to be morally good; the defect of any one circumstance is sufficient in order that (the act) should be morally bad.' 'Evil should not be done in order that good (results) may eventuate.' For an act to be good, then, it must be free, and it must be objectively good and be done with the right intention.[3]

By separating the ideas of freedom and justice, while presenting both as necessary conditions of moral conduct, Duns Scotus took an important step. He was not alone, however. Through preoccupation with the will and the conditions of its exercise, a distinctive Franciscan philosophical tradition had formed by the fourteenth century. This emerges unmistakably in the work of the greatest Franciscan theologian and philosopher, William of Ockham.

Just as Duns Scotus distinguishes two elements within the idea of 'Christian liberty', Ockham distinguishes two meanings of the term dominium, meanings that had previously often been run together.

Ockham benefited from the work of canon lawyers. They had begun to refer to the 'rights' of dominium (*jus dominii*) – a usage unknown in antiquity when dominium or lordship was understood as a privileged social fact rather than an individual right. Dominium then conjured up a superior social position, a position which, by definition, was not shared by all. Once the term 'right' was introduced by the canonists, however, a new universality entered. And that, in Ockham's eyes, revealed an ambiguity in the ancient usage. He argues that the ancient use of dominium combined, in 'modern' terms, two different meanings: a right to rule and the right to own. These two meanings have to be separated, Ockham implies, if thinking is to be clear.[4]

In effect, Ockham adjusts the traditional use of dominium to the new assumption of moral equality. As long as thinking rested on the assumption of natural inequality, there had been no need to separate the two meanings – indeed, no possibility of doing so. For dominium had then conveyed the inherent mastery or domination of some over others, a domination that combined ownership and rule. Thus, the patrician's ownership of his slaves was also the power to rule, while the role of the paterfamilias meant that the father not only governed but also in a sense owned his family. Such radical inequality had been fundamental to ancient societies. Radical differences of status were conveyed by the term dominium, differences so fundamental that they constrained all other social arrangements.

If such radical differences of status were not taken for granted, however, then the need to distinguish different meanings became urgent. It was especially urgent for Ockham, because he wished to probe the grounds of obligation to obey both secular and religious authorities, particularly the emperor and the pope. When we examine his arguments, it becomes clear how far moral intuitions had changed since the Carolingian period. Ockham cannot accept what might be called the schizophrenia of the Carolingians, oscillation between egalitarian emphasis on the 'care of souls' and a universal oath of allegiance to the ruler on the one hand; and on the other hand, reliance on dominium or lordship (mastery or de facto power) as the means of preserving social order.

Ockham insisted on the difference between mere power and a 'licit' or rightful power, power understood as a *jus* or 'right'. To call a power 'rightful' implies a higher norm – 'right reason' or justice. That norm introduces the God-given belief in moral equality, that is, recognition of freedom of the will and individual moral agency.[5] Thus, if dominium is to be understood as a *jus* or 'right', and not merely mastery or de facto power, it has to respect the norms of equality and reciprocity. And the right to rule must be distinguished from rights of ownership.

This introduction of the language of rights into discussions of government and property paved the way for a clear distinction between 'the state' and 'civil society'. While not understanding it in our terms, the Franciscans Duns Scotus and Ockham put into place the basic building blocks of modern secularism. In refining the idea of Christian liberty – separating the idea of freedom from that of justice and making both conditions of morality as well as distinguishing rights of ownership from a right to rule – they prepared a revolution in the understanding of the 'proper' ground of all authority. They moved from an aristocratic towards a democratic idea of authority.

The canon lawyers had contributed greatly to this development, through their dialogue with theologians. By the thirteenth century something else was added. Philosophy was emerging out of theology, leading to ever more intense debate about the 'proper' relationship between reason and faith. But not only that. The developments in both theology and philosophical argument testified to the presence of a new institution which fostered intellectual ambition and achievement, giving far more reality to talk of 'schools of thought' or 'traditions'.

Such traditions required more than the curiosity, moral seriousness and dialectical skills of individuals. They were made possible by the emergence of a new form of association that gave thinking greater discipline and continuity. For in addition to the growth of urban centres and trade during this period – spreading the seeds of a social class intermediate between the feudal aristocracy and serfs – the European university made its appearance.

The university was something almost unprecedented. It gave the claims of individual reason and dissent a public space which had previously been lacking. It made possible a new social role, the intellectual, thinkers who 'navigated' between the claims of church and secular government. For one of the striking things about the early history of universities is their success in generating a competition of favours from church and state. Both popes and princes went out of their way to encourage and protect the fledgling universities. Both sought to benefit from the new institution. But neither succeeded in mastering it.[6]

The more complex social division of labour which resulted from the growth of urban centres and market exchanges had created both a new setting for learning and greater demand for it. As a consequence, the traditional centres of learning – the cathedral and monastic schools – were becoming anachronistic. The twelfth century presided over these changes. Details of how what became the 'masters' and 'scholars' of a new corporation – a *universitas* in canon law – first took form are tantalizingly few. But two things are clear from the oldest universities. First, in Bologna it was the students, organized into 'nations', who employed their teachers, while in Paris it was the teachers who joined together and shaped the emerging university. Secondly, different subjects led the way in different places, law at Bologna, theology at Paris, natural philosophy at Oxford, medicine at Montpellier.

During the thirteenth century the new universities were given charters by the pope or a secular ruler and their structures were formalized in statutes. The charters conferred privileges on both students and professors, protecting them from local policing, feudal services and taxation by granting them an independent jurisdiction and giving them the right to confer degrees after a carefully regulated course of study.[7] Usually a student had to complete a degree in arts before moving to the study of theology, law or medicine, culminating in the doctorate which qualified him for university teaching. It was not long before the university-educated came to occupy many of the most important posts in both ecclesiastical and secular government in Europe.

The assembly of minds which the new universities promoted gave a tremendous fillip to argument. The marshalling of arguments 'for' and 'against' – which had roots in the dialectics championed by Abelard and the methods applied in Gratian's *Decretum* – shaped the form of university teaching. 'Disputations' were as important as lectures on required texts. In a disputation some proposition had a 'defender' who was confronted with an 'objector', while the arguments put forward on both sides were finally arranged and assessed by the presiding professor.

During the twelfth century the recovery of Aristotle's major works – especially his *Physics*, *Metaphysics* and *Ethics* – also raised intellectual sights. To the advantages derived from the association of minds in universities was added the example of close argument of the highest order. Translated from Arabic texts rather than from the original Greek, Aristotle's works offered at once a model and a challenge. Could Christian thinkers expound their doctrine with the same subtlety and precision? The combination of a university education and the challenge offered by Aristotle's philosophical writings led to far more ambitious works combining theology and philosophy being undertaken by the second half of the thirteenth century. The goal was to create a synthesis which reconciled faith and reason by showing how philosophy could generate a 'natural' theology consistent with Christian revelation.

The most remarkable thinkers who pursued this goal are now remembered as saints: Bonaventure, Albert the Great and Thomas Aquinas. Yet despite sharing that status, there were important differences in the use they made of Aristotle. No doubt all of them claimed to reject 'pagan' philosophy when it conflicted with Christian revelation. Yet Bonaventure remained within the Augustinian tradition – concerned, above all, with relating the individual will to God's will – while adapting some arguments from Aristotle. Albert the Great and Thomas Aquinas, on the other hand, sought to integrate far more of Aristotle ('The Philosopher' as he was called) with Christianity.[8]

It is striking that these thinkers (as well as Duns Scotus and William of Ockham) were all either Franciscans or Dominicans. The mendicant orders had at first encountered strong opposition when they sought – as 'regular' rather than 'secular' clergy – to integrate 'houses' of study into the new universities and take an important part in the teaching of theology. Yet by the mid-thirteenth century they succeeded in establishing 'chairs' at Paris and gaining recognition for their houses at Oxford and Bologna.

The mendicant orders can lay claim to great intellectual achievements in the thirteenth and the fourteenth centuries. However, the Franciscan and Dominican traditions in theology and philosophy came to differ in an ever more fundamental way. And that difference was to have extraordinary influence on the future development of Europe, both on its thought and on its institutions. The fourteenth century saw this difference emerge in the form of intractable tensions between the claims of philosophy and theology, tensions which jeopardized the attempt to create a synthesis of Aristotle and Christian beliefs.

The importance of the difference between the two traditions can hardly be overstated. Examining this difference and its source requires some oversimplification, for neither the Franciscans nor the Dominicans offered a uniform point of view. Nonetheless, by the fourteenth century many Dominicans revered Thomas Aquinas as their 'Doctor' and his synthesis of Aristotle and Christian beliefs as definitive for the church. While the Franciscans never proclaimed a 'Doctor' in the same way, they tacitly recognized Duns Scotus and William of Ockham as their outstanding thinkers and spokesmen.

The difference between the two traditions has been described as that between 'Augustinians' and 'Aristotelians', between 'conservatives' and 'radicals' as well as between contrasting accounts of the relationship between will and reason. The latter description gets nearest to the source of the difference. Yet even it does not go deep enough.

What did the contrast between the Dominican emphasis on 'reason' and the Franciscan emphasis on 'will' spring from? It sprang from radically different assessments of the extent to which 'pagan' philosophy could safely be appropriated for the understanding and exposition of Christian doctrine. But behind that difference lay another that was even more fundamental. What were the consequences of such appropriation for the Christian-inspired belief in moral equality?

The Franciscan tradition harboured serious doubts about wholesale borrowing from Aristotle's theory of knowledge and his metaphysics of 'nature'. Ancient rationalism seemed to re-emerge in Aquinas' view that 'the root of freedom has the will as its subject, but reason as its cause'.[9] The Franciscans detected in such borrowings a residue of the ancient assumption that reason could 'command' reality, and that, out of its own resources, reason could demonstrate the deepest metaphysical and moral truths. In Franciscan eyes, that assumption was arrogant. It elevated human fiat above the facts of moral experience, the complexity of human motivation and dependence of the will on 'grace'. Franciscans found such arrogance lurking in Aristotle's teleological model of nature. For its hierarchical framework – postulating 'essences' and 'final causes' – threatened the humility required by the truth revealed in the Christ. It threatened the assumption of moral equality.

The Franciscan tradition held that belief in moral equality entailed humility in the use of reason. For if humans are equal, they are also equally fallible. This duality of moral experience led Franciscans – following Augustine – to pay closer attention to the nature of human agency. Their insistence on the importance of the will was balanced by recognition of its inconstant nature. Humans are free and endowed with rationality. But an upright will also depends on the support of revelation to supply motive force.

In contrast to Dominican emphasis on rationality and 'correct' doctrine, Franciscan emphasis on human agency involved a revised view of the role of reason. Reason became the companion of the will rather than its arrogant master. For the mere use of reason could not guarantee what mattered most, an upright will. Left entirely to its own resources, reason could not take us to the heart of the matter. Such access required the union of individual wills with a higher will, through the practice of humility, prayer and the gift of grace. A kind of spiritual training or 'pilgrimage' was needed. Reason acquired the status of 'right reason' only when it submitted to the moral law revealed by revelation, enjoining brotherly love and humility about its own claims when exploring a world it has not created.

In Franciscan eyes, excessive borrowing from pagan philosophy – associated with Thomas Aquinas' *Summa Theologica* (1273) – jeopardized the originality of Christianity. It obscured what had led the early Christian Fathers to reject even Stoic ethics. The tentative universalism in Stoicism did not reach the deepest layers of the self as the Christian revelation did. Nor did Judaism — for all of its emphasis on God's will – go so deep. While pregnant with further moral development, Judaism remained tribal. By contrast, Christianity held up the prospect of an essentially individual rather than a tribal relationship with divinity. It called individual wills into existence and gave them a glimpse of the transcendent. It offered a relationship that informed social life rather than being determined by it. Franciscan arguments implied that neither pagan philosophy nor Judaism could fully emancipate the individual from conventional social roles. Both failed to reach the depths that only humility – illustrated by the life of Francis, who sought to imitate the Christ – could plumb. For Franciscans, that was the significance of the incarnation. The idea of 'God with us' linked human agency with a higher agency.

It was no accident that Augustine was a major source of inspiration for the Franciscan tradition. For it is only a slight exaggeration to say that Augustine, drawing on Paul, invented the idea of the will. Arguably, the Christian assumption of moral equality made such an idea indispensable. It distanced individuals from whatever social roles they might occupy. As we have seen, the individual became the 'primary' role, while other social roles became secondary. Such roles became the attributes of a subject endowed with a will. But they could not exhaust the subject's identity. Thus individual identity was deemed to be extrinsic to social relations and the rightful criterion of them. The will acquired a privileged status as the threshold of divinity, the precondition for entering what Augustine called the city of God.

If we are to understand the Franciscans, we must again look back at Augustine.

Augustine introduced a more complex notion of human agency than that to be found in ancient philosophy, a notion incorporating both the freedom and the weakness of the will. Influenced by Augustine, Franciscans such as William of Ockham adopted a view of human agency which stripped reason of the motivational power often attributed to it by the ancient schools of philosophy. Reason could and should shape action. But it could not, by itself, determine action. Instead, the practice of humility and an infusion of grace had to supplement upright intentions, 'right reasons' for acting. For humans were equal, not least in their weakness.

Franciscan thinkers benefited from the abstracting potential that the Church Fathers had drawn from pagan philosophy when creating Christian theology, with its moral universalism. But they also accepted Augustine's assessment of the limitations of ancient philosophy, limitations emerging especially in its model of human agency. What disturbed the Franciscans was that Aquinas' attempt to assimilate the larger part of Aristotle might reintroduce (even if only implicitly) the model of human agency characteristic of ancient rationalism. Why was Aquinas less concerned about this possibility? The reason is clear enough. Aquinas' intellectual formation and that of Augustine resulted in each having a very different relationship with ancient philosophy. They had moved in opposite directions.

Augustine had worked his way through the pagan schools and become dissatisfied with them before he became a Christian. Aquinas, on the other hand, was a believer before he discovered in Aristotle a range of speculation far exceeding that in previous Christian theology. So Aquinas sought to extend and strengthen Christian thinking with the help of 'The Philosopher'.[10] Was Aquinas over-impressed by Aristotle as a result? He could hardly fail to be. The translation of many more of Aristotle's works into Latin by the thirteenth century had revealed the extraordinary range and rigour of his thought. Nonetheless, the Franciscans came to draw on Augustine's critique of ancient philosophy precisely because it mirrored their own doubts about Aristotle's influence.

Before his conversion, Augustine had taken the schools of ancient philosophy – Stoic, Peripatetic and Platonic – on their own terms. He had not judged them from the standpoint of Christian belief. Yet by the time Augustine took up residence in Milan and came under the influence of its bishop, Ambrose, he remained unsatisfied. The true nature and needs of the self seemed to elude the ancient schools. They failed to identify a relationship which, Augustine began to suspect, is the only relationship that can liberate and satisfy the self. It was his study of St Paul's letters that enabled Augustine to escape from what he saw as the limits of ancient philosophy. For Paul took the idea of the self down to a deeper, pre-social level. Paul's conception of the Christ – a mystical union of individuals through love of the Christ – made possible a descent into the self and a fuller understanding of human agency. Thus, the will and the conditions of its exercise became Augustine's preferred study. For him, God's grace, revealed by the Christ, provided the means of entry into a truer self offered to all equally.

This discovery enabled Augustine to identify the assumption affecting all the pre-Christian schools of philosophy, the assumption of natural inequality, which Paul's conception of the Christ overturned. Even the tentative universalism in Stoicism now struck Augustine as redolent of pagan pride rather than Christian humility. It was a matter for speculation rather than the source of a moral imperative. Whether the assumption of natural inequality took the form of Plato's division of society into guardians, warriors and workers, Aristotle's distinction between citizens and slaves ('living tools') or the Stoics' aristocratic view that only a few could ever attain 'true' knowledge and virtue, that assumption effectively ruled out the moral universalism which, for Augustine, was the crux of Paul's message.

Even before incorporating this contrast into his greatest work, the *City of God*, Augustine had combated what he regarded as elitist temptations surviving from pagan philosophy. That can be seen in his attack on Pelagianism as well as his critique of early monasticism. At first glance Pelagius' vindication of free will might seem far more egalitarian than Augustine's emphasis on grace. For Pelagius held that God's gift to man was a free will, which enabled him to choose and follow the good: 'Once the accretion of evil habits contracted through contact with the "world" had been washed away through the transformative effects of baptism, every Christian believer was both able and obliged to reach out for perfection. For Pelagius, every Christian was the master craftsman of his or her own soul.'[11] For Augustine, by contrast, Pelagius' account of human agency was dangerously oversimplified. Pelagius misunderstood the implications of free will. He assumed that Christians could simply decide to be good and become so. In Augustine's eyes, this view was contaminated by ancient rationalism, by the assumption that reason, on its own, could motivate. This was to misunderstand the complex nature of the will and the extent to which grace was required to reinforce good intentions. Humility, rather than the pride of ancient reason, provided the key.

The Pelagian controversy brings out the nature of Augustine's egalitarianism, his sensitivity to the enormous difficulties humans face in reforming their wills. For Augustine, the genius of Christianity lay in its understanding of and compassion for human weakness. For Augustine, freedom of the will did not exclude recognizing the importance of other causes, in particular, the impact of habits acquired over a lifetime. Such habits posed terrible obstacles to any lasting reformation of the will. Pelagianism, with its exclusive emphasis on self-control, led to a kind of elitism. It separated Christians into two groups, the more perfect and the less.

> His [Augustine's] instinctive suspicion of any form of spiritual elitism was reinforced by the theology of human action and divine grace which he developed in the course of his debate with Pelagius . . . Thus Augustine came to realize that he had to abandon the old idea that what distinguished the monastic life from other forms of Christian living was the pursuit of perfection through self-denial. The question of perfection could not be allowed to be the monopoly of one group of Christians. The Christian community could not be allowed to be divided by a double standard, one for the ordinary Christian, another for an ascetic elite . . .[12]

Seeking to create a spiritual elite drew implicitly on the assumption of natural inequality, threatening to reintroduce an inherent superiority of some over others (dominium). As Peter Brown remarks, for Augustine, however, the support of grace for an upright will was a need shared by all Christians equally, 'a source of comfort to the humble and a warning to the proud'.

Ancient philosophers, living in societies founded on the belief in human inequality, had projected hierarchy onto the 'natural' order of things. It infected their ideas of nature and social order. How could it have been otherwise? It was 'natural' for them to conflate the dictates of reason with the commands of a superior social position. Christian beliefs dispelled that confusion. If Christian belief provides the foundation for the individual as a moral status and a social role, it helps to explain Franciscan anxiety about the results of trying to merge ancient rationalism with those beliefs. For many ideas associated with ancient rationalism – the unequal distribution of reason among men, the eternity of the world and reliance on a theory of essences – pointed back to the belief in natural inequality.

Would the enthusiasm for Aristotle lead to the Christian God being made subject to rationality as understood by the ancients? If so, seeking a synthesis of Aristotle and Christianity came at too high a price for the Franciscans. It risked extracting from Christianity its Jewish roots: the idea of creation and a God who acts in history, the emphasis on a higher will and distrust of human pride. By contrast, Aristotle's account of man as a social being could remove any appeal beyond the norms of particular societies, however unequal. The attempt of Aquinas to join Aristotelian rationalism with Christian doctrine might in that way subvert the idea of human agency defended by Paul and Augustine, a pre-social basis for individual identity.

At risk was the role of conscience created by Christian beliefs, a domain which required principles higher than merely social norms. Had not the ancient Greeks called anyone who sought to stand outside the norms of his society 'an idiot'? Was the Christ therefore (as well as his follower, St Francis) an idiot? The crux of the Franciscan tradition was its defence of egalitarian moral intuitions. But that raised another question. What kind of society and what form of the church could satisfy the intuition that there is something in every man that goes beyond the social, creating a rightful domain for individual conscience and choice?

Such was the momentous question emerging in Europe by the fourteenth century. It was prompted by the erosion of feudal status differences, through papal and royal claims to a 'sovereign' authority, as well as the challenge posed by Aristotle's account of citizenship and 'the good life'. It was a question with unprecedented subversive potential, opening a kind of Pandora's Box. For it led to Christian moral intuitions being turned against authoritarian forms of both church and state. It was a question that created powerful pressures for reform and ushered in a new world.

23

God's Freedom and Human Freedom Joined: Ockham

Things are not always what they seem to be. This is especially true of the fourteenth century. The fourteenth century witnessed intellectual developments which make it the gateway to modern Europe. It introduced themes that became central in the following centuries: the rightful claims of conscience and civil liberty, the importance of government by consent as well as the difference between understanding 'nature' and 'culture'. Yet at first glance the fourteenth century can seem to be trapped in rather arid debates about the attributes of God, debates that involved, in turn, disagreements about the role of philosophy as distinct from that of theology.

Why did these debates have such unexpected and far-reaching consequences? We have already encountered a deeper stratum of argument. Lying under the surface was an attempt by Franciscan thinkers to purge the remains of ancient rationalism from Christian thinking. In their view, such elements contaminated Christian thinking, leading it into a framework of ideas shaped by the assumption of natural inequality. For Franciscans, this emerged whenever theologians tried to explain the world in terms of 'rational necessity' rather than divine and human liberty.

So what was meant by 'rational necessity' and why had that notion come to seem unacceptable for understanding the relationship of God to the world?

By the later thirteenth century Franciscans were criticizing Aquinas for relying too much on Aristotle's philosophy in his *Summa Theologica*. At first their criticisms were piecemeal, but this situation soon changed. During the fourteenth century Franciscan 'nominalism' – the philosophical movement increasingly dubbed 'the modern way'–

became more ambitious and assertive. We have already met its leading thinker, William of Ockham, who had studied and taught at Oxford. Summoned to Avignon to defend his ideas in 1324, Ockham came in for papal censure for defending the Franciscan position over the renunciation of property rights. He felt obliged to take refuge with the German emperor. Despite the papal censure, which led to his excommunication, Ockham's influence spread rapidly. In the church at large, his nominalism became associated with the 'Spiritual Franciscans', who embraced a moral radicalism distrusted by the papacy.

The surest way of understanding the nominalist movement and its appeal is to look more closely at Ockham's differences with Aquinas. For this will enable us to come to grips with systems of thought which began to pull Europe in different directions. It will also enable us to understand better what was meant by 'rational necessity' and why that notion became the focus of Ockham's attempt to root out the remains of ancient rationalism from Christian thinking.

Let us start with questions about the nature of God – for it is important to remember that both Aquinas and Ockham were theologians as well as philosophers. What was the issue between them? It turned on the question of God's rationality versus God's freedom. William of Ockham sought, above all, to assert God's freedom, believing that the world we experience and the moral duties we acknowledge are the results of his choices as creator. They are not the result of ideas or 'essences' which can be known a priori and which constrain even God's actions. For Ockham, God's creation cannot be 'second-guessed'. We have not created ourselves, but we have been created with free will. Is that not the clue given to us about the nature of things? Ockham's nominalism celebrated contingency rather than rational necessity.

The nominalists thus turned their back on a long-standing form of philosophical argument. Postulating 'eternal ideas' or essences can be traced back to Plato's doctrine of forms – archetypes deemed to be more real than our day-to-day experience of things. These forms provided, *ex hypothesi*, the keys to metaphysical truth which could be identified by minds sufficiently philosophical. Such minds were able to break through mere appearances to the nature of things. While differing from Plato in other respects, Aristotle preserved the idea of forms or essences when he postulated the 'final causes' of things, that towards which 'by nature' they tend as their goal.

Early Christian thinkers, educated in Greek philosophy, revised these arguments by lodging such forms or essences as 'eternal ideas' in the mind of God. And medieval theologians such as Bonaventure had continued to postulate such ideas. For them, it was by means of eternal ideas that God had constructed the world.[1] Thus, the form or eternal idea of a 'human nature' constrained even God when it was a question of man's duty or obligation. The moral law was dictated by man's nature. Not even God could alter it.

Augustine too had referred to eternal ideas in the mind of God. Yet his insistence on a direct, intimate relationship between God's will and individual wills suggested another direction – a direction which could potentially overturn the basis of the theory of essences or eternal ideas. Ockham moved in that direction. It is true that Aquinas' references to eternal ideas in the mind of God were nuanced. But they were enough to convince Ockham that Greek rationalism – with its belief in the eternity of the world and essences – posed a threat to belief in God's freedom as creator.[2] That freedom was at the heart of Ockham's voluntarist philosophy, the source of his defence of freedom against necessity.

Aquinas could hardly deny that Aristotle had assumed the eternity of the world, a permanent structure to which superior minds had access.[3] Did that not compromise Christian belief in a God who acts freely in time rather than being constrained by pre-established rational forms? And did not such forms imply an overly unified structure of rationality which ran contrary to the idea of individual human souls endowed with a free will? In Aristotle's system, immortality belonged to essences or ideas rather than to individual souls. For Ockham, such conclusions subverted the vision of a God who acts in history and has a direct relationship with souls, a vision turning on freedom.[4]

Why did Ockham insist, above all, on God's freedom? The biblical argument that freedom reveals the way humans are made 'in the image of God' suggests one possible answer. The nominalists were reasserting the Jewish sources of Christian thought against Greek influences. But there is another possibility. The canonist conversion of natural law into a theory of natural rights, founded on the assumption of moral equality, was feeding back into the conception of divinity itself. Emphasizing the claims of the will in human agency led Ockham to emphasize the same trait in divine agency. Human freedom and God's freedom were becoming mutually reinforcing characteristics. That is why contingency and choice, rather than eternal ideas and a priori knowledge, loomed so large in his thinking. Ockham denied that the kind of a priori knowledge of the universe required by the doctrine of eternal ideas or 'essences' is possible. Exaggerating the capabilities of human reason, it compromises God's freedom and power, his 'sovereignty'.

In order to defend God's sovereignty, Ockham (developing a tradition initiated by Abelard) insisted on the difference between two types of reasoning: deductive and inductive. Deductive reasoning explores the relations between the meaning of words, and turns on issues of consistency and logical entailment. By contrast, inductive reasoning is concerned with the relations between words and 'things', the world of sense experience. Its propositions are at best probable, requiring verification by the senses, what Ockham calls 'intuitions' of the external world. So it follows that 'necessary' truth belongs only to the former, and not to the world of things.

In Ockham's eyes, the doctrine of necessary or a priori knowledge misleads the human mind by privileging its capacity for definition over the contingent facts of experience. The assumption that universal categories such as 'man' are more real than the experiences of 'men' jeopardizes belief in God's direct relation to individuals. Such philosophical 'realism' fosters the illusion of a corporate human mind. Thus, belief in universals or concepts as eternal 'things in themselves' does not only put God's freedom at risk. But the doctrine is also a threat to individual freedom, to the belief in equal moral agency.

By emphasizing the role of the will, Ockham associated reason with individual experience and choice rather than with 'legislating' about a timeless 'nature' of things. But he does not present the will as unconstrained. Rather, the self, which is a gift of God, is obligated by the principles of equality and reciprocity, by 'right reason'.[5] That, indeed, is fundamental to understanding ourselves as creatures of God. So while accepting that human reason can be distinguished from the will for certain purposes, Ockham, like Augustine, denies that intellect and will are entirely distinct faculties. Rather, they are companions. Human agency is a unity. Acts spring from the whole self or soul.

That is how Ockham recast the role of reason. It is tempting to see his attack on the doctrine of eternal ideas as another stage in the prolonged struggle between polytheism and monotheism, for the rejection of essences and 'final causes' bears some resemblance to the attack on belief in 'demons' conducted by the early church. Both sprang from an aversion to populating the world with agencies intermediate between God and humans, agencies endowed with purpose or goals. In Ockham's eyes, belief in such agencies obscured the direct relationship between the Creator and the created.

That is the background to the principle of explanation associated with his name: 'Ockham's Razor'. It calls for economy in explanation, avoiding the introduction of unnecessary entities or terms. Sharing with other nominalists the belief that 'it is futile to work with more entities when it is possible to work with fewer', Ockham argued that 'a plurality must not be asserted without necessity'. And, with more than a little sarcasm, he used his 'razor' to remove Aristotle's 'final causes': 'The special characteristic of a final cause is that it is able to cause when it does not exist; from which it follows that this movement towards an end is not real but metaphorical.'[6] Ockham concluded that even Aquinas' sophisticated use of Aristotelian philosophy offended against the principle of economy in explanation. It exemplified what we would call the pathetic fallacy or anthropomorphism, by projecting categories drawn from human action, such as goals or purposes, onto the physical world and misrepresenting the location of moral agency.

The fourteenth century saw a bitter contest develop between doctrines associated with Aquinas and Ockham, between ideas which continued to carry the impress of the 'ancient' assumption of natural inequality and 'modern' ideas that divine and human liberty are indissolubly joined. The protagonists remained the Dominican and Franciscan traditions. While the Dominicans increasingly accepted Aquinas' status as the uniquely authoritative 'doctor' of the church, the Franciscans followed a path which distanced the use of reason from the constraints imposed by Aquinas' attempt to synthesize reason and faith. Ockham, in particular, held that any attempt to create a 'natural' theology by drawing on ancient rationalism and the idea of 'necessary truth' was doomed to fail, for it required reason to prove more than it was capable of proving.

We have seen that in the ancient world belief in natural inequality contributed to a teleology which associated rationality with hierarchy. Hierarchy had come to shape the image of both nature and society. The model it held up was 'everything in its proper place'. For Ockham, by contrast, Christian understanding of the soul's relationship to God founded the claim of 'equal liberty'. Rational agency became a birthright, shared by all humans equally.

Ancient rationalism had not conferred freedom and responsibility on individuals as such. That is why it had never fully generated a morality founded on the notion of individual 'rights'. Rather, ancient philosophers had emphasized fate, pride and shame, an entirely social matrix for morality.[7] They took for granted the privileged life of the citizen in the polis. The ancient citizen acted out a role in the presence of his inferiors. Even Aristotle's account of virtue as 'moderation' or the austere ethic of Stoicism carried messages different from that of Christianity. 'Virtue' understood as proud self-control and a will regenerated by humility through belief in human equality are not the same thing.

Ockham drew on the Augustinian tradition which portrayed a descent into the self as leading, paradoxically, to discovery of a higher will. That tradition presented the individual will, when properly directed, as a vehicle of divine agency. Such continuity of agency had no place in the polytheism of the ancient world, nor in the model of reason fostered by a society which rested on the assumption of natural inequality. That is why Ockham rejected the doctrine of rational necessity in the name of God's sovereignty and human freedom.

Did Ockham also benefit from social changes when developing his 'modern' critique of ancient rationalism? Probably. By the fourteenth century permanent differences of social status were under threat in Europe. They no longer seemed unavoidable. The moral intuitions 'carried' by Christian beliefs had acquired deeper roots. We have already seen how a corporate conception of society was giving way to the image of society as an association of individuals. The new 'sovereign' legal systems in church and state propagated that image. And the rapid growth of cities and commerce – with the emergence of a 'middling' class which advertised the advantages of social relations based on choice rather than inherited status – made it vivid.

Plague, in the form of the Black Death in mid-century, reinforced this trend by creating a sudden scarcity of labour. But decades before its arrival, a French king, Louis le Hutin, had declared in 1315 his determination to end serfdom and ensure that all the French were 'free'. The words of his decree reveal the extent of the revolution in minds:

> Louis, by the Grace of God King of France and Navarre ... As according to the law of nature each must be born free, and that by some usages and customs, which of great antiquity have been introduced and hitherto preserved in our kingdom ... many of our common people have fallen into servitude and diverse conditions which very much displease us; we, considering that our kingdom is called ... the kingdom of the Franks [free men], and wishing that the fact should be truly accordant with the name ... upon deliberation of our great council, have ordered and order that generally through our kingdom ... such servitudes be brought back to freedom and that to all those who from origin or recently from marriage or from residence in places of servile condition are fallen ... into bonds of servitude, freedom be given. ... [8]

No doubt rulers appreciated that such an appeal could be useful in their struggle against feudal lords. But it is clear, in any case, that personal identity was increasingly being joined to the idea of freedom. The world had begun to seem more open-ended, even the world of serfs.

If so, was God to be less free than his creatures? Was it plausible that a 'sovereign' God's actions could be subject to necessity? As we have just seen, Ockham and his Franciscan followers thought not. For them, the core of Christian revelation was the 'grace' which the Christ offered to all equally. That grace held out the prospect of an individual relationship with divinity which transcended social relations and required a new understanding of the role of reason. It was this conviction that turned Ockham and his followers into harbingers of 'modernity'.

For a millennium the doctrines of the church and the role of its priesthood had – without any socially subversive intention – weakened the association of hierarchy with reason. Ockham and his nominalist followers brought this development to a climax. They did two remarkable things: they reconstructed the idea of justice and revised the test for scientific truth. Their work was truly revolutionary. Nominalists laid the foundations for what we now call 'liberal secularism' as well as for what we call experimental or 'empirical' science.

Taking the moral autonomy of individuals as their weapon, the nominalists broke through a set of assumptions which had confined the structure of society and the pursuit of knowledge within an hierarchical or corporate framework. Ockham replaced those assumptions with the assertion of individual rights (justifying a private sphere of choice) and the verification principle (which made knowledge of the external world always subject to disproof by further experience). In drawing a sharper contrast between the terms in which we understand our own actions and our knowledge of external, physical processes, the nominalists, in effect, began to separate 'culture' from 'nature' – emphasizing the central role of reasons and intentions in the former, while driving explanations in terms of purpose from the latter.

It was a bittersweet moment. Distinguishing between knowledge of nature and knowledge of culture did not merely challenge traditional assumptions about the unity of knowledge. It also called into question the possibility of proving God's existence by constructing a 'natural' theology, the enterprise which Aquinas, under the influence of Aristotle, had pursued. Thus, Ockham's emphasis on faith and freedom confronted Aquinas' rationalist account of natural law.

We can see this by looking more closely at two respects in which Ockham differed radically from Aquinas. The first is Ockham's emphasis on natural rights and liberty rather than on traditional natural law. The second is his insistence on the difference between demonstrative reasoning and causal explanation, between 'rational science' and 'experimental science'. In each case, we see the human mind embarking on a new voyage, a voyage of discovery.

Ockham's understanding of justice emerged as the claim for 'equal liberty'. Freedom became a birthright, a right founded on the nature of human agency. For two hundred years canon lawyers had been converting the ancient doctrine of natural law into a theory of natural rights. They had come close to asserting a general right to freedom. But it was left to Ockham and his followers to take that final step. That is why the 'poverty debate', which involved the Franciscan order in repeated conflicts with the papacy, became so important. It was the Franciscan emphasis on a natural right to freedom, justifying their claim to renounce property of any kind, that finally led to Ockham's excommunication.

Freedom was central to Ockham's understanding of rational agency. He defined it as the power 'by which I can indifferently and contingently produce an effect in such a way that I can cause or not cause that effect, without any difference in that power having been made'.[9] Knowledge of freedom comes not from a priori reasoning but from experience of ourselves as agents. That knowledge, in turn, underpins our sense of moral responsibility. 'No act is blameworthy unless it is in our power. For no one blames a man born blind, for he is blind by sense (*caecus sensu*). But if he is blind by his own act, then he is blameworthy.'[10] The human will does not will anything *necessarily* – not the pursuit of happiness or even the enjoyment of God for those with faith! For Ockham, this radical character of freedom makes it both possible and important to distinguish between acting out of conviction and mere conformity of behaviour.

In Ockham's eyes, it was no accident that Paul had spoken of 'Christian liberty'. By linking freedom to a regenerated will, the idea of 'Christian liberty' undermined the ancient meaning of freedom, freedom understood as a form of privilege, a social status or rank. However, the idea of Christian liberty had not merely been egalitarian. It had also, by definition, been fully moralized. To be truly free, for Paul, was to be moral. But the nominalists' emphasis on the will led them to revise this account of 'Christian liberty', and to abandon a fully moralized definition of freedom.

We have seen how Duns Scotus distinguished freedom from 'right reason' or justice, arguing that freedom and upright intentions are separable ideas, while each is a necessary condition for moral action. But if freedom is separable from the idea of 'right reason' or justice, what is to be done if it conflicts with some claim of justice? Here Ockham goes further than Duns Scotus, for he celebrates autonomy as such. We can see this in two remarkable turns taken by his argument.

The first is his defence of mistaken moral judgements, while the second emerges in his insistence that individuals can choose to renounce some natural rights.

In order to protect the sphere of conscience, Ockham argues that allowance must be made for well-intentioned conduct, even if it conflicts with a dictate of 'right reason' or justice. When an agent believes – mistakenly – that his intention accords with justice, he is obligated to follow his conscience. That is why promoting the claims of justice must not lead to the extinction of freedom, for freedom remains a necessary condition of moral action. So Ockham defends what might be called 'conscientious mistakes' of judgement.

'Right reason' – the canonists' golden rule – continued to provide the standard of justice for Ockham. But he argues that the sphere of conscience, with the freedoms required to sustain that sphere, should be defended against interpretations of 'right reason' which jeopardize liberty: 'A created will which follows an invincibly erroneous conscience is a right will; for the divine will wills that it should follow its reason when this reason is not blameworthy. If it acts against that reason (that is, against an invincibly erroneous conscience), it sins. . . .'[11] If the role of conscience is to be protected by society, there must be room for such mistaken judgements. By insisting that intentions formed in a 'conscientious' way deserve respect, Ockham implies that in the absence of freedom, the notion of moral conduct itself becomes incoherent. 'Enforced' morality becomes a contradiction in terms.

That does not mean there are no enforceable moral limits to choice. Ockham makes it clear that some actions remain 'blameworthy', providing grounds for social intervention and punishment. Thus, acting in good faith involves accepting constraints imposed by equality and reciprocity. But if society is to encourage acting in good faith, without making the mistake of assuming that morality can be enforced, a system of individual rights – allowing considerable freedom of judgement and conduct – becomes indispensable. For only a system of rights can protect the role of conscience and foster self-respect.

Some of these rights are 'natural' rights. Ockham distinguishes three types. The first are those which free and equal individuals carry into any association, but which they can modify by express or tacit agreement. Thus, the right to choose rulers in church and state can be lodged in some intermediate body, such as the college of cardinals or the electors of the German empire. But 'the people' can always claim back their residual rights if that body fails to act appropriately. The second type of natural right is inoperative, for it is a right that humans might claim (to take whatever they need, for example) if they were fully moralized agents, as in the Garden of Eden before sin and imperfection entered the world.

The third type of natural right recognized by Ockham takes us into a morally imperfect world, as well as into a major controversy involving the Franciscan order and the papacy. It is the type of natural right bound up with a moral principle such as self-preservation. The duty to preserve one's life creates a right to do so, a right which cannot be renounced. However, there are some natural rights, Ockham argues, which can be renounced. That is the case with the right to property. The Franciscans argued that they renounced all property rights, even the 'rights' of use in favour of a 'precarious' use of temporal things, that is, a use which depends upon the permission of others and which can be withdrawn at any time. This was deemed to be central to the 'apostolic poverty' of the Franciscan order, its charitable nature and dependence on alms. 'There is, indeed, a precept of right reason that temporal goods should be appropriated and owned by men; but it is not necessary for the fulfilment of the precept that every individual man should exercise the right of private property, and he can, for a just and reasonable cause, renounce all rights to the possession of property.'[11] The crucial requirement for Ockham is that such a renunciation be voluntary, for that makes it legitimate.

As in his defence of conscientious mistakes, Ockham again lays radical emphasis on personal autonomy, subordinating even one natural right to its preservation. This emphasis gives Ockham's nominalism its historical importance. For it is the moment when we can observe the egalitarian moral intuitions generated by Christianity being turned against doctrines and institutions that do not acknowledge the difference between acting from conviction and mere conformity of behaviour – even if they are doctrines and institutions of the church. It is, in effect, the birth of liberal secularism.

I am not claiming that Ockham's argument is entirely coherent or that he foresaw all of the implications of secularism. For example, he does not develop the possibility – raised by his argument – that our intuitions of justice may not be clear enough or may come into conflict with one another. But one thing is certain. Ockham placed such importance on moral autonomy that he was willing to defend, within limits, mistaken judgements about what justice requires. Such a radical emphasis on autonomy had been gathering force for some time. But if anyone has a claim to be its leading spokesman, it is William of Ockham.

Ockham has often been accused of a kind of authoritarianism by emphasizing God's freedom over God's rationality. For the followers of Aquinas, Ockham's critique of reason's ability to reveal metaphysical truth makes his subsequent appeal to 'right reason' inconsistent. Does not Ockham here reintroduce the rationality which he had rejected along with 'essences' and 'eternal ideas'? Yet Thomists fail to understand what Ockham understood, that the theory of natural rights involves subjecting the ancient idea of natural law to a new distributive principle, the biblical golden rule, with its stipulation in favour of equality and reciprocity. Human autonomy is authorized 'by God and nature'. The golden rule introduced a principle of justice which overthrew the assumption of natural inequality. And, in Ockham's eyes, that move is at the heart of Christian revelation. It is God's will.

The subject of excommunication himself, Ockham turned his defence of natural rights against abuses of authority, especially against what he considered to be the danger of exaggerated papal pretensions. For him, it was axiomatic that the power of rulers was limited by the rights of their subjects. 'Ockham's favourite way of proving this was to argue that the evangelical liberty proclaimed in scripture limited papal power by safeguarding the natural and civil rights of the pope's subjects.'[12] But such limits also applied to secular rulers, even to the emperor who had given Ockham shelter and protection. Individuals cannot alienate their moral autonomy because it is God-given.

Human agency and divine agency were joined in Ockham's mind by the claims of 'right reason' and natural rights. Those claims protected the role of individual conscience. A disciple of Augustine rather than Aristotle, Ockham found his own way of defending the city of God from the city of man. To be fair, in seeking to combine Aristotle with Christian beliefs, Aquinas had been aware that Aristotle's polis-inspired conception of citizenship might compromise Christian commitment to an order 'beyond this world'. The more positive value that Aquinas attributed to secular order was not meant to detract from the claims of the 'soul'. Yet despite his precautions, Aquinas imbibed more of the ancient sense of justice as natural inequality than perhaps he realized. That emerges not least in his use of the idea of natural law. For, unlike Ockham, Aquinas did not convert moral agency into a full-blown theory of natural rights.

For Ockham, the role of reason itself had to be revised to accord with the assumption of moral equality. How does this emerge in his writings? Ockham goes out of his way to argue that God might have created a different moral order, commanding moral inequality or even hatred of himself. Logic cannot rule out the possibility that God might have imposed a different moral imperative. *But he did not*. That was crucial for Ockham. It is why he defended God's freedom against rational necessity.

Ockham's attack on the habit of projecting terms drawn from human action (especially 'goals' or 'purposes') into our understanding of the non-human world accounts for his second step into modernity. As we have seen, he drew attention to the difference between 'reasons' for human actions and the 'causes' of external events. The two ideas, 'reasons' and 'causes', should not be confused. For the human mind operates in different ways when shaping action and when investigating the non-human world. Ockham's argument, elaborated by his followers, helped to foster a new curiosity about the physical world, freeing its study from preordained conclusions. A rationalist mind-set would no longer prescribe the roles of physical processes, by lodging them within an assumed 'great chain of being'.

Ockham and his followers moved the analysis of causation from the model of 'rational' science to that of 'empirical' or 'experimental' science. In that respect Ockham considered himself the heir of Aristotle, but not an uncritical heir. He took up one type of cause identified by Aristotle – 'efficient' causes – and turned it into the paradigm of empirical explanation. Yet Ockham insisted that concepts which summarize the attributes of external 'things' must be constrained by observable facts. That is why he applied his 'razor' to such concepts, rejecting the introduction of entities unless they can be verified through our repeated experience of things. That, indeed, became his test for causal explanations.

Is it far-fetched to see Ockham anticipating the eighteenth-century philosopher David Hume's account of causation as 'constant conjunction' – one thing repeatedly following another? His words seem clear enough. 'I say that this is sufficient for something being an immediate cause, namely that when it is present the effect follows, and when it is not present, all other conditions and dispositions being the same, the effect does not follow.'[13] While he did not use the term himself, Ockham presents knowledge of the relations between things as 'hypothetical', always subject to revision in the light of further experience. That is why 'demonstrative knowledge' – certitude which springs necessarily from the very meaning of the words used – differs in its nature from 'probable knowledge', or what we now call 'empirical' knowledge. For Ockham, therefore, it is a category mistake to postulate necessary truths about the world of sense experience. It confuses the claims of inductive and deductive reasoning.

There is no simple connection between Ockham's nominalism and his account of natural rights. Yet his insistence on the difference between deductive and inductive reasoning served the same purpose as his defence of human autonomy. Both served to establish that God's activity in the world is a work of freedom in which humans can and should participate. Just as Ockham's insistence on the reality of freedom had led him to limit the claims of 'right reason' or justice, so it shaped his account of the limits of deductive reasoning. Acknowledging the right to make conscientious mistakes and insisting on the merely probable nature of empirical knowledge were both rooted in his belief in the reality of God's freedom and the fact of human fallibility.

Ockham and other nominalists did not renounce reason. Rather, they refined its uses. Their work amounted to a protest against the 'domestication' of reality, against a rationalism which claimed to contain God's activity within a framework of human assumptions and definitions: what has been called 'Greek necessity'. For Ockham and his followers, such claims to capture the world of experience in a system of essences or final causes was an example of hubris. So if we are to grasp the originality of nominalism, we must look both backward and forward.

Looking backward, Ockham's critique of essences and eternal ideas can be seen as the ultimate stage of a war which from its outset the Christian church had waged against polytheism. For polytheism survived as a temptation to multiply the non-material agencies at work in the world, agencies that interposed in the relations between God and man. Ockham wielding his 'razor' preserved something of the spirit of that war against 'pagan' superstition. Looking forward, there is little doubt that Ockham's analysis of empirical reasoning – his understanding of causation in terms of regular succession or constant conjunction of events – contributed to developments in the following century which provided the bridge between Aristotle's physics and modern physics. Ockham's insistence on the difference between 'reasons' and 'causes' prepared the way for a kind of Christian positivism, and for the disenchantment of the physical world.

Yet Ockham's programme was not reductionist. He was no materialist. Underpinning his analysis of the difference between understanding 'culture' and 'nature' was a firm faith that God's free activity lay beneath each. Ockham would have been dismayed to see how, a few centuries later, his analysis of causation became joined to materialist assumptions directed against theism, a combination he would have dismissed as a new form of rationalist arrogance.

Ockham's defence of both natural rights and the limitations of human reason sprang from his belief in the omnipresence of God's freedom. If we were to put this defence in contemporary scientific terms, we might say that Ockham took up his stand on the principle of indeterminacy. He would have welcomed evidence of a 'big bang' at the beginning of things and the difficulty of capturing space-time in a single, unified theory. In our time, freedom has moved cosmology beyond a mechanistic model of the universe.

24

Struggling for Representative Government in the Church

We are nearing the end of our story. We have seen how Christian egalitarianism (the 'care of souls') first shaped the distinction between spiritual and temporal authority, creating a sphere for individual conscience. We then followed the gradual but far from complete penetration of this egalitarianism into traditional beliefs – emerging as a kind of schizophrenia among the Carolingians. Finally, we discovered its full potential for transforming institutions in the papal revolution of the twelfth century, when the idea of a 'sovereign' authority over individuals, embodied in a coherent legal system, not only transformed the church, but also began to inspire secular rulers with the project of creating 'states' out of the jumble of feudal jurisdictions.

The egalitarian moral intuitions generated by the 'care of souls', which had helped to undermine ancient slavery, became a far more formidable weapon once they were defined into the idea of sovereignty. Permanent inequalities of social status came under increasing threat. But if creating a sovereign authority provided the means of liberating people from the ties of inherited status and custom, it also created a new threat. Would the claim of 'sovereignty' create a monopoly of power as well as of final legal authority? Would the idea of sovereignty become an instrument of tyranny rather than liberation? Would 'equal subjection' crush the claims of 'equal liberty'?

These questions arose first in the church. For by the fourteenth century there was considerable disquiet in the Church about the growth of papal 'absolutism'. What, after all, had been the crux of the papal revolution? Identifying the papacy as the final judge and supreme legislator of the church had been necessary to create a self-contained system of canon law. Such a postulate was necessary to establish the 'equal subjection' of all Christians to church authority. The pope, as the 'sovereign' pontiff, could then address his subjects individually – as members of the *ecclesia christiana* – rather than through intermediaries.

Yet what had been the result of acknowledging papal sovereignty? During the twelfth and thirteenth centuries papal power and pretensions had escalated. Developments since the papal revolution revealed only too clearly the centralizing potential of the idea of sovereignty. Increasing papal control over dioceses, monasteries and religious orders – especially control over the granting of benefices – had led to ever greater papal claims. At the outset of his pontificate, in 1198, Innocent III declared that he was 'lower than God, but higher than man'.

> According to Innocent III, the Pope's *plenitudo potestatis* not only set him above all other prelates but also above the law, *supra jus* . . . Innocent IV went still further, asserting that the possession of *plenitudo potestatis* enabled the Pope to exercise temporal power as well as spiritual power . . . The ground was thus well prepared for the concept of *plenitudo potestatis* as an illimitable, all-embracing sovereignty . . .[1]

This expansion of papal claims led to conflicts with secular rulers, the dramatic disputes between Innocent IV and the Emperor Frederick II and between Boniface VIII and the French king, Philip the Fair. Secular rulers complained that the papacy was itself endangering the distinction between sacred and secular authority. Yet even before these conflicts, opposition to extreme papal claims had developed within the church itself. The church had existed for more than a thousand years. It had developed with a multiplicity of jurisdictions, such as those of bishops, cathedral chapters and monasteries, a multiplicity reflected in the ever-increasing amount of litigation coming before church courts. Recognizing the papacy as the final legal arbiter was one thing, but abandoning claims long sanctioned by custom or earlier church 'law' was another.

Papal ambitions ran up against not only the traditional autonomy of diocesan bishops but also the new importance of the college of cardinals. In due course, both of these contributed to the reaction against extreme papal claims. But it was a reaction prepared by the canonists who, while developing the system of church law, had also been debating the extent of papal authority. How should the church respond to papal claims, if exaggerated? Canon lawyers commenting on Gratian's *Decretum* (the Decretists) did not doubt papal 'headship' of the church. They cited gospel accounts of the Christ describing Peter as the 'rock' on which he would build the church and giving Peter the 'keys' to the kingdom of God.

Yet, while respecting the primacy of the papacy, the canonists, as lawyers, were also concerned to identify the limits of papal authority, a concern emerging in their discussions of whether a heretical pope could be removed and whether crimes or scandalous conduct could also justify replacing a pope. However, the procedure for doing any such thing remained uncertain for these canonists, who acknowledged that a pope could not normally be judged by his legal 'inferiors'.[2]

Questions about papal authority were becoming increasingly specific and urgent. Could popes, on their own authority, redefine the articles of faith? Did a heretical pope cease, *ipso facto*, to be pope? Could a pope be judged or deposed by a general council of the church? And what became of papal authority when a pope died, resigned, or, worse still, if there were rival pontiffs? Did not ultimate authority reside in the church as a whole, the *ecclesia christiana*?

Worries about the centralizing of power in the papacy may have contributed to the canonists translating the ancient theory of natural law into a theory of natural rights. In their eyes, the protection of moral agency – and with it, God's claim on man – was the justification for investing sovereign authority in the papacy. Running through the canonists' writings was a concern for the quality of intentions. They began to stake out the difference between a legitimate authority, resting on consent, and mere conformity of behaviour, resulting from coercion or the fear of power. The strong implication of such canonist thinking was that natural rights provided a framework which constrained the exercise of authority within the church.

To answer questions about the limits of papal authority, canonists fell back on the egalitarian moral intuitions that had given rise to the idea of sovereignty. They drew on the belief in moral equality in order to review claims that popes were not subject to any human authority, to censure or deposition. The canonists began to argue that only the whole church or 'congregation of the faithful' could be considered unerring in faith. Typically, William of Ockham would later make this point with his cutting irony, saying that even if the entire church hierarchy became corrupt, the faith would be preserved by 'women, children and idiots . . .'

Brian Tierney has shown how canonistic thinking about the limits of papal authority developed through several stages. In the twelfth century, among the Decretists, there was a widespread, if only tacit, acceptance that papal authority could not extend to redefining the articles of faith. These had been defined by the four earliest 'universal' councils of the Church. 'The Pope, it was held, was supreme judge in cases involving articles of faith, but the Pope himself was required to judge in accordance with the canons of the General Councils.'[3]

Nor was that all. The protection of God's claims on conscience – what St Paul had called 'Christian liberty' – also limited the papal claim to a sovereign authority. Thus, while the twelfth-century canonists regularly asserted papal primacy, the well-being of the whole church remained their final criterion. 'It was commonly held that he [the pope] could not dispense against the decree of a Council in any matter that affected the general well-being of the Church.'[4] And for canonists that well-being was now understood partly in terms of natural rights. But how was excessive centralizing of power in the papacy to be avoided in practice? That was the rub. The Decretists did not succeed in finding a solution.

By the thirteenth century the accumulation of papal legislation, or decretals, ushered in a new phase of canonist commentary. At first glance this phase – described as that of Decretalists rather than of the Decretists– seemed to represent the triumph of extreme papal claims. For the discussion of papal sovereignty was shaped by popes Innocent III and Innocent IV, who were themselves canon lawyers and laid a radical emphasis on *plenitudo potestatis*.

That was not the whole story, however. At the same time the canonists developed a new theory about the nature of 'corporations', a theory which had the potential to undermine extreme interpretations of papal sovereignty. It was a theory which sought to defend the moral agency of individuals by limiting the claims to authority of those governing 'corporations'. 'In the first half of the thirteenth century they [the canonists] built up the doctrine, denied only by Innocent IV and hardly challenged after Hostiensis, that authority in a corporation was not concentrated in the head but resided in all the members . . .'⁵

The theory developed out of reflections about the authority of bishops, in relation to their diocese and to the canons of their cathedral. This was interpreted as a 'delegated' authority, limited by the purposes for which it was delegated and always subject to the best interests of those whom it represented. Corporations were no longer understood as having a reality apart from their members. 'Medieval lawyers described corporations as a fiction of the law precisely because they attributed actual reality only to the individual persons who composed it.'⁶ This was a fundamental change. For it involved passing from representation understood as personification – relying on the metaphor of the 'head' ruling the body – to representation understood as the explicit delegation of authority from the members of the community to its head. Representation ceased to be a metaphor.

The development of this theory of corporation law amounted to the emergence of a theory of representative government. It was driven by the needs of the church, contending with complex relations between its multiple jurisdictions. These needs sprang not only from ancient associations such as the diocese and the monastery, but new forms of association such as the friars and the universities. The new understanding of the nature of a corporation was applied to these associations, and involved attributing an underlying equality of status to their members. Claims to authority could therefore no longer be taken for granted.

> Questions . . . were constantly arising on the level of practical litigation. Where did authority in a church reside, in the head or in all the members? And who were the 'members' of a church in this sense? Could a bishop act in the affairs of his diocese without consulting his canons? If so, in what types of business? If not, did he need the consent of the canons or only their counsel? Could an abbot take an oath on behalf of his whole convent of monks? Did he require consent of the monks to act as their representative in so doing? What was the source of a prelate's jurisdiction? How could a bishop be prevented from acting against the interests of his church? Did the rights of a bishop devolve to his canons during an episcopal vacancy? Did they so devolve if the bishop was negligent?⁷

The theory of corporation law developed in response to these questions was at first applied only to parts of the church, rather than to the church as a whole. But it reshaped legal language and thinking in a way that was fraught with consequences. Canonists insisted that the authority of bishops must no longer be understood in terms of ownership. It was not dominium in the ancient sense of the word, with the radical subordination that implied. Only the community of the faithful as a whole could be said to have dominium over the church and its goods.

By contrast, the bishop's authority was a conditional authority, founded on and respecting the moral agency of those subject to his authority. The bishop began to be described as an agent or 'proctor', a term drawn from Roman law, but reinterpreted by the canonist Hostiensis so that the most important transactions by their bishop required the express consent of the canons. In other decisions, the proctor was deemed to have a mandate from those he represented, but even so it was a mandate which restricted his authority to the defence of their interests, the purposes for which they had, explicitly or implicitly, granted the authority.

What were the implications of Hostiensis' – who had lectured on canon law and became a cardinal – adaptation of the idea of proctorship?

> It may be that in this refinement of the proctorial concept is to be found an important link between the earlier medieval concept of representation as mere personification and the later idea, growing ever more explicit in the fourteenth century, that a true representative needed an actual delegation of authority from his community; for it was generally agreed among the canonists that the jurisdiction and administrative authority of a bishop were derived from election, not from consecration to the episcopal order.[8]

Hostiensis' reinterpretation reveals how rapidly a corporate understanding of society was eroding: representation was one thing, personification quite another.

Not only the claims of bishops but the claims of the heads of other legally constituted bodies increasingly came to be understood in terms of proctorship rather than ancient dominium. The idea of a 'head' thus ceased to convey an inherent and unquestionable superiority.

And if at first this reinterpretation of the Roman law notion of proctorship was applied only to parts of the church, the fourteenth century saw bolder thinkers begin to apply it to the church as a whole, with dramatic consequences for views of the papacy.

In effect, canon lawyers had encountered a problem which, centuries later, would come to haunt modern liberalism. The new understanding of society as an association of individuals – its 'individuated' image – could easily become a threat to the role of intermediate associations, located, that is, between the association 'of all' and the individual. The identification of a sovereign authority had a radical centralizing potential because it was a claim to speak for 'all equally'. By identifying sovereign authority with universality – in the manner of popes Innocent III and Innocent IV – the autonomy of associations that were less than universal became problematic.

So the intellectual challenge which canonists faced was the need to reconcile their egalitarian moral intuitions with a defence of intermediate associations. How could the authority of such associations be made legitimate in the face of a sovereign agency representing, *ex hypothesi*, the claims of all? The canon lawyers developed a powerful response: an original theory about the nature of corporations, paving the way for a more general case for representative government in the church. They turned the moral intuitions that originally gave rise to the idea of sovereignty against 'absolutist' interpretations of the form of government it entailed.

Inadvertently, the canonists thereby laid another part of the foundation of modern liberal thought. They extended and refined earlier arguments about the difference between ownership and political authority, between ancient dominium and the right to rule. They did this by demonstrating that an egalitarian understanding of society implied by the idea of sovereignty dispersed moral authority in a way that was incompatible with the interpretation of papal authority as a form of ownership or dominium. The canonists appealed to the ideal of a church ('the community of the faithful') in which reason and freedom are dispersed against the assumption of unlimited authority by any human agency. This vision, in turn, provided the 'deep' moral foundation for constitutionalism in the church, for a formal dispersal of authority and power.

By the fourteenth century an increasing number of voices were calling for something like representative government in the church. Calls for reform focused on the role of general councils. Was not a general council of the church the supreme authority in matters concerning the faith and well being of the church? Did not the authority of such a council constrain even the pope's ordinary jurisdiction, his claim to be the final judge and legislator of the church?

The struggle between Boniface VIII and Philip the Fair, which began in 1297, gave these questions a new urgency. The French king – urged on by many cardinals and Franciscans – appealed to a general council, contending that Boniface was a usurper (that is, that the resignation of his predecessor, Celestine V, was 'forced' and invalid) and a heretic. Ironically, both sides of the argument that followed drew on the new theory of corporations to make their case. The relationship between the papacy and church authorities – as well as papal relations with secular rulers asserting their sovereignty – came under unprecedented critical scrutiny.

Had the concentration of power as well as authority in the papacy created a monster? Philip the Fair's resistance to the theocratic claims in Boniface's bull, Unam Sanctam, drew the attention of the whole of Europe to constitutional issues. As a result, the papal attempt to submit all nations to its sovereign authority suffered a serious and lasting reverse, while within the church critics of the papacy gained in confidence. Stimulated by the new theory of corporations as well as their own interests, many bodies – not least the bishops and the college of cardinals – felt the need for a more collegiate governance of the church. They were ready to welcome a retreat from the 'extravagant' papal claims in the name of the 'community of the faithful'. Thus, the absolutist version of papal authority was coming under threat even before the schism which created the conciliar movement.

Late in the fourteenth century an extraordinary series of events gave such voices in the church not only an opportunity to express their views, but forced them to do so. In April 1378 the cardinals elected as pope the archbishop of Bari, who took the name of Urban VI. His conduct, however, soon led many cardinals to regret their decision, and a few months later they declared the election null and void. When Urban refused to accept their decision, the cardinals proceeded to elect a new pope, Clement VII. Neither 'pope' would give way to the other, and before long Clement established his own rival curia at Avignon. The previous decades, when popes had governed the church from Avignon, had greatly increased French influence in the curia. Clement gained French support, while the Italian cardinals supported Urban VI. The secular rulers of Europe responded differently to these rival claims of legitimacy, moved not least by national rivalries. Europe was torn apart by schism.

The constitutional question lurking in earlier canonist speculation suddenly became central and unavoidable. It drew attention to the possible role of a general council of the church, as offering far the most likely way of putting an end to schism.

By 1409 such a council, at Pisa, proceeded to depose both 'popes' and elect another, who styled himself Alexander V. The result, however, merely complicated the schism, with three contenders for the papal throne. Five years later the emperor Sigismund summoned another council at Constance. Its aim was no longer simply to end the schism, but to undertake a general reform of the church, to give the church what would amount to a constitution, clearly dispersing authority and power. The council comprised not only representatives of the secular clergy and the monastic orders, but also doctors of the new universities, who introduced a powerful voice in support of 'conciliarism', that is, regular meetings of general councils, to be recognized as the ultimate authority in the church.

This conciliar movement, drawing on canonist thinking and the writings of Ockham, won the support of some of Europe's leading intellectuals. With growing confidence, the Council of Constance 'proclaimed the indissolubility of the general council, and its superiority over the papal power; it undertook to make these principles prevalent in the church, and to reform the abuses which had crept into it, above all the exactions by which the court of Rome had procured supplies'.[9] To achieve these ends, the Council of Constance appointed a commission of reform, drawing its members from across the orders and nations of the church.

At this point, however, the papal party rallied, insisting that such a comprehensive programme could not be carried out without the participation of the pope. So the rivals were finally induced to give way, and a new pope, Martin V, was elected. However, his proposals for reform proved unsatisfactory to the council, which dissolved, not having achieved its programme. The meeting of a new council at Basle in 1431 met with no greater success. The papal party then brought about a rupture in the council by moving it to Italy, while the unreconciled partisans of reform remained at Basle.

By the mid-fifteenth century the papacy had – relying on the centralized administration that had been created since the twelfth century – regained control over the church. The project of reform which the church had failed to carry through did not die, however. The cause of church reform was almost immediately taken up by secular rulers who drew their own conclusions from the series of frustrated general councils and the resurgence of papal pretensions. The French king, in the Pragmatic Sanction of Bourges (1438), and the German empire, at the Diet of Mayence in 1439, introduced greater autonomy and more collegiate government into national churches. But even these national reforms championed by secular rulers were soon abandoned as a result of papal pressure and diplomacy, returning the situation in the church, at least in appearance, to one of papal absolutism.

But it was only an appearance. For the project of reform, which had eluded both the leaders of the church and secular rulers, had now taken root among the people.

Was it mere chance that the fourteenth and fifteenth centuries saw such widespread popular agitation within the church, with Pietist movements in the Netherlands and Germany fostering a distrust of clerical authority, while the Lollards in England and the Hussites in Prague openly criticized the established church hierarchy, especially the papacy? In the eyes of John Wycliffe, leader of the Lollards, the church had lost its way, preoccupied with legal supremacy and the accumulation of wealth rather than the care of souls, its proper role. Wycliffe spoke for many across Europe when he called for translation of the scriptures into popular languages, so that they could be widely read and properly understood, giving people a basis for judging the claims of the clerical establishment. The understanding of 'authority' was taking a dramatic turn, away from aristocracy towards democracy.

Christian egalitarianism had already more than once fostered a kind of populism. But what is striking about movements in the fourteenth and fifteenth centuries is the way they combined the promotion of individual devotion through real knowledge of the scriptures with a deep-seated anti-clericalism. The belief that claims of authority had to make themselves both intelligible and acceptable to individual consciences was on the rise. That is why the programme of devolving authority and power within the church had exposed a popular need, even before the invention of printing added its 'democratic' influence. That is also why forcible repression of the Lollards and the Hussites was not the end of the story.

The fact that the Council of Constance condemned Huss and his associates as heretics cannot conceal a deep affinity between their projects. By defining a direction for reform of the church, the conciliarists had unleashed – only half-wittingly – what amounted to an impulse which could no longer be contained.

> The popular reform of John Huss was for the instant stifled . . . But as the reforms of the councils had failed, as the end which they had pursued had not been attained, popular reform ceased not to ferment. It watched the first opportunity, and found it at the commencement of the sixteenth century. If the reform undertaken by the councils had been well carried out, the Reformation might have been prevented. But one or the other must have succeeded; their coincidence shows a necessity.[10]

These observations by François Guizot should give us pause to reflect. We have the advantage of far longer experience of European history, when considering consequences of the 'failure' of the conciliar movement.

How great a difference would the success of the conciliar movement have made to the future of Europe? Might it have preserved the unity of European Christianity? And how would that have affected the emergence of liberal secularism, often held to be the outcome of Protestantism? Would a united church that had adopted conciliarism – a decentralized church in which national churches and interests had freer play and greater influence – have developed with a form of secularism less strident and aggressive than the form which developed in post-Reformation Europe? These questions are fascinating, but finally unanswerable. In any case, they should not be allowed to obscure the argument of this book: that in its basic assumptions, liberal thought is the offspring of Christianity. It emerged as the moral intuitions generated by Christianity were turned against an authoritarian model of the church.

The roots of liberalism were firmly established in the arguments of philosophers and canon lawyers by the fourteenth and early fifteenth centuries: belief in a fundamental equality of status as the proper basis for a legal system; belief that enforcing moral conduct is a contradiction in terms; a defence of individual liberty, through the assertion of fundamental or 'natural' rights; and, finally, the conclusion that only a representative form of government is appropriate for a society resting on the assumption of moral equality.

These roots of liberalism were, however, dispersed in the fifteenth century. They had not yet been combined to create a coherent programme or theory for reform of the sovereign state, into what we have come to call 'secularism'. That development awaited developments in the sixteenth and the seventeenth centuries – the Renaissance and the Reformation – when the fragmentation of Christianity led to religious wars, civil and international. In an attempt to restore a broken unity, Catholic and Protestant churches resorted to force. It was an appeal to force which led sensitive minds gradually to put together the credo of secularism, drawing on the insights of so-called 'medieval' thinkers.

Increasingly, the adjective 'barbarous' – which in earlier centuries had been applied by churchmen to the beliefs and practices of the tribes overrunning the Western Roman empire – would be reapplied to the attitudes and actions of the churches.

25

Dispensing with the Renaissance

If liberalism can be described as the child of Christianity, should it be called a 'natural' rather than a 'legitimate' child? There is good reason for thinking so. The reason is that liberalism as a coherent doctrine was not born willingly. It was certainly never a project of the church. Indeed, as a political theory it developed against the fierce resistance of the Catholic and even, for a long time, most Protestant churches. Its emergence was the result of a 'civil war' in early modern Europe, a war in which 'liberal' moral intuitions generated by Christianity were increasingly turned against attempts to 'enforce' belief.

The civil war has distorted our understanding of the relationship between liberalism and Christianity. And that is because the proto-liberal beliefs which had developed within the church by the fifteenth century – the belief in moral equality and a range of natural rights, in a representative form of government and the importance of freer enquiry – only came together when they were deployed against the church's claim to have a right to 'enforce' belief, with the help of secular rulers.

Mounting opposition to that claim from the sixteenth to the eighteenth century – after the Reformation put an end to confessional unity in Europe – played a crucial part in the birth of modern liberalism. It shaped liberalism as a coherent doctrine directed against the idea of an authoritarian church, whether Catholic or Protestant. Liberalism became a doctrine which paved the way for a far more systematic separation of church and state – that is, for secularism. Indeed, the two terms became almost inseparable. Liberal secularism sought to limit the role of government through a structure of fundamental rights, rights that create and protect a sphere of individual freedom, a private sphere. Religion thus became a matter for the private sphere, a matter of conscience. Liberal secularism sought to protect that private sphere, moreover, by means of constitutional arrangements that would disperse and balance powers in the state.

This profound moral and intellectual development did not take place overnight. It emerged by fits and starts over several hundred years. The story of its development – from sixteenth-century natural rights theory, through the writings of Grotius and Hobbes, Locke and Montesquieu, to early nineteenth-century thinkers such as Constant, Tocqueville and J. S. Mill – has often been told. It is a story about what might be called the liberal 'moment' in European history.

Understandably, the story presents the development of liberal secularism largely in terms of opposition to 'illegitimate' claims of the church. Yet that is not the whole story. For the story often begins with what it calls a 'rebirth' rather than a 'birth'. It begins with the Renaissance in Italy, the rediscovery of ancient 'humanism'. And it presents the Renaissance as marking a decisive break with what had gone before in Europe.

The Renaissance is presented as the end of the middle ages, a crucial step in the process of individual liberation. We have inherited from historians such as Burckhardt the view that the individual re-emerged and burst into bloom in the Italian Renaissance. The Renaissance is held to have marked the end of a kind of religious tyranny, a tyranny of the mind – opening European eyes to the apparently far wider range of values and interests exhibited in classical antiquity. And there can be no doubt that a passion for the ancient world did seize many minds.

In Burckhardt's eloquent account, fourteenth- and fifteenth-century Italian city-states witnessed the unabashed pursuit of fame, wealth and beauty, an inversion of values, a rehabilitation of self-assertion. Surrounded by physical remains of ancient cities, and themselves living in city-states, Italian humanists came to take as models of refined taste the achievements of antiquity in sculpture, painting, architecture and writing. This rebirth of humanism revealed man to himself, freeing him to explore new needs, create new ambitions and taste new pleasures.[1] It fostered an unabashed enjoyment of this world, free of religious guilt.

While the earliest Italian humanists may have sought to merge Christian and ancient values, by the late fifteenth century humanists often displayed a contempt for the church. Machiavelli went further than most. He contrasted favourably the patriotism of the ancient citizen with the virtue of the Christian. Other humanists displayed impatience with the arid 'scholastic' preoccupations of the universities, with the 'obscure' arguments about logic and natural law pursued by canon lawyers and philosophers. Such arguments seemed to them too remote from human affairs, from real desires, needs and – not least – pleasures. Their preferred philosopher was Plato, whose dialogues conjured up a civilized, urban world rather than the austere monastic setting suggested by scholastic disputations about Aristotle.

If the Renaissance is understood as a first step towards liberal secularism because it began to throw off the shackles of religion authority, the next step identified is the growth of scepticism after the religious wars issuing from the Reformation, with their attempts to enforce uniformity of belief. This new scepticism – epitomized in the writings of Montaigne – fuelled anti-clericalism and calls for toleration. Such calls were soon made by invoking fundamental or 'natural' rights. The language of rights thus became integral to the growth of liberal secularism. The sphere of freedom defended in this way widened gradually until it included even atheism. By the eighteenth century anti-clericalism had become so virulent in parts of Europe that it led to an onslaught on religious belief as such. The result was that liberal secularism in Europe came to be understood as essentially anti-religious. Its roots were interpreted in that light, with the help of the idea of the Renaissance. Any suggestion that the roots might be traced to Christianity became outlandish.

Yet justifying the process of secularization – the separation of a private realm from the public sphere – was the distinction between outward conformity and inner, authentic belief. That distinction was based, in turn, on the conviction that freedom is a prerequisite of moral conduct, that moral obligation presupposes an area of choice. It was that conviction, after all, which had led to the ancient theory of natural law being recast as a doctrine of natural rights.

And that is the rub. For the conviction that uncoerced belief provides the true foundation for 'legitimate' authority was itself the product of

Christianity. It was the test of 'internal acceptance' that had gradually made 'enforced belief' a contradiction in terms, encapsulating reflections on the role of individual conscience by canon lawyers, theologians and philosophers from the twelfth to the fifteenth century. And as we have seen, their reflections rested on rejection of the assumption of natural inequality which had permeated ancient thinking. That is why presenting the process of secularization as a 'rebirth' of ancient humanism can be so misleading. For it ignores the moral conviction that led to the ancient theory of natural law being recast. It was that moral conviction which led to 'rights' becoming fundamental to the discourse of liberal secularism.

But an understanding of that connection was lost in the heat of early modern battles against the church. That is why we have to reconsider the view that the Renaissance marked a decisive break in European history, separating a period of ignorance and superstition (the 'middle ages') from one of freedom and progress.

The forms of ancient thought, feeling and expression that excited Italian humanists had sprung from and reflected an altogether different type of society: a society of citizens and slaves, of families rather than souls. This difference was often ignored by the humanists, many of whom were mostly interested in what we would call the 'fine arts'. But ignoring this difference prevented them from exploring the deepest respects in which the ancient world differed from Christian Europe. Philosophical argument about 'foundational' moral assumptions was not to their taste. Italian humanists drew on the ancient world as a kind of quarry, without asking too much about its original structure.

To be fair, their eclecticism enabled humanists to mix ancient and 'modern' features in ways that are often very striking. But they are striking partly because they juxtapose elements drawn from utterly different types of society, from mind-sets resting on the contrary assumptions of natural inequality and moral equality. Yet the humanists were not immune to moral intuitions of their own society. Probably unconsciously, Renaissance painters turned the idealized types found in surviving ancient statuary into beautiful individuals. Take the treatment of male nudity. Italian painters transformed what had been a celebration of social superiority – of citizens' muscular fitness to dominate their inferiors – into the graceful and touching figures we find, for example, in Botticelli. Botticelli's figures look as if they might have a conscience!

So I am not suggesting that the Renaissance did not matter, that it did not channel human thought, feeling and expression into new forms. Nor am I suggesting that it has no place in understanding the development of sculpture, painting and architecture. That would be absurd. But what I am maintaining is that as an historiographical concept the Renaissance has been grossly inflated. It has been used to create a gap between early modern Europe and the preceding centuries – to introduce a discontinuity which is misleading.

If the fundamental feature of modernity is an individuated model of society – a model in which the individual rather than the family, clan or caste is the basic social unit – then it is important to distinguish that test from other criteria. Celebration of the Renaissance has confused the emergence of what is better called the pursuit of 'individuality' – an aesthetic notion – with the invention of the individual – a moral notion. This invention was the product of what philosophers call 'ontological' argument, argument about how reality is understood. And that was not the work of the humanists, though they too drew on its achievements. The humanists did introduce a new emphasis on cultivating the self, on the refinement of taste and self-expression. This was an emphasis that shaped what might be called the cult of individuality, depicting the individual as the 'victim' of social pressures and heroism as resistance to such pressures. Social institutions were presented as a threat to the self.

This new sensibility contributed to developments in seventeenth- and eighteenth-century moral philosophy and political theory which are often 'held against' liberalism. They encouraged an 'atomized' picture of the world, separating the individual from a social context and obscuring the normative developments which had led to the emergence of liberalism. A kind of 'physicalism' did, it is true, invade liberal thinking during these centuries. It was reinforced by developments in the physical sciences which placed the individual mind in nature rather than culture, making the test of valid knowledge observable regularities rather than social norms.[2] The philosophical tradition we call utilitarianism turned this into an 'atomized' model of society, a model in which individual wants or preferences are taken as given, with little interest in the role of norms or the socializing process.

There is good reason for considering these later intellectual developments as a liberal heresy, because it deprives liberal secularism of its profoundly moral roots, cutting it off from the tradition of discourse which had generated it. Yet liberalism rests on the moral assumptions provided by Christianity. It preserves Christian ontology without the metaphysics of salvation.

We have found that the 'deep' foundation for the individual as the organizing social role – a status which broke the chains of family and caste – was laid by lawyers, theologians and philosophers from the twelfth to the fifteenth century. Their picture of reality gave individual conscience and intentions, the moral life of the individual, a foundational role. Let us recall just one example. Through innovations in thirteenth-century canon law, corporations came to be understood as associations of individuals, ceasing to have an identity radically independent of and superior to that of their members. A freer spirit and the sense that institutions could be reshaped owed more than a little to the demolition of that older, reified meaning of corporation. This was no atomized individualism. Self-reliance and the habit of association were joined.

The view that the Renaissance and its aftermath marked the advent of the modern world – the end of the 'middle ages' – is mistaken. By the fifteenth century canon lawyers and philosophers had already asserted that 'experience' is essentially the experience of individuals, that a range of fundamental rights ought to protect individual agency, that the final authority of any association is to be found in its members, and that the use of reason when understanding processes in the physical world differs radically from normative or a priori reasoning. These are the stuff of modernity.

As we have seen, these elements were still 'free-standing' in the fifteenth century. They had not yet been fused together in a coherent and militant programme. But even in the absence of such a programme, these elements began to spread from the clerical elite into university education and affect popular attitudes. In doing so, they sharpened egalitarian moral intuitions that were to be turned against an authoritarian church. Paul's notion of 'Christian liberty' had returned with a vengeance.

The foundation of modern Europe lay in the long, difficult process of converting a moral claim into a social status. It was pursuit of belief in the equality of souls that made the conversion possible. A commitment to individual liberty sprang from that. Combining the two values gave rise to the principle which more than any other has defined modern liberal thinking, the principle of 'equal liberty'. Yet it is far from clear that the Italian Renaissance did much to explore or develop that principle.

Renaissance humanists did little to further the logical and ontological enquiries which had enabled medieval thinkers to replace one conception of society with another. Yet, by the fourteenth and the fifteenth centuries, canon lawyers and philosophers had laid the foundation for a more radical separation of the spiritual and temporal spheres than hitherto imagined. They had laid the foundation for a private, rights-based sphere, where freedom and conscience prevailed. This would be a sphere which had implications for both church and state. For it first established that authority in the church rested ultimately in the congregation of the faithful represented by general councils, while the new model it offered to secular society was a 'sovereign' government caring for and responsive to individuals rather than families or castes.

Understanding of the nature of 'the state' had already stimulated re-thinking of traditional 'co-proprietorship' of church and state. In the fourteenth century the philosopher and publicist Marsiglio of Padua began to insist that as an institution the church must be subject to the laws of the state. He argued that 'law' properly so called is backed by visible sanctions in this world. He denied that moral precepts, however exalted, should be described as laws. While rulers of the state ought to be guided by morality, they should not tolerate clerical interference in their affairs. Papal ambitions had, in Marsiglio's view, extended and perverted the jurisdictions of the church, creating unnecessary wars and civil discord. He therefore saw the legal autonomy of the state as essential, if it was to preserve the peaceful and orderly association of individuals.[3]

By the fifteenth century, this new image of society as an association of individuals was breaking through the surface of European life. It was a blurred image, doubtless more blurred in some areas than in others. It was more distinct in the commercial, urbanized areas, less distinct in rural areas of southern Europe than in the north. But even in 'backward' rural areas, the decline of serfdom and the growth of market economies projected the image to some extent. Increased social mobility – abetted by a scarcity of labour after the Black Death – eased the way for intellectual changes 'carried' by this new image of society. So did the centralizing of authority by national monarchs in France, England and Spain. The envy felt by many Italian humanists, when they compared this with the failure of attempts to unify Italy, is indirect evidence of the impact of this new image of society.

But there is more direct evidence of the impact. In fourteenth- and fifteenth-century Europe, fundamental changes can be seen in several spheres: in attitudes towards the self, in attitudes towards the natural world, and in attitudes towards government. Let us look briefly at each.

First is the extraordinary emphasis on 'innerness' which suddenly marked popular religious movements across Europe. Being guided by an 'inner light' became the almost standard form of aspiration. It was as if individuals, glimpsing a world in which differences of status and social roles might no longer be assigned at birth, felt the need for a more secure moral foundation – something that would not fail them. For when personal identity cannot be exhausted by the roles an individual 'occupies', where can that individual look for support?

Emphasis on the mystical union of God and the individual soul – famously asserted by Meister Eckhart, for whom 'the creature exists only by and through God' as creator – became a leitmotiv among the German and the Dutch pietists, as well as among the followers of Wycliffe in England and Huss in Prague. Religion understood merely as ritual practice came under growing threat. The conviction that religion meant nothing when it did not transform the feelings and motives of the individual was expressed memorably by Thomas à Kempis, who belonged to a Dutch movement called the Brethren of the Common Life and wrote the *Imitation of Christ*: 'I desire to feel compunction rather than to know its definition . . .'

The emphasis on innerness, on something felt, contributed to a new kind of humility and a revaluation of the role of the mind: 'A humble rustic who serves God is certainly better than a proud philosopher who, neglecting himself, considers the movement of the heavens.' The revealing phrase here is 'neglecting himself'.

The disciplining of the self was becoming the primary moral imperative. Reason could not simply command feelings. That conviction – with its roots in Paul and Augustine – stood in contrast to the ambitions of theologians who had sought to capture Christian beliefs within the structure of ancient rationalism. For the pietists, a personal relationship with God was the fundamental experience open to every individual, the true source of morality. It was the relationship which should inform all others. 'God is in all creatures . . . and yet he is above them.' Transforming feeling was more than the mind on its own could accomplish. It would be a mistake to call this pietist response anti-intellectual, however. For these popular movements laid great emphasis on self-discipline, through education and reading the scriptures. What they pointed out, though, were the limits of the mind in shaping moral action. Their emphasis on a devoted life and on the role of grace was a warning against the pride of the intellect. Work and daily dedication should be the companions of study.[4] Virtue then became a matter of practice.

A thinker like Jean Gerson, chancellor of the University of Paris in 1395, deemed individual moral agency – rather than the systems of theologians over-impressed by the achievements of ancient philosophy – to be the introduction to God. Gerson considered that the concept of God elaborated by theologians such as Aquinas, seeking to emulate Aristotle, had departed from the God proclaimed by Paul, the biblical God who spoke through Abraham and the prophets, before taking on human form in the Christ. For the biblical God was a God who transformed motives and action. The experience of such a God was always available to those with faith. And that experience of motives transformed was just as real as experience of the physical world.

This remarkable upsurge of emphasis on 'innerness' led to a preoccupation with the will. Here the direction taken by popular opinion parallels that taken by philosophical argument during the same period. We have seen that the criticisms levelled at Aquinas by Duns Scotus and Ockham amounted to a rejection of Thomism in the name of God's freedom. Aquinas' conception of natural law seemed to entail that God could not have chosen or acted other than the way he did. For Aquinas, natural law consisted of rational principles that governed God's will as well as the human will. For Duns Scotus and Ockham, however, that position both threatened divine omnipotence and misunderstood role of reason. They saw God's will as limited only by his free nature. And it was God's will, revealed in the Christian faith, that humans should be equal and free agents. Thus, freedom became the bond between God and man. God, not any 'necessary' dictates of reason, created our world. Reason is a part of creation. But reason by itself is not the creator.

Here we meet the second fundamental change, for this revised view of the role of reason had other important consequences. It helped to reshape understanding of the physical world. It created a sharper distinction between an inner, moral life –'wrestling' with the will – and the processes of the physical world. That emerges clearly in the direction taken by thought in the fourteenth and fifteenth centuries. For these centuries witnessed the almost irresistible spread of Ockham's nominalist philosophy across Europe, sending down deep roots in the universities, where it competed with 'official' Thomism. At Paris, Oxford, Heidelberg, Prague and Cracow, nominalism became ascendant. Those who defended more 'realist' philosophical positions – the 'ancient way' rather than the 'modern way'– even sought at times, in desperation, to ban the teaching of nominalism.

Ockham's emphasis on individual experience and observation as the only legitimate basis of empirical or 'probable' knowledge had distinguished such knowledge from deductive or 'demonstrative' truth, which did not provide factual knowledge of the world. This separation of two forms of knowledge worked against metaphysical speculation, in particular, 'natural' theology. For Ockham, the natural world became instead something to be investigated, in a search for the causes of things. The causes of external events could not, he held, be discovered by a priori reasoning, which produced certainty only in the sense that it drew the consequences of its own assumptions and definitions. This separation of contingent from formal truth created a threshold for much freer thinking. It was a spur to curiosity about the natural world of experience.

Followers of Ockham pursued this separation of two types of reasoning, and rejected 'realist' positions which clung to the belief that a structure of the universe knowable by reason alone could be identified. We have already encountered Ockham's attack on the misuse of definitions, taking as premises terms such as 'final cause', which correspond to nothing that is verifiable. Thus, Ockham's insistence on the difference between reasons and causes, the latter turning on observable sequences of events, liberated enquiry about the natural world by providing the conceptual basis for distinguishing 'nature' from 'society'. This was a death blow to traditional teleological thinking, for it separated norms and the conditions of human action from the requirements for explaining external, physical events.

So it was no accident that, by the fourteenth century, previous understanding of the physical world had come under review in the universities. A newly critical approach to Aristotle's physics developed, an approach which noticed anomalies in the theory by relying on direct observation. The first response was to introduce additional assumptions to account for the anomalies and 'rescue' Aristotelian theory. Yet the multiplication of such assumptions in order to 'save appearances' gradually raised doubts about the fundamental assumption on which Aristotelian theory was based, that everything in the universe tends to find a resting place, its purpose or 'final cause'.

Ockham's Razor – the principle that the best explanation is one that does not multiply assumptions needlessly – took its toll of confidence in Aristotle's physical theory. Aristotle's assumption that everything has a rightful 'place' had sprung from the ancient natural law tradition, with its underlying assumption of inequality. Thus, Aristotle had distinguished 'natural' from 'unnatural' motion (for example, throwing a stone upwards, when it 'naturally' falls). Ockham rejected this distinction, suggesting instead something like the idea of inertia. Stimulated by Ockham's arguments, his followers Nicholas Oresme, Pierre d'Ailly and Jean Buridan developed an account of motion in terms of impetus: the energy given to an object by its mover.

The idea that motion was as fundamental as rest in 'nature' was emerging. By the fourteenth century, it had begun to subvert the ancient model of the cosmos. Buridan, for example, applied the theory of impetus to argue that it could explain the movement of heavenly bodies in precisely the same way that it accounted for the movement of bodies on earth: 'There is no need to suppose that the heavenly bodies are made of a special element (the quintessence or fifth element) which can only move with a circular motion. Nor is it necessary to postulate Intelligences of the spheres to account for the spheres' movements.'[5] Thus, Buridan abandoned the assumption that heavenly bodies have a superior nature – the usual assumption of ancient teleology – and that their role springs from a higher intelligence ('the music of the spheres') than any available on earth. 'Motion on earth and motion in the heavens can be explained in the same way.' It is as if the moral intuitions behind social levelling on earth were being applied to the celestial sphere. There was no need to postulate 'aristocracy' in nature!

Oresme was even bolder than Buridan. He called into question another basic ancient assumption – the assumption that while the heavens move, the earth itself is stationary. 'I conclude that one could not show by any experience that the heaven was moved with a daily motion and that the earth was not moved in this way.'[6] Altogether, fourteenth-century physical theories reveal how understanding of the physical world began to profit from abandoning the assumption of natural inequality.

Let us now look at a third series of changes revealing the impact of the new image of society. This series was political rather than moral or scientific. The question hanging over Europe by the fifteenth century was this: how would it be organized as feudal institutions eroded? Feudalism had not sent down the same roots everywhere. It was never as strong in Italy or in southern France, as in the north of France or Germany. The Italian city-states or republics, together with the cities of Flanders and Catalonia, suggested a different basis for political organization than the feudal north, while in England, still another model was on offer, that of a royal power traditionally stronger than the leading feudatories.

The outstanding political fact of fifteenth-century Europe was the centralizing of authority and power by monarchs seeking to leave feudal constraints behind and become 'sovereigns' properly so called. Louis XI of France, Henry VII of England and Ferdinand and Isabella in Spain all took remarkable steps in that direction. Why did they have such success? How did they overcome the resistance of other institutions? For they certainly met with resistance. In effect, there were four institutions which might have provided a model for the political organization of Europe: feudalism, the church, the boroughs and monarchy.

However, after the frustration of the theocratic ambitions of Innocent IV and Boniface VIII, neither the feudal nobility nor the cities were able to shape the political organization of Europe. By the fourteenth century, it was clear that feudal 'law' could not provide the basis for a stable political system. Its incoherence and constant reliance on force made that impossible. Yet at the same time the feudal nobility was strong enough to prevent anything like the generalizing of 'republican' civic institutions. That was a development improbable in any case, for the burghers of the cities lacked wider political ambitions. In the face of the feudal nobility, burghers exhibited a sense of inferiority. Fierce as they were if it was a question of defending their own boroughs, they had no vision of a republican organization for society at large, though the Netherlands was perhaps an exception.

So there was a stand-off. Before the triumph of monarchy, however, there was a last quasi-feudal attempt to organize Europe. It took the form of bringing together the representatives of these different institutions with a view to their cooperating, while retaining their original character.[7] Thus, awareness of centralizing pressures led to the creation of assemblies which sought to reflect and organize the diversity of European institutions – the Estates-General in France, the English Parliament, the Cortes of Spain and an Imperial Diet in Germany. These assemblies were organized according to rank, with the nobility, clergy and burghers each in their assigned place.

But these attempts at national organization – with the signal exception of England's Parliament (which benefited from a stronger crown) – failed. The assemblies were too heterogeneous. While the feudal nobles were accustomed to exercising political will, neither the clergy nor the representatives of the boroughs were used to direct political power, and they had little taste for it, fearing new taxes. As a result, these assemblies failed to become effective instruments of government.

But these assemblies did not fail merely because of their diversity, their clinging to traditional privileges. There was a deeper reason. It was because the new idea of a 'sovereign' authority vested in monarchs projected a different image of society, an egalitarian image which now had a popular resonance that it had previously lacked. The appeal of royalty released and reinforced new aspirations. Popular attitudes had changed enough to deprive the traditional corporate model of society of its legitimacy. That is why 'equal subjection' to a sovereign was perceived not as loss but as gain. So we have to be careful when speaking of the 'triumph' of royalty in the fifteenth century. For, indirectly, it was also the triumph of moral intuitions generated by the church.

The task of organizing Europe fell to monarchy because its way had been prepared by the church. It was not merely that the royal ambition to acquire a sovereign authority had been shaped by the papal revolution. At the deepest level – the moral and intellectual level – the church had won the struggle for the future of Europe. The church had projected the image of society as an association of individuals, an image which unleashed the centralizing process in Europe.

Of course, monarchs were not disinterested exponents of an egalitarian form of society. They rapidly came to understand how much they stood to gain in power from the centralizing of legal authority. For them, the prospect of subduing leading feudal magnates and controlling the church within their realms was as important as moral considerations generated by Christian beliefs – often far more important. Nonetheless, unintended consequences overtook the monarchs. In the process of centralizing laws, manners and ideas – forging a single society out of what had been separate, parochial societies – the monarchs not only created states, but also the foundation for a 'public' or 'national' opinion. The partial emergence of national opinions in the fifteenth century provides further evidence of the impact of the new image of society as an association of individuals.

How was this manifest? The prestige of royalty grew because royal power became the symbol of social progress, the abolition of privilege through 'equal subjection'. The Third Estate in France or the 'Commons' in England were at times prepared to sacrifice even local self-government in order to destroy feudal privilege. The creation of a 'sovereign' agency seemed far the most important objective. This was the pattern that marked the growth of royal power, especially in France. But across Europe it invested royalty with a kind of idealism. Equal subjection to a sovereign was seen as developing at the expense of subordinations based on 'mere' custom.

It would be a mistake therefore to see only the tyrannical potential of the growth of sovereign authorities, that royal 'absolutism' which came to the fore during the sixteenth and seventeenth centuries. For it contained the seeds of individual liberty. By claiming a monopoly of legal authority, sovereigns deprived many traditional attitudes and practices of legal status. What royal commands did not positively enjoin or forbid, defined – at least potentially – a sphere of choice and personal freedom.

Of course, full awareness of the model of society entailed by the claim of 'sovereignty' did not develop overnight. Even the late sixteenth-century French theorist of sovereignty Jean Bodin wavered over the nature of the unit of subordination entailed by the claim. Yet the time of Thomas Hobbes, in the next century, the distinctive nature of the claim to a sovereign authority was made clear, not least by Hobbes's referring to sovereigns as secular deities.

There is one final, formidable piece of evidence about 'inventing the individual' available. It comes from what remains the most reliable source about social change, language itself. If we look at the word 'individual' in historical dictionaries of the English or French languages, we will find that it first became current in the fifteenth century. The word 'state', with its stipulation of a sovereign authority, became current at about the same time. And that is no accident, for the meanings of these two words depend upon each other. It was through the creation of states that the individual was invented as the primary or organizing social role.

It should not come as a surprise, therefore, that we often find the motives and actions of Europeans by the fifteenth century easier to understand – more familiar and more 'modern'. The kind of means/end rationality or thinking that we associate with market relations was emerging clearly, even to the point of caricature in the calculations of Louis XI and Henry VII. That is because the beliefs and institutions shaping action were changing dramatically.

It would not be long before Cervantes was able to parody as illusions the motives and patterns of behaviour belonging to a hierarchical society that no longer existed, while Shakespeare could create human characters by plumbing the depths below the social roles they happened to occupy. Christian egalitarianism had prepared this revolution in the structure of society. Social positions could no longer be regarded as 'fated' or inescapable.

This was the secular translation of the Christian idea of the 'soul'. And we are living with its consequences even now.

Epilogue: Christianity and Secularism

Like other cultures, Western culture is founded on shared beliefs. But, in contrast to most others, Western beliefs privilege the idea of equality. And it is the privileging of equality – of a premiss that excludes permanent inequalities of status and ascriptions of authoritative opinion to any person or group – which underpins the secular state and the idea of fundamental or 'natural' rights. Thus, the only birthright recognized by the liberal tradition is individual freedom.

Christianity played a decisive part in this. Yet the idea that liberalism and secularism have religious roots is by no means widely understood. Evidently, the separation of church and state – the first great objective of the liberal tradition – has itself drawn attention away from these roots of secularism. But so too has a 'civil war' that long raged in Europe, and may now be spreading to the United States. What is this civil war? It is a war in which religious belief and 'godless' secularism are understood as irreconcilable opponents, an understanding that was long fed by memories of the burning of Protestant 'martyrs' in sixteenth-century England, by the legend of the Spanish Inquisition and by a 'holy alliance' between churches (especially the Roman Catholic Church) and socially conservative forces in reaction to the French Revolution.

Those memories may have dimmed, but the perception of profound conflict between secularism and religious belief has been reawakened and taken a new form in Western societies recently. In Europe, massive immigration and the growth of large Muslim minorities have widened the range of non-Christian beliefs dramatically. And such beliefs have consequences. Quite apart from the acts of terrorism which invoke – more or less dubiously – the name of Islam, Muslims are frequently encouraged to look forward to replacing the laws of the nation-state with shariah 'law'. Islam seems to sit uneasily with secularism.

It is hardly surprising, therefore, that questions about the relationship between religious belief and secularism have re-entered public debate. When referring to the Christian roots of Europe in a proposed constitution for the European Union became an issue in 2001–2, there were strong voices in support, for example from Poland. There were also strong voices opposed, notably from France. Yet far the most widespread reaction was one of embarrassment, an uneasy wish that the question would go away. With the defeat of the proposed constitutional treaty in referendums, the question has gone away. But the embarrassment remains. And it is an important phenomenon, something which merits closer examination. For when examined, it throws light on why Europe does not project a more coherent identity onto the world today. It throws light on what I have called Europe's 'civil war'.

So let us try to get at the source of this embarrassment. For it seems to me that the widespread sense of discontinuity that Europeans at least tacitly acknowledge when reconsidering their past – and even more revealingly, their reluctance to embark on such a reconsideration – weakens Europe's voice in the conversation of mankind. But not only that. It also helps to explain major differences between European and American attitudes. By what route have we got to where we are today? What is the relation of the secular state, liberal democracy and market economics to the European past? In answering these questions, we have become the victims of our own historiography – and not simply at a professional, academic level.

What is characteristic about historical writing in recent centuries? It is an inclination to minimize the moral and intellectual distance between the modern world and the ancient world, while at the same time maximizing the moral and intellectual distance between modern Europe and the middle ages. That inclination first appeared, we have seen, in the Italian Renaissance, with its admiration for antiquity and hostility to the 'scholasticism' of the universities and the church. But it was in the eighteenth century, especially among the French philosophes, that this inclination developed into a passionate anti-clericalism, which reshaped the understanding of European history.

An overriding temptation for many eighteenth-century historians was to present the ancient world as 'secular', and in that way provide a point of contact with European states in which the role of the church and of the clergy was contested and being redefined. In Protestant countries this had long been under way, but by the eighteenth century even Catholic countries were involved, as the expulsion of the Jesuits from several of them reveals.

Understanding the ancient world as secular – with citizens 'free' from the oppression of priests and a privileged, dogmatic church – became an important weapon in the arsenal of political argument. In the same way, the conception of the medieval church as aspiring to, if not always achieving, a theocratic regime in which thought was stifled by 'superstition' and clerical self-interest provided another weapon. Neither of these conceptions was baseless. Yet both were, I think, more wrong than right. For each overlooked something fundamental, something radically inconsistent with their account of the past. So let us review what we have discovered.

Let us take the account of antiquity as 'secular' first. The trouble with this account is that it looks in the wrong place for religion, applying inappropriate tests for its organization and its expression. As Fustel de Coulanges demonstrated in *The Ancient City*, the religion of the Greek and Roman pre-history did not speak to the individual conscience. Rather, it spoke to and through the family. And it is to the family that we have to look to find religion and priesthood. The ancient family was itself a religious cult, with the father as its high priest tending the family altar and its 'sacred flame', the flame that made his ancestors visible. Ancient religion thus consisted in worship of divine ancestors through the paterfamilias, a radical inequality of roles within the family and a series of elaborate ritual requirements. The family was, at least originally, a self-contained moral universe. It did not seek or welcome any deep or 'moral' connection with humans outside.

In time, this kind of hermetic family cult was altered by the emergence of the polis or city-state. But it was altered only to the extent that the bond of association constituting the city was itself a religious bond. The city was an association of families and tribes, each defined by a shared worship of ancestors. Little wonder, then, that the formation of a city required the emergence of a new cult or worship, through discovery of a 'hero' as founder of the city. As the family had its gods, and the tribe its gods, so the city had to become the domain of gods, its 'protecting deities'.

So instead of an antiquity free of religion, priesthood and superstition – a 'secular' inspiration for modern Europe – we find on closer examination that the family, tribe and city were each a kind of church. Each had its own rites, a worship with very elaborate requirements. 'Faith and purity of intention counted for very little, and the religion consisted entirely in the minute practice of innumerable rules . . .' Because of that, the constant fear in each association was that some detail of ritual requirement might be neglected and the god of the association offended. Hence the need for frequent rites of purification and expiation. These became the duties of the civic magistrates in both Greece and Rome.

Altogether, the most distinctive thing about Greek and Roman antiquity is what might be called 'moral enclosure', in which the limits of personal identity were established by the limits of physical association and inherited, unequal social roles. This moral enclosure is illustrated by the Greek term describing anyone who sought to live outside such associations and such roles: such a person was called an 'idiot'.

More than anything else, I think, Christianity changed the ground of human identity. It was able to do that because of the way it combined Jewish monotheism with an abstract universalism that had roots in later Greek philosophy. By emphasizing the moral equality of humans, quite apart from any social roles they might occupy, Christianity changed 'the name of the game'. Social rules became secondary. They followed and, in a crucial sense, had to be understood as subordinate to a God-given human identity, something all humans share equally. Thus, humans were to live in 'two cities' at the same time.

We can see this breaking out of moral enclosure everywhere in the New Testament. In particular, we can glimpse the merger of Judaism and Greek philosophy in St Paul's conception of the Christ, a conception remarkable for its universalism. For Paul, the love of God revealed in the Christ imposes opportunities and obligations on the individual as such, that is, on conscience. The Christ thus becomes the medium of a new and transformed humanity. In one sense, Paul's conception of the Christ introduces the individual, by giving conscience a universal dimension. Was Paul the greatest revolutionary in human history?

Through its emphasis on human equality, the New Testament stands out against the primary thrust of the ancient world, with its dominant assumption of 'natural' inequality. Indeed, the atmosphere of the New Testament is one of exhilarating detachment from the unthinking constraints of inherited social roles. Hence Paul's frequent references to 'Christian liberty'. This was not simply an opposition to the Jewish law. It was a fulfilment, made possible by the discovery of a ground for existence antecedent to inherited social rules and roles. This is the moral atmosphere revealed when Jesus restricts even the claims of the family if the service of God requires it, something which churches have since often toned down.

In contrast to some later Hellenic philosophy, the New Testament assertion of a basic human equality ceased to be a speculative stripping away of social conventions, an exercise which had at times served chiefly to demonstrate the superiority of the philosopher to local prejudice. Instead, this stripping away revealed the need for a moral response to the individual freedom implied by equal standing in the eyes of God. Jesus' insistence that 'the kingdom of God is within you' (as the early church often proclaimed) was designed to invoke such a response, to create an individual will. Thus, to earlier speculations about equality, the New Testament added the duty of reciprocity – the obligation 'to love thy neighbour as thyself'.

That is why I argued in an earlier book, *Democracy in Europe* (2000), that the Christian conception of God provided an ontological foundation for the individual, first as a moral status, and then, centuries later, as the primary social role. 'The interiority of Christian belief – its insistence that the quality of personal intentions is more important than any fixed social rules – was a reflection of this. Rule following – the Hebraic "law" – was downgraded in favour of action governed by conscience. In that way, the Christian conception of God provided the foundation for what became an unprecedented form of human society.' Christian moral beliefs emerge as the ultimate source of the social revolution that has made the West what it is.

In *Democracy in Europe*, I suggested an analogy to understand what Christian beliefs introduced into the world. It is an analogy with an argument in Marxism – the distinction Marx drew between a 'class in itself' and a 'class for itself'. Marx meant that a class could exist objectively – identified by income or occupation – without necessarily having any consciousness of itself as a class. He illustrated this by contrasting medieval peasants with the townspeople or burghers, the 'bourgeoisie', who became conscious of themselves as a class by struggling against feudal privileges. So I then applied this distinction to the role of Christianity.

> Christianity took humanity as a species in itself and sought to convert it into a species for itself. Thus, the defining characteristic of Christianity was its universalism. It aimed to create a single human society, a society composed, that is, of individuals rather than tribes, clans or castes. The fundamental relationship between the individual and his or her God provides the crucial test, in Christianity, of what really matters. It is, by definition, a test which applies to all equally. Hence the deep individualism of Christianity was simply the reverse side of its universalism. The Christian conception of God became the means of creating the brotherhood of man, of bringing to self-consciousness the human species, by leading each of its members to see him- or herself as having, at least potentially, a relationship with the deepest reality – viz., God – that both required and justified the equal moral standing of all humans.

This was the revolutionary promise of Christian beliefs.

It is hardly too much to claim that this framework of ideas provided the original constitution of Europe. It is a framework that can be glimpsed as early as Augustine's famous work, the *City of God*. For Augustine, following Paul, belief in the moral equality of men created a role for conscience, and that set limits to the claims of any social organization. This is the source of the dualism that has distinguished Christian thinking about society and government, a preoccupation with the different claims of the sacred and the secular spheres. It rests on the conviction that we ought to recognize and respect the difference between inner conviction and external conformity, a distinction which would not have served any function or perhaps even been intelligible in much of the ancient world.

But if Christian beliefs provided the ontological foundation for the individual as a moral status and primary social role, why did the latter take more than a millennium to develop? We should not be surprised by this fact. There were many other causes at work. The implications of moral intuitions generated by Christianity had to be worked out against prejudices and practices sometimes as old as the social division of labour. That, in turn, involved learning how to create and protect a public role for conscience, first of all by forging a conceptual framework that could be deployed to criticize existing social practices. It was something that took centuries. And it involved fierce controversy, frequent back-tracking and frustration. It is that process we have been examining.

We do not have to suppose that the process was always self-conscious. Nonetheless, outstanding minds among the clergy clung to one framework of ideas, even during what I have called the 'schizophrenic' Carolingian period, when there was an unstable mixture of ancient and Christian thought and practice. The framework emerges in the voice of a leading Carolingian churchman, Agobard, the archbishop of Lyons:

> There is neither Gentile nor Jew, Scythian nor Aquitainian, nor Lombard, nor Burgundian, nor Alaman, nor bond, nor free. All are one in Christ ... Can it be accepted that opposed to this unity which is the work of God, there should be an obstacle in the diversity of laws in one and the same country, in one and the same city, and in one and the same house? It constantly happens that of five men walking or sitting side by side, no two have the same terrestrial law, although at root – on the eternal plane – they belong to Christ.

In this urgent voice from the early ninth century we can still hear the moral heart of Christianity beating beneath the surface of social conventions.

This brings us to another historical 'moment'. For just as modern historical writing has often underestimated the role of religion in the ancient world, so it has failed to draw attention to a remarkable development during the so-called 'middle ages'. This was the moment when the idea of natural rights emerged and began to provide a new conceptual tool for criticizing established social beliefs and practices, including, eventually, even the church as an institution. Historians of social and political thought have usually located such a moment in the sixteenth and seventeenth centuries. This 'early modern' period is the period when it is conventional to say that the doctrines of liberalism and secularism first raised their heads, not least because of the needs of nation-states struggling with bitter confessional conflicts arising from the Reformation.

The conventional interpretation also relates the emergence of liberalism and secularism to a new scepticism bred by the interest in and sympathy with antiquity. The increasingly sceptical turn taken by the humanist movement at the end of the fifteenth century saw a writer like Machiavelli draw on Roman sources when interpreting the events of his own time, an interpretation that gave less attention to Christian beliefs and more attention to the failures of the church as an institution. Borrowing the idea of an inexorable historical cycle drove out worries about individual salvation. Corruption of the citizenry, their loss of civic spirit, came to seem more important than the Christian idea of virtue. The clergy, suspected of manipulating beliefs to their own advantage, were often charged with 'weakening' the citizens' valour.

So humanism became increasingly associated with anti-clericalism, at about the same time as religious wars resulting from the Reformation provided further motive for secular authorities to intervene, in order to establish a framework that might contain the violence unleashed by confessional differences. Taken together, these trends suggested that the emergent secularism or proto-liberalism had little to do with the moral intuitions generated by Christianity, but rather that their inspiration should be located in antiquity and paganism. Suddenly, 'superstition' was associated more with the church than with paganism.

The trouble with this view is that it ignores the fact that, by the fifteenth century, there was already operating in Europe a theory of justice that did, indeed, have roots in ancient 'pagan' philosophy. But it was a doctrine that had for several centuries been reshaped by Christian moral intuitions – by, put most simply, the golden rule of 'doing unto others what you would have them do unto you', with its strikingly egalitarian underpinnings. That doctrine was the doctrine of natural law. Long before the fifteenth century it had been revived and revised by canon lawyers in the universities of Bologna, Padua, Paris and Oxford.

How was this doctrine revised? It was revised, as we have seen, by being turned into a theory of natural rights, rights which belong to the individual as such, rights which are in that sense pre-social and ought to serve as a criterion of legitimate social organization. Drawing on Roman law, and under the patronage of the papacy, canon lawyers from the late eleventh century began to create a system of law for Christians founded on the assumption of moral equality. This system was to privilege the conception of what has been called 'subjective rights', that is, rights inhering in the individual, starting with the claim to freedom. That claim amounted to a rejection of the ancient assumption of natural inequality.

Brian Tierney shrewdly observes that 'the idea of subjective rights has become central to our political discourse, but we still have no idea of the origin and early development of the idea'. Tierney argues that Gratian's *Decretum* and its impact on the twelfth- and thirteenth-century canonists is the correct point of departure, quoting the first words of the *Decretum*: 'The human race is ruled by two (means) namely by natural law and by usages. Natural law is what is contained in the law and the Gospel by which each is commanded to do to another what he wants done to himself and forbidden to do to another what he does not want done to himself.' Tierney shows how canonists following Gratian constantly moved between two senses of the word *jus* – between *jus* understood as objective law (whether divine or human in origin) and *jus* understood as individual subjective right:

> A decisive shift of meaning and emphasis occurred in the twelfth century. For some of the Stoics and for Cicero there was a force in man through which he could discern jus naturale, the objective natural law that pervaded the whole universe, but for the canonists jus naturale itself could be defined as a subjective force or faculty or power or ability inherent in human persons.

Where the Stoics had construed natural law to refer to a cosmic order of things, the canonists of the twelfth century construed it to mean free will or power, an 'area of licit choice' for individuals justified by the nature of human agency.

Thus, by the twelfth century a sense of *jus* was emerging that was not far removed from the modern sense of a right. There is no need for us here to go again into the complicated story of how the doctrine of natural rights developed from Gratian to Ockham and beyond. For our purposes, as Voltaire said about the miracle of St Denis (who, after being decapitated, picked up his head and walked away), it is 'only the first step that is difficult'.

Why have these origins of the theory of natural rights not been appreciated sooner? The answer, I suspect, turns on the hostility shown by fifteenth- and sixteenth-century humanists to what was going on in the universities of their day. The blanket condemnation of 'scholasticism' (understood as an obsession with Aristotle and logic) led to quite different forms of enquiry being bundled together and confused. Theology, civil and canon law, logic and physical theory suffered under the same term of opprobrium, which became a stock-in-trade of eighteenth-century historical writing.

Yet we can now see that not only did an identification of anomalies in Aristotelian physical theory in the universities pave the way for the sixteenth- and seventeenth-century revolution in physics, but the origins of natural rights language which became central to modern political discourse can also be traced back to innovations in canon law during the twelfth, thirteenth and fourteenth centuries.

The identity of the individual – of a status which creates a space for the legitimate exercise of personal judgement and will – had broken through the surface of social life by the fifteenth century. Equality was no longer consigned to the arrangements of 'another world', to an afterlife in which unjustifiable (that is, in the sight of God) inequalities of status and treatment would disappear. The papal claim of sovereignty, embodied in a legal system founded on the assumption of moral equality, had thus achieved more than the papacy either imagined or intended. It had generated a new conception of society, a conception which had, in turn, created unprecedented moral needs in the population at large. That is the most striking thing about the fifteenth century. Such needs were seizing the popular mind. They took the form of new claims in both the religious and secular spheres, claims anticipating the Reformation.

What at least some of the conciliarists grasped was that the moral intuitions generated by Christianity were transforming the traditional idea of 'authority'. Embodied in the legal system created by canonists, and inspiring secular rulers to create comparable systems based on the claims to 'sovereignty', the introduction of an underlying equality of status – the invention of the individual – was turning the source of authority upside down. Increasingly it was to be found 'below', in human agency and conscience, rather than 'above' in coercive eternal ideas.

Why is all this important? It reveals how Christian moral intuitions played a pivotal role in shaping the discourse that gave rise to modern liberalism and secularism. Indeed, the pattern by which liberalism and secularism developed from the sixteenth to the nineteenth century resembles nothing so much as the stages through which canon law developed from the twelfth to the fifteenth century. The sequence of argument is quite extraordinarily similar. The canonists, so to speak, 'got there first'.

The sequence began with insistence on equality of status, moved on to the assertion of a range of basic human rights, and concluded with the case for self-government. Thus, from Hobbes's insistence on basic human equality, in preparation for defining sovereignty in terms of 'equal subjection', through Locke's defence of human freedom by identifying a range of natural rights, to Rousseau's making the case for the sovereignty of the people and self-government, each of these three steps in modern political thought had its counterpart in the evolution of medieval canon law.

To be sure, there remains an important difference between the two traditions of thought. The Pauline moral source is frequently asserted in canon law, whereas developing liberal thought often conflated assumptions about God and nature. As the historian Carl Becker once remarked, in *The Heavenly City of the Eighteenth-Century Philosophers* (1932) the eighteenth century 'denatured God and deified nature'. The foundation for the claim to liberty became 'human nature' and personal conscience. Yet the conception of human agency relied upon – and elaborated by the great philosopher Immanuel Kant at the end of the eighteenth century – continued to have a markedly Christian impress.

What, then, has led to a 'war' between religion and secularism, a struggle which can plausibly be called a 'civil war' because of the moral roots shared by the two sides? Why do Europeans feel happier referring to the role of ancient Greece and Rome than to the role of the church in the formation of their culture? The answer can be found in the way secularism has come to be understood – and misunderstood – in Europe.

Attitudes towards secularism were shaped by anti-clericalism in the eighteenth and nineteenth centuries. The French Revolution, in particular, had a decisive effect on attitudes. It created two hostile camps. On the one hand were followers of Voltaire, who sought to *écraser l'infâme*, as they described the authoritarian and privileged church of the *ancien régime*. On the other hand were those, such as Joseph de Maistre, who saw the separating of church and state as nothing less than an 'insurrection' against God, public denial of beliefs which had shaped Europe.

Of course, the last two hundred years have overlaid the hostility between the two camps. The religious camp has come, by and large, to accept civil liberty and religious pluralism. The anti-clericals have – with the exception of hardline Marxists and writers such as Richard Dawkins – given up on the attempt to extirpate religious belief. But the old antagonism still lurks under the surface. The visceral reaction of the French left to the prospect of acknowledging the Christian roots of Europe has its counterpart in much church rhetoric deploring the growth of 'Godless' secularism. Even Benedict XVI, a most learned pope, was not free of this habit. He called for an understanding between religions in order to 'combat' secularism.

This is Europe's undeclared 'civil war'. And it is as tragic as it is unnecessary. It is tragic because, by identifying secularism with non-belief, with indifference and materialism, it deprives Europe of moral authority, playing into the hands of those who are only too anxious to portray Europe as decadent and without conviction. It is unnecessary because it rests on a misunderstanding of the nature of secularism. Properly understood, secularism can be seen as Europe's noblest achievement, the achievement which should be its primary contribution to the creation of a world order, while different religious beliefs continue to contend for followers. Secularism is Christianity's gift to the world, ideas and practices which have often been turned against 'excesses' of the Christian church itself.

What is the crux of secularism? It is that belief in an underlying or moral equality of humans implies that there is a sphere in which each should be free to make his or her own decisions, a sphere of conscience and free action. That belief is summarized in the central value of classical liberalism: the commitment to 'equal liberty'. Is this indifference or non-belief? Not at all. It rests on the firm belief that to be human means being a rational and moral agent, a free chooser with responsibility for one's actions. It puts a premium on conscience rather than the 'blind' following of rules. It joins rights with duties to others.

This is also the central egalitarian moral insight of Christianity. It stands out from St Paul's contrast between 'Christian liberty' and observance of the Jewish law. Enforced belief was, for Paul and many early Christians, a contradiction in terms. Strikingly, in its first centuries Christianity spread by persuasion, not by force of arms – a contrast to the early spread of Islam.

When placed against this background, secularism does not mean non-belief or indifference. It is not without moral content. Certainly secularism is not a neutral or 'value-free' framework, as the language of contemporary social scientists at times suggests. Rather, secularism identifies the conditions in which authentic beliefs should be formed and defended. It provides the gateway to beliefs properly so called, making it possible to distinguish inner conviction from mere external conformity.

Nor is this just a hypothetical understanding of secularism. This is the way secularism has traditionally been understood in the United States. It has been understood as a condition for authentic belief presupposed by Christianity. In contrast to views formed by Europe's 'civil war', secularism in the United States has been identified with moral intuitions generated by Christianity.

Why has this not been the view in Europe? For centuries a privileged, monolithic church which was almost inseparable from an aristocratic society, confronted Europeans. So the church became associated in the popular mind with social hierarchy and deference, even at times with coercion, rather than with the moral equality and role of conscience that provide, in fact, the foundation of its beliefs.

A kind of intellectual incoherence – especially noticeable in Catholic

Europe – was the consequence. Religiously minded people struggled against the claims of civil liberty as threatening the church, while those who defended liberty looked upon the church as their enemy. Both sides failed to appreciate the extent to which promoting secularism in Europe amounted to turning the moral intuitions generated by Christianity against a privileged, coercive role for the church. By contrast, the United States has largely escaped from this 'civil war'. The absence of both a monolithic church and aristocracy in the United States meant that Americans instinctively grasped the moral symmetry between secularism, with its prized civil liberty, and Christianity, accepting that secularism identifies a necessary condition of authentic belief. At times Muslim commentators themselves perceive that symmetry when they speak of 'Christian secularism'.

What will happen to its 'civil war' now that Europe is faced with the challenge of Islam? Will Europeans come to understand better the moral logic that joins Christianity with civil liberty? It is important that they do so if they are to counter the argument that European secularism is a form of non-belief or indifference. Their self-understanding is at stake. If Europeans understand 'secularism' in the terms favoured by its critics – as mere consumerism, materialism and amorality – they lose touch with their own moral intuitions. They forget why they value freedom.

And what of the United States? There is no room for complacency. The rapid growth of Christian fundamentalism – in part, no doubt, a reaction to the threat of radical Islam – may now jeopardize the traditional American understanding of secularism as the embodiment of Christian moral intuitions. In the Southern and Western states especially, 'born-again' Christians are coming to identify secularism as an enemy rather than a companion. In struggling against abortion and homosexuality, they risk losing touch with the most profound moral insights of their faith. If good and evil are contrasted too simply, in a Manichaean way, charity is the loser. The principle of 'equal liberty' is put at risk.

It is a strange and disturbing moment in Western history. Europeans – out of touch with the roots of their tradition – often seem to lack conviction, while Americans may be succumbing to a dangerously simplistic version of their faith. On neither side of the Atlantic is there an adequate understanding of the relationship between liberal secularism and Christianity.

Failure to understand that relationship makes it easier to underestimate the moral content of liberal secularism. In the Western world today, it contributes to two temptations, to what might be called two 'liberal heresies'. The first is the temptation to reduce liberalism to the endorsement of market economics, the satisfaction of current wants or preferences without worrying much about the formation of those wants or preferences. In doing so, it narrows the claims of justice. This temptation reduces liberalism to a crude form of utilitarianism. The second temptation is best described as 'individualism', the retreat into a private sphere of family and friends at the expense of civic spirit and political participation. This weakens the habit of association and eventually endangers the self-reliance which the claims of citizenship require. Both of these heresies focus on the second word of the core liberal value – 'equal liberty' – at the expense of the first word. They sacrifice the emphasis on reciprocity – on seeing ourselves in others and others in ourselves – which we have seen to be fundamental to inventing the individual and which gives liberalism its lasting moral value.

If we in the West do not understand the moral depth of our own tradition, how can we hope to shape the conversation of mankind?

Select Bibliography and Endnotes

I want first to acknowledge a number of works which have had the courage – some might say audacity – to provide a large-scale account of the development of Western ideas and institutions. F. Guizot's *History of Civilisation in Europe* (Harmondsworth, 1996); A. O. Lovejoy, *The Great Chain of Being* (Cambridge, Mass., 1936); H. Maine, *Ancient Law* (many edns.); P. Brown, *The Rise of Western Christendom*, 2nd edn. (Oxford, 2003); D. MacCulloch, *A History of Christianity* (London, 2010); W. E. H. Lecky, *History of European Morals*, 2 vols. (London, 1869); R. W. and A. J. Carlyle, *A History of Medieval Political Theory in the West*, 2 vols. (London, 1928); P. A. Rahe, *Republics Ancient and Modern* (Chapel Hill, NC, 1994). Over the years, I have benefited from all of them. However, my greatest debt is to the writings of Guizot and Brown.

CHAPTER I. THE ANCIENT FAMILY

This chapter is crucially indebted to N. D. Fustel de Coulanges, *The Ancient City* (New York, n.d.). Because his prose is so closely aligned with his ancient sources, I have tried to preserve it as much as possible – even if at times that means resorting to what is little more than paraphrase. For I am anxious to retain his power of drawing the contemporary reader into another, utterly remote world. Aspects of Fustel's account have been criticized, not least by Marxist historians such as M. I. Finley (*The Ancient Economy*, London, 1985) and G. E. M. de Sainte Croix (*The Class Struggle in the Ancient Greek World*, Ithaca, NY, 1981) who emphasize the motive force of property rather than religious belief. More restrained correctives can be found in a recent collection edited by O. Murray and S. Price, *The Ancient City: From Homer to Alexander* (Oxford, 1990) and A. Momigliano's article in S. Humphreys, *The Family, Women and Death: Comparative Studies* (London,1983). Yet even these can fall victim at times to a form of reductionism. In my view, none of what has been added or corrected approaches the depth of Fustel's account.

The self-understanding of any society remains of the first importance when studying it.

1. Fustel, *The Ancient City*, p. 117.
2. Murray and Price (eds.), *The Ancient City*, p. 268.
3. Fustel, *The Ancient City*, p. 134.
4. Murray and Price (eds.), *The Ancient City*, pp. 265–94.
5. Fustel, *The Ancient City*, p. 42.
6. Ibid., p. 25.
7. Ibid., p. 61.
8. Ibid., p. 63.
9. Murray and Price (eds.), *The Ancient City*, pp. 295–322.
10. Fustel, *The Ancient City*, p. 99.
11. Ibid., p. 211.
12. Ibid., p. 67.
13. Quoted ibid., p. 81.
14. Ibid., p. 87.

CHAPTER 2. THE ANCIENT CITY

Much attention has been devoted to the difference between ancient and modern conceptions of liberty since Benjamin Constant's essay 'On the Liberty of the Ancients compared to that of the Moderns' was published early in the nineteenth century. Constant's argument made a profound impression on other French thinkers such as Alexis de Tocqueville and Fustel de Coulanges. But Constant's influence did not end with them. It has continued to inform philosophical works such as Isaiah Berlin's *Two Concepts of Liberty* and historical studies such as P. Rahe's *Republics Ancient and Modern,* 2 vols. (Chapel Hill, NC, 1994). Constant's essay can be found in B. Constant, *Political Writings* (Cambridge, 1988). See also J.-J. Rousseau, 'On the Arts and Sciences', in *The Social Contract and Discourses* (London, 1966); J. G. A. Pocock, *The Machiavellian Moment* (Princeton, 1975). I am unconvinced by the attempts of K. Popper, *The Open Society and its Enemies* (London, 1966) and E. Havelock, *The Liberal Temper of Greek Politics* (New York, 1957) to give a liberal interpretation of ancient Greek politics, while M. I. Finley's *Democracy Ancient and Modern*(London, 1985) relies on Marxist distinctions which downplay the role of beliefs informing action in the polis.

1. O. Murray and S. Price (eds.), *The Ancient City: From Homer to Alexander* (Oxford, 1990), p. 12.
2. N. D. Fustel de Coulanges, *The Ancient City* (New York, n. d.), p. 148.
3. Quoted ibid., p. 152.

4. Ibid., pp. 128–9.

5. Ibid., p. 194.

6. Ibid., p. 191.

7. Ibid., p. 198.

8. Ibid., pp. 135–6.

9. Ibid., p. 217.

10. Ibid., p. 261.

11. Ibid., p. 259.

12. Ibid., p. 206.

13. Ibid., p. 207.

CHAPTER 3. THE ANCIENT COSMOS

The chief primary sources here are Herodotus, *The Histories* (Harmondsworth, 1994) and Thucydides, *The History of the Peloponnesian War* (Harmondsworth, 1972); for Plato and Aristotle, convenient editions are Plato, *The Republic*, ed. and trans. H. D. P. Lees (Harmondsworth, 1955), and Aristotle, *The Nicomachean Ethics*, ed. and trans. R. Crisp (Cambridge, 2000), and *The Politics*, ed. and trans. C. Lord (Chicago, 1984). For general background, I suggest E. Barker, *Plato and his Predecessors* (Cambridge, 1925) and his *Political Thought of Plato and Aristotle* (London, 1959); F. M. Cornford, *Plato's Theory of Knowledge* (London, 1935); E. R. Dodds, *The Greeks and the Irrational* (Berkeley, 1973); A. H. M. Jones, *The Greek City from Alexander to Justinian* (Oxford, 1940); K. R. Popper, *The Open Society and its Enemies* (London, 1966); J.–J. Rousseau, *The Social Contract and Discourses* (London, 1966); B. Snell, *The Discovery of the Mind: The Greek Origins of European Thought* (Oxford, 1953); B. Williams, *Shame and Necessity* (Berkeley, Calif., 1993); P. Rahe, *Republics Ancient and Modern*, 2 vols. (Chapel Hill, NC, 1994); and W. K. C. Guthrie, *The Sophists* (Cambridge, 1971). A larger context is provided by W. E. H. Lecky, *History of European Morals*, 2 vols. (London, 1869).

1. Quoted in Rahe, *Republics Ancient and Modern*, vol. 1, p. 31.

2. Quoted in W. H. C. Frend, *The Early Church* (London, 2003), p. 8.

3. Williams, *Shame and Necessity*, p. 33.

4. Quoted in Rahe, *Republics Ancient and Modern*, vol. 1, pp 37–8.

5. Quoted in Lecky, *History of European Morals,* vol 1, p. 211, fn.

6. Thucydides, *History of the Peloponnesian War*, p. 131.

7. Herodotus, *The Histories*, p. 450.

8. See I. Ridpath (ed.), *Oxford Dictionary of Astronomy* (Oxford, 2003), esp. p. 28.

9. P. Brown, 'The Risks of Being Christian', *Times Literary Supplement* (20 Dec. 2012).

10. Guthrie, *The Sophists*, *passim*.

CHAPTER 4. THE WORLD TURNED UPSIDE DOWN: PAUL

Quotations from Paul's letters are from the Revised Standard Version of the Bible. The studies of Paul are legion – from great theologians such as Rudolf Bultmann to students of the relations between Judaism and Christianity such as Albert Schweitzer and W. D. Davies. See especially R. Bultmann, 'The Theology of Paul', in *Theology of the New Testament* (London, 1952). Recent works which I have found helpful include D. E. H. Whiteley, *The Theology of Saint Paul* (Oxford, 1972), E. P. Sanders, *Paul, the Law and the Jewish People* (London, 1985) as well as his brief *Paul* (Oxford, 1991), Geza Vermes, *The Religion of Jesus the Jew* (1993) and M. D. Hooker and S. G. Wilson (eds.), *Paul and Paulinism* (London, 1982). A. N. Wilson's *Paul: The Mind of the Apostle* (London, 1998) is especially sensitive to Paul's personality and the poetic potential of his letters. Though not primarily concerned with Paul's thought, A. Dihle's *The Theory of the Will in Classical Antiquity* (Berkeley, 1982) provides a fascinating philosophical context for it. Even broader background is provided by F. Millar, *The Roman Near East, 331 BC–AD 337* (Cambridge, Mass., 1993) and by D. MacCulloch's *A History of Christianity* (London, 2010).

1. Dihle, *The Theory of the Will in Classical Antiquity*, pp. 10–19.
2. Quoted in Dihle, *The Theory of the Will in Classical Antiquity*, p. 1.
3. Ibid., chapters 1 and 2.
4. Ibid., pp. 1–2.
5. 2 Corinthians 5: 16–17.
6. Romans 8: 35–9.
7. Galatians 2: 19–20.
8. 1 Corinthians 3: 11.
9. Galatians 3: 28.
10. 1 Corinthians 13: 1–8.
11. Galatians 3: 24–6.
12. Romans 7: 15.
13. 1 Corinthians 1: 23–4.
14. 1 Corinthians 7: 31.
15. Galatians 5: 13–14.

CHAPTER 5. THE TRUTH WITHIN:
MORAL EQUALITY

A most useful volume of translations from early Christian thinkers (chiefly Greek-speaking) is that of M. Wiles and M. Santer, *Documents in Early Christian Thought* (Cambridge, 1975). *The Gospel of Thomas*, trans. S. Davies (London, 2009) is another fascinating source. For studies of the Church Fathers, I have consulted H. Chadwick, *Early Christian Thought and the Classical Tradition* (Oxford, 1966); W. H. C. Frend, *Rise of the Monophysite Movement* (Cambridge, 1972); R. M. Grant, *A History of Early Christian Literature* (Chicago, 1966), *The Letter and the Spirit* (London, 1957) and *Gnosticism and Early Christianity* (New York, 1959); M. Wiles, *The Christian Fathers* (London, 1966); A. von Harnack, *History of Dogma* and J. N. D. Kelly, *Early Christian Doctrines* (London, 1968); and P. Brown, *The Body and Society* (London, 1989). Among more general works, W. H. C. Frend's *The Early Church* (London, 2003) is especially sensitive to doctrinal issues, while H. Chadwick, *The Early Church* (Harmondsworth, 1967) is also helpful.

1. Wiles and Santer, *Documents in Early Christian Thought*, p. 186.
2. Ibid., p. 6.
3. Ibid., p. 10.
4. Ibid., p. 100.
5. Ibid., p. 228.
6. Quoted in Frend, *The Early Church*, p. 63.
7. Wiles and Santer, *Documents in Early Christian Thought*, p. 174.
8. Ibid., p. 11.
9. Ibid., pp. 13–14.
10. Ibid., pp. 14–15.
11. Frend, *The Early Church*, chapter 5; see also Chadwick, *The Early Church*, pp. 33–41.
12. Frend, *The Early Church*, pp. 55–57, 72–73; Chadwick, *The Early Church*, pp. 38–40.
13. *Gospel of Thomas*, 22b.
14. Wiles and Santer, *Documents in Early Christian Thought*, p. 229.
15. Ibid., p. 230.
16. Ibid., p, 229.
17. Ibid., pp. 226–7.
18. Quoted by Brown, *The Body and Society*, p. 83.
19. Wiles and Santer, *Documents in Early Christian Thought*, p. 227.

CHAPTER 6. HEROISM REDEFINED

This period has been illuminated by the writings of Peter Brown. Brown's combination of imaginative sympathy and command of the sources puts him, in my view, on a level with Fustel de Coulanges. They share a rare ability to enter and animate the minds of the agents making history. Both move between minds and institutions without being either naive or reductionist. Thus, Brown's *Power and Persuasion in Late Antiquity* (Madison, 1992), *The Rise of Western Christendom* (Oxford, 2003) and *The Cult of the Saints: Its Rise and Function in Early Christianity* (Chicago, 1981) are essential reading. A much earlier work which remains significant is W. Jaeger, *Early Christianity and Greek Paideia* (Cambridge, Mass., 1962). See also R. Lane-Fox, *Pagans and Christians* (New York, 1987). Marilyn Dunn, *The Emergence of Monasticism* (Oxford, 2003) provides an excellent introduction to the remarkable developments in Egypt, while some of the literature of early monasticism is collected by W. Harmless in *Desert Christians* (Oxford, 2004).

1. Quoted in W. H. C. Frend, *The Early Church* (London, 2003), p. 63.
2. H. Chadwick, *The Early Church* (Harmondsworth, 1967), p. 46.
3. Brown, *Power and Persuasion in Late Antiquity*, p. 50.
4. Ibid., p. 77.
5. Ibid., p. 78.
6. Ibid., p. 91.
7. Quoted in Harmless, *Desert Christians*, p. 158.
8. Quoted ibid., p. 19.
9. Chadwick, *The Early Church*, p. 180.
10. Brown, *Power and Persuasion*, p. 71.
11. Quoted ibid., p. 72.

CHAPTER 7. A NEW FORM OF ASSOCIATION: MONASTICISM

M. Dunn's account in *The Emergence of Monasticism* (Oxford, 2003) should be supplemented with P. Brown, *The Body and Society* (London, 1989) and *Power and Persuasion in Late Antiquity* (Madison, 1992) as well as R. A. Markus's fascinating study, *The End of Ancient Christianity* (Cambridge, 1990). Markus explores the complex reactions of Christians moving from being a threatened minority to a privileged position within the Roman empire after the conversion of Constantine. He reveals how monasticism came to absorb the cult of the martyr and stimulated Augustine's thinking about asceticism and Christian vocation – thus looking both backward and forward.

1. W. H. C. Frend, *The Early Church* (London, 2003), p. 164.
2. Quoted ibid., pp. 174–5.
3. Brown, *Power and Persuasion*, p. 157.
4. Quoted in Dunn, *The Emergence of Monasticism*, p. 15.
5. Brown, *The Body and Society*, pp. 83–102.
6. Quoted in Dunn, *The Emergence of Monasticism*, p. 27.
7. Quoted ibid.
8. Quoted ibid., p. 38.
9. Ibid., p. 37.
10. Quoted ibid., p. 39.
11. Ibid., pp. 25–41.

CHAPTER 8. THE WEAKNESS OF THE WILL: AUGUSTINE

My preferred translation of Augustine's *Confessions* is that by R. S. Pine-Coffin (Harmondsworth, 1961), while there is a reliable edition of *The City of God*, ed. R. W. Dyson (Cambridge, 1998). Once again Peter Brown's writings are central here. His original study, *Augustine of Hippo* (London, 1967), has recently been expanded, while (unsurprisingly) Augustine also looms large in his *The Rise of Western Christendom*, 2nd edition (Oxford, 2003). Other studies of Augustine worth consulting include E. Gilson, *The Christian Philosophy of Saint Augustine* (London, 1961), G. Bonner, *Saint Augustine of Hippo: Life and Controversies* (London, 1963), F. van der Meer, *Augustine the Bishop* (London, 1962), R. W. Battenhouse (ed.), *A Companion to the Study of Saint Augustine* (1955), and A. Momigliano (ed.), *The Conflict between Paganism and Christianity in the Fourth Century* (Oxford, 1963). A larger backdrop is provided by R. Pasman (ed.), *The Cambridge History of Medieval Philosophy* (Cambridge, 2010). Guglielmo Verdirame drew my attention to the important parallels between Augustine's moral thinking and that of Kant.

1. Augustine, *Confessions*, p. 178; also Brown, *Augustine of Hippo*, p. 109.
2. Quoted in Brown, *Augustine of Hippo*, p. 154.
3. Quoted ibid., p. 155.
4. Ibid., p. 156.
5. Ibid., p. 168.

6. Brown, *Rise of Western Christendom*, p. 88.
7. Quoted in Brown, *Augustine of Hippo*, p. 152.
8. Quoted ibid., p. 150.
9. Quoted ibid.
10. Quoted ibid.
11. Brown, *Rise of Western Christendom*, pp. 88–91.
12. Quoted in Brown, *Augustine of Hippo*, pp. 347–8.
13. *Cambridge History of Medieval Philosophy*, p. 414.
14. Quoted in P. Brown, *Power and Persuasion in Late Antiquity* (Madison, 1992), p. 18.
15. Brown, *Augustine of Hippo*, pp. 324–7.
16. Ibid., p. 324.

CHAPTER 9. SHAPING NEW ATTITUDES AND HABITS

R. A. Markus, *The End of Ancient Christianity* (Cambridge, 1990), explores Christian fears of over-assimilation to pagan Roman *mores* after Constantine's conversion – the ways in which the cult of martyrs and Christian 'festivals' were among the means used to keep the threat at bay. P. Garnsey, *The Idea of Slavery from Aristotle to Augustine* (Cambridge, 1990), examines the variety of attitudes towards slavery and emphasizes that the absence of a frontal confrontation was not the same as acquiescence in the institution. F. Guizot, *History of Civilization in Europe* (Harmondsworth, 1997) and his *Histoire de la civilisation en France*, 3 vols. (Paris, 1840) still provide the subtlest account of the attitudes and habits of patricians in post-Roman Gaul who had embraced Christianity without abandoning classical culture and a leisured lifestyle. See also P. Brown, *The Rise of Western Christendom* (Oxford, 2003), and W. E. Klingshirn, *Caesarius of Arles* (Cambridge, 1994).

1. Markus, *The End of Ancient Christianity*, pp. 87–135.
2. W. H. C. Frend, *The Early Church* (London, 2003), p. 196.
3. H. Chadwick, *The Early Church* (Harmondsworth, 1967), p. 60.
4. Quoted in Garnsey, *The Idea of Slavery from Aristotle to Augustine*, p. 82.
5. Quoted in Guizot, *History of Civilization in Europe*, p. 41.
6. Guizot, *Histoire de la civilisation en France*, vol. 1, p. 101.
7. Quoted ibid., p. 102.
8. Ibid., p. 104.
9. Ibid., p. 106.

CHAPTER 10. DISTINGUISHING SPIRITUAL FROM TEMPORAL POWER

François Guizot remains a remarkable guide to this period. His formidable intelligence, his training in law as well as history, his familiarity with the work of German historians of Roman law such as Savigny and his special interest in the Visigoths give his discussion of the law codes of the post-invasion Germanic kingdoms an enduring interest. It is a pity that there has been no English edition of his *Histoire de la civilisation en France*, 3 vols. (Paris, 1840), since Hazlitt's translation was published (London and New York, 1892). More recent and useful studies include P. D. King, *Law and Society in the Visigothic Kingdom* (Cambridge, 1972); I. N. Wood, *The Merovinigian Kingdom 450–751* (London, 1994); and E. James, *The Origins of France: From Clovis to the Capetians* (London, 1982).

1. Guizot, *Histoire de la civilisation en France,* vol. 1, pp. 325–6.
2. Quoted ibid., pp. 90–91.
3. Quoted in P. Brown, *The Rise of Western Christendom* (Oxford, 2003), p. 260.
4. Quoted ibid., p. 249.
5. F. Guizot, *History of Civilization in Europe* (Harmondsworth, 1997), p. 42.
6. Ibid.
7. Brown, *Rise of Western Christendom*, p. 237.
8. Guizot, *Histoire de la civilisation en France*, vol. 1, pp. 358–9.
9. Ibid., p. 121.
10. Brown, *Rise of Western Christendom*, p. 112.
11. Ibid., p. 237.
12. Guizot, *Histoire de la civilisation en France*, vol. 1, p. 310.
13. Guizot, *History of Civilization in Europe*, p. 60.
14. D. Ayers and A. S. T. Fisher, *Records of Christianity* (Oxford), vol.2, p. 17.
15. Quoted in Brown, *Rise of Western Christendom*, p. 225.
16. Ibid., p. 211.
17. Ibid., p. 212.

CHAPTER 11. BARBARIAN CODES, ROMAN LAW AND CHRISTIAN INTUITIONS

Gregory of Tours, *History of the Franks* (Harmondsworth, 1974), is a fascinating and often very amusing chronicle of a period when the diversity of minds and manners can scarcely be exaggerated: it describes people of often credulous piety trying to live together with feuds, incest and unashamed violence among the Germanic invaders. I. N. Wood provides a background to Gregory's account in *The Merovingian Kingdom 450–751* (London, 1994); E. James, *The Origins of France: From Clovis to the Capetians* (London, 1982) provides a balanced, well-judged general account of this tumultuous period. F. Guizot, *History of Civilization in Europe* (Harmondsworth, 1997), draws attention to legal changes encouraged by the church in the Visigothic kingdom, while P. Brown, in *The Rise of Western Christendom* (Oxford, 2003), emphasizes what he calls the 'Christianising' of death – that is, the individualist implications of the day of judgement awaiting every soul.

1. Quoted in James, *The Origins of France*, p. 45.
2. Ibid., p. 47.
3. Quoted ibid., p. 86.
4. Ibid., p. 96.
5. Brown, *The Rise of Western Christendom*, pp. 263–4.
6. Ibid.
7. Guizot, *History of Civilization in Europe*, pp. 106–7.
8. Ibid., p. 107.
9. Quoted ibid., p. 107.
10. Ibid., pp. 60–61.

CHAPTER 12. THE CAROLINGIAN COMPROMISE

Einhard's contemporary *Life of Charlemagne* – with its echoes of the Lives of the Caesars – is the obvious starting point. Beyond that there is an embarrassment of choice: H. Fichtenau, *The Carolingian Empire* (Oxford, 1968); F.-L. Ganshof, *Frankish Institutions under Charlemagne* (New York, 1968); J. L. Nelson, *The Frankish World, 750–900* (London, 1996); H. Pirenne, *Mohammed and Charlemagne* (London, 1937); R. Collins, *Charlemagne* (London, 1998); J. M. Wallace-Hadrill, *The Frankish Church* (Oxford, 1983); and W. Ullmann, *The Carolingian Renaissance and the Idea of Kingship* (Cambridge, 1969). A useful collection of readings from the period, in E. Dutton (ed.), *Carolingian Civilization: A Reader* (Peterborough, Ont., 1993), conveys the atmosphere. And, as always, P. Brown, *The Rise of Western Christendom* (Oxford, 2003), offers subtle insights into the ambitions, both moral and intellectual, of Charlemagne and his clerical advisers. The influence of Gregory the Great and his writings on Carolingian ambitions and rhetoric was considerable. For an examination of Gregory's life and times, see J. Richards, *Consul of God* (London, 1980).

1. Brown, *The Rise of Western Christendom*, p. 451.
2. Quoted ibid., p. 454.
3. Quoted in F. Donald Logan, *History of the Church* (London, 2013), p. 75.
4. L. Olson, *The Early Middle Ages* (Basingstoke, 2007), p. 89.
5. Quoted in E. James, *The Origins of France: From Clovis to the Capetians* (London, 1982), p. 164.
6. Quoted in Dutton (ed.), *Carolingian Civilization*, p. 74.
7. Quoted in James, *The Origins of France*, p. 199.
8. Quoted in Dutton (ed.), *Carolingian Civilization*, p. 372.
9. Brown, *The Rise of Western Christendom*, p. 212.
10. Dutton (ed.), *Carolingian Civilization*, pp. 189–91.
11. Brown, *The Rise of Western Christendom*, pp. 443–5.
12. James, *The Origins of France*, p. 199.

CHAPTER 13. WHY FEUDALISM DID NOT RECREATE ANCIENT SLAVERY

I have tried to avoid sinking into the bog of dispute about the meaning of 'feudal' by contrasting different conditions of labour with ancient slavery. Readers can pursue the origins of vassalage in F.-L. Ganshof's *Feudalism* (London, 1964). Two important further studies are M. Bloch, *Feudal Society* (London, 1962), and G. Fourquin, *Lordship and Feudalism in the Middle Ages* (London, 1976). A recent work by the economic historian G. Bois, *The Transformation of the Year 1000* (Manchester, 1992), reveals the difficulty of generalizing about social change by a close study of landowning and status in villages near Cluny. In *The Origins of France: From Clovis to the Capetians* (London, 1982), E. James prefers to avoid using the term 'feudalism' altogether.

1. F. Guizot, *Histoire de la civilisation en France*, 3 vols. (Paris, 1840), vol. 3, pp. 121–34.
2. M. Bloch, 'How and Why Ancient Slavery Came to an End', in his *Slavery and Serfdom in the Middle Ages*, trans. W. R. Beer (Berkeley, 1975), pp. 1–31.
3. Bois, *Transformation of the Year 1000*, pp. 14–17.
4. E. Dutton (ed.), *Carolingian Civilization* (Peterborough, Ont., 1993), p. 469.
5. James, *The Origins of France*, pp. 193–6.
6. Quoted ibid., p. 201.
7. Ibid., p. 74.
8. P. Brown, *The Rise of Western Christendom* (Oxford, 2003), p. 441.

9. Quoted in L. Olson, *The Early Middle Ages* (Basingstoke, 2007), p. 103.

10. Bois, *Transformation of the Year 1000*, pp. 164, 28–9.

11. James, *The Origins of France*, p. 200.

12. Quoted in Abbé Loupot, *Hincmar: Sa vie, ses œuvres, son influence* (Reims, 1869), pp. 265–6.

13. Quoted in Guizot, *Histoire de la civilisation en France*, vol. 3, p. 143.

CHAPTER 14. FOSTERING THE 'PEACE OF GOD'

Studying the tenth century is fascinating and frustrating, for it is marked by violence, ambiguity and innovation. However, whether it is a question of the condition of labour, the emergence of a market economy or urban revival, the importance of the tenth century is increasingly recognized. What I have tried to bring out is its 'moral' importance – how the efforts of the Carolingian clergy in the previous century to embed the church in the countryside and internalize the Christian faith began to bear fruit, despite the fragmenting of the empire. The important 'Peace of God' and 'Truce of God' movements are discussed by E. James, *The Origins of France: From Clovis to the Capetians* (London, 1982), and G. Bois, *The Transformation of the Year 1000* (Manchester, 1992). A particularly vivid account can be found in T. Holland, *Millennium* (London, 2008). For the influence of Cluny, see N. Hunt (ed.), *Cluniac Monasticism in the Central Middle Ages* (Basingstoke, 1971). Three more general studies are F. D. Logan, *A History of the Church in the Middle Ages* (London, 2013); W. Blockmans and P. Hoppenbrouwers, *Introduction to Medieval Europe, 300–1550* (London, 2007); and M. Deanesly, *A History of the Medieval Church 590–1500* (London, 1990). A symptom of growing interest in the tenth century is the semi-popular account by P. Collins, *The Birth of the West* (New York, 2013).

1. Quoted in R. W. Southern, *Western Society and the Church in the Middle Ages* (Harmondsworth, 1970), p. 152.

2. Quoted in K. H. Digby, *Ages of Faith* (Cincinnati, 1841), vol. 1, p. 183.

3. Quoted in James, *The Origins of France*, p. 204.

4. Quoted in F. Guizot, *Histoire de la civilisation en France*, 3 vols. (Paris, 1840), vol. 3, p. 144.

5. James, *The Origins of France.*, p. 78–81.

6. Ibid., pp. 117–19, 205–6.

7. Ibid., pp. 206–8.

8. Deanesly, *A History of the Medieval Church 590–1500*, p. 98.

9. James, *The Origins of France*, p. 207.

10. Ibid., p. 206.
11. Blockmans and Hoppenbrouwers, *Introduction to Medieval Europe, 300–1550*, p. 146.
12. James, *The Origins of France*, p. 208.

CHAPTER 15. THE PAPAL REVOLUTION: A CONSTITUTION FOR EUROPE?

Two leading students of the 'papal revolution' are Brian Tierney and Harold Berman. Indeed, it is Berman who promoted the description as part of his larger argument about the formation of the Western legal tradition in *Law and Revolution*, 2 vols. (Cambridge, Mass., 1983). Tierney has written a magisterial study of the originality of canon lawyers from the twelfth to the sixteenth century, *The Idea of Natural Rights* (Grand Rapids, Mich., 1997). He has also edited a useful collection of primary sources about Gregory VII and the struggle between the empire and the reformed papacy in *The Crisis of Church and State, 1050–1300* (Toronto, 1988). A detailed study of the context of that struggle can be found in I. S. Robinson, *The Papacy 1073–1198* (Cambridge, 1990). For another look at Pope Gregory VII and his reign, see J. Richards, *Consul of God* (London, 1980) and W. Ullmann, *A Short History of the Papacy in the Middle Ages* (London, 1972). For a broader study of the Cluniac movement, see N. Hunt (ed.), *Cluniac Monasticism in the Central Middle Ages* (London 1971).

1. E Prestage (ed.), *Chivalry* (London, 1928), p. 10.
2. F. Guizot, *History of Civilization in Europe* (Harmondsworth, 1997), p. 141.
3. Ibid., p. 41.
4. E. James, *The Origins of France: From Clovis to the Capetians* (London, 1982), p. 207.
5. Tierney (ed.), *The Crisis of Church and State, 1050–1300*, p. 9.
6. Quoted ibid., p. 10.
7. R. W. Southern, *Western Society and the Church in the Middle Ages* (Harmondsworth, 1970), p. 98.
8. Quoted in Tierney (ed.), *The Crisis of Church and State, 1050–1300*, p. 43.
9. Quoted ibid., p. 41.
10. Quoted ibid., pp. 49–50.
11. Ibid., pp. 61–2.
12. Ibid., p. 57.

13. Quoted ibid., p. 68.
14. Quoted ibid., p. 70.
15. Quoted ibid., pp. 70–71.
16. Quoted ibid., p. 72.
17. Quoted ibid., p. 71.

CHAPTER 16. NATURAL LAW AND NATURAL RIGHTS

Harold Berman and Brian Tierney continue to be crucial sources for understanding the construction of a legal system by the papacy. See Berman's *Law and Revolution*, 2 vols. (Cambridge, Mass., 1983), especially vol.1, pp. 85–119, 199–224; and Tierney's *The Crisis of Church and State, 1050–1300* (Toronto, 1988), especially pp. 45–53, 116–38, 150–58. See also R. Tuck, *Natural Rights Theories* (Cambridge, 1979). A general account of the importance of Roman law and its adaptation by canon lawyers can be found in P. Stein, *Roman Law in European History* (Cambridge, 1999). For more detailed accounts see P. Vinogradoff, *Roman Law in Medieval Europe* (Oxford, 1929), and J. Brundage, *Medieval Canon Law* (London, 1995). Also useful is I. Robinson (trans. and ed.), *Papal Reform in the Eleventh Century* (Manchester, 2004). Some of the implications for secular government and lordship in Europe are explored by T. Bisson in *The Crisis of the Twelfth Century* (Princeton, 2009).

1. Quoted in Tierney, *The Crisis of Church and State, 1050–1300*, pp. 78–9, 98.
2. Quoted ibid., p. 92.
3. Ibid., p. 97.
4. Quoted ibid., p. 15.
5. Ibid., p. 138.
6. R. W. Southern, *Western Society and the Church in the Middle Ages* (Harmondsworth, 1970), pp. 104–5.
7. Quoted in Tierney, *The Crisis of Church and State, 1050–1300*, p. 135.
8. F. Copleston, *A History of Philosophy* (London, 1993–), vol. 3, p. 33.

CHAPTER 17. CENTRALIZATION AND THE NEW SENSE OF JUSTICE

Centralization in the twelfth- and thirteenth-century Church, with the papacy becoming the apex of a judicial and administrative structure spread across Europe, is a fascinating story. It was, to some extent, an unintended consequence of the declaration of papal sovereignty. In addition to the works by Berman and Tierney cited in Chapter 15, Tierney's *Foundations of the Conciliar Theory* (Cambridge, 1955; repr. 1968) explores the intellectual repercussions of that declaration, for the relations between popes on the one hand, and cardinals, bishops and religious corporations on the other. Berman emphasizes how canon lawyers modified the very idea of a corporation in his *Law and Revolution*, 2 vols. (Cambridge, Mass., 1983). A different set of repercussions on ideas of sin, crime, punishment, intentionality and personal responsibility are explored by both Guizot and Berman. These intellectual developments contributed to the emergence of philosophy from theology – as the career and writings of Abelard reveal. See, inter alia, A. Kenny, *Medieval Philosophy* (Oxford, 2005), pp. 44–8, 123–7, 260–63; F. Copleston, *A History of Philosophy* (London, 1993–), vol. 2, pp. 205–11; and A. de Libera, *La Philosophie médiévale* (Paris, 1993).

1. Berman, *Law and Revolution*, vol. 1, pp. 113–15.
2. R. W. Southern, *Western Society and the Church in the Middle Ages* (Harmondsworth, 1970), pp. 107–9.
3. Ibid., p. 116.
4. P. Stein, *Roman Law in European History* (Cambridge, 1999), *passim*.
5. Quoted in Berman, *Law and Revolution*, vol. 1, p. 184.
6. F. Guizot, *History of Civilization in Europe* (Harmondsworth, 1997), p. 108.
7. Berman, *Law and Revolution*, vol. 1, pp. 185–6.
8. Quoted ibid., pp. 186–9.
9. B. Tierney, *The Idea of Natural Rights* (Grand Rapids, Mich., 1997), p. 56.
10. Berman, *Law and Revolution*, vol.1, pp. 215–24; also Tierney, *Foundations of the Conciliar Theory*, pp. 127–30, 222–3, 235–7.

CHAPTER 18. THE DEMOCRATIZING OF REASON

One of the remarkable things about H. Berman's *Law and Revolution*, 2 vols. (Cambridge, Mass., 1983) is that he seeks to bridge the gaps between developments in theology, law (both canon and secular) and philosophy. That ambition makes his work stimulating. B. Tierney's *The Idea of Natural Rights* (Grand Rapids, Mich., 1997) is ambitious in a different way – written with a view to demonstrating how canon lawyers from the twelfth century onwards laid the foundations for a rights-based theory of justice ('human rights'), a theory which had previously been assigned to the early modern period. Tierney brings to our attention, in particular, the originality of the canonist Huguccio and the development of what might be called an early form of 'judicial review'. The assimilation of rights to powers (*jus* to *potestas*) is central to rights theory and indispensable for discussing the invention of the individual. It avoids collapsing that story into discussions of the more diffuse terms 'individualism' and 'individuality'– something that plagues the accounts to be found in C. Morris, *The Discovery of the Individual, 1050–1200* (London, 1972) and A. MacFarlane, *The Origins of English Individualism* (Cambridge, 1979).

1. Berman, *Law and Revolution*, vol. 1, p. 229.
2. Ibid., p. 232.
3. Quoted in B. Tierney, *The Crisis of Church and State, 1050–1300* (Toronto, 1988), p. 135.
4. Berman, *Law and Revolution*, vol. 1, pp. 166–72.
5. Ibid., p. 139.
6. Ibid.
7. Tierney, *The Idea of Natural Rights*, pp. 4–5.
8. Quoted ibid., pp. 43–77.
9. Quoted ibid., p. 62.
10. Quoted ibid.
11. Quoted ibid., pp. 63–4.
12. Quoted ibid., p. 67.
13. Ibid., p. 64.
14. Quoted ibid., pp. 64–5.
15. Quoted ibid., p. 231.
16. Quoted ibid., p. 72.
17. Quoted ibid., p. 74.
18. Ibid.
19. Tierney, *The Crisis of Church and State, 1050–1300*, p. 79.
20. Quoted in Berman, *Law and Revolution*, vol. 1, p. 141
21. Ibid.

CHAPTER 19. STEPS TOWARDS THE CREATION OF NATION-STATES

The process of creating the modern state took different forms in Sicily, France, England and Spain. I have tried to identify what the rulers in these nations had in common and what they owed to the example of the church. Influenced by the papal revolution, their conception of right rule or 'sovereignty' came to turn on legal supremacy over 'individuals' rather than the traditional model of rule over families and 'estates' of the realm. For a subtle overview of that process, see F. Guizot, *The History of Civilization in Europe* (Harmondsworth, 1997), where class conflict and 'centralization' inspired by a new (rights-based) sense of justice are presented as the keys to the transformation of a corporate society into a society based on equality before the law – an argument which had a great impact on Alexis de Tocqueville, Karl Marx and J. S. Mill. See also J. R. S. Strayer, *The Medieval Origins of the Modern State* (Princeton, 1970); H. Mitteis, *The State in the Middle Ages* (Amsterdam, 1975); D. C. Douglas, *The Norman Achievement 1050–1100* (Berkeley, 1969); C. Petit-Dutaillis, *The Feudal Monarchy in France and England: From the Tenth to the Thirteenth Century* (London, 1936); J. E. A. Jolliffe, *The Constitutional History of Medieval England* (London, 1961); and F. D. Logan, *A History of the Church in the Middle Ages*, 2 vols. (London, 2013).

1. H. Berman, *Law and Revolution*, 2 vols. (Cambridge, Mass., 1983), vol. 1, p. 404. See also Strayer, *The Medieval Origins of the Modern State* (esp. chapter 1).

2. B. Tierney, *The Crisis of Church and State, 1050–1300* (Toronto, 1988), p. 155.

3. P. Stein, *Roman Law in European History* (Cambridge, 1999), p. 73.

4. Tierney, *The Crisis of Church and State, 1050–1300*, p. 118.

5. Berman, *Law and Revolution*, vol. 1, p. 419.

6. Stein, *Roman Law in European History*, p. 64.

7. Ibid., pp. 65–6.

8. R. W. Southern, *Western Society and the Church in the Middle Ages* (Harmondsworth, 1970), p. 81.

9. Stein, *Roman Law in European History*, p. 74.

CHAPTER 20. URBAN INSURRECTIONS

The theme of F. Guizot's *History of Civilization in Europe* (Harmondsworth, 1997) is the gradual collapse of the classes of an aristocratic society derived from feudalism into a new intermediate social condition, 'the middle class'. The revival of urban life from the tenth century, with the struggle of boroughs for enfranchisement across Europe, provided a foundation for this new, more egalitarian form of society and a market economy. H. Berman, *Law and Revolution*, 2 vols. (Cambridge, Mass., 1983), devotes a chapter in vol. 1 (pp. 357–403) to the development of 'urban law' and its distinctive features. A worthy companion to these studies is D. Nicholas, *The Growth of the Medieval City* (London, 1997). See also G. Duby (ed.), *Histoire de la France urbaine*, vol. 2 (Paris, 1980); R. Hodges, *Dark Age Economics: The Origins of Towns and Trade 600–1000* (New York, 1982); D. Nicholas, *Medieval Flanders* (London, 1992); and H. Pirenne, *Medieval Cities: Their Origins and the Revival of Trade* (New York, 1956).

1. Guizot, *History of Civilization in Europe*, p. 124.
2. Berman, *Law and Revolution*, vol. 1, p. 395.
3. Guizot, *History of Civilization in Europe*, p. 125.
4. Ibid., p. 126.
5. Ibid., p. 127.
6. Berman, *Law and Revolution*, vol. 1, pp. 357–403.
7. Ibid., pp. 389, 394–5.
8. Ibid., p. 396.
9. Guizot, *History of Civilization in Europe*, pp. 129–30.

CHAPTER 21. POPULAR ASPIRATIONS AND THE FRIARS

N. Cohn's *The Pursuit of the Millennium* (London, 1970) is a fascinating book. Cohn balances a sensitivity to ideas with an interest in practices, and so is able to portray the variety of popular 'protest' movements in medieval Europe. Combining millenarianism with mysticism and, quite often, social subversion, these movements – and the threat they represented – helped to give rise to the more familiar movements of the friars, the Dominicans and Franciscans. The debate about 'apostolic' poverty and property rights which the Franciscans engendered led them into confrontation with the papacy. The result was the emergence of a more socially radical stream of thought within the church, which had important repercussions in the following centuries – both in philosophy and in disputes about church government, preparing the way for reformation. A brief introduction to the friars movement can be found in R. W. Southern, *Western Society and the Church in the Middle Ages* (Harmondsworth, 1970), pp. 272–99. Consequences of that movement for the development of the language of natural rights are analysed by B. Tierney in *The Idea of Natural Rights* (Grand Rapids, Mich., 1997). For more extended treatment of the movement, see M. D. Lambert, *Franciscan Poverty: The Doctrine of the Absolute Poverty of Christ and the Apostles in the Franciscan Order, 1210–1323* (London, 1961); J. Moorman, *History of the Franciscan Order* (Oxford, 1968); and M. Villey, *La Formation de la pensée juridique moderne* (Paris, 1975).

1. Cohn, *The Pursuit of the Millennium*, pp. 37–9.
2. Ibid., pp. 39–40.
3. Ibid., pp. 47–8.
4. Ibid., p. 45.
5. Southern, *Western Society and the Church in the Middle Ages*, p. 281.
6. Tierney, *The Idea of Natural Rights*, pp. 94, 149.
7. Ibid., p. 150.
8. Ibid., p. 153.
9. Ibid., pp. 154–5.
10. Ibid., p. 147.
11. Ibid.

CHAPTER 22. THE DEFENCE OF EGALITARIAN MORAL INTUITIONS

The recovery of many Aristotelian texts forms the background to this chapter. Leading Franciscan thinkers such as Duns Scotus and William of Ockham reacted to what they saw as a growing over-reliance on Aristotle, a trend which seemed to threaten the morally distinctive features of Christianity. The attempt by Aquinas to assimilate Aristotelianism and Christianity in his *Summa Theologica* therefore became the object of their criticisms. For this background and an exposition of Aquinas's thought, see F. Copleston, *A History of Philosophy* (London, 1993–), vol. 2, or, more briefly, A. Kenny, *Medieval Philosophy* (Oxford, 2005). For an exposition of the philosophies of Duns Scotus and William of Ockham, see Copleston, *A History of Philosophy*, vol. 3, and J. Marenbon, *Later Medieval Philosophy* (London, 1987). The development of distinct 'schools' of thought in theology and philosophy strikes me as a symptom of the emergence of universities across Europe. H. Rashdall's *The Universities of Europe in the Middle Ages* (Oxford, 1936) can hardly be bettered on that subject.

1. Quoted in Copleston, *A History of Philosophy*, vol. 2, p. 545.
2. Ibid., pp. 545–6.
3. Ibid., p. 546.
4. B. Tierney, *The Idea of Natural Rights* (Grand Rapids, Mich., 1997), pp. 16–19, 29–32, 34–7.
5. Ibid., pp. 99–100.
6. R. W. Southern, *Western Society and the Church in the Middle Ages* (Harmondsworth, 1970), pp. 277–9; also H. Berman, *Law and Revolution*, 2 vols. (Cambridge, Mass., 1983), vol. 1, pp. 120–31.

7. Rashdall, *The Universities of Europe in the Middle Ages*, pp. 87–267; also, Copleston, *A History of Philosophy*, vol. 2, pp. 212–18.

8. Ibid., pp. 240–50, 423–34, 476–86.

9. R. Pasnau (ed.), *The Cambridge History of Medieval Philosophy* (Cambridge, 2010), p. 415.

10. Copleston, *A History of Philosophy*, vol. 2, pp. 423–34.

11. P. Brown, *The Rise of Western Christendom* (Oxford, 2003), p. 88.

12. R. A. Markus, *The End of Ancient Christianity* (Cambridge, 1990), p. 77.

CHAPTER 23. GOD'S FREEDOM AND HUMAN FREEDOM JOINED: OCKHAM

Ockham's adult life was divided between Oxford and 'exile' in Germany under the emperor's protection. It is hardly surprising that his later writings have a more political and polemical character than his earlier writings on logic and epistemology. P. Boehner (ed.), *Selected Philosophical Writings* (London, 1952), draws on this earlier work. F. Copleston's chapters on Ockham's philosophy in his *History of Philosophy* (London, 1993–), vol. 3, provides a careful commentary on the full range of thought. A. S. McGrade's *The Political Thought of William of Ockham* (Cambridge, 1974) is impressive because it draws together his moral philosophy and his political ideas – providing a nuanced account of his understanding of the role of 'right reason'. See also McGrade's (trans. J. Kilcullen) edition of Ockham's *A Letter to the Friars Minor and Other Writings* (Cambridge, 1995). Yet it is B. Tierney's *The Idea of Natural Rights* (Grand Rapids, Mich., 1997) which makes the most of Ockham's contribution to the development of rights theory, through his formidable defence of the Franciscan position on poverty. The story of Ockham and the nominalists' contribution to the emergence of modern physics is best told by A. C. Crombie, *From Augustine to Galileo* (London, 1979), vol. 2: Science in the Middle Ages.

1. Copleston, *A History of Philosophy*, vol. 2, pp. 259–62, 358–62.

2. Ibid., pp. 90–91.

3. Ibid., vol. 3, pp. 4–6.

4. Ibid., pp. 88–95.

5. Tierney, *The Idea of Natural Rights*, pp. 99–100.

6. Quoted in Crombie, *From Augustine to Galileo*, vol. 2, p. 46; see also Copleston, *A History of Philosophy*, vol. 3, pp. 71–6.

7. B. Williams, *Shame and Necessity* (Berkeley, 1993), *passim*.

8. Quoted in F. Guizot, *Histoire de la civilisation en France*, 3 vols. (Paris, 1840), vol. 3, pp. 149–50.

9. Quoted in Copleston, *A History of Philosophy*, vol. 3, p. 101.

10. Quoted ibid.

11. Quoted ibid., pp. 113–14.

12. Tierney, *The Idea of Natural Rights*, p. 187; William of Ockham, 'On the Power of the Pope and Clergy' in McGrade and Kilcullen (ed. and trans.), *A Letter to the Friars Minor and Other Writings*, pp. 118–229.

13. Quoted in Crombie, *From Augustine to Galileo*, vol. 2, p. 45.

CHAPTER 24. STRUGGLING FOR REPRESENTATIVE GOVERNMENT IN THE CHURCH

The variety and depth of canonist thinking emerges clearly from its contributions to the conciliar movement – to the critique of papal absolutism and the exploration of the requirements of a more representative government in the church. Brian Tierney leads the way in insisting that there is much more to be discovered in canonist writings – as the list of the leading canonists, most of whose names are unfamiliar, at the end of his *Foundations of the Conciliar Theory* (Cambridge, 1955; repr. 1968) suggests. Early in the twentieth century the brothers R. W. and A. J. Carlyle's *A History of Medieval Political Theory in the West* (London, 1928) also began to mine this rich deposit, as did J. N. Figgis, *Churches in the Modern State* (London, 1913) and E. F. Jacob, *Essays in the Conciliar Epoch* (Manchester, 1953). But the most striking thing about twentieth-century study of the conciliar movement is how it was dominated by German scholars – itself perhaps a symptom of the connection with the Reformation. Apart from Tierney, F. W. Maitland's introduction to Otto von Gierke's *Political Theories of the Middle Ages* (Cambridge, 1938) and W. Ullmann, *Origins of the Great Schism* (London, 1948) are useful studies in English.

1. Tierney, *Foundations of the Conciliar Theory*, p. 147.

2. Ibid., pp. 23–46.

3. Ibid., p. 49.

4. Ibid., p. 50.

5. Ibid., p. 117.

6. B Tierney, *The Idea of Natural Rights* (Grand Rapids, Mich., 1997), p. 110.

7. Tierney, *Foundations of the Conciliar Theory*, p. 126.

8. Ibid., p. 126.

9. F. Guizot, *History of Civilization in Europe* (Harmondsworth, 1997), p. 192.

10. Ibid., p. 194.

CHAPTER 25. DISPENSING WITH THE RENAISSANCE

While I have emphasized Burckhardt's seminal work, other studies of the Renaissance have become legion and reveal the expansion of the concept beyond humanism, from art and cultural history to almost every aspect of change from the fourteenth to the later sixteenth century. For an elegant, if orthodox study of these centuries, see J. Hale's *Civilization of Europe in the Renaissance* (London, 1993), while Q. Skinner's *Foundations of Modern Political Thought* (Cambridge, 1979) provides a comprehensive, lucid examination of the development of political doctrines. Although the sixteenth century is beyond the scope of this book, Thomas More's *Utopia* and Erasmus's *In Praise of Folly* stand out as classic examples of humanist thinking and attitudes, while Montaigne's *Essays* reveal the scepticism aroused by religious wars following the Reformation.

1. J. Burckhardt, *Civilisation of the Renaissance* (London, 1944).
2. L. Siedentop, 'Two Liberal Traditions', in A. Ryan (ed.), *The Idea of Freedom* (Oxford, 1979).
3. Marsilius of Padua, *Defensor Pacis*, trans. A. Gewirth (New York, 1991). See also his *Writings on the Empire: Defensor Minor and De Translatione Imperii*, ed. C. Nederman (Cambridge, 1993).
4. Thomas à Kempis, *Imitation of Christ* (Harmondsworth, 2005), *passim*.
5. Quoted in F. Copleston, *A History of Philosophy* (London, 1993–), vol. 3, p. 159.
6. Quoted ibid., p. 161.
7. F. Guizot, *History of Civilization in Europe* (Harmondsworth, 1997), pp. 166–81.

Index

Kant, Immanuel 107
Kempis, Thomas à 340
kingship (*see also* sovereignty)
  and the aristocracy 29, 31
  and bureaucracy 260
  and canonists 265
  and the cause of justice 256
  and centralization of authority
    229, 340, 344–5
  change to local lordship 169
  creation of 'sovereign' agency
    and growth of royal power
    346–7
  de-sacralizing of kingship 220,
    253, 256, 273
  equal subjection to monarchs
    346, 347
  and feudalism 254, 265, 344–6
  French/Capetian 169, 254,
    255–6, 262–3
  and idealism 347
  and individual subjects 255
  jurisdiction/legal supremacy
    claims 261–2
  and lawyers 260, 263
  and liberty 347
  and nostalgia 254
  and the organization of Europe
    344–7
  and papacy *see* papacy: and
    kingship
  philosopher-kings 36, 43
  and priesthood 23
  and royal councils 260, 263
  and tyranny 31
  and a unified legal system 254
knights 178, 186, 193–4

labour
  ancient contempt for 36, 39
  changes leading to feudalism
    165–8
  and *coloni* 166–73, 181–2
  monasticism and the
    rehabilitation of 95–6, 188
  rural labour and the church 171
  scarcity 312, 340
  serfs *see* serfdom
  slaves *see* slaves/slavery
  and warfare 39
Languedoc 286, 287
Last Judgement 240
Lateran Council, fourth 230, 233
law
  and the ancient city 23–4
  Carolingian 154, 172; *capitula*
    of Charlemagne 156–7, 170,
    172, 173; 'Christian law' in the
    Carolingian empire 159,
    172, 200
  centralization of legal authority
    346 (*see also* justice: and
    centralization)
  and charters 272–4
  church law *see* church law
  church subject to laws of the
    state 339
  civil–canon law interaction
    253–64
  corporation law 234–5,
    324–8, 338
  customary 137, 142, 212, 216,
    227, 229, 230–31, 234, 262,
    263
  developing a unified legal system
    253–64
  disagreements in Western Europe
    about meaning of 253
  and distinguishing spiritual from
    temporal power 126–40

liberalism – *cont.*

rulers to enforce belief 333; in 'civil war' against secularism 333, 349–63; foundation in canon law 244, 327, 332, 359; and moral equality 244, 292, 336, 338, 339 (*see also* moral equality: Christian intuitions of); preserving Christian ontology without metaphysics of salvation 338; separation of church and state and the shaping of liberalism 333–4, 349, 360

development 334

and equality: equal liberty and moral equality 244, 292, 339, 361 (*see also* liberty: equal liberty; moral equality); of status 237–8, 274, 332, 359

and the individual *see* individualism/the individual

liberal secularism 3, 313, 316–17, 331, 333–8, 349–63 (*see also* secularism)

Marxist infiltration of liberal thinking 2

and 'physicalism' 337–8

reduced to endorsement of market economics 363

and the Renaissance 334–48

and retreat into individualism 363

and rights *see* human rights; rights

and secularism as non-belief 2, 360–62

liberty

and the borough and its individual inhabitants 268–77

and citizenship 19–20, 30

civil liberty claims 306, 362

divine and human freedom joined 306–20

divine freedom vs divine rationality 307

from dogma 8

equal liberty: in Christian apologetics 77; civil and political liberty and equal rights 277; emergence from Christian moral intuitions 244, 292, 339; and liberalism/ secularism 244, 292, 339, 361; and moral equality 244; and Ockham 311, 313–14, 342; and the soul's relationship to God 311

and faith 69, 76

from feudal social hierarchies 8

free will *see* free will

freedom of conscience *see* conscience: freedom of

human nature as foundation for claim to 359

liberation of clients 30

and monastic obedience 98

moral freedom 245

and moral responsibility 65–6, 71

and Ockham 311, 313–14, 342

in Pauline conceptions: and canon law 244; 'christian liberty' 63–4, 65–6, 98, 213, 244, 245, 292, 294–6, 314, 324, 339, 353, 361; of dying in Christ 61; of freedom of conscience 62; of new creation 61, 65; of service 65–6; of submission to God's will 64–6;